The Virtual Community

The Virtual Community
Homesteading on the Electronic Frontier
revised edition

Howard Rheingold

The MIT Press
Cambridge, Massachusetts
London, England

First MIT Press edition, 2000

Originally published in 1993 by Addison Wesley.

First paperback edition published by Harper Collins, 1994.

This book was set in Sabon by Mary Reilly Graphics.

Printed and bound in the United States of America.

Library of Congress Cataloging-in-Publication Data

Rheingold, Howard.
  The virtual community : homesteading on the electronic frontier / Howard
  Rheingold.—Rev. ed.
    p. cm.
  Includes bibliographical references and index.
  ISBN 0-262-68121-8 (pbk.)
    1. Internet (Computer network) 2. Computer networks—Social aspects.
    I. Title.

TK5105.875.157 R45   2000
303.48'33—dc21   00-041851

To the friends and family I've met through the WELL, our virtual community.

We know the rules of community; we know the healing effect of community in terms of individual lives. If we could somehow find a way across the bridge of our knowledge, would not these same rules have a healing effect upon our world? We human beings have often been referred to as social animals. But we are not yet community creatures. We are impelled to relate with each other for our survival. But we do not yet relate with the inclusivity, realism, self-awareness, vulnerability, commitment, openness, freedom, equality, and love; of genuine community. It is clearly no longer enough to be simply social animals, babbling together at cocktail parties and brawling with each other in business and over boundaries. It is our task—our essential, central, crucial task—to transform ourselves from mere social creatures into community creatures. It is the only way that human evolution will be able to proceed.

M. Scott Peck
The Different Drum: Community-Making and Peace

Contents

Preface to the MIT Press Edition   xi

Acknowledgments   xiii

Introduction   xv

1 The Heart of the WELL   1

2 Daily Life in Cyberspace: How the Computerized Counterculture
Built a New Kind of Place   25

3 Visionaries and Convergences: The Accidental History of the
Net   57

4 Grassroots Groupminds   109

5 Multi-User Dungeons and Alternate Identities   149

6 Real-time Tribes   181

7 Japan and the Net   205

8 *Télématique* and *Messageries Roses*: A Tale of Two Virtual
Communities   231

9 Electronic Frontiers and Online Activists   255

10 Disinformocracy   295

11 Rethinking Virtual Communities   323

Afterword (1994)   393

Bibliography   405

Index   427

Preface to the MIT Press Edition

When *The Virtual Community* was first published in 1993, social cyber-spaces and the Internet were new phenomena to most people. Now, the entire world seems to be undergoing an Internet-enabled transformation. This new edition has afforded me the opportunity to try to cover some of the enormous new territory that has opened up over the past seven years. My update is at the end of the book, in an afterword that the MIT Press generously allowed me to add. (Note that there is also a 1994 after-word—the Web was an interesting little cloud on the horizon in 1992, when I was writing the first edition.)

New people and a new virtual community need to be acknowledged in regard to the additional material. First and foremost, Moya Mason, bib-liographic researcher extraordinaire, has helped me compile an extensive new bibliography that is meant to serve as a guide to further research for those who are setting out to map the vast new social cyberspaces. In addition, members of the Brainstorms virtual community offered invalu-able advice. Some of those who were helpful in that context are Bryan Alexander, Andrea Baker, Valerie Bock, Glen Blankenship, Michael Boyle, Timothy Burke, Steve Cisler, Sherwood A. Dowling, Robert F. Johnson, Gary Jones, Tim Jordan, Thorsten Kogge, Jon Lebkowsky, Elizabeth Lewis, Geert Lovink, Del Rickel, Mike Sellers, Sharon Shaw, David Silver, Dana Still, John Suler, Paul Waterhouse, Bob Watson, Michael Wilson.

Acknowledgments

A few of the many people who helped make this book possible: Izumi Aizu, the Allison family, John P. Barlow, Richard Bartle, John Brockman, Amy Bruckman, the Catalfo family, Steve Cisler, John Coate, Kathleen Creighton, Mary Clemmey, Paul Dourish, Cliff Figallo, Dan Franklin, Katsura Hattori, David Hawkins, Herestoby, Dave Hughes, Hiroshi Ishii, Joicho Ito, Tom Jennings, Peter and Trudy Johnson-Lenz, Kevin Kelly, David Kline, Barry Kort, Lionel Lumbroso, Tom Mandel, Annick Morel, Blair Newman, Tim Oren, William Patrick, Adam Peake, Tim Pozar, Judy Rheingold, Mamie Rheingold, Jeff Shapard, Marc Smith, the staff of *Whole Earth Review*, the staff of the WELL, Dave Winder, the Weird conference.

Introduction

"Daddy is saying 'Holy moly!' to his computer again!"

Those words have become a family code for the way my virtual community has infiltrated our real world. My seven-year-old daughter knows that her father congregates with a family of invisible friends who seem to gather in his computer. Sometimes he talks to them, even if nobody else can see them. And she knows that these invisible friends sometimes show up in the flesh, materializing from the next block or the other side of the planet.

Since the summer of 1985, for an average of two hours a day, seven days a week, I've been plugging my personal computer into my telephone and making contact with the WELL (Whole Earth 'Lectronic Link)—a computer conferencing system that enables people around the world to carry on public conversations and exchange private electronic mail (e-mail). The idea of a community accessible only via my computer screen sounded cold to me at first, but I learned quickly that people can feel passionately about e-mail and computer conferences. I've become one of them. I care about these people I met through my computer, and I care deeply about the future of the medium that enables us to assemble.

I'm not alone in this emotional attachment to an apparently bloodless technological ritual. Millions of people on every continent also participate in the computer-mediated social groups known as virtual communities, and this population is growing fast. Finding the WELL was like discovering a cozy little world that had been flourishing without me, hidden within the walls of my house; an entire cast of characters welcomed me to the troupe with great merriment as soon as I found the secret door. Like others who fell into the WELL, I soon discovered that

I was audience, performer, and scriptwriter, along with my companions, in an ongoing improvisation. A full-scale subculture was growing on the other side of my telephone jack, and they invited me to help create something new.

The virtual village of a few hundred people I stumbled upon in 1985 grew to eight thousand by 1993. It became clear to me during the first months of that history that I was participating in the self-design of a new kind of culture. I watched the community's social contracts stretch and change as the people who discovered and started building the WELL in its first year or two were joined by so many others. Norms were established, challenged, changed, reestablished, rechallenged, in a kind of speeded-up social evolution.

The WELL felt like an authentic community to me from the start because it was grounded in my everyday physical world. WELLites who don't live within driving distance of the San Francisco Bay area are constrained in their ability to participate in the local networks of face-to-face acquaintances. By now, I've attended real-life WELL marriages, WELL births, and even a WELL funeral. (The phrase "in real life" pops up so often in virtual communities that regulars abbreviate it to IRL.) I can't count the parties and outings where the invisible personae who first acted out their parts in the debates and melodramas on my computer screen later manifested in front of me in the physical world in the form of real people, with faces, bodies, and voices.

I remember the first time I walked into a room full of people IRL who knew many intimate details of my history and whose own stories I knew very well. Three months after I joined, I went to my first WELL party at the home of one of the WELL's online moderators. I looked around at the room full of strangers when I walked in. It was one of the oddest sensations of my life. I had contended with these people, shot the invisible breeze around the electronic watercooler, shared alliances and formed bonds, fallen off my chair laughing with them, become livid with anger at some of them. But there wasn't a recognizable face in the house. I had never seen them before.

My flesh-and-blood family long ago grew accustomed to the way I sit in my home office early in the morning and late at night, chuckling and cursing, sometimes crying, about words I read on the computer screen. It might have looked to my daughter as if I were alone at my desk the night she caught me chortling online, but from my point of view I was in living contact with old and new friends, strangers and colleagues:

I was in the Parenting conference on the WELL, participating in an informational and emotional support group for a friend who just learned his son was diagnosed with leukemia.

I was in MicroMUSE, a role-playing fantasy game of the twenty-fourth century (and science education medium in disguise), interacting with students and professors who know me only as "Pollenator."

I was in TWICS, a bicultural community in Tokyo; CIX, a community in London; CalvaCom, a community in Paris; and Usenet, a collection of hundreds of different discussions that travel around the world via electronic mail to millions of participants in dozens of countries.

I was browsing through Supreme Court decisions, in search of information that could help me debunk an opponent's claims in a political debate elsewhere on the Net, or I was retrieving this morning's satellite images of weather over the Pacific.

I was following an eyewitness report from Moscow during the coup attempt, or China during the Tiananmen Square incident, or Israel and Kuwait during the Gulf War, passed directly from citizen to citizen through an ad hoc network patched together from cheap computers and ordinary telephone lines, cutting across normal geographic and political boundaries by piggybacking on the global communications infrastructure.

I was monitoring a rambling real-time dialogue among people whose bodies were scattered across three continents, a global bull session that seems to blend wit and sophomore locker-room talk via Internet Relay Chat (IRC), a medium that combines the features of conversation and writing. IRC has accumulated an obsessive subculture of its own among undergraduates by the thousands from Adelaide to Arabia.

People in virtual communities use words on screens to exchange pleasantries and argue, engage in intellectual discourse, conduct commerce, exchange knowledge, share emotional support, make plans, brainstorm, gossip, feud, fall in love, find friends and lose them, play games, flirt, create a little high art and a lot of idle talk. People in virtual communities do just about everything people do in real life, but we leave our bodies behind. You can't kiss anybody and nobody can punch you in the nose, but a lot can happen within those boundaries. To the millions who have been drawn into it, the richness and vitality of computer-linked cultures is attractive, even addictive.

There is no such thing as a single, monolithic, online subculture; it's more like an ecosystem of subcultures, some frivolous, others serious. The cutting edge of scientific discourse is migrating to virtual communities, where you can read the electronic pre-preprinted reports of molecular biologists and cognitive scientists. At the same time, activists and educational reformers are using the same medium as a political tool. You can use virtual communities to find a date, sell a lawnmower, publish a novel, conduct a meeting.

Some people use virtual communities as a form of psychotherapy. Others, such as the most addicted players of Minitel in France or Multi-User Dungeons (MUDs) on the international networks, spend eighty hours a week or more pretending they are someone else, living a life that does not exist outside a computer. Because MUDs not only are susceptible to pathologically obsessive use by some people but also create a strain on computer and communication resources, MUDding has been banned at universities such as Amherst and on the entire continent of Australia.

Scientists, students, librarians, artists, organizers, and escapists aren't the only people who have taken to the new medium. The U.S. senator who campaigned for years for the construction of a National Research and Education Network that could host the virtual communities of the future is now vice president of the United States. As of June 1993, the White House and Congress have e-mail addresses.

Most people who get their news from conventional media have been unaware of the wildly varied assortment of new cultures that have evolved in the world's computer networks over the past ten years. Most people who have not yet used these new media remain unaware of how profoundly the social, political, and scientific experiments under way today via computer networks could change all our lives in the near future.

I have written this book to help inform a wider population about the potential importance of cyberspace to political liberties and the ways virtual communities are likely to change our experience of the real world, as individuals and communities. Although I am enthusiastic about the liberating potentials of computer-mediated communications, I try to keep my eyes open for the pitfalls of mixing technology and human relationships. I hope my reports from the outposts and headquarters of this new kind of social habitation, and the stories of the people I've met in cyberspace, will bring to life the cultural, political, and ethical implications of virtual communities both for my fellow explorers of cyberspace and for those who never heard of it before.

The technology that makes virtual communities possible has the potential to bring enormous leverage to ordinary citizens at relatively little cost—intellectual leverage, social leverage, commercial leverage, and most important, political leverage. But the technology will not in itself fulfill that potential; this latent technical power must be used intelligently and deliberately by an informed population. More people must learn about that leverage and learn to use it, while we still have the freedom to do so, if it is to live up to its potential. The odds are always good that big power and big money will find a way to control access to virtual communities; big power and big money always found ways to control new communications media when they emerged in the past. The Net is still out of control in fundamental ways, but it might not stay that way for long. What we know and do now is important because it is still possible for people around the world to make sure this new sphere of vital human discourse remains open to the citizens of the planet before the political and economic big boys seize it, censor it, meter it, and sell it back to us.

The potential social leverage comes from the power that ordinary citizens gain when they know how to connect two previously independent, mature, highly decentralized technologies: It took billions of dollars and decades to develop cheap personal computers. It took billions of dollars and more than a century to wire up the worldwide telecommunication network. With the right knowledge, and not too much of it, a ten-year-old kid today can plug these two vast, powerful, expensively developed technologies together for a few hundred dollars and instantly obtain a bully pulpit, the Library of Congress, and a world full of potential coconspirators.

Computers and the switched telecommunication networks that also carry our telephone calls constitute the technical foundation of computer-mediated communications (CMC). The technicalities of CMC, how bits of computer data move over wires and are reassembled as computer files at their destinations, are invisible and irrelevant to most people who use it, except when the technicalities restrict their access to CMC services. The important thing to keep in mind is that the world-wide, interconnected telecommunication network that we use to make telephone calls in Manhattan and Madagascar can also be used to connect computers together at a distance, and you don't have to be an engineer to do it.

The Net is an informal term for the loosely interconnected computer networks that use CMC technology to link people around the world into public discussions.

Virtual communities are social aggregations that emerge from the Net when enough people carry on those public discussions long enough, with sufficient human feeling, to form webs of personal relationships in cyberspace.

Cyberspace, originally a term from William Gibson's science-fiction novel *Neuromancer*, is the name some people use for the conceptual space where words, human relationships, data, wealth, and power are manifested by people using CMC technology.

Although spatial imagery and a sense of place help convey the experience of dwelling in a virtual community, biological imagery is often more appropriate to describe the way cyberculture changes. In terms of the way the whole system is propagating and evolving, think of cyberspace as a social petri dish, the Net as the agar medium, and virtual communities, in all their diversity, as the colonies of microorganisms that grow in petri dishes. Each of the small colonies of microorganisms—the communities on the Net—is a social experiment that nobody planned but that is happening nevertheless.

We now know something about the ways previous generations of communications technologies changed the way people lived. We need to understand why and how so many social experiments are coevolving today with the prototypes of the newest communications technologies. My direct observations of online behavior around the world over the past ten years have led me to conclude that whenever CMC technology becomes available to people anywhere, they inevitably build virtual communities with it, just as microorganisms inevitably create colonies.

I suspect that one of the explanations for this phenomenon is the hunger for community that grows in the breasts of people around the world as more and more informal public spaces disappear from our real lives. I also suspect that these new media attract colonies of enthusiasts because CMC enables people to do things with each other in new ways, and to do altogether new kinds of things—just as telegraphs, telephones, and televisions did.

Because of its potential influence on so many people's beliefs and perceptions, the future of the Net is connected to the future of community, democracy, education, science, and intellectual life—some of the human institutions people hold most dear, whether or not they know or care about the future of computer technology. The future of the Net has become too important to leave to specialists and special interests. As it influences the lives of a growing number of people, more and more citizens must contribute to the dialogue about the way public funds are applied to the development of the Net, and we must join our voices to the debate about the way it should be administered. We need a clear citizens' vision of the way the Net ought to grow, a firm idea of the kind of media environment we would like to see in the future. If we do not develop such a vision for ourselves, the future will be shaped for us by large commercial and political powerholders.

The Net is so widespread and anarchic today because of the way its main sources converged in the 1980s, after years of independent, apparently unrelated development, using different technologies and involving different populations of participants. The technical and social convergences were fated, but not widely foreseen, by the late 1970s.

The wide-area CMC networks that span continents and join together thousands of smaller networks are a spinoff of American military research. The first computer network, ARPANET, was created in the 1970s so that Department of Defense-sponsored researchers could operate different computers at a distance; computer data, not person-to-person messages, were the intended content of the network, which handily happened to serve just as easily as a conduit for words. The fundamental technical idea on which ARPANET was based came from RAND, the think tank in Santa Monica that did a lot of work with top-secret thermonuclear war scenarios; ARPANET grew out of an older RAND scheme for a communication, command, and control network that could survive nuclear attack by having no central control.

Computer conferencing emerged, also somewhat unexpectedly, as a tool for using the communication capacities of the networks to build social relationships across barriers of space and time. A continuing theme throughout the history of CMC is the way people adapt technologies designed for one purpose to suit their own, very different, communication needs. And the most profound technological changes have come from the fringes and subcultures, not the orthodoxy of the computer industry or academic computer science. The programmers who created the first computer network installed electronic mail features; electronic mail wasn't the reason ARPANET was designed, but it was an easy thing to include once ARPANET existed. Then, in a similar, ad hoc, do-it-yourself manner, computer conferencing grew out of the needs of U.S. policymakers to develop a communications medium for dispersed decision making. Although the first computer conferencing experiments were precipitated by the U.S. government's wage-price freeze of the 1970s and the consequent need to disseminate up-to-date information from a large number of geographically dispersed local headquarters, computer conferencing was quickly adapted to commercial, scientific, and social discourse.

The hobbyists who interconnect personal computers via telephone lines to make computer bulletin-board systems, known as BBSs, have home-grown their part of the Net, a true grassroots use of technology. Hundreds of thousands of people around the world piggyback legally on the telecom network via personal computers and ordinary telephone lines. The most important technical attribute of networked BBSs is that it is an extremely hard network to kill—just as the RAND planners had hoped. Information can take so many alternative routes when one of the nodes of the network is removed that the Net is almost immortally flexible. It is this flexibility that CMC telecom pioneer John Gilmore referred to when he said, "The Net interprets censorship as damage and routes around it." This way of passing information and communication around a network as a distributed resource with no central control manifested in the rapid growth of the anarchic global conversation known as Usenet. This invention of distributed conversation that flows around obstacles— a grassroots adaptation of a technology originally designed as a doomsday weapon—might turn out to be as important in the long run as the hardware and software inventions that made it possible.

The big hardwired networks spend a lot more money to create high-speed information conduits between high-capacity computing nodes. Internet, today's U.S. government-sponsored successor to ARPANET, is growing in every dimension at an astonishing pace. These "data super-highways" use special telecommunication lines and other equipment to send very large amounts of information throughout the network at very high speeds. ARPANET started around twenty years ago with roughly one thousand users, and now Internet is approaching ten million users.

The portable computer on my desk is hundreds of times less expensive and thousands of times more powerful than ARPANET's first nodes. The fiber-optic backbone of the current Internet communicates information millions of times faster than the first ARPANET. Everything about Internet has grown like a bacterial colony—the raw technical capacity to send information, the different ways people use it, and the number of users. The Internet population has grown by 15 percent a month for the past several years. John Quarterman, whose book *The Matrix* is a thick guide to the world's computer networks, estimates that there are nine hundred different networks worldwide today, not counting the more than ten thousand networks already linked by the Internet "network of networks."

Real grassroots, the kind that grow in the ground, are a self-similar branching structure, a network of networks. Each grass seed grows a branching set of roots, and then many more smaller roots grow off those; the roots of each grass plant interconnect physically with the roots of adjacent plants, as any gardener who has tried to uproot a lawn has learned. There is a grassroots element to the Net that was not, until very recently, involved with all the high-tech, top-secret doings that led to ARPANET—the BBSers.

The population of the grassroots part of the Net, the citizen-operated BBSs, has been growing explosively as a self-financed movement of enthusiasts, without the benefit of Department of Defense funding. A BBS is the simplest, cheapest infrastructure for CMC: you run special software, often available inexpensively, on a personal computer, and use a device known as a modem to plug the computer into your regular telephone line. The modem converts computer-readable information into audible beeps and boops that can travel over the same telephone wires that carry your voice; another modem at the other end decodes the beeps and boops into computer-readable bits and bytes. The BBS turns the bits and bytes into human-readable text. Other people use their computers to call your BBS, leave and retrieve messages stored in your personal computer, and you have a virtual community growing in your bedroom. As the system operator (sysop) of the BBS, you contribute part of your computer's memory and make sure your computer is plugged into the telephone; the participants pay for their own communication costs.

Boardwatch magazine estimates that sixty thousand BBSs operated in the United States alone in 1993, fourteen years after the first BBSs opened in Chicago and California. Each BBS supports a population of a dozen to several hundred, or even thousands, of individual participants. There are religious BBSs of every denomination, sex BBSs of every proclivity, political BBSs from all parts of the spectrum, outlaw BBSs, law enforcement BBSs, BBSs for the disabled, for educators, for kids, for cults, for nonprofit organizations—a list of the different flavors of special-interest BBSs is dozens of pages long. The BBS culture has spread from the United States to Japan, Europe, Central and South America.

Each BBS started out as a small island community of a few people who dialed into a number in their area code; by their nature, like a small-wattage radio station, BBSs are localized. But that's changing, too. Just as several different technologies converged over the past ten years to create CMC—a new medium with properties of its own—several different online social structures are in the process of converging and creating a kind of international culture with properties of its own.

Technical bridges are connecting the grassroots part of the network with the military-industrial parts of the network. The programmers who built the Net in the first place, the scholars who have been using it to exchange knowledge, the scientists who have been using it for research, are being joined by all those hobbyists with their bedroom and garage BBSs. Special "gateway" computers can link entire networks by automatically translating communications from the mechanical languages used in one network to the languages (known as protocols) used in another network. In recent years, the heretofore separate groups of Internet and BBS pioneers worked together to gateway the more than ten thousand computers of the worldwide FidoNet, the first network of small, private BBSs, with Internet's millions of people and tens of thousands of more powerful computers.

The Net and computer conferencing systems are converging too, as medium-size computer conferencing communities like the WELL join Internet. When the WELL upgraded to a high-speed connection to Internet, it became not just a community-in-progress but a gateway to a wider realm, the worldwide Net-at-large. Suddenly, the isolated archipelagos of a few hundred or a few thousand people are becoming part of an integrated entity. The small virtual communities still exist, like yeast in a rapidly rising loaf, but increasingly they are part of an overarching culture, similar to the way the United States became an overarching culture after the telegraph and telephone linked the states.

The WELL is a small town, but now there is a doorway in that town that opens onto the blooming, buzzing confusion of the Net, an entity with properties altogether different from the virtual villages of a few years ago. I have good friends now all over the world who I never would have met without the mediation of the Net. A large circle of Net acquaintances can make an enormous difference in your experience when you travel to a foreign culture. Wherever I've traveled physically in recent years, I've found ready-made communities that I met online months before I traveled; our mutual enthusiasm for virtual communities served as a bridge, time and again, to people whose language and customs differ significantly from those I know well in California.

I routinely meet people and get to know them months or years before I see them—one of the ways my world today is a different world, with different friends and different concerns, from the world I experienced in premodem days. The places I visit in my mind, and the people I communicate with from one moment to the next, are entirely different from the content of my thoughts or the state of my circle of friends before I started dabbling in virtual communities. One minute I'm involved in the minutiae of local matters such as planning next week's bridge game, and the next minute I'm part of a debate raging in seven countries. Not only do I inhabit my virtual communities; to the degree that I carry around their conversations in my head and begin to mix it up with them in real life, my virtual communities also inhabit my life. I've been colonized; my sense of family at the most fundamental level has been virtualized.

I've seen variations of the same virtualization of community that happened to me hitting other virtual groups of a few hundred or a few thousand, in Paris and London and Tokyo. Entire cities are coming online. Santa Monica, California, and Cleveland, Ohio, were among the first of a growing number of American cities that have initiated municipal CMC systems. Santa Monica's system has an active conference to discuss the problems of the city's homeless that involves heavy input from homeless Santa Monica citizens who use public terminals. This system has an electronic link with COARA, a similar regional system in a remote province of Japan. Biwa-Net, in the Kyoto area, is gatewayed to a sister city in Pennsylvania. The Net is only beginning to wake up to itself.

Watching a particular virtual community change over a period of time has something of the intellectual thrill of do-it-yourself anthropology, and some of the garden-variety voyeurism of eavesdropping on an endless amateur soap opera where there is no boundary separating the audience from the cast. For the price of a telephone call, you can take part in any kind of vicarious melodrama you can dream of; as a form of escape entertainment, the Minitel addicts in Paris and the MUDders of Internet and the obsessive IRC participants on college campuses everywhere have proved that CMC has a future as a serious marketplace for meterable interactive fantasies.

CMC might become the next great escape medium, in the tradition of radio serials, Saturday matinees, soap operas—which means that the new medium will be in some way a conduit for and reflector of our cultural codes, our social subconscious, our images of who "we" might be, just as previous media have been. There are other serious reasons that ordinary nontechnical citizens need to know something about this new medium and its social impact. Something big is afoot, and the final shape has not been determined.

In the United States, the Clinton administration is taking measures to amplify the Net's technical capabilities and availability manyfold via the National Research and Education Network. France, with the world's largest national information utility, Minitel, and Japan, with its stake in future telecommunications industries, have their own visions of the future. Albert Gore's 1991 bill, the High Performance Computing Act, signed into law by President Bush, outlined Gore's vision for "highways of the mind" to be stimulated by federal research-and-development expenditures as a national intellectual resource and carried to the citizens by private enterprise. The Clinton-Gore administration has used the example of the ARPA (Advanced Research Projects Agency) venture of the 1960s and 1970s that produced the Net and the foundations of personal computing as an example of the way they see government and the private sector interacting in regard to future communications technologies.

In the private sector, telecommunication companies, television networks, computer companies, cable companies, and newspapers in the United States, Europe, and Japan are jockeying for position in the nascent "home interactive information services industry." Corporations are investing hundreds of millions of dollars in the infrastructure for new media they hope will make them billions of dollars. Every flavor of technological futurist, from Alvin Toffler and John Naisbitt to Peter Drucker and George Gilder, base utopian hopes on "the information age" as a techno-fix for social problems. Yet little is known about the impact these newest media might have on our daily lives, our minds, our families, even the future of democracy.

CMC has the potential to change our lives on three different, but strongly interinfluential, levels. First, as individual human beings, we have perceptions, thoughts, and personalities (already shaped by other communications technologies) that are affected by the ways we use the medium and the ways it uses us. At this fundamental level, CMC appeals to us as mortal organisms with certain intellectual, physical, and emotional needs. Young people around the world have different communication proclivities from their pre-McLuhanized elders. MTV, for example, caters to an aesthetic sensibility that is closely tuned to the vocabulary of television's fast cuts, visually arresting images, and special effects. Now, some of those people around the world who were born in the television era and grew up in the cellular telephone era are beginning to migrate to CMC spaces that better fit their new ways of experiencing the world. There is a vocabulary to CMC, too, now emerging from millions and millions of individual online interactions. That vocabulary reflects something about the ways human personalities are changing in the age of media saturation.

The second level of possible CMC-triggered change is the level of person-to-person interaction where relationships, friendships, and communities happen. CMC technology offers a new capability of "many to many" communication, but the way such a capability will or will not be used in the future might depend on the way we, the first people who are using it, succeed or fail in applying it to our lives. Those of us who are brought into contact with each other by means of CMC technology find ourselves challenged by this many-to-many capability—challenged to consider whether it is possible for us to build some kind of community together.

The question of community is central to realms beyond the abstract networks of CMC technology. Some commentators, such as Bellah et al. (*Habits of the Heart, The Good Society*), have focused on the need for rebuilding community in the face of America's loss of a sense of a social commons.

Social psychologists, sociologists, and historians have developed useful tools for asking questions about human group interaction. Different communities of interpretation, from anthropology to economics, have different criteria for studying whether a group of people is a community. In trying to apply traditional analysis of community behavior to the kinds of interactions emerging from the Net, I have adopted a schema proposed by Marc Smith, a graduate student in sociology at the University of California at Los Angeles, who has been doing his fieldwork in the WELL and the Net. Smith focuses on the concept of "collective goods." Every cooperative group of people exists in the face of a competitive world because that group of people recognizes there is something valuable that they can gain only by banding together. Looking for a group's collective goods is a way of looking for the elements that bind isolated individuals into a community.

The three kinds of collective goods that Smith proposes as the social glue that binds the WELL into something resembling a community are social network capital, knowledge capital, and communion. Social network capital is what happened when I found a ready-made community in Tokyo, even though I had never been there in the flesh. Knowledge capital is what I found in the WELL when I asked questions of the community as an online brain trust representing a highly varied accumulation of expertise. And communion is what we found in the Parenting conference, when Phil's and Jay's children were sick, and the rest of us used our words to support them.

The third level of possible change in our lives, the political, derives from the middle, social level, for politics is always a combination of communications and physical power, and the role of communications media among the citizenry is particularly important in the politics of democratic societies. The idea of modern representative democracy as it was first conceived by Enlightenment philosophers included a recognition of a living web of citizen-to-citizen communications known as civil society or the public sphere. Although elections are the most visible fundamental characteristics of democratic societies, those elections are assumed to be supported by discussions among citizens at all levels of society about issues of importance to the nation.

If a government is to rule according to the consent of the governed, the effectiveness of that government is heavily influenced by how much the governed know about the issues that affect them. The mass-media-dominated public sphere today is where the governed now get knowledge; the problem is that commercial mass media, led by broadcast television, have polluted with barrages of flashy, phony, often violent imagery a public sphere that once included a large component of reading, writing, and rational discourse. For the early centuries of American history, until the telegraph made it possible to create what we know as news and sell the readers of newspapers to advertisers, the public sphere did rely on an astonishingly literate population. Neil Postman, in his book about the way television has changed the nature of public discourse, *Amusing Ourselves to Death*, notes that Thomas Paine's *Common Sense* sold three hundred thousand copies in five months in 1775. Contemporary observers have documented and analyzed the way mass media ("one to many" media) have "commoditized" the public sphere, substituting slick public relations for genuine debate and packaging both issues and candidates like other consumer products.

The political significance of CMC lies in its capacity to challenge the existing political hierarchy's monopoly on powerful communications media, and perhaps thus revitalize citizen-based democracy. The way image-rich, sound-bite-based commercial media have co-opted political discourse among citizens is part of a political problem that communications technologies have posed for democracy for decades. The way the number of owners or telecommunication channels is narrowing to a tiny elite, while the reach and power of the media they own expand, is a converging threat to citizens. Which scenario seems more conducive to democracy, which to totalitarian rule: a world in which a few people control communications technology that can be used to manipulate the beliefs of billions, or a world in which every citizen can broadcast to every other citizen?

Ben Bagdikian's often-quoted prediction from *The Media Monopoly* is that by the turn of the century "five to ten corporate giants will control most of the world's important newspapers, magazines, books, broadcast stations, movies, recordings and videocassettes." These new media lords possess immense power to determine which information most people receive about the world, and I suspect they are not likely to encourage their privately owned and controlled networks to be the willing conduits for all the kinds of information that unfettered citizens and nongovernmental organizations tend to disseminate. The activist solution to this dilemma has been to use CMC to create alternative planetary information networks. The distributed nature of the telecommunications network, coupled with the availability of affordable computers, makes it possible to piggyback alternate networks on the mainstream infrastructure.

We temporarily have access to a tool that could bring conviviality and understanding into our lives and might help revitalize the public sphere. The same tool, improperly controlled and wielded, could become an instrument of tyranny. The vision of a citizen-designed, citizen-controlled worldwide communications network is a version of technological utopianism that could be called the vision of "the electronic agora." In the original democracy, Athens, the agora was the marketplace, and more— it was where citizens met to talk, gossip, argue, size each other up, find the weak spots in political ideas by debating about them. But another kind of vision could apply to the use of the Net in the wrong ways, a shadow vision of a less utopian kind of place—the Panopticon.

Panopticon was the name for an ultimately effective prison, seriously proposed in eighteenth-century Britain by Jeremy Bentham. A combination of architecture and optics makes it possible in Bentham's scheme for a single guard to see every prisoner, and for no prisoner to see anything else; the effect is that all prisoners act as if they were under surveillance at all times. Contemporary social critic Michel Foucault, in *Discipline and Punish*, claimed that the machinery of the worldwide communications network constitutes a kind of camouflaged Panopticon; citizens of the world brought into their homes, along with each other, the prying ears of the state. The cables that bring information into our homes today are technically capable of bringing information out of our homes, instantly transmitted to interested others. Tomorrow's version of Panoptic machinery could make very effective use of the same communications infrastructure that enables one-room schoolhouses in Montana to communicate with MIT professors, and enables citizens to disseminate news and organize resistance to totalitarian rule. With so much of our intimate data and more and more of our private behavior moving into cyberspace, the potential for totalitarian abuse of that information web is significant and the cautions of the critics are worth a careful hearing.

The wise revolutionary keeps an eye on the dark side of the changes he or she would initiate. Enthusiasts who believe in the humanitarian potential of virtual communities, especially those of us who speak of electronic democracy as a potential application of the medium, are well advised to consider the shadow potential of the same media. We should not forget that intellectuals and journalists of the 1950s hailed the advent of the greatest educational medium in history—television.

Because of its potential to change us as humans, as communities, as democracies, we need to try to understand the nature of CMC, cyberspace, and virtual communities in every important context—politically, economically, socially, cognitively. Each different perspective reveals something that the other perspectives do not reveal. Each different discipline fails to see something that another discipline sees very well. We need to think together here, across boundaries of academic discipline, industrial affiliation, nation, if we hope to understand and thus perhaps regain control of the way human communities are being transformed by communications technologies.

We can't do this solely as dispassionate observers, although there is certainly a strong need for the detached assessment of social science. Community is a matter of emotions as well as a thing of reason and data. Some of the most important learning will always have to be done by jumping into one corner or another of cyberspace, living there, and getting up to your elbows in the problems that virtual communities face.

I care about what happens in cyberspace, and to our freedoms in cyberspace, because I dwell there part of the time. The author's voice as a citizen and veteran of virtual community-building is one of the points of view presented in this book: I'm part of the story I'm describing, speaking as both native informant and as uncredentialed social scientist. Because of the paucity of first-person source material describing the way it feels to live in cyberspace, I believe it is valuable to include my perspective as participant as well as observer. In some places, like the WELL, I speak from extensive experience; in many of the places we need to examine in order to understand the Net, I am almost as new to the territory as those who never heard about cyberspace before. Ultimately, if you want to form your own opinions, you need to pick up a good beginner's guidebook and plunge into the Net for yourself. It is possible, however, to paint a kind of word-picture, necessarily somewhat sketchy, of the varieties of life to be found on the Net.

Much of this book is a tour of widening circles of virtual communities as they exist today. I believe that most citizens of democratic societies, given access to clearly presented information about the state of the Net, will make wise decisions about how the Net ought to be governed. But it is important to look in more than one corner and see through more than one set of lenses. Before we can discuss in any depth the way CMC technology is changing us as human beings, as communities, and as democracies, we need to know something about the people and places that make the Net what it is.

Our journey through the raucous immensity of Usenet, the subcultures of the MUDs and IRC channels, the BBSs, mailing lists, and e-journals, starts with a glimpse over my shoulder at the WELL, the place where cyberspace started for me. The ways I've witnessed people in the virtual community I know best build value, help each other through hard times, solve (and fail to solve) vexing interpersonal problems together, offer a model—undoubtedly not an infallible one—of the kinds of social changes that virtual communities can make in real lives on a modestly local scale. Some knowledge of how people in a small virtual community behave will help prevent vertigo and give you tools for comparison when we zoom out to the larger metropolitan areas of cyberspace. Some aspects of life in a small community have to be abandoned when you move to an online metropolis; the fundamentals of human nature, however, always scale up.

1

The Heart of the WELL

In the summer of 1986, my then-two-year-old daughter picked up a tick. There was this blood-bloated *thing* sucking on our baby's scalp, and we weren't quite sure how to go about getting it off. My wife, Judy, called the pediatrician. It was eleven o'clock in the evening. I logged onto the WELL. I got my answer online within minutes from a fellow with the improbable but genuine name of Flash Gordon, M.D. I had removed the tick by the time Judy got the callback from the pediatrician's office.

What amazed me wasn't just the speed with which we obtained precisely the information we needed to know, right when we needed to know it. It was also the immense inner sense of security that comes with discovering that real people—most of them parents, some of them nurses, doctors, and midwives—are available, around the clock, if you need them. There is a magic protective circle around the atmosphere of this particular conference. We're talking about our sons and daughters in this forum, not about our computers or our opinions about philosophy, and many of us feel that this tacit understanding sanctifies the virtual space.

The atmosphere of the Parenting conference—the attitudes people exhibit to each other in the tone of what they say in public—is part of what continues to attract me. People who never have much to contribute in political debate, technical argument, or intellectual gamesmanship turn out to have a lot to say about raising children. People you knew as fierce, even nasty, intellectual opponents in other contexts give you emotional support on a deeper level, parent to parent, within the boundaries of Parenting, a small but warmly human corner of cyberspace.

Here is a short list of examples from the hundreds of separate topics available for discussion in the Parenting conference. Each of these entries is the name of a conversation that includes scores or hundreds of individual contributions spread over a period of days or years, like a long, topical cocktail party you can rewind back to the beginning to find out who said what before you got there.

Great Expectations: You're Pregnant: Now What? Part III
What's Bad About Children's TV?
Movies: The Good, the Bad, and the Ugly
Initiations and Rites of Passage
Brand New Well Baby!!
How Does Being a Parent Change Your Life?
Tall Teenage Tales (cont.)
Guilt
MOTHERS
Vasectomy—Did It Hurt?
Introductions! Who Are We?
Fathers (Continued)
Books for Kids, Section Two
Gay and Lesbian Teenagers
Children and Spirituality
Great Parks for Kids
Quality Toys
Parenting in an Often-Violent World
Children's Radio Programming
New WELL Baby
Home Schooling
Newly Separated/Divorced Fathers
Another Well Baby—Carson Arrives in Seattle!
Single Parenting
Uncle Philcat's Back Fence: Gossip Here!
Embarrassing Moments
Kids and Death
All the Poop on Diapers
Pediatric Problems—Little Sicknesses and Sick Little Ones
Talking with Kids About the Prospect of War
Dealing with Incest and Abuse
Other People's Children
When They're Crying
Pets for Kids

People who talk about a shared interest, albeit a deep one such as being a parent, don't often disclose enough about themselves as whole individuals online to inspire real trust in others. In the case of the sub-community of the Parenting conference, a few dozen of us, scattered across the country, few of whom rarely if ever saw the others face-to-face, had a few years of minor crises to knit us together and prepare us for serious business when it came our way. Another several dozen read the conference regularly but contribute only when they have something important to add. Hundreds more every week read the conference without comment, except when something extraordinary happens.

Jay Allison and his family live in Massachusetts. He and his wife are public-radio producers. I've never met any of them face-to-face, although I feel I know something powerful and intimate about the Allisons and have strong emotional ties to them. What follows are some of Jay's postings on the WELL:

Woods Hole. Midnight. I am sitting in the dark of my daughter's room. Her monitor lights blink at me. The lights used to blink too brightly so I covered them with bits of bandage adhesive and now they flash faintly underneath, a persistent red and green, Lillie's heart and lungs.

Above the monitor is her portable suction unit. In the glow of the flashlight I'm writing by, it looks like the plastic guts of a science-class human model, the tubes coiled around the power supply, the reservoir, the pump.

Tina is upstairs trying to get some sleep. A baby monitor links our bedroom to Lillie's. It links our sleep to Lillie's too, and because our souls are linked to hers, we do not sleep well.

I am naked. My stomach is full of beer. The flashlight rests on it, and the beam rises and falls with my breath. My daughter breathes through a white plastic tube inserted into a hole in her throat. She's fourteen months old.

Sitting in front of our computers with our hearts racing and tears in our eyes, in Tokyo and Sacramento and Austin, we read about Lillie's croup, her tracheostomy, the days and nights at Massachusetts General Hospital, and now the vigil over Lillie's breathing and the watchful attention to the mechanical apparatus that kept her alive. It went on for days. Weeks. Lillie recovered, and relieved our anxieties about her vocal capabilities after all that time with a hole in her throat by saying the most extraordinary things, duly reported online by Jay.

Later, writing in *Whole Earth Review*, Jay described the experience:

Before this time, my computer screen had never been a place to go for solace. Far from it. But there it was. Those nights sitting up late with my daughter, I'd go to my computer, dial up the WELL, and ramble. I wrote about what was happening that night or that year. I didn't know anyone I was "talking" to. I had never laid eyes on them. At 3:00 a.m. my "real" friends were asleep, so I turned to this foreign, invisible community for support. The WELL was always awake.

Any difficulty is harder to bear in isolation. There is nothing to measure against, to lean against. Typing out my journal entries into the computer and over the phone lines, I found fellowship and comfort in this unlikely medium.

Over the years, despite the distances, those of us who made heart-to-heart contact via the Parenting conference began to meet face-to-face. The WELL's annual summer picnic in the San Francisco Bay area grew out of a face-to-face gathering that was originally organized in the Parenting conference. We had been involved in intense online conversations in this conference all year. When summer rolled around we started talking about doing something relaxing together, like bringing our kids somewhere for a barbecue. In typical WELL fashion, it quickly amplified to a WELLwide party hosted by the Parenting conference. Phil Catalfo reserved a picnic site and the use of a softball field in a public park.

Parents talk about their kids online—what else?—and therefore we all already knew about my daughter Mamie and Philcat's son Gabe and Busy's son, the banjo player, but we had not seen many of them before. I remember that when I arrived at the park, Mamie and I recognized one particular group, out of the first half-dozen large parties of picnickers we saw in the distance. There was just something about the way they were all standing, talking with each other in knots of two or three, while the kids ran around the eucalyptus grove and found their way to the softball diamond. I remember playing on the same team with a fellow who never ceases to annoy me when he wrenches every conversation online around to a debate about libertarianism; I remember thinking, after we had darn near accomplished a double play together, that he wasn't such a bad guy.

It was a normal American community picnic—people who value each other's company, getting together with their kids for softball and barbecue on a summer Sunday. It could have been any church group or PTA. In this case, it was the indisputably real-life part of a virtual community. The first Parenting conference picnic was such a success that it became an annual event, taking place around the summer solstice. And kids became a fixture at all the other WELL parties.

Another ritual for parents and kids and friends of parents and kids started in the winter, not long after the picnic tradition began. For the past four or five years, in December, most of the conference participants within a hundred miles, and their little ones, show up in San Francisco for the annual Pickle Family Circus benefit and potluck. One of the directors of this small circus is a beloved and funny member of the WELL community; he arranges a special block of seats each year. After the circus is over and the rest of the audience has left, we treat the performers, the stagehands, and ourselves to a potluck feast.

Albert Mitchell is an uncommonly fierce and stubborn fellow—many would say pugnacious—who argues his deeply felt principles in no uncertain terms. He can be abrasive, even frightening, in his intensity. He gets particularly riled up by certain topics—organized religion, taxation, and circumcision—but there are other ways to cross him and earn some public or private vituperation. I discovered that I could never again really be too frightened by Albert's fierce online persona—the widely known and sometimes feared "sofia"—after seeing him and his sweet daughter, Sofia, in her clown suit, at a Pickle potluck. He gave me a jar of honey from his own hive at that event, even though we had been shouting at each other online in ways that probably would have degenerated into fisticuffs face-to-face. At the Pickle Family Circus or the summer picnic, we were meeting in the sacred space of Parenting, not the bloody arenas of WELL policy or politics.

The Parenting conference had been crisis-tested along with the Allisons, and had undergone months of the little ups and downs with the kids that make up the normal daily history of any parent, when one of our most regular, most dear, most loquacious participants, Phil Catalfo, dropped a bombshell on us.

Topic 349: Leukemia

By: Phil Catalfo (philcat) on Wed, Jan 16, '91
404 responses so far

<linked topic>

I'd like to use this topic for discussing leukemia,
the disease, both as it affects my family and what
is known about it generally.

We learned early last week that our son Gabriel, 7
(our middle child), has acute lymphocytic leukemia,
aka ALL. I will be opening one or more additional
topics to discuss the chronology of events,
emotions and experiences stirred up by this newly
central fact of our lives, and so on. (I'm also
thinking of opening a topic expressly for everyone
to send him get-well wishes.) I intend for this
topic to focus on the disease itself—his diagnosis
and progress, but also other cases we know about,
resources (of all types) available, etc. etc.

If Tina has no objection, I'd like to ask the
hosts of the Health conf. to link any/all of these
topics to their conf. I can't think offhand of
where else might be appropriate, but I'm sure
you'll all suggest away.

The first thing I want to say, regardless of how
it does or doesn't pertain to this particular
topic, is that the support and love my family and
I, and especially Gabe, have been receiving from
the WELL, have been invaluable. This turns out to
have a medical impact, which we'll discuss in good
time, but I want to say out loud how much it's
appreciated: infinitely.

With that, I'll enter this, and return as soon as
I can to say more about Gabe's case and what I've
learned in the past week about this disease and
what to do about it.

404 responses total.

```
# 1: Nancy A. Pietrafesa (lapeche)   Wed, Jan 16,
'91 (17:21)

Philcat, we're here and we're listening. We share
your hope and a small part of your pain. Hang on.

# 2: Tina Loney (onezie)   Wed, Jan 16, '91 (19:09)

Phil, I took the liberty of writing to flash (host
of the Health conf) and telling him to link
whichever of the three topics he feels appropriate.
I very much look forward to you telling us all
that you can/are able about Gabe. In the meanwhile,
I'm thinking about Gabriel and your entire family.
Seems I remember Gabe has quite a good Catalfic
sense of humor, and I hope you're able to aid him
in keeping that in top form. . . . Virtual hugs
are *streaming* in his direction. . . .
```

The Parenting regulars, who had spent hours in this conference trading quips and commiserating over the little ups and downs of life with children, chimed in with messages of support. One of them was a nurse. Individuals who had never contributed to the Parenting conference before entered the conversation, including a couple of doctors who helped Phil and the rest of us understand the daily reports about blood counts and other diagnostics and two other people who had firsthand knowledge, as patients suffering from blood disorders themselves.

Over the weeks, we all became experts on blood disorders. We also understood how the blood donation system works, what Danny Thomas and his St. Jude Hospital had to do with Phil and Gabe, and how parents learn to be advocates for their children in the medical system without alienating the caregivers. Best of all, we learned that Gabe's illness went into remission after about a week of chemotherapy.

With Gabe's remission, the community that had gathered around the leukemia topic redirected its attention to another part of the groupmind. Lhary, one of the people from outside the Parenting conference who had joined the discussion of leukemia because of the special knowledge he had to contribute, moved from the San Francisco area to Houston in order to have a months-long bone-marrow transplant procedure in an attempt to abate his own leukemia. He continued to log onto the WELL from his hospital room. The Catalfos and others got together and personally tie-dyed regulation lab coats and hospital gowns for Lhary to wear around the hospital corridors.

Many people are alarmed by the very idea of a virtual community, fearing that it is another step in the wrong direction, substituting more technological ersatz for yet another natural resource or human freedom. These critics often voice their sadness at what people have been reduced to doing in a civilization that worships technology, decrying the circumstances that lead some people into such pathetically disconnected lives that they prefer to find their companions on the other side of a computer screen. There is a seed of truth in this fear, for virtual communities require more than words on a screen at some point if they intend to be other than ersatz.

Some people—many people—don't do well in spontaneous spoken interaction, but turn out to have valuable contributions to make in a conversation in which they have time to think about what to say. These people, who might constitute a significant proportion of the population, can find written communication more authentic than the face-to-face kind. Who is to say that this preference for one mode of communication—informal written text—is somehow less authentically human than audible speech? Those who critique CMC because some people use it obsessively hit an important target, but miss a great deal more when they don't take into consideration people who use the medium for genuine human interaction. Those who find virtual communities cold places point at the limits of the technology, its most dangerous pitfalls, and we need to pay attention to those boundaries. But these critiques don't tell us how Philcat and Lhary and the Allisons and my own family could have found the community of support and information we found in the WELL when we needed it. And those of us who do find communion in cyberspace might do well to pay attention to the way the medium we love can be abused.

Although dramatic incidents are what bring people together and stick in their memories, most of what goes on in the Parenting conference and most virtual communities is informal conversation and downright chitchat. The model of the WELL and other social clusters in cyberspace as "places" is one that naturally emerges whenever people who use this medium discuss the nature of the medium. In 1987, Stewart Brand quoted me in his book *The Media Lab* about what tempted me to log onto the WELL as often as I did: "There's always another mind there. It's like having the corner bar, complete with old buddies and delightful newcomers and new tools waiting to take home and fresh graffiti and letters, except instead of putting on my coat, shutting down the computer, and walking down to the corner, I just invoke my telecom program and there they are. It's a place."

The existence of computer-linked communities was predicted twenty-five years ago by J. C. R. Licklider and Robert Taylor, research directors for the Department of Defense's Advanced Research Projects Agency (ARPA), who set in motion the research that resulted in the creation of the first such community, the ARPANET: "What will on-line interactive communities be like?" Licklider and Taylor wrote in 1968: "In most fields they will consist of geographically separated members, sometimes grouped in small clusters and sometimes working individually. They will be communities not of common location, but of common interest. . . ."

My friends and I sometimes believe we are part of the future that Licklider dreamed about, and we often can attest to the truth of his prediction that "life will be happier for the on-line individual because the people with whom one interacts most strongly will be selected more by commonality of interests and goals than by accidents of proximity." I still believe that, but I also know that life online has been unhappy at times, intensely so in some circumstances, because of words I've read on a screen. Participating in a virtual community has not solved all of life's problems for me, but it has served as an aid, a comfort, and an inspiration at times; at other times, it has been like an endless, ugly, long-simmering family brawl.

I've changed my mind about a lot of aspects of the WELL over the years, but the sense of place is still as strong as ever. As Ray Oldenburg proposed in *The Great Good Place*, there are three essential places in people's lives : the place we live, the place we work, and the place we gather for conviviality. Although the casual conversation that takes place in cafes, beauty shops, pubs, and town squares is universally considered to be trivial, idle talk, Oldenburg makes the case that such places are where communities can come into being and continue to hold together. These are the unacknowledged agorae of modern life. When the automobilecentric, suburban, fast-food, shopping-mall way of life eliminated many of these "third places" from traditional towns and cities around the world, the social fabric of existing communities started shredding.

Oldenburg explicitly put a name and conceptual framework on that phenomenon that every virtual communitarian knows instinctively, the power of informal public life:

Third places exist on neutral ground and serve to level their guests to a condition of social equality. Within these places, conversation is the primary activity and the major vehicle for the display and appreciation of human personality and individuality. Third places are taken for granted and most have a low profile. Since the formal institutions of society make stronger claims on the individual, third places are normally open in the off hours, as well as at other times. The character of a third place is determined most of all by its regular clientele and is marked by a playful mood, which contrasts with people's more serious involvement in other spheres. Though a radically different kind of setting for a home, the third place is remarkably similar to a good home in the psychological comfort and support that it extends.

Such are the characteristics of third places that appear to be universal and essential to a vital informal public life....

The problem of place in America manifests itself in a sorely deficient informal public life. The structure of shared experience beyond that offered by family, job, and passive consumerism is small and dwindling. The essential group experience is being replaced by the exaggerated self-consciousness of individuals. American life-styles, for all the material acquisition and the seeking after comforts and pleasures, are plagued by boredom, loneliness, alienation, and a high price tag....

Unlike many frontiers, that of the informal public life does not remain benign as it awaits development. It does not become easier to tame as technology evolves, as governmental bureaus and agencies multiply, or as population grows. It does not yield to the mere passage of time and a policy of letting the chips fall where they may as development proceeds in other areas of urban life. To the contrary, neglect of the informal public life can make a jungle of what had been a garden while, at the same time, diminishing the ability of people to cultivate it.

It might not be the same kind of place that Oldenburg had in mind, but so many of his descriptions of third places could also describe the WELL. Perhaps cyberspace is one of the informal public places where people can rebuild the aspects of community that were lost when the malt shop became a mall. Or perhaps cyberspace is precisely the *wrong* place to look for the rebirth of community, offering not a tool for conviviality but a life-denying simulacrum of real passion and true commitment to one another. In either case, we need to find out soon.

* * *

The feeling of logging into the WELL for just a minute or two, dozens of times a day, is very similar to the feeling of peeking into the café, the pub, the common room, to see who's there, and whether you want to stay around for a chat. As social psychologist Sara Kiesler put it in an article about networks for *Harvard Business Review*: "One of the surprising properties of computing is that it is a social activity. Where I work, the most frequently run computer network program is the one called 'Where' or 'Finger' that finds other people who are logged onto the computer network."

Because we cannot see one another in cyberspace, gender, age, national origin, and physical appearance are not apparent unless a person wants to make such characteristics public. People whose physical handicaps make it difficult to form new friendships find that virtual communities treat them as they always wanted to be treated—as thinkers and transmitters of ideas and feeling beings, not carnal vessels with a certain appearance and way of walking and talking (or not walking and not talking).

One of the few things that enthusiastic members of virtual communities in Japan, England, France, and the United States all agree on is that expanding their circle of friends is one of the most important advantages of computer conferencing. CMC is a way to *meet* people, whether or not you feel the need to affiliate with them on a community level. It's a way of both making contact with and maintaining a distance from others. The way you meet people in cyberspace puts a different spin on affiliation: in traditional kinds of communities, we are accustomed to meeting people, then getting to know them; in virtual communities, you can get to know people and then choose to meet them. Affiliation also can be far more ephemeral in cyberspace because you can get to know people you might never meet on the physical plane.

How does anybody find friends? In the traditional community, we search through our pool of neighbors and professional colleagues, of acquaintances and acquaintances of acquaintances, in order to find people who share our values and interests. We then exchange information about one another, disclose and discuss our mutual interests, and sometimes we become friends. In a virtual community we can go directly to the place where our favorite subjects are being discussed, then get acquainted with people who share our passions or who use words in a way we find attractive. In this sense, the topic is the address: you can't simply pick up a phone and ask to be connected with someone who wants to talk about Islamic art or California wine, or someone with a three-year-old daughter or a forty-year-old Hudson; you can, however, join a computer conference on any of those topics, then open a public or private correspondence with the previously unknown people you find there. Your chances of making friends are magnified by orders of magnitude over the old methods of finding a peer group.

You can be fooled about people in cyberspace, behind the cloak of words. But that can be said about telephones or face-to-face communication as well; computer-mediated communications provide new ways to fool people, and the most obvious identity swindles will die out only when enough people learn to use the medium critically. In some ways, the medium will, by its nature, be forever biased toward certain kinds of obfuscation. It will also be a place that people often end up revealing themselves far more intimately than they would be inclined to do without the intermediation of screens and pseudonyms.

The sense of communion I've experienced on the WELL is exemplified by the Parenting conference but far from limited to it. We began to realize in other conferences, facing other human issues, that we had the power not only to use words to share feelings and exchange helpful information, but to accomplish things in the real world.

The power of the WELL's community of users to accomplish things in the real world manifested itself dramatically when we outgrew our first computer. The computing engine that put-putted us around as a group of seven hundred users in 1985 was becoming inadequate for the three thousand users we had in 1988. Things started slowing down. You would type a letter on your keyboard and wait seconds for the letter to be displayed on your screen. It quickly became frustrating.

Because we had such a large proportion of computer experts among the population, we knew that the only solution to the interminable system lag that made it agonizing to read and even more agonizing to write on the WELL's database was to move to more up-to-date hardware, better suited to keeping up with the communication tasks of a hive numbering in the thousands. But the WELL's managing director, Clifford Figallo, himself an active member of the WELL community, reported that the WELL as a business entity was unable to find the kind of financing we'd need to upgrade our system.

That's when some of the armchair experts online started talking about their back-of-the-envelope calculations. If the hard-core users who had grown so irritated about the system's performance (but had realized that there was no place remotely like the WELL to turn to as an alternative) were willing to pay their next few months bills in advance, how much money would it take to buy the big iron? Half-seriously, Clifford Figallo named a figure. Within a few days, enough people had pledged hundreds of dollars each, thousands of dollars cumulatively, to get the show on the road. The checks arrived, the computer was purchased, the hardware was installed, and the database—the living heart of the community—was transferred to its new silicon body.

After suffering through the last months of the Vax, the first months of our new computer, the Sequent, was like switching from a Schwinn to a Rolls. And we had flexed our first barn-raising muscles in a characteristically unorthodox way: here were the customers, and the producers of the value that the customers buy, raising money among themselves to loan the owners of the business so they could sell themselves more of each other.

Casey's operation was another barn raising. This one was her idea. Casey was another WELL old-timer who had a job—freelance transcription and word processing services—that enabled her to work at home. Nobody ever doubts her intelligence, although her manner is often indelicate. The way she would say it, I'm sure, is that she has a "relatively low need for affiliation." The way others might say it is that Casey is a tough cookie.

Casey, whose real name is Kathleen, needed an operation that she could almost, but not quite, afford; her ability to walk was at stake. So she put up $500 to have a poster of her own design printed. The poster showed the silhouette of a head, with the title "This Is Your Mind on the WELL," and the head was filled with words and phrases that WELL users would recognize. She offered copies for sale as a benefit for her operation at $30 each. She raised the money she needed.

The most dramatic barn raising, however, was the saga of Elly, a shy and gentle and much-loved WELLite who left the virtual community, possibly forever, to travel to the farthest reaches of the Himalayas. Her saga, her crisis, and the WELL's response unfolded over period of months, and climaxed over a few intensely active days:

Topic 198: News from Elly
By: Averi Dunn (vaxen) on Wed, Aug 28, '91
    263 responses so far

<linked topic>

This is the place to post any news which may come
your way about Northbay's vacationing host, Elly
van der Pas.

1: Elly van der Pas (elly) Wed, Aug 28, '91
(18:03)

Right now, I'm almost finished moving out of my
house. Later tonight, I'm going to look at my
stuff, and see if I have what I need for my trip,
and maybe do last minute shopping tomorrow.
Cleaning Friday. Gone Saturday to parts unknown.
The plane leaves Monday morning. Phew!

6: Averi Dunn (vaxen)   Mon, Sep 23, '91
(18:44)

I got another postcard from Elly on Saturday:
        13 Sept
        Amsterdam
    So far, so good. The weather's been beautiful,
and I've been riding all over by bike. Tomorrow I'm
going to London for a few days, and then to Italy
by train. Should be an adventure. I went to a
piano concert last night with friends of a friend,
and may be sailing today. Greetings to everyone.
Elly

22: Averi Dunn (vaxen) Thu, Nov 7, '91 (23:25)

Well, Kim, you can post the parts that don't
repeat. It's good to hear any news from Elly. And
with that in mind I post the following from her-
own-self:
        27 Oct 1991

I got your letter from Sept 14 yesterday, forwarded from Italy. Apparently they were having a post office strike of something, because one of the workers drowned in the elevator. Anyway, they didn't process mail for at least a week, so I didn't get any letters.

Anyway, you have no idea how weird it is to be sitting on a mountain in Kathmandu reading about AP2 and the WELL. Oh, I took a picture of the WELL coffee shop in London and sent it to the office. I hope they get it. I thought it was quite appropriate. Janey Fritsche showed up about a week ago, and then took off trekking. It was good to see her. My friend Peter will be here, too, in a few days, and I guess I'll come down off the mountain to spend some time renewing visas and stocking up for the month-long course. We have to stay put for that, and no mail, either, so this might be it for awhile. Happy Thanksgiving, Merry Christmas, and Happy New Year. They've just finished their big holiday here—everyone was off work for a week, and dressed in new clothes. The kids made huge bamboo swings and went out kite flying.

I've been studying Dzogchen, which is like Tibetan Zen—meditating on the empty mind. Different from what I've done before. We stayed for awhile at a monastery way up in the hills, where there's an old abbot who specializes in pointing out the nature of the mind. It was rather an unusual opportunity.

You guys are all asleep now, except maybe for you. It's 2 pm—too late for lunch and too early for tea. Just about bath time, though, because we have a solar heater on the roof. I'm taking all my baths now, because in a week, 300 people will come here for the course, and bathing will be a fond dream. Or showering, that is.

Tell Brian and June and Josephine I said hi, and that I'm OK. I hope they got my card. I'll try to write, but don't know when I'll get time.

Take care of yourself and be happy,
      Elly

\# 26: Averi Dunn (vaxen) Sat, Dec 28, '91 (01:26)
The following are excerpts from a letter I received from Elly on Dec 21.
****
      7 Nov
The course starts today so I'm incommunicado for a month.
      13 Dec
Hmmm. I guess I never finished this. Lots of things have happened since then. Mainly, I've become a nun. I sent details to Hank so he could post, because I have to write about 10 letters for Peter to take back when he goes.
***
It's a little strange, but I feel really good about it, and I really feel it's the right move for me. Even Peter agrees.
***
I never wanted to be a nun (at least not before now). I always felt a little sorry for the Catholic nuns. This is a little different, though—much more freedom. It's interesting to have short hair, though. I think I'll grow it out to about 3/4".:-)
***
PPS. My ordination name is Jigme Palmo: Glorious fearless woman (!!!?)
****
She also sent an address she can be reached at for the next six months. Drop me Email if you want it.

So Elly had decided to become a Buddhist nun in Asia, and therefore threatened to pass into the annals of WELL legend. The topic stayed dormant for six months. In June, former neighbor Averi Dunn, who had been typing Elly's correspondence into the WELL, reported hearing that Elly had some kind of amoeba in her liver. At the end of July 1992, Flash Gordon reported that Elly was in a hospital in New Delhi. In a coma. She had severe hepatitis and reportedly suffered liver failure. If that report turned out to be true, Flash and the other doctors online agreed that the prognosis was not good.

Within hours, people started doing things in half a dozen directions on their own initiative. The raw scope and diversity of the resources available to us by pooling our individual networks was astonishing. People who had medical connections in New Delhi were brought in; airline schedules and rates for medical evacuation were researched; a fund was started and contributions started arriving. Casey used the Net to find a possible telecommunications site in New Delhi where they could relay information for Frank, Elly's ex-husband, who had flown to Asia to help with what was looking like a grave situation.

After a tense few days, the news made its way through the network that she did have some liver function left and might need access to special blood-filtering equipment before she could be moved. Within hours, we knew how to get such medical equipment in New Delhi and whose name to mention. We knew whom to call, how to ask, what it cost, and how to transfer funds to get Elly delivered to a hospital in the San Francisco region. "It gives me goosebumps," reported Onezie, as the topic unfolded on the WELL. "This is love in action."

Elly recovered enough strength to travel without medical evacuation. Her next message was direct, via the WELL:

```
#270: Elly van der Pas (elly) Fri, Sep 11, '92
(16:03)

Thanks to everyone for your generous WELLbeams,
good wishes, prayers, advice, and contributions of
green energy. The doctor thought the fast recovery
was due to Actigall, but in fact it was due to
beams, prayers, and pujas. He even said I might be
able to go back to India in February or so.|-)
```

If paying attention to other people's interests is a kind of attracting force in cyberspace, Blair Newman was a superconducting megamagnet. He acted the same way in person that he acted in his online persona of Metaview. Metaview had a jillion wonderful schemes for what you could do with new technology. Friends of his had become billionaires. How could you make a million on the blanking interval in television signals? How about a service that records only the television programs you want to watch? How many other intelligent crazies would pay good money for Compconf Psychserv?

He had a story to tell you. His eyes would get wide, and his overgrown mustache would twitch with excitement. His hair, a magnificent and irrevocably unruly dirty-blond mop, seemed to reflect his mental state; the curlier and more out of control his hair looked, the faster it seemed his mind had been moving. At WELL parties, his mental state was manic. He'd grab you, laugh in your face, drag you halfway through the crowd to introduce you to somebody. He would start laughing at somebody's joke, and the laughter would turn into a spasm of coughing that went on for frightening lengths of time.

To me, Blair Newman's defining characteristic was his habit of calling me—and any of several dozen people he liked and admired—via telephone if I wasn't online, to tell me to turn my television or radio to one channel or the other, *immediately*, because there was something on that I simply must pay attention to. He was often right, and it was well meant, but there was always something eerie about it. Here is an acquaintance of many years, but not a bosom buddy, who was thinking about what television program he knew I would really like to watch at 11:30 p.m. on a weeknight. That's the way he acted on the WELL, too.

My most important bond with Blair was the kind of bond that regulars in any informal public space share. In the late 1980s, Blair and I were among a floating group of ten to thirty WELLites you could count on at any time of day to be online. We often joke about the addictive qualities of the WELL. And there always seem to be several nonjoking discussions about WELL addiction going on in different parts of the WELL. At two bucks an hour, obsessive computer conferencing is cheaper than every other addiction except tobacco.

According to my recollection of Blair's own account, he had been a newly minted Harvard M.B.A. with a high daily cocaine intake, working with Howard Hughes's notoriously abstemious legal staff, deep in their Vegas bunkers. A chain-smoker and died-in-the-wool pothead (and also, according to his own account, one of the founders of the National Organization for the Reform of Marijuana Laws), Blair had been, in his past, a paradigm of the classic addictive personality. He was clean in regard to his cocaine problem when he came to the WELL, however. In a series of postings, Blair related to us how he'd realized that the WELL was for him more insidiously addictive than cocaine had been.

Years after he had kicked his cocaine habit, he claimed, somebody put a line of the substance next to Blair's computer while he was logged on. It dawned on him, several hours later, that the white crystals were still there, and he had known about them, but had not mustered the energy necessary to sniff them. It wasn't a moral decision but a battle of obsessions, Blair explained—he couldn't tear his hands from the keyboard and his eyes from the screen of his current, deeper addiction long enough to ingest the cocaine. Blair shared his insight with us, as he shared every single thing that crossed his unpredictable and unrelenting mind for hours a day, every day, for years.

You have to be careful with the addiction model as applied to the range of human behavior. Is a prodigy who practices day and night a violin addict? Perhaps. Is a great actor addicted to the attention of audiences? Probably. Is addiction the proper lens for evaluating the violinist's or actor's behavior? Probably not. But nobody who has let her meal grow cold and her family grow concerned while she keeps typing furiously on a keyboard in full hot-blooded debate with a group of invisible people in faraway places can dismiss the dark side of online enthusiasm. If a person has a compelling—even unhealthily compelling—need for a certain kind of attention from intelligent peers, the WELL is a great place to find it. Blair called it Compconf Psychscrv. It was cheaper than drugs, cheaper than shrinks, and it kept him off the street. He was smart enough to know what had happened to him, even as it tightened its grip.

Going after the juice of people's attention, especially large groups of intelligent people, was always part of Blair's story. He wanted to help. He wanted to impress.

Blair also got on people's nerves. His good-natured and totally unbelievably bald-faced self-promotion was part of it. He had a mythology about himself. One of his roommates had started one of the most successful software companies, according to Blair. He had worked for the upper echelons of the Howard Hughes organization, according to Blair. He had been a principal organizer of the marijuana legalization movement, according to Blair. He introduced famous computer entrepreneurs to one another in dramatic circumstances, according to Blair. It wasn't difficult to do a parody of a Blair Newman rap.

Then, after years online, and dozens of parties and excursions with other WELL members, and all the late-night phone calls with television recommendations to fellow WELLites, Blair Newman removed everything he had ever written on the WELL. For a day and a night and a day, most of the conversation on the WELL was about the trauma of mass-scribbling—the term that had emerged for the act of removing years' worth of postings. It seemed an act of intellectual suicide. A couple of weeks later, in real life, Blair Newman killed himself. A kind of myth seems to have grown up around this event, on the Net and in the mass media. The story has been distorted into a more dramatic form. In the urban folklore version that has been printed in some magazine articles, people from the WELL allegedly desperately tried to find Blair as his postings disappeared, and when his last comment was scribbled, the legend has it that he killed himself.

Most of the people at the funeral were from the WELL. But there was a surprising number of odd characters. We who were there remember the thoroughly slick fellow in the thousand-dollar suit and the three-hundred-dollar sunglasses who flew the corporate jet in from L.A. to the funeral, to tell the kind of story about Blair that Blair so frequently had told about himself. White Rastafarians showed up—marijuana legalization activists. Founders of successful software companies arrived. It was a great last laugh. As that amazing parade of people stood up in the funeral home and said their piece about Blair, it dawned on all of us that he had been telling the outrageous truth.

But when he was alive and in our faces, metaphorically speaking, in every conference on the WELL, many of us struck back with words: "Calm down, Blair," was something I said to him publicly. Bandy, who later gave Blair the software tool that enabled him to mass-scribble, started a topic in the Weird Conference (the WELL's subconscious free-fire zone) on "Day Sixteen of Your Lithium Holiday." Other remarks were even less kind, on my own part and the part of others. When you grab people's attention often, and monopolize the public soapbox, the response can be cruel. Like the legendary audience at the Apollo theater in Harlem, the WELL's audience can create a star or boo a bad performer off the stage. Blair experienced both reactions at the same time.

Sometimes, when the online banter got a little cruel, I would call Blair on the telephone and try to see what might really be the matter. We'd talk. He'd ramble until his beeper wrenched him off to another tangent. Blair was always one step ahead of the state of the art in message-forwarding technology.

It was after some weeks of fairly stormy psychic weather on the WELL that Blair obtained the virtual suicide weapon, the scribble tool. Weeks before that, Bandy, one of the WELL's technical staff, quit his job in a dispute over a personal relationship with another online character. When he quit, he used his programming expertise to create a tool that searched out everything he had ever posted to any public conference on the WELL, and deleted it, all of it. Quite a fancy trick, that, an act of programming virtuosity calculated to test the structural integrity of the social system. Bandy posted the source code for the scribble tool to the Net, which means that forevermore, anybody who wants to obtain the scribble weapon can post a request on the Net and sooner or later somebody will point to an archive where the program is stored.

The WELL's early history had established a strong relationship between the WELL and the anarchic subcommunity of volunteer programmers. For years, people had created tools, for free, and for the prestige, and because we needed them. Bandy was the first to create a weapon.

Every person who posts words in the WELL has the right to remove—scribble—those words later. Hosts have the power to scribble other people's words, but that power is severely constrained by the knowledge that the act is likely to be followed by weeks of acrimonious and repetitive debate. Hosts traditionally have scribbled comments written by other WELL users no more than once a year. Scribbling one's own comment is not as rare, but it is still far from the norm. Better to think twice before saying something, instead of saying too many things that you regret enough to scribble them, seems to be the unwritten law. Perhaps one in a thousand comments is scribbled.

You used to have to track down each comment, then follow a series of steps to scribble it. Of course, everybody should have the right to automatically remove every comment they've ever posted, now that the tool/weapon to do that exists, we decided in the endless arguments that followed its first use by Bandy, then Blair. But to actually do it is, in the eyes of many, despicably antisocial.

When Metaview used Bandy's scribble tool, the shock of ripping out several years' worth of postings from a very prolific writer made the fabric of recorded conversations, the entire history of the WELL's discourse to that point, look...moth-eaten. Often, as in particularly Metaview-intense topics, so much is missing that the entire thread is rendered indecipherable. It's annoying. Why be an enthusiastic member of a multiperson, multiyear word-weaving project if you plan to rip out your contributions to the conversational fabric when you leave?

The novelty of the act tempered our reactions, I think, when Bandy first mass-scribbled. The design problem of rebuilding our mental models of the WELL was perversely intriguing. The idea that the WELL seems to have a critical mass of thought-force in it that is greater than the destructive power of any one person is reinforced by the way it can withstand assaults on the commons. A lot of people cursed Blair for vandalizing the WELL that had nourished him for so long. I picked up the telephone and called him.

"Why did you do it, Blair?" I asked.

"It seemed like the thing to do at the time" is precisely what he told me. There was a flatness of affect to the way he said it. Nothing unusual there for Blair, who jumped from mood to mood during the course of a conversation. I think he really meant it. It was an impulse. The tool/weapon made it possible to follow the impulse. And that's what I reported back to the WELL community.

Nobody mistakes virtual life for real life, even though it has an emotional reality to many of us. Some kinds of impulses are simply more serious than others. Impulsive acts in real life can have more permanent consequences than even the most drastic acts in cyberspace. I asked Blair if he was feeling suicidal. He talked about it. I told him the old cliche, about suicide being a permanent solution to a temporary problem. After that conversation with Blair, I talked with his friend and psychiatrist. His toying with suicide was not new. One of these times, Blair was bound to succeed. This time he did.

From the moment we heard the news, the population of the WELL went through a period of transformation. Joking around with words on a computer keyboard is one thing. Going to Blair's funeral and talking to his family face-to-face was another.

Several topics on the WELL were devoted to Blair. One of the topics, at his family's request, was for people to post eulogies. Many of the other topics, those that were not donated to his parents, were hideously violent flamewars over the way people behaved and did not behave. In the heat of argument over one topic, people who had simmering resentments dating back to previous arguments took the opportunity to haul out the big guns. Suicide brings up unusual feelings in any family or social group. Fortunately, there were one or two among us who knew exactly how to understand what was happening to us; a fellow who had struggled with years of feelings over his brother's suicide was able to offer wise and caring and credible counsel to many of us.

There was the real-life funeral, where we brought our physical bodies and embraced each other and Blair's family. We were learning how fond we had grown of Blair, and how his death put a milestone in cyberspace. Marriages had happened and others had unraveled. Businesses had started and failed. We had parties and picnics. But death seems somehow more real, even if your only participation is in the virtual funeral. How could any of us who looked each other in the eye that afternoon in the funeral home deny that the bonds between us were growing into something real?

The feelings ran just as high during the virtual part of the grieving rituals as they did during the face-to-face part—indeed, with many of the social constraints of proper funeral behavior removed, the online version was the occasion for venting of anger that would have been inappropriate in a face-to-face gathering. There were those who passionately and persistently accused the eulogizers of exhibiting a hypocrisy that stank unto the heavens, because of our not altogether charitable treatment of Blair online when he was alive. Those of us who had made the calls to Blair and his shrinks, who went out and met his brother and his mother and tried to provide them some comfort, had a different attitude toward those who couldn't bring themselves to attend the painful event in person but didn't hesitate to heckle others online. People who had to live with each other, because they were all veteran addicts of the same social space, found themselves disliking one another.

For me, it was one particularly important lesson that has been reinforced many times since then. Words on a screen can hurt people. Although online conversation might have the ephemeral and informal feeling of a telephone conversation, it has the reach and permanence of a publication.

Years have passed. Megabytes of conversation have been added to the WELL. It isn't easy to find one of the parts of the old fabric where Blair's holes are still visible. But feelings that people online have toward one another are still profoundly influenced. As one WELLite, John P. Barlow, said at the time, you aren't a real community until you have a funeral.

2

Daily Life in Cyberspace:
How the Computerized Counterculture
Built a New Kind of Place

I was still toting around my 1969 edition of the *Whole Earth Catalog* when I read an article about a new computer service that *Whole Earth* publisher Stewart Brand and his gang were starting in the spring of 1985. For only $3 an hour, people with computers and modems could have access to the kind of online groups that cost five or ten times that much on other public telecommunication systems. I signed up for an account. I had previously suffered the initiation of figuring out how to plug in a modem and use it to connect to computer bulletin-board systems, or BBSs, and the Source (an early public information utility), so I was only a little dismayed that I had to learn a whole new set of commands to find my way through the software to the people. But established WELL users were extraordinarily helpful to newcomers, which more than made up for the bewilderment caused by the software. I started reading the conferences and began to post my own messages. Writing as a performing art! I was hooked in minutes.

Over a period of months, I fell into the habit of spending an hour or two every day gazing in fascination at this window into a community that was creating itself right in front of my eyes. Although the system was only a few months old, the air of camaraderie and pioneer spirit was evident among the regulars. Those three-dollar hours crept up on me in ten- to thirty-minute minivisits during the workday and hourlong chunks in the evening. Still, my daily telecommunicating expenses were less than the price of a couple of drinks or a double capuccino. The cumulative economic impact of my new habit came home to me when my first month's bill was over $100.

As it happened, a friend of mine had to deliver some artwork to the *Whole Earth Catalog* people, at the Sausalito office where the WELL also was located. So I went along for the ride. When we got to the rambling series of ancient offices in one of the last bohemian enclaves of the Sausalito houseboat district, I asked for the WELL. I was led to a small room and the staff of one, Matthew McClure. I talked with Matthew about the possibility of diminishing my monthly bill by starting and hosting a conference about the mind.

Hosts are the people who serve the same role in the WELL that a good host is supposed to serve at a party or salon—to welcome newcomers, introduce people to one another, clean up after the guests, provoke discussion, and break up fights if necessary. In exchange for these services, WELL hosts are given rebates on their bills. I was worried that my hosting duties might take up too much of my time.

Matthew smiled at my question. I know the meaning of that smile now, although it puzzled me then. He recognized what was happening to me. He judged it to be a good thing to happen to me, and to the WELL. He was right. But it was still Mephistophelian. He said, "Some hosts get away with less than an hour a week."

That was the fall of 1985. By the fall of 1986, the WELL was a part of my life I wasn't willing to do without. My wife was concerned, then jealous, then angry. The night we had the climactic argument, she said, referring to the small, peculiar, liberal arts college where we first met: "This is just like Reed. A bunch of intelligent misfits have found each other, and now you're having a high old time." The shock of recognition that came with that statement seemed to resolve the matter between us.

The WELL is rooted in the San Francisco Bay area and in two separate cultural revolutions that took place there in past decades. The *Whole Earth Catalog* originally emerged from the Haight-Ashbury counterculture as Stewart Brand's way of providing access to tools and ideas to all the communards who were exploring alternate ways of life in the forests of Mendocino or the high deserts outside Santa Fe. The *Whole Earth Catalog*s and the magazines they spawned—*Co-Evolution Quarterly* and its successor, *Whole Earth Review*—seem to have outlived the counterculture itself, since the magazine and catalogs still exist after twenty-five years.

One of *Whole Earth*'s gurus, Buckminster Fuller, was fond of using the analogy of the tiprudder—the small rudder on very big ships that is used to control the larger, main rudder. The tiprudder people who steer the movements and disciplines that steer society—the editors and engineers, scientists and science-fiction writers, freelance programmers and perma-culture evangelists, grassroots political activists and congressional aides—continued to need new tools and ideas, even though they were no longer a counterculture but part of the mainstream. These cultural exper-imenters continued to feed *Co-Evolution Quarterly* and then *Whole Earth Review* through decades when magazines died by the thousands. Even the idea that you could publish books on the West Coast was a rev-olution when it happened; in 1992, when *Publishers Weekly* ran an arti-cle on the history of West Coast publishing, it started with the *Whole Earth Catalog*. The first *Whole Earth Catalog* was the first idealistic enterprise from the counterculture, besides music, that earned the cul-tural legitimation of financial success.

The *Whole Earth Catalog* crew, riding on the catalog's success, launched a new magazine, *The Whole Earth Software Review*, and, after the WELL was started, received a record-breaking $1.4 million advance for the *Whole Earth Software Catalog*. It was time for the string of suc-cesses to take another turn: the WELL was the only one of the three proj-ects to succeed. The *Whole Earth Review* is what survived in print; the WELL did more than survive.

The inexpensive public online service was launched because two com-rades from a previous cultural revolution noticed that the technology of computer conferencing had potential far beyond its origins in military, scientific, and government communications. Brand had been part of the faculty at an online institute devoted to stretching the imaginations of business leaders—the Western Behavioral Sciences Institute (WBSI)—which introduced him to the effectiveness of computer conferencing. WBSI was also where he connected with Larry Brilliant.

Brilliant and Brand shared a history at the center of several of the most colorful events of the 1960s: Brand was "on the bus" with Ken Kesey and the Merry Pranksters (Kesey's pot bust, as described in Tom Wolfe's *Electric Kool-Aid Acid Test*, happened on the roof of Brand's apartment; Brand was one of the organizers of the seminal Trips Festival that gave birth to Bill Graham Presents and the whole rock concert scene). Brilliant had been part of the Prankster-affiliated commune, the Hog Farm (which had organized the security arrangements for Woodstock around the judicious use of cream pies and seltzer bottles and had whipped up "breakfast in bed for 400,000"). After his Hog Farm days, Brilliant became a doctor and an epidemiologist and ended up spearheading the World Health Organization's successful effort to eliminate smallpox.

Brilliant was involved with another health-care effort aimed at curing blindness in Asia, the Seva Foundation, and he had found that Seva's far-flung volunteers, medical staff, and organizational directors could meet and solve problems effectively through computer conferencing. When a medical relief helicopter lost an engine in a remote region of Nepal, the organization's online network located the nearest spare parts, gained key information about ways to cut through local bureaucracies, and transported the needed parts to the crippled aircraft. Brilliant became one of the principles of NETI, a business that created and licensed computer conferencing systems. After they met via WBSI's conferencing system, Brilliant offered Brand the license to Picospan (the WELL's conferencing software) and the money to lease a minicomputer, in exchange for a half interest in the new enterprise. The new enterprise started out in the *Whole Earth Review*'s charming but ramshackle office, leased a dozen incoming telephone lines, installed what was then a state-of-the-art minicomputer, and set up modems, and in 1985 the WELL was born.

Brand and Brilliant both hoped the WELL would become a vehicle for social change, but instead of trying to mold it in a specific image, they wanted to see the vehicle emerge spontaneously. The WELL was consciously a cultural experiment, and the business was designed to succeed or fail on the basis of the results of the experiment.

The person Stewart Brand chose to be the WELL's first director—technician, manager, innkeeper, and bouncer—was Matthew McClure, not coincidentally a computer-savvy veteran of the Farm, one of the most successful communes that started in the 1960s. Brand and McClure started a low-rules, high-tone discussion, where savvy networkers, futurists, intelligent misfits of several kinds who had learned how to make our outsider status work for us in one way or another, could take the technology of CMC to its cultural limits. When McClure left a year and a half later, another Farm veteran, Cliff Figallo, took over. While Figallo managed the business, yet another Farm veteran, John "Tex" Coate, was charged with building the community.

The Farm veterans had tried for more than a decade to create a self-sufficient colony in Tennessee. At the Farm's height, more than one thousand people worked together to try to create their own agricultural society. It still exists and is still surprisingly self-sufficient. They home-birthed and homeschooled, built laundries for washing hundreds of diapers, grew soybeans, and even extended their efforts to other countries —Cliff Figallo had spent years in Guatemala on behalf of Plenty, the Farm's international development arm, helping Maya villages install hygienic water systems. Matthew and Cliff and John and their families, including eight children, left the Farm after twelve years, partially out of disagreement with the way it was governed, partially out of weariness. Self-sufficiency is very hard work.

Brand thought the Farm alumni were perfect choices for their jobs at the WELL. Matthew was the only one with prior computer experience, but what they knew from the front lines of communal living about the way people reach decisions and create cultures collectively—and the ways people fail to reach decisions and create cultures—more than made up for their lack of computer savvy. By 1992, the WELL staff had grown to fifteen, the original minicomputer was long gone, and all the Farm veterans had moved on to other enterprises.

By the time I had been esconced in the WELL for a year, it seemed evident to me that the cultural experiment of a self-sustaining online salon was succeeding very well. At that point, as I was becoming convinced that we were all setting some sort of cultural precedent, I interviewed online both Matthew McClure and Kevin Kelly, who had been part of the original group that founded the WELL.

One of the advantages of computer conferencing is the community memory that preserves key moments in the history of the community. Sure enough, although I had not looked at it in years, the online oral history was still around, in the archives conference. The responses were dated October 1986.

Matthew McClure recalled that "Stewart's vision was very important in the design." The vision that McClure and Brand agreed on involved three goals: to facilitate communications among interesting people in the San Francisco Bay area, to provide sophisticated conferencing at a revolutionary low price, and to bring e-mail to the masses. To reach a critical mass, they knew they would need to start with interesting people having conversations at a somewhat more elevated level than the usual BBS stuff. In Matthew's words, "We needed a collection of shills who could draw the suckers into the tents." So they invited a lot of different people, gave them free accounts, called them "hosts," and encouraged them to re-create the atmosphere of a Paris salon—a bunch of salons. Brand, a biologist, insisted on letting the business grow instead of artificially stimulating it. Instead of spending money on glossy advertising, they gave free accounts to journalists.

McClure recalled two distinct growth spurts. First, the word about the WELL spread among the more adventurous members of the bay area's computer professionals, and the free journalist accounts paid off as WELLites began to write and publish articles about the WELL. Brand went to Cambridge to write a book, and the hosts seemed to have the run of the place.

"The next major event," McClure recalled, "was the organization of the Deadhead conference and subsequent promotion via interview and occasional remarks on local radio. Suddenly we had an onslaught of new users, many of whom possessed the single characteristic that most endears a user to a sysop [system operator]: ratchet jaws [habitual talkativeness]. The Deadheads came online and seemed to know instinctively how to use the system to create a community around themselves, for which I think considerable thanks are due to Maddog, Marye, and Rosebody. Not long thereafter we saw the concept of the online superstar taken to new heights with the advent of the True Confessions conference.... Suddenly our future looked assured.... "

Kevin Kelly had been editor of *Whole Earth Review* for several years when the WELL was founded. The Hackers' Conference had been his idea. Kelly recalled the original design goals that the WELL's founders had in mind when they opened for business in 1985.

The design goals were:

1. That it be free. This was a goal, not a commitment. We knew it wouldn't be exactly free but it should be as free (cheap) as we could make it....
2. It should be profit making...After much hard, low-paid work by Matthew and Cliff, this is happening. The WELL is at least one of the few operating large systems going that has a future.

3. It would be an open-ended universe...

4. It would be self-governing...

5. It would be a self-designing experiment.... The early users were to design the system for later users. The usage of the system would co-evolve with the system as it was built....

6. It would be a community, one that reflected the nature of Whole Earth publications. I think that worked out fine.

7. Business users would be its meat and potatoes. Wrong....

"The system is the people" is what you see when you log into TWICS, an English-language conferencing system in Tokyo. The same turned out to be true for the WELL, both by design and by happenstance. Matthew McClure understood that he was in the business of selling the customers to each other and letting them work out everything else. This was a fundamental revelation that stood the business in good stead in the years to follow. His successor, Farm alumnus Clifford Figallo, also resisted the temptation to control the culture instead of letting it work out its own system of social governance.

People who were looking for a grand collective project in cyberspace flocked to the WELL. The inmates took over the asylum, and the asylum profited from it. "What it is is up to us" became the motto of the nascent WELL community.

Some kind of map of what "it" is can help you to understand the WELL. Here is a snapshot of the WELL's public conference structure. Keep in mind that each conference can have as many as several hundred different topics going on inside it (like the Parenting conference topic list in chapter 1), and each topic can have several hundred responses. For the sake of space, this listing does not include sixteen conferences on social responsibility and politics, twenty conferences on media and communications, twelve conferences about business and livelihood, eighteen conferences about body-mind-health, eleven conferences about cultures, seventeen conferences about place, and seventeen conferences about interactions.

List of Public Conferences on the WELL

ARTS AND LETTERS

Art Com Electronic Net	(g acen)	Photography	(g pho)
		Poetry	(g poetry)
Art and Graphics	(g gra)	Radio	(g rad)
		Science	(g sf)
Beatles	(g beat)	Fiction	(g sf)
Books	(g books)	Songwriters	(g song)
Comics	(g comics)	Theater	(g theater)
Design	(g design)	Words	(g words)
Jazz	(g jazz)	Writers	(g wri)
MIDI	(g midi)	Zines/Fanzine Scene	(g f5)
Movies	(g movies)	Scene<td	
Muchomedia	(g mucho)		
NAPLPS	(g naplps)		

RECREATION

Bicycles	(g bike)	Gardening	(g gard)
Boating	(g boat)	Music	(g music)
Chess	(g chess)	Motoring	(g car)
Cooking	(g cook)	Pets	(g pets)
Collecting	(g collect)	Outdoor Recreation	(g out)
Drinks	(g drinks)		
Flying	(g flying)	Sports	(g sports)
Games	(g games)	Wildlife	(g wild)

ENTERTAINMENT

Audio-videophilia	(g aud)	Jokes	(g jokes)
Bay Area		Movies	(g movies)
Tonight	(g bat)	Music	(g music)
CDs	(g cd)	Potato!	(g spud)
Comics	(g comics)	Restaurants	(g rest)
Fun	(g fun)	Star Trek	(g trek)
		Television	(g tv)

EDUCATION AND PLANNING

Apple Library Users	(g alug)	Earthquake	(g quake)
Brainstorming	(g brain)	Homeowners	(g home)
Biosphere II	(g bio2)	Indexing	(g indexing)
Co-Housing	(g coho)	Network Integrations	(g origin)
Design	(g design)	7Science	(g science)
Education	(g ed)	Transportation	(g transport)
Energy	(g power)	Whole Earth	
Environment	(g environ)	Review	(g we)

GRATEFUL DEAD

Grateful Dead	(g gd)	Tapes	(g tapes)
Deadlit	(g deadlit)	Tickets	(g tix)
GD Hour	(g gdh)	Tours	(g tours)
Feedback	(g feedback)	Tours	(g tours)

COMPUTERS

AI/Forth/		Mac System7	(g mac7)
Realtime	(g real-time)	MIDI	(g midi)
Amiga	(g amiga)	NAPLPS	(g naplps)
Apple	(g apple)	NeXt	(g next)
Arts and		OS/2	(g os2)
Graphics	(g gra)	Printers	(g print)
Computer Books	(g cbook)	Programmer's	
CP/M	(g cpm)	Net	(g net)
Desktop		Scientific	
Publishing	(g desk)	Computing	(g scicomp)
Hacking	(g hack)	Software	
Hypercard	(g hype)	Design	(g sdc)
IBM PC	(g ibm)	Software/	
Internet	(g internet)	Programming	(g software)
LANs	(g lan)	Software	
Laptop	(g lap)	Support	(g ssc)
Macintosh	(g mac)	Unix	(g unix)
Mactech	(g mactech)	Virtual	
Mac Network		Reality	(g vr)
Admin	(g macadm)	Windows	(g windows)
		Word Processing	(g word)

THE WELL ITSELF

Deeper tech-		Virtual	
nical view	(g deeper)	Communities	(g vc)
MetaWELL	(g metawell)	Hosts	(g host)
General		Policy	(g policy)
technical	(g gentech)	System News	(g sysnews)
WELLcome and		Test	(g test)
help	(g well)	Public	
		programmers	(g public)

SOME POPULAR PRIVATE CONFERENCES ON THE WELL
Mail the hosts listed for information on their criteria
for admission.

BODY - MIND - HEALTH

Crossroads	(g xroads)	mail rabar for entry
Gay (private)	(g gaypriv)	mail hudu for entry
Men on the WELL	(g mow)	mail flash for entry
Recovery	(g recovery)	mail dhawk for entry
Women on the WELL	(g wow)	mail reva for entry
Sacred Sites Int'l.	(g ssi)	mail rebop or mandala for entry/td

ARTS, RECREATION

Aliens on the Well	(g aliens)	mail flash for entry
Band (for working musicians)	(g band)	mail tnf or rik for entry
WELL Writer's Workshop	(g www)	mail sonia for entry

GRATEFUL DEAD

Deadplan	(g dp)	mail tnf dor entry
Producers (radio)	(g grape)	mail rebop or phred for entry

COMPUTERS, COMMUNICATIONS

The Matrix	(g mids)	mail estheise for entry
Producers (radio)	(g pro)	mail jwa for entry

The *Whole Earth* crowd—the granola-eating utopians, the solar-power enthusiasts, the space-station crowd, immortalists, futurists, gadgeteers, commune graduates, environmentalists, social activists— constituted a core population from the beginning. But a couple of other populations of early adopters made the WELL an open system as well as a specific expression of one side of San Francisco culture. One such element was the subculture that had been created by a cultural upheaval ten years after the counterculture era—the personal computer (PC) revolution.

"The personal computer revolutionaries *were* the counterculture," Brand reminded me when I asked him about the WELL's early cultural amalgam. Apple cofounder Steve Jobs had traveled to India in search of enlightenment; Lotus 1–2–3 designer and founder Mitch Kapor had been a transcendental meditation teacher. They were five to ten years younger than the hippies, but they came out of the zeitgeist of the 1960s, and embraced many of the ideas of personal liberation and iconoclasm championed by their slightly older brothers and sisters. The PC was to many of them a talisman of a new kind of war of liberation: when he hired him from Pepsi, Steve Jobs challenged John Sculley, "Do you want to sell sugared water to adolescents, or do you want to change the world?"

Personal computers and the PC industry were created by young iconoclasts who had seen the LSD revolution fizzle, the political revolution fail. Computers for the people was the latest battle in the same campaign. The *Whole Earth* organization, the same Point foundation that owned half the WELL, had honored the PC zealots, including the outlaws among them, with the early Hackers' conferences. Although the word *hacker* has taken on criminal overtones in the popular parlance, restricting it to urchins who break into other people's computer systems, the original hackers were young programmers who flouted conventional wisdom, delighted in finding elegant solutions to vexing technical problems, and liked to create entire new technologies. Without them, the Department of Defense's ARPA research never would have succeeded in creating computer graphics, computer communications, and the antecedents of personal computing.

The young computer wizards and the grizzled old hands who were still messing with mainframes showed up early at the WELL because the guts of the system itself—the Unix operating system and "C" language programming code—were available for tinkering by responsible craftspersons. The original hackers looked around the system for security holes and helped make the WELL secure against the darkside hackers. Making online tools available to the population, rather than breaking into other systems, was their game.

A third cultural element making up the initial mix of the WELL, which otherwise has drifted far from its counterculture origins in many ways, were the Deadheads. Books and theses have been written about the subculture that has grown up around the band the Grateful Dead. They had their origins in the same milieu that included the Merry Pranksters, the Hog Farm, and the *Whole Earth Catalog*. The Deadheads, many of whom weren't born when the band started touring, have a strong feeling of community that they can manifest only in large groups when the band has concerts. Deadheads can spot each other on the road via the semiotics of window decals and bumper stickers, or on the streets via tie-dyed uniforms, but Deadheads didn't have a *place*.

Then several technology-savvy Deadheads started a Grateful Dead conferenceon the WELL. GD, as it came to be known, was so phenomenally successful that for the first several years, Deadheads were by far the single largest source of income for the enterprise. Because of the way the WELL's software allowed users to build their own boundaries, many Deadheads would invest in the technology and the hours needed to learn the WELL's software, solely in order to trade audiotapes or argue about the meaning of lyrics—and remain blithely unaware of the discussions of politics and technology and classical music happening in other conferences. Those Deadheads who did "go over the wall" ended up having strong influence on the WELL at large. But very different kinds of communities began to grow in other parts of the technological-social petri dish that the Deadheads were keeping in business.

Along with the other elements came the first marathon swimmers in the new currents of the online information streams, the professional futurists and writers and journalists. Staff writers and editors for the *New York Times, Business Week*, the *San Francisco Chronicle, Time, Rolling Stone, Byte, Harper's*, and the *Wall Street Journal* use the WELL as a listening post; a few of them are part of the community. Journalists tend to attract other journalists, and the purpose of journalists is to attract everybody else: most people have to use an old medium to hear news about the arrival of a new medium.

One important social rule was built into the software that the WELL lives inside: Nobody is anonymous.Everybody is required to attach their real userid to their postings. It is possible to use pseudonyms to create alternate identities, or to carry metamessages, but the pseudonyms are always linked in every posting to the real userid. The original PicoSpan software offered to the WELL had an option for allowing users to be anonymous, but one of Stewart Brand's strong influences on system design was to insist that the anonymity option should *not* be offered.

Two of the first WELLites I met were Dhawk and Mandel. Like new recruits or rookies in any ongoing enterprise, we found ourselves relating to each other as a kind of cohort. A lot of that early fraternization was necessitated by the confusing nature of the WELL's software. The development of human-user interfaces for CMC was in the Pleistocene era when PicoSpan was designed. It isn't easy to find your way around the WELL, and at first there is always the terrifying delusion that everybody else on the WELL can see all the mistakes you make as you learn your way. The WELL's small staff was available to help confused newcomers via telephone, but the more computer-savvy among the newcomers were eager to actively encourage others. David Hawkins had worked as an engineer and electrician, and found that he quickly learned enough about the WELL's software to act as an unpaid guide for many of us who joined around the same time he did.

David Hawkins was studying to be a Baptist minister, and he was recently married to Corinne, a woman he had met at the seminary. He was from the Deep South. I had never known a Baptist minister or a good old boy. David changed his original career plans to enter the ministry, and Dhawk spent more and more time online, helping the lost, comforting the afflicted. The real people behind the online personae were important to him. I remember that no more than a year after he joined the WELL, David Hawkins drove for nearly an hour, every day for most of a week, to visit an online acquaintance who had undergone minor surgery. Dhawk helped me find my way around, and he visited me face-to-face early in the game. I was one of many who felt obligated to pass along the favor when we noticed newcomers floundering around, looking for a way to connect with each other through the WELL's software.

Tina Loney, userid Onezie, is another dedicated community-builder. A single mother of two daughters, a public school teacher, and a proud resident of Berkeley, she is a zealous nurturer of the heart elements of the WELL, as the host of the Parenting conference, and one of the people who showed up at the first WELL real-life party and still rarely misses the face-to-face get-togethers. She's a fierce fighter with a temper that comes through her words. I've "watched" her daughters grow up and leave the nest, via Onezie's online reports, and she has watched my daughter grow from toddler to schoolgirl. We've been on the same side of many online battles, and on a few occasions have struggled against each other over one issue or another.

Maddog named himself after something a friend had called him once, in reference to his occasional verbal ferocity. He's a sweet guy if you meet him in person, but online, David Gans in the Maddog days did his best to live up to the moniker. He is a dedicated and educated Deadhead, by profession as well as avocation. His book about the band is required reading for hitchhiking tour rats and limousine Deadheads alike. He produced an hourly radio program of Grateful Dead music and lore for a San Francisco station. It was at a Dead concert that he and two of his companions, Mary Eisenhart (marye), a computer journalist-editor, and Bennett Falk (rosebody), a programmer, received the inspiration to start a Grateful Dead conference on the WELL.

The WELL drew me into the Deadhead milieu and real-life contact with David Gans. I watched and participated as the WELL's Deadhead community helped him grow through a major life crisis. The management of the local radio station canceled his show. David was devastated. He loved to do radio, he loved to evangelize about his favorite band, and the cancellation hit him hard. After much commiseration and anguish online, somebody suggested that David syndicate the show to other stations. That way, he could have revenge on the station that canceled and reach even more people than he had reached before.

He was skeptical at first, but so many of his online cohorts urged him to do it that he couldn't very well refuse to try. The idea turned out to be a good one; Gans started Truth 'N Fun productions to distribute his weekly programs to scores of public radio stations around the country, and along the way he changed his userid from Maddog to tnf. The Maddog persona is still latent, and jumps out snarling online every once in a while, but tnf continues to be one of the people who most visibly reinvents himself on the WELL's center stage.

David Gans is one of several dozen people who seem to influence strongly the WELL's conversational flavor, simply because we spend so much time reading and posting. David in particular sometimes seems to have his frontal lobe directly wired into the WELL. It helps to see him at work in real life. Like many of us, he works at home, in a custom-designed office-studio. He has a wraparound audio console in front of him—the control center for his radio production. Studio speakers are on either side, focused on the one chair in the middle of all the equipment. A television is mounted at eye level, above the audio monitor. A telephone is at his right hand. And directly in front of him is the computer and modem. David Gans marinates himself in media for a living. Not exactly what Peter Drucker envisioned when he coined the term *knowledge worker*, I'd bet. David Gans, like a lot of others these days, is multitasking. The WELL is just part of the information flow.

Then there is Mandel, who appears at first glance to better fit the image of the information-age specialist. He brought some kind of intellectual respectability to the high-tech bull session. He was a professional futurist at a real live think tank. He had solid research, facts and figures, to back up his assertions. If you wanted to argue with him, you'd better do your homework. Mandel, who joined the WELL the same day as Dhawk, a few weeks before I joined, was another one of the instant online regulars, along with me, the freelance writer, and Onezie, the schoolteacher, and Dhawk, the Baptist minister turned Unix hacker, and Maddog, the Deadhead radio producer, and a dozen others.

Mandel's employer is SRI International (which started out as Stanford Research Institute, where Jacques Vallee and Doug Engelbart did some of the pioneering research in computer conferencing in the 1970s). Municipal and national governments and the biggest corporations in the world pay SRI for a few hours of Tom Mandel's pontifications about the future of publishing or paper or transportation or—and here I can see his wicked grin—communication. Tom not only is paid well for his WELL addiction, he was applauded for it by his clients and the consulting firm that employs him. He doesn't even have to feel guilty. When he is having fun, he is still working.

You can't talk about the WELL as a community without meeting Tex, the innkeeper, bartender, bouncer, matchmaker, mediator, and community-maker, another communard who emerged from twelve years on the

Farm with a reality-tempered commitment to community-building and a deep distaste for anything less than democratic governance. I knew all about him long before I set eyes on him. He was a born online autobiographical entertainer, and what he said about the way things ought to be had some bite because he had put more than a decade into living his communal ideals. I knew he had worked as an interstate truck driver, as a carpenter restoring houses in the poorer sections of Washington, D.C., as an activist in the South Bronx. He was working as an automobile mechanic when Matthew McClure hired him to help deepen and broaden the WELL community. He had four children. And I had constructed my own mental image of him from what he had disclosed about himself online. When I met him in real life, his boyish looks surprised me. I was prepared for a grizzled, tobacco-chewing, potbellied guy—the kind of guy who would call himself Tex even though he's from California.

One big part of Tex's persona, to everybody who knows him in person, is his friendly disregard for other people's personal space. Online and off, Tex likes to shed formalities and talk person to person, to say what's really on his mind and in his heart. In person, he does this very close up, literally "in your face." He's over six feet tall and big boned. It isn't easy to keep your distance when he gets a grip on your shoulder and talks to you earnestly from less than three inches away. When Tex left the WELL in 1992 to take a position in another online service, the WELL community threw a combination testimonial, bon voyage party, and roast. One by one, people came up to the podium, grabbed Tex, and talked to him from about three inches away.

His "in your face" style and his anecdotes from twelve years of trying to make a real-life intentional community work represented a core value of the WELL that has survived beyond the years of Farm-vet management: a commitment to using the medium to make real human connections, and more—to try to find better and better ways to live with each other in cyberspace. From the beginning, the exchange of information and the sharing of emotional sympathy exemplified by the Experts on the WELL topic and the Parenting conference were accompanied by some of the less attractive attributes of human groups. Whatever community is, it is not necessarily a conflict-free environment. There has always been a lot of conflict in the WELL, breaking out into regular flamefests of interpersonal attacks from time to time. Factionalism. Gossip. Envy. Jealousy. Feuds. Brawls. Hard feelings that carry over from one discussion to another.

When one of those online brouhahas happened and people started choosing sides and unkind words were being said, Tex and I often walked in the hills above Sausalito and talked about how and why onlife life can become unpleasant and how to make it work. We kept concluding that simple, corny, all-powerful love was the only way to make a community work when it is diverse, thus guaranteeing friction, and at the same time committed to free expression, which can and does get out of hand. A core of people must flat-out believe in the possibility of community and keep coming back to that amid the emotional storms in order for the whole loosely coupled group to hold together at all. When you complicate the situation with the real-life courtships and marriages and divorces and affairs and breakups that tend to happen to the same cohort of people when they stay in touch over a number of years, you have an atmosphere that can get overheated at times.

Who are the WELL members in general, and what do they talk about? I can tell you about the individuals I have come to know over seven years, but only a few of them, and the WELL has long since been something larger than the sum of everybody's friends. On the WELL, I subscribe to an automatic service created by another WELLite who likes to build tools for the community; the Blair Newman Memorial Newuser Report collects the biographical descriptions that new WELL members publish in a public file when they join, and sends them to me in one long electronic message every day or two. If I'm too busy to bother, I just delete those electronic messages. E-mail makes it very easy not to read something. But it gives me a sense of who is joining the WELL, and why, when I let those bios scroll by at 2,400 bits per second. Every once in a while I save a few to a file, as a methodologically sloppy kind of survey.

The following is a very small random sample of the different user biographies I culled over a few months in 1991 and 1992.

* * *

```
I am a self-employed productivity consultant. I
live out in the country overlooking the ocean near
Bodega Bay. The phone, fax, and e-mail let me work
here, and still be in the business community.
```

***

I reside in Seoul Korea where I practice public
relations for the U.S. government.

***

I am a physician, specializing in women's health,
including contraception, abortion, and estrogen
replacement therapy after menopause. I am the
medical director of an abortion clinic. I was a
member of the Mid-Peninsula Free University in the
70's and organized concerts, including the Dead,
Big Brother, Quicksilver, Jefferson Airplane, etc.
I am interested in philosophical/ethical issues
surrounding the beginning of life and the end of
life and the functional value of rituals and
traditions.

***

I am a 19 year old college student struggling to
find myself. I enjoy sitting in a field of
dandelions with no socks. I spend too much time
playing on my computer. I am an advertising/
business major so I will be here for five or more
years. I am trying to find the meaning of life
. . . helpful hints are appreciated. I wish that
penguins could have wings that worked (Breathed),
solutions are being contemplated . . .

***

I am a student from Prague, Czechoslovakia,
studying in San Francisco's Center for Electronic
Art computer graphic and design program.

***

Librarian for USDA, sysop of "ALF" bbs

***

I am a lawyer, working as a law clerk to 3 state
judges in Duluth. I am 31 and single. I graduated
from the Naval Academy in 1982, and the University
of Minnesota Law School in 1990. I opposed the Gulf
War, and I was Paul Wellstone's deputy campaign

director in the 8th Congressional District. I like
sailing and long hikes in the woods and the shore.
My other interests include law and Italy. My
biggest issues today are single payer universal
health care and proportional representation.

***

I'm interested in land-use planning (I'm helping to
put together the Sacramento County General Plan),
and in Management of Information Systems (I'm
writing an article about this, and am interested in
a career in it). I'm a real estate broker and
developer now, with several years experience using
and reviewing software for IBM-compatibles.

***

I am a born-again phreak, at age 33. My modem is
my life! OK, the weightlifting, the fast car, they
are all fun, but the modem is the biggie! As a
matter of fact, I met my husband on a bbs! But, I
realize that I have only tapped the surface of what
my little Hayes can do, and I want to learn it
all!

***

I am a self-employed systems and software
consultant, primarily on large military command-
and-control systems. My newest interests are in
neural networks and fuzzy logic, with parallel
processing as an enabling technology. I am usually
interested in discussing new technologies and new
applications of technology, along with the societal
implications, with almost anybody, anywhere,
anytime.

***

Music Store owner, Secretary of Ecological
Economics of Alaska.

***

Captain, US Army

```
* * *
```

```
I am a Japanese writer who are very much interested
in ecology and the electronic democracy. I am going
to spend two years with studying (joining?) ecolog-
ical movement and sharing network as a tool for
making the new world here in Berkeley.
```

```
* * *
```

```
I work at the only hospital dedicated to the cure
and eradication of leprosy in the United States. I
also spent 6 months in Romania after the December,
1989, Revolution.
```

One of the reasons people value places like the WELL is the intellectual diversity it offers. With a divergent group, you get separate, nonoverlapping personal networks of expertise. If you could use that diversity as a kind of living encyclopedia, you would find that communication, the immeasurable matters of the heart that the Parenting conference provides, is not the only kind of value that people derive from virtual communities. The knowledge-sharing leverage of a large, diverse group of people who are motivated to help one another, and whose differences of place and time are erased by CMC, can be considerable.

Gift Economies and Social Contracts in Cyberspace

No single metaphor completely conveys the nature of cyberspace. Virtual communities are places where people meet, and they also are tools; the place-like aspects and tool-like aspects only partially overlap. Some people come to the WELL only for the community, some come only for the hard-core information, and some want both. The WELL contains places of the heart for me, but it is also a valuable and unemotional information-seeking device that has become an integral part of my professional routine. The Parenting conference might be a sacred circle, but the News conference can be much more like a combination of intellectual marketplace and mind-game parlor. When I first found my way into the WELL, I was looking for information and I found it. By that time, I realized that the people who have the information are more interesting than the information alone; the game-like and tool-like aspects of sharing information online drew me in further. Later, I began meeting some of the knowledge traders in more communitarian places online.

I was hungry for intellectual companionship as well as raw information. While many commuters dream of working at home, telecommuting, I happen to know what it's like to work that way. I never could stand to get out of my pajamas if I didn't have to, so I've always worked at home. It has its advantages and its disadvantages. But the occupational hazard of the self-employed, home-based symbolic analyst of the 1990s is isolation. Information-age hunters and gatherers were lone wolves until we found the Net.

The kind of people that Robert Reich, in *The Work of Nations*, called "symbolic analysts" are natural matches for online communities: computer programmers, writers and journalists, freelance artists and designers, independent radio and television producers, editors, researchers, librarians. For some time now, these early adopters have been joined by the first ranks of the mainstream CMC users. Increasingly, many people who paint houses or build boats or work in an office or hospital or sell real estate, but who are curious about new cultural phenomena and not afraid of using a computer keyboard to express themselves, are mixing it up with the knowledge workers. People who work for themselves, whether it is with their hands or their symbols, have been plugging into the Net for the kind of tactical and emotional support others get at the office or factory.

Since so many members of virtual communities are workers whose professional standing is based on what they know, virtual communities can be practical instruments. If you need specific information or an expert opinion or a pointer to a resource, a virtual community is like a living encyclopedia. Virtual communities can help their members, whether or not they are information-related workers, to cope with information overload. The problem with the information age, especially for students and knowledge workers who spend their time immersed in the info flow, is that there is too much information available and few effective filters for sifting the key data that are useful and interesting to us as individuals.

Programmers are trying to design better and better software agents that can seek and sift, filter and find, and save us from the awful feeling one gets when it turns out that the specific knowledge one needs is buried in fifteen thousand pages of related information. The first software agents are now becoming available (e.g., Archie, Gopher, Knowbots, WAIS, and Rosebud are the names for different programs that search through the vast digital libraries of Internet and the real-time feed from the news services and retrieve items of interest), but we already have far more sophisticated, if informal, social contracts among groups of people that allow us to act as software agents for one another.

If, in my wanderings through information space, I come across items that don't interest me but I know would interest one of my worldwide affinity group of online friends, I send the appropriate friend a pointer or simply forward the entire text (one of the new powers of CMC is the ability to publish and converse via the same medium). In some cases I can put the information in exactly the right place for ten thousand people I don't know, but who are intensely interested in that specific topic, to find it when they need it. And sometimes, one of the ten thousand people I don't know does the same thing for me.

This informal, unwritten social contract is supported by a blend of strong-tie and weak-tie relationships among people who have a mixture of motives and ephemeral affiliations. It requires one to give something, and enables one to receive something. I have to keep my friends in mind and send them pointers instead of throwing my informational discards into the virtual scrap heap. It doesn't take much energy to do that, since I have to sift that information anyway to find the knowledge I seek for my own purposes; it takes two keystrokes to delete the information, three keystrokes to forward it to someone else. And with scores of other people who have an eye out for my interests while they explore sectors of the information space that I normally wouldn't frequent, I find that the help I receive far outweighs the energy I expend helping others: a marriage of altruism and self-interest.

Lee Sproull and Sara Kiesler, two social scientists who have been observing the ways people in organizations use CMC, point out in their book *Connections: New Ways of Working in the Networked World* that this kind of informal lore exchange is a key, if invisible, part of every organization:

"Does anybody know...?" is a common phrase in organizations— typically heard in informal encounters in office hallways, before meetings begin, at the water cooler, coffeepot, and lunchrooms. In the terms of the general information procedure, one person asks a search question that may be vague or ambiguous.

Usually the asker is seeking a piece of current or arcane information, not easily found in official documents. The audience for such questions usually knows the asker and is sympathetic or at least tolerant because the behavior is conventional, the questions are not onerous, and answerers themselves may one day need to ask a question.

In the conventional world, if the asker's acquaintances cannot provide an answer, the asker is stymied. But with electronic communication, the asker has access to a much broader pool of information sources. An oceanographer broadcast a message to an electronic network of oceanographers: "Is it safe and reasonable to clamp equipment onto a [particular type of insulating] wire?" The official instructions said, "Do not clamp." Right away the sender got several messages from other places saying, "Yes, we do it all the time, but you have to use the following type of clamp." The oceanographer did not know the people who responded and would never have encountered them in a face-to-face setting, but through electronic communication, he benefited from their knowledge and experience. Folklore is an important part of science and technology, consisting of idiosyncratic information about how equipment really works and what tricks you have to know to get the experiment to come out right. It never appears in journal articles or manuals, and it is typically conveyed by word of mouth. With electronic communication, folklore can be more broadly accessible.

Early in my history with the WELL, I was invited to join a panel of experts who advise the U.S. Congress's Office of Technology Assessment (OTA) on the subject of communication systems for an information age. I'm not an expert in telecommunications technology or policy, but I do know where to find a group of such experts and how to get them to tell me what they know. Before I went to Washington for my first panel meeting, I opened a conference in the WELL and invited assorted information freaks, technophiles, and communications experts to help me come up with something to say. An amazing collection of minds flocked to that topic, and some of them created whole new communities when they collided.

By the time I sat down with the captains of industry, government advisers, and academic experts at the panel table, I had more than two hundred pages of expert advice from my own panel. I wouldn't have been able to integrate that much knowledge of my subject in an entire academic or industrial career, and it took me (and my virtual community) only a few minutes a day for six weeks. In my profession I have found the WELL to be an outright magical resource. An editor or producer or client can call and ask me if I know much about the Constitution, or fiber optics, or intellectual property. "Let me get back to you in twenty minutes," I say, reaching for the modem.

The same strategy of nurturing and making use of loose information-sharing affiliations across the Net can be applied to an infinite domain of problem areas, from literary criticism to software evaluation. It's a good way for a sufficiently large, sufficiently diverse group of people to multiply their individual degree of expertise, and I think it could be done even if the people aren't involved in a community other than their place of employment or their area of specialization. But I think it works better when the community's conceptual model of its own activities includes a healthy amount of barn raising along with the horse trading.

Reciprocity is a key element of any market-based culture, but the arrangement I'm describing feels to me more like a kind of gift economy in which people do things for one another out of a spirit of building something between them, rather than a spreadsheet-calculated quid pro quo. When that spirit exists, everybody gets a little extra something, a little sparkle, from their more practical transactions; different kinds of things become possible when this mind-set pervades. Conversely, people who have valuable things to add to the mix tend to keep their heads down and their ideas to themselves when a mercenary or hostile zeitgeist dominates an online community.

In the virtual community I know best, elegantly presented knowledge is a valuable currency. Wit and use of language are rewarded in this medium, which is biased toward those who learn how to manipulate attention and emotion with the written word. Sometimes you give one person more information than you would give another person in response to the same query, simply because you recognize one of them to be more generous or funny or to-the-point or agreeable.

I give useful information freely, and I believe my requests for information are met more swiftly, in greater detail, than they would have been otherwise. A sociologist might say that my perceived helpfulness increased my pool of social capital. I can increase your knowledge capital and my social capital at the same time by telling you something that you need to know, and I could diminish the amount of my capital in the estimation of others by transgressing the group's social norms. The person I help might never be in a position to help me, but someone else might be. That's why it is hard to distinguish idle talk from serious context-setting. In a virtual community, idle talk is context-setting. Idle talk is where people learn what kind of person you are, why you should be trusted or mistrusted, what interests you. The agora—the ancient Athenian market where the citizens of the first democracy gathered to buy and sell—was more than the site of transactions; it was also a place where people met and sized up one another. It's where the word got around about those who transgress norms, break contracts. Markets and gossip are historically and inextricably connected.

Parents, libertarians, Deadheads, radio producers, writers, homeowners, and sports fans all have particular places to hang out in the WELL. But in the News conference, the WELL's town square, there is a deliberately general topic, Experts on the WELL, that continues to be a paradigm of one of the ways people can spin banter into an unstructured repository of valuable unclassifiable expertise.

The premise of Experts on the WELL is simple. If you have a problem or a question concerning any topic, from plumbing to astrophysics, you pose it. Then you wait seven minutes or a week. Sometimes nothing happens, and sometimes you get exactly what you want. In many instances, the answer already exists elsewhere in the WELL, and the topic serves as a kind of community librarian service that points the query toward the right part of the WELL's collection of information. And in some instances, the information requested exists in someone's head, and that person takes the time to type it.

The reward for knowing the answer and taking the time to enter it into the WELL is symbolic but not inconsequential. People who come up with accurate and well-worded answers win prestige in front of the whole virtual stadium. Experts compete to solve problems; the people who harvest solutions become believers. For $2 an hour, you gain access to your own think tank. You just have to know how to prime it and mine it.

Most topics on the WELL are about something specific. A topic in the Pets conference might be about places to board dogs; a topic in the Parenting conference might be about discipline or coping with measles. Experts on the WELL is about several things at the same time, and the topic is expected to change regularly. The topic serves as an intelligent community filter, where people seeking information can be directed to the specific part of the WELL where their area of inquiry is a topic of discussion. This is how social norms of helpfulness to newcomers contend against the ponderous difficulty of the WELL's software that makes it difficult for new people to find their way. In a surprising number of cases, somebody from the WELL's diversity happens to know the definitive answer to a question about angelology or automatic transmissions or celestial navigation or where to find a good martini. Many of us read the topic for amusement and for the odd bits of expertise we can pick up along the way.

Experts on the WELL is about more than simple fact-finding. It is also about the pleasure of making conversation and creating value in the process. Although all these responses were originally typed on a terminal or computer keyboard, and are available for people to read long after they were typed, the postings in a computer conference are experienced by those who read and write them as a form of conversation as well as a form of publication. In the case of the WELL, it's a conversation in which 16 percent of the people contribute 80 percent of the words, but many people are listening invisibly and all are free to join. In that sense, there's a theatrical element to this medium—written conversation as a performing art. One of CMC's distinguishing characteristics is the way it mixes aspects of informal, real-time communication with the more formally composed, write-once-read-forever mode of communication.

Computer conference conversations are dialogues that are situated in a specific place (the conferencing system, the conference, the topic) and time. The place is a cognitive and social one, not a geographic place. The WELL is a kind of place to those who come to it, and within the WELL, the News conference is a more specific kind of place inside the larger place, and within the news conference, the Experts on the WELL topic has its own flavor, its own cast of characters, its own norms and rhythms. The way casual conversation is organized in a hierarchical structure, with descriptive names at every level, enables people to use the record of the conversation as a database in which to search for specific information. The way words and ideas are structured by computer conferencing systems is different from more familiar structures, such as books or face-to-face discussions, so we don't have a default mental model that helps us think about the structure.

An architectural model of the WELL can help you create a mental model of these spaces within spaces. If you think of the WELL as a building, you can walk down the halls and look at the signs on the doors to different rooms of various sizes. The sign on the door tells you about the general subject of the conversations that take place inside—sex or art or politics or sports or literature or childrearing. The building is the conferencing system. The rooms are the conferences. And within each conference room, imagine a number of blackboards covered with writing. Approach one of the blackboards, and you will see a sign at the top that indicates which subtopic of the conference room's specified domain is under discussion. In the health conference, you might have topics about medicines, topics about different diseases, topics about medical discoveries, topics about the politics and economics of health care. Each of those topics has its own blackboard, known in the WELL as the topic level. That's where Experts on the WELL exists, as a topic in the News conference.

At the top of the blackboard, a person begins a new topic of conversation by asserting a proposition or asking a question or more generally describing an area for general discussion. Immediately after and under the introduction, somebody writes a response. On the WELL, that is the response level. When you know how to navigate the different levels of such a system, and use tools provided by the system to automate that navigation, the sense of place helps you structure the system in your memory.

Reading a computer conference transcript in hard copy—on paper—misses the dynamism of the conversation as it is experienced by regulars; the back-and-forth dialogue over a period of time that regular participants or observers experience can be reconstructed by looking at the time stamps of the postings, however. In terms of communication rhythms, e-mail and computer conferencing can be levelers. This is one way in which computer conferencing differs from other communications media. The ability to think and compose a reply and publish it within the structure of a conversation enables a group of people to build the living database of Experts on the WELL, in an enterprise where contributors all work at their own pace. This kind of group thinks together differently from how the same group would think face-to-face or in real time.

Sara Kiesler, a social psychologist who studied how e-mail systems changed the nature of organizations, was one of the first to observe businesses systematically and study the impact of CMC on the organization. Dr. Kiesler confirmed and legitimated what CMC pioneers had known from personal experience when she noted in *Harvard Business Review* that "computer-mediated communications can break down hierarchical and departmental barriers, standard operating procedures, and organizational norms." Kiesler's observations supported the theory long popular among online enthusiasts that people who often dominate conversations face-to-face, because of rank or aggressive demeanor, are no more visible than those who would remain silent or say little in a face-to-face meeting but say a lot via CMC. Businesses are the next organizations to be subjected to the same new kinds of social forces that were experienced by the research and academic communities when they went online.

Kiesler also offered evidence that people communicate across and around traditional hierarchical organizational boundaries if their mutual interest in a particular subject matter is strong enough; groups make more daring decisions via CMC than they do face-to-face; work that later turns out to be important is sometimes accomplished in informal conversations as well as in structured online meetings.

Clearly, people in the Parenting conference are enmeshed in a social interaction different from that of people in Experts on the WELL, and a college student indulging in the online role-playing games known as Multi-User Dungeons lives in a different virtual society from a participant in a scholarly electronic mailing list. Point of view, along with identity, is one of the great variables in cyberspace. Different people in cyberspace look at their virtual communities through differently shaped keyholes. In traditional communities, people have a strongly shared mental model of the sense of place—the room or village or city where their interactions occur. In virtual communities, the sense of place requires an individual act of imagination. The different mental models people have of the electronic agora complicates the question of why people seem to want to build societies mediated by computer screens. A question like that leads inexorably to the old fundamental questions of what forces hold any society together. The roots of these questions extend farther than the social upheavals triggered by modern communications technologies.

When we say "society," we usually mean citizens of cities in entities known as nations. We take those categories for granted. But the mass-psychological transition that people made to thinking of ourselves as part of modern society and nation-states is historically recent. Could people make the transition from the close collective social groups, the villages and small towns of premodern and precapitalist Europe, to a new form of social solidarity known as society that transcended and encompassed all previous kinds of human association? Emile Durkheim, one of the founders of sociology, called the premodern kind of social group *gemeinschaft*, which is closer to the English word *community*, and the new kind of social group he called *gesellschaft*, which can be translated roughly as *society*. All the questions about community in cyberspace point to a similar kind of transition that might be taking place now, for which we have no technical names.

Sociology student Marc Smith, who has been using the WELL and the Net as the laboratory for his fieldwork, pointed me to Benedict Anderson's work *Imagined Communities*, a study of nation-building that focuses on the ideological labor involved. Anderson points out that nations and, by extension, communities are imagined in the sense that a given nation exists by virtue of a common acceptance in the minds of the population that it exists. Nations must exist in the minds of its citizens in order to exist at all. "Virtual communities require an act of imagination to use," points out Marc Smith, extending Anderson's line of thinking to cyberspace, "and what must be imagined is the idea of the community itself."

It's far too early to tell what the tools of social psychology and sociology will help us make of the raw material of group interaction that proliferates in cyberspace. This is an area where adroit use of the Net by scholars could have a profound effect on the nature of the Net. One of the great problems with the atmosphere of free expression now tolerated on the Net is the fragility of communities and their susceptibility to disruption. The only alternative to imposing potentially dangerous restrictions on freedom of expression is to develop norms, folklore, ways of acceptable behavior that are widely modeled, taught, and valued, that can give the citizens of cyberspace clear ideas of what they can and cannot do with the medium, how they can gain leverage, and where they must beware of pitfalls inherent in the medium, if we intend to use it for community-building. But all arguments about virtual community values take place in the absence of any base of even roughly quantified systematic observation.

Right now, all we have on the Net is folklore, like the Netiquette that old-timers try to teach the flood of new arrivals, and debates about freedom of expression versus nurturance of community. About two dozen social scientists, working for several years, might produce conclusions that would help inform these debates and furnish a basis of validated observation for all the theories flying around. A science of Net behavior is not going to reshape the way people behave online, but knowledge of the dynamics of how people do behave is an important social feedback loop to install if the Net is to be self-governing at any scale.

3

Visionaries and Convergences: The Accidental History of the Net

While driving to work one day in 1950, Douglas Engelbart started thinking about how complicated civilization had become. What were humans going to do about managing this complex new world that technology had helped us create? Engelbart asked himself what kinds of tools we use to help us think. "Symbols" was the answer that came to him, the answer he had been taught as an engineer. Could we use machines to help us deal with symbols? Why not computers? Could computers automate symbol-handling tasks, and thus help people think faster, better, about more complex problems? To the right person, the line of thought was inevitable, even in 1950; it never ceases to amaze Engelbart that other people didn't see it, too.

Engelbart, who had been a radar operator during World War II, began to see an actual picture come into focus in his mind's eye, like a snapshot of the future: "When I first heard about computers, I understood, from my radar experience, that if these machines can show you information on punchcards and printouts on paper, they could write or draw that information on a screen. When I saw the connection between a cathode-ray screen, an information processor, and a medium for representing symbols to a person, it all tumbled together in about a half an hour." He saw groups of people at desks and in theaterlike environments where people could control the computer by pointing at it.

The scene in his imagination grew more vivid and detailed. Knowledge and information and thinking tools not yet invented could be available at the touch of a keyboard, the twist of a dial. With a setup like that, Engelbart dreamed, groups of people might have a real handle on solving complex problems. By the time he arrived at work at the end of that commute in December 1950, Engelbart's internal logic had taken him to the threshold of a crusade that has lasted almost half a century. By the 1990s, as a direct result of Engelbart's crusade, tens of millions of people around the world use computers and telecommunications to extend their abilities to think and communicate. Computers as mind amplifiers are something we take for granted today.

The problem in the 1950s was getting somebody to listen—somebody who could give him access to a computer and some research funding. His friends warned him that talking too much about his science-fiction schemes when he was interviewing for jobs might not be good for his career as an electrical engineer. Traveling from university to private industry to entrepreneurship, he spent over a decade trying and failing to convince computer scientists, psychologists, librarians, that computers could become marvelous problem-solving assistants to people who work with their minds.

In 1950, there were less than a dozen electronic computers. The first "electronic brains" were so big and generated so much heat that they filled air-conditioned warehouses, and in terms of computing power, all of them put together couldn't compete with the cheapest microchip in a twenty-dollar toy today. Nobody thought anybody would need many more computers or very much more powerful ones than that to fill the world's computational needs. By 1960, people were convinced that computers were useful tools, and the slightly less enormous, less expensive devices proliferated, but strictly as high-tech instrumentation for scientists or payroll devices for businesses.

In 1957, the Soviet launching of the first artificial satellite, Sputnik, shifted some funding paradigms in Washington, D.C.; two direct side effects of that shift were the personal computer revolution and computer-mediated communications. In 1963, Engelbart was funded to create the thinking machines he had dreamed about. Engelbart was just the first of a lineage of stubborn visionaries who insisted that computers could be used by people other than specialists. It is very unlikely that we would have the computers and CMC systems we have today if it weren't for these few people who stuck stubbornly to their desire to build better thinking tools, computers designed for most people to use, in order to do the things most people do.

The essential elements of what became the Net were created by people who believed in, wanted, and therefore invented ways of using computers to amplify human thinking and communication. And many of them wanted to provide it to as many people as possible, at the lowest possible cost. Driven by the excitement of creating their own special subculture below the crust of the mass-media mainstream, they worked with what was at hand. Again and again, the most important parts of the Net piggybacked on technologies that were created for very different purposes.

The most important parts of the Net began as dreams in the imaginations of a few specific people, who acted on inspiration rather than orders. Computer networks started with a former MIT professor working in a small technical funding office in the Pentagon; the global Usenet was created by a couple of students in North Carolina who decided it was possible for computer communities to communicate with each other without the benefit of an expensive Internet connection; hobbyists in Chicago triggered the worldwide BBS movement because they wanted to transfer files from one PC to another without driving across town.

In the 1960s and 1970s, the U.S. Department of Defense's Advanced Research Projects Agency (ARPA) funded a small group of unorthodox computer programmers and electronic engineers who wanted to redesign the way computers were operated. With keyboards and screens and graphics, people could interact directly with computers instead of laboring through the time-consuming and arcane mediation of punched cards and printouts. Some young programmers felt their virtuosity required the kinds of computers that a good mind could play like a musical instrument, in real time. They called their crusade "interactive computing," and still speak in terms of the "conversion experience" that led their research. When the ARPA-funded crusaders succeeded in creating the computers they wanted, they discovered that they also wanted to use their computers as communication devices.

It took two more decades of research and development for interactive personal computers and CMC to mature, proliferate, and converge into the increasingly citizen-accessible Net of the 1990s. It took another couple of revolutions beyond interactive computing to get that far.

By the late 1970s, the personal computer revolution, built on the technical foundations created by the ARPA researchers a decade previously, had created a new industry and a new subculture. The old ARPA stars were creating new companies and running research laboratories by the time their younger brothers and sisters decided to turn computers from business machines and scientific workstations into thinking tools "for the rest of us," as Apple put it in their first Macintosh commercials.

Again, changes in the way computers were designed and used led to the expansion of the computer-using population from a priesthood in the 1950s, to an elite in the 1960s, to a subculture in the 1970s, and to a significant, still growing part of the population in the 1990s. Again, it wasn't the mainstream of the existing computer industry that created affordable personal computing, but teenagers in garages. And it was neither national defense nor the profit motive but the desire to make a tool for changing the world that motivated the young entrepreneurs who built the PC industry.

When enough people brought sufficiently powerful computers into their homes, it was inevitable that somebody would figure out a way to plug PCs into telephones. All the off-the-shelf devices that you could plug together to make that work, the "enabling technologies" for personal telecommunications, were available and the price was dropping. With the powerful computers available to citizens today and affordable modems, you don't need an expensive, high-speed conduit like Internet uses. You just plug right into your telephone line, perfectly legally—so far—and publish your manifestos or organize your meetings.

The BBS enthusiasm spread among a wholly different population from the research roots of the Net. BBSers benefited from the research and development that made PC technology possible because it is unlikely that microchips and interactive computers would have been available to civilians today if the Department of Defense had not found them essential to national security decades ago. But BBS enthusiasts aren't interested in ARPA or big laboratories. They want to know what they can do at home with their own hands and affordable technology.

By the 1980s, it wasn't just computer scientists using the Net or BBSers scattered across the globe. Internet, the successor to ARPANET, sponsored in the 1980s by the National Science Foundation, already included tens of thousands of researchers and scholars in private industries and universities connected to the Net through their institutions' computer centers. Each computer center is a community of individuals who share computer resources, and when it joins the high-speed backbone of Internet, each community is virtually/connected to every other, via private e-mail, public real-time chat, and worldwide public conversations such as Usenet. Net culture took on a global, youthful, often heavily American flavor as so many colleges worldwide came online, starting in the United States.

In the future, that's where the net culture in the rest of society will come from worldwide—those who connected with it in college. Will the future see an increasing gap between the information-rich and the information-poor? Access to the Net and access to college are going to be the gateways, everywhere, to a world of communications and information access far beyond what is accessible by traditional media.

Through the 1980s, significant computing power became available on college campuses, and everybody, not just the programming, science, and engineering students, began using networked personal computers as part of their intellectual work, along with textbooks and lectures. Not only did many university computer centers join the high-speed backbone of the Net, millions of students gained dial-up access to the Net. Thousands got hooked on Usenet, MUDs, Internet Relay Chat, and electronic mailing lists.

More efficient means of communicating traditional forms of information, such as research papers, from place to place or performing routine knowledge-gathering tasks, such as searching for a reference, were facilitated by the Net's campus infrastructure. The Net was also a gateway to purely social realms. Two of the most important and popular cultural experiments—MUD (which first appeared at the University of Essex, England) and Usenet—originated on college campuses in 1979–1980.

In 1979, computer science students at Duke University and the University of North Carolina experimented with a simple scheme by which these two computer communities, which were not connected via Internet, could automatically exchange information via modem at regular intervals. By 1990, Usenet brought tens of millions of words daily to several million people in more than forty countries, sprouting from the experiment in North Carolina and propagating itself like a virus from campus to campus, research lab to research lab, around the world, more or less unofficially, via the sympathetic managers who ran the computer centers. A few private-sector institutions—AT&T's Bell Laboratories and DEC foremost among them—helped boost the growth of Usenet by paying the bill for increased telecommunications among its key backbone sites. The people in those companies who were the most passionate advocates of CMC use were also valuable enough to their employers to allow for a few interesting experiments.

Usenet is not a network or a BBS but a way of managing multiple public conversations about specific topics, conversations that are not located or controlled in a central site but spread throughout the system. It is a network-scale computer conferencing system. It rides on the computer networks but doesn't need them. You can read Usenet newsgroups from Internet, or you can read them from your desktop PC, if you can talk a medium-size system like the WELL into feeding the stream of conversations to your PC. Usenet enables people to read and respond to specific conversations about specific topics, similar to the way they read and respond to e-mail, but Usenet postings are public rather than private; in this way Usenet is related to other efforts to use computers as many-to-many group communication devices. Usenet is more like the WELL than Internet because it's about conversation—hundreds of thousands of conversations a day about thousands of different subjects.

ARPANET, the BBSs, and the conferencing systems that had separate origins ten and twenty years ago are growing together now into one system with many parts—the Net. In the 1990s, the role of government and private industry in the creation and regulation of the next level of Internet, the National Research and Education Network (NREN), is becoming the focus of increased public debate about how to manage that convergence.

As big government and big business line up to argue about which information infrastructure would be better for citizens, it is the right of the citizens to remind elected policymakers that these technologies were created by people who believed that the power of computer technology can and should be made available to the entire population, not just to a priesthood. The future of the Net cannot be intelligently designed without paying attention to the intentions of those who originated it.

From ARPANET to NREN: The Toolbuilders' Quest

Douglas Engelbart might have remained a voice in the wilderness, one of the myriad inventors with world-changing devices, or at least the plans for them, gathering dust in their garages. And you might still be required to wear a lab coat and speak FORTRAN in order to gain access to a computer. But Engelbart got a job in the early 1960s doing some respectably orthodox computer research at a new think tank in Menlo Park, California, the Stanford Research Institute. And a few years later, the paper he wrote, "The Augmentation of Human Intellect," fell into the hands of J. C. R. Licklider, another man with foresight who was in a historically fortunate position to do something about their shared vision of the future. Licklider had written a paper of his own in 1960, "Man-Computer Symbiosis," predicting that "in not too many years, human brains and computing machines will be coupled together very tightly, and that the resulting partnership will think as no human being has ever thought and process data in a way not approached by the information-handling machines we know today."

Licklider was an MIT and Harvard professor who studied psychoacoustics. Like Engelbart, he was captured by a picture in his mind's eye of a new kind of intellectual tool involving computers. Licklider's revelation came to him as he was sitting in his office. He was spending hours creating a graphic plot of some experimental data when he realized that he spent far more time fiddling with data, drawing graphs, finding citations, than he did thinking. A friend of Licklider's worked at Bolt, Beranek, and Newman, a Cambridge computer consulting company that had a special kind of computer known as a DEC PDP–1. DEC—Digital Equipment Corporation—was a new computer company that a couple of MIT graduates had created. And the PDP–1 was the first commercial computer that showed information on a screen.

Licklider realized, as had Engelbart, that if he could get the right information into the computer's memory, he would be able to fiddle with data, draw graphs, and find citations—what he called "getting into position to think"—far more efficiently. In 1983, I interviewed Licklider and he recalled his encounter with the PDP–1 as the beginning of his involvement with the interactive computing crusade. "I guess you could say I had a religious conversion," he said.

Licklider became involved himself with computer display technology at Lincoln Laboratory, an MIT facility that did top-secret work for the Department of Defense. The new computers and displays that the North American Defense Command required in the early 1960s needed work on the design of information displays. Out of that work, one of Licklider's junior researchers, a graduate student named Ivan Sutherland, created the field of computer graphics. Through Lincoln Laboratory, Licklider met the people who later hired him at ARPA.

In October 1957, when the Soviet Union launched Sputnik, the people who were responsible for maintaining the state of the art in U.S. military technology were shocked into action. To keep up with the pace of technical developments, the Department of Defense created the Advanced Research Projects Agency with a specific mandate to leapfrog over existing technology, bypassing, if necessary, the standard process of peer-reviewed research proposals. ARPA had a license to look for visionaries and wild ideas and sift them for viable schemes. When Licklider suggested that new ways of using computers not only were valuable to weapons and air defense technologies but also could improve the quality of research across the board by giving scientists and office workers better tools, he was hired to organize ARPA's Information Processing Techniques Office.

Licklider knew there was a whole subculture of unorthodox programming geniuses clustered at the new Artificial Intelligence Laboratory at MIT and graphics geniuses like Ivan Sutherland at Lincoln. There were others around the country, chafing to get their hands on the kind of computing resources that didn't exist in the punched card and mainframe era. They wanted to reinvent computing; the computer industry giants and the mainstream of computer science weren't interested in reinventing computing. So Licklider and his successors at ARPA, Robert Taylor and Ivan Sutherland (both in their twenties), started funding the young hackers—the original hackers, as chronicled in Steven Levy's book *Hackers*, not the ones who break into computer systems today. They also funded Engelbart, whose Augmentation Research Center (ARC) at Stanford Research Institute lasted for more than a decade and created the first word processors, conferencing systems, hypertext systems, mouse pointing devices, mixed video and computer communications—the technical foundation for half a dozen of the biggest high-tech industries today. When the first ARPANET went online, Engelbart's ARC was the original network information center that centralized all information gathering and record keeping about the state of the network.

During the 1960s, ARPA-funded groups worked on different aspects of interactive computing at different research centers scattered around the country. At MIT, they concentrated first on time-sharing, the scheme by which many individuals could interact directly with a central computer through a terminal, instead of waiting in line to submit their programs to computer operators. When you build a computer system that enables fifty or a hundred programmers to sit around a computer room and interact individually and directly with the main computer, you are automatically building in the potential for a community, because they are going to want to exchange lore and wisecracks while they do their programming. Electronic mail was one of the features built into the new time-sharing systems. Once they had e-mail in place, they were loathe to give it up. Later, they built e-mail into the system that linked the computer communities across geographical boundaries. The earliest users of CMC systems also were the people who built the first CMC systems; as users as well as designers of this thinking tool, they were reluctant to build in features that took power away from individual users, so they designed a degree of user autonomy into the system that persists in the architecture of cyberspace today.

At Lincoln Lab and the University of Utah, where Ivan Sutherland and a younger generation of crusaders such as Alan Kay ended up, interactive computer graphics was the quest. The jump from alphabetic printout to graphic screen display was a major leap in the evolution of the way computers are designed to be operated by people, the "human-computer interface." Humans process the world visually extremely well; we can extract far more information from color and pattern than we can from a page full of numbers. This breakthrough of manipulating patterns on a screen to display computer information involved more than graphics, because once you could display graphic information on a screen, you could display words as well. The capability of using the graphics to control the computer, as well as using the computer to control graphics, also led to further breakthroughs that made computers easier for nonprogrammers to use. Instead of a computer command that requires a person to type in an arcane code phrase, the computer user can point to a picture and press a button and issue the same command—now known as "point and click" commands.

Engelbart's team at SRI put graphics and time-sharing and group communication together in a new kind of research environment that Engelbart named "bootstrapped research": the researchers' goal was to design better tools for themselves; then they would test and debug their own tools and use them to create better tools. Other ARPA projects produced essential hardware for ARC. There were major nodes of the research network at a dozen different universities, and private research institutions such as RAND in Santa Monica and Bolt, Beranek, and Newman in Cambridge, the consulting firm that first showed Licklider the PDP–1. Under the ARPA direction of Licklider, Taylor, and Ivan Sutherland, a community of interdisciplinary toolbuilders collaborated for a decade to produce what they were then calling multiple-access computers.

The ARPA researchers from all the major projects got together in the same place once or twice a year. Through the 1960s, directly from their efforts, the original dreams of interactive computing and augmentation of human intellect began to turn into the kind of computers people use today. After six or seven years, the different projects initiated and supported by ARPA were beginning to converge. Each computer center had special hardware or software or data that other centers didn't have. A programmer using a powerful interactive computer in Illinois might make good use of the computer graphics software at another ARPA-sponsored computer center in Utah. In the previous era, the bottleneck was the way people had to stand in line to use the computer. Time-sharing made it possible for individuals to interact directly with the computer. The next bottleneck was the geographic distance between user and computer, and between computer and computer. In the era of time-sharing, it was natural to ask, Why not extend the line of control and link computers up, through telecommunication lines, at a distance?

Could computers send data fast enough through copper wires to allow remote operation of computers and resource-sharing? If it could be done through the short wire that connected all the terminals to the central time-shared computer, it could, in theory, be done with a wire as long as a continent. The telecommunications orthodoxy of the 1960s was as pessimistic about the ARPA quest as the computer orthodoxy had been uninterested in interactive computing. The ARPA planners adopted a particular way of sending chunks of computer information over a network, a scheme known as packet-switching.

Packet-switching is yet another case of a technology invented for one purpose evolving into purposes beyond the intentions of the inventors. It started in the 1950s, when the RAND Corporation performed top-secret studies on thermonuclear war scenarios. They focused on the survivability of the communications system that made command and control possible on local and national levels. In an all-out nuclear war, communications infrastructure—networks of wires, command centers, antennae—would become prime targets. RAND's Paul Baran proposed that the threat of the unreliability of any communications network under nuclear combat conditions could be dealt with by decentralizing authority for keeping communications flowing. The key idea he proposed was "that messages be broken into units of equal size and that the network route these message units along a functioning path to their destination where they would be reassembled into coherent wholes." Baran's scheme was made public in 1964.

Instead of having a hierarchy of command centers in the communications system to match the hierarchical organization of military command and control, Baran proposed eliminating the command center for communications. Chop all the communications into small packets of data, and precede the message data in each packet with information about where it originated and where it is going and which other packets it connects with when it gets there. Then distribute routers throughout the network that know how to read the addressing information on the packets and send them on their way. In this way, the routers could update each other about the state of the network at very short intervals. What any node knows about routing information, all other nodes know soon thereafter. Packets can take alternate paths through the network. If nodes go down, the network routes around it. If the receiving node does not receive all the packets it expects in a message, it can ask the transmitting node to retransmit specific packets. If you build a message-passing network on this scheme, and use computers to do the routing, you can build a network that will survive as node after node is blasted away.

The National Physical Laboratory in Great Britain tested packet-switching principles in practice in 1968. At the same time, ARPA issued a request for proposals (RFP) for a system to link geographically remote research computers into a network. Robert Taylor hired Lawrence Roberts from MIT's Lincoln Laboratory to write the RFP and choose the sites for the first network nodes. Roberts made the decision to use the packet-switching scheme. Robert Kahn, a mathematics professor at MIT, took a leave to work at Bolt, Beranek, and Newman (BBN), a government-funded think tank that ended up designing and running key components of ARPANET. Kahn wrote the proposal that won the first contract from ARPA for BBN. The first node was delivered to UCLA in 1969, and the network expanded to four nodes by the end of the year. In 1970, Harvard and MIT came online. By the middle of 1971, more than thirty different computers (and their communities) were linked to the network. Many of the people involved in funding and building the first network, such as Robert Taylor and Robert Kahn, are still actively involved in creating the next generation of network technology, more than twenty years later.

The significance of packet-switching technology to nontechnologists is twofold. First, this invention creates the building block for a communications system with no central control because you don't need a central controller when each packet and the entire network of routers all know how to get information around. Second, as the world's information becomes digitized, those packets can carry everything that humans can perceive and machines can process—voice, high-fidelity sound, text, high-resolution color graphics, computer programs, data, full-motion video. You can even send packets over the airwaves.

In research-and-development laboratories today, one popular buzzphrase is "digital convergence," which means that a lot more than virtual communities and libraries of text are going to live on the Net in the near future. Digitization is where the future of the Net is likely to collide with other computer-amplified forces in the world. As John P. Barlow is fond of saying, "Cyberspace is where your money is." Money is already an abstraction, part of a huge, incessant, worldwide flow of electronic messages. The value gained now by knowing how to move these abstract money messages around the world's telecommunications networks dwarfs the original value of the goods and services that produced the money.

Cyberspace is where global entertainment and communications are headed; large colonies of those industries already live there. Televisions and newspapers rely on a slightly different flavor of the same basic electronic signals traveling through the same worldwide network. The cable companies are in on it. Everybody knows that only those whose networks connect to everybody else's have a chance to reach the enormous world market, but nobody knows yet which set of interests—newspapers, television networks, entertainment conglomerates, communication giants—will dominate the mass-market networks of the future.

At the same time, many of the same powerful financial interests are investing in providing subject matter—"content," in telecom jargon—for universal, high-speed digital networks of the future. Entertainment and communications industries are both eyeing the same technological pipelines for delivering their products. In laboratories in Palo Alto and Cambridge, England, today, CMC communities are including video clips and voice mail with their e-mail and conferencing.

The fact that these new technical conduits for information had the potential to create new kinds of communities was noted and encouraged by the very top leaders of the research projects that created it. Before ARPANET went online in 1969, the people who had sponsored its initial development, J. C. R. Licklider and Robert Taylor, wrote an article with E. Herbert, "The Computer as a Communication Device," in which they set forth their vision for the future of computer-linked communities:

Although more interactive multiaccess computer systems are being delivered now, and although more groups plan to be using these systems within the next year, there are at present perhaps only as few as half a dozen interactive multiaccess computer communities...

For the society, the impact will be good or bad, depending mainly on the question: Will "to be on-line" be a privilege or a right? If only a favored segment of the population gets a chance to enjoy the advantage of "intelligence amplification," the network may exaggerate the discontinuity in the spectrum of intellectual opportunity.

On the other hand, if the network idea should prove to do for education what a few have envisioned in hope, if not in concrete detailed plan, and if all minds should prove to be responsive, surely the boon to human kind would be beyond measure.

As soon as ARPANET went online, people started sending electronic mail, far beyond the requirements of maintaining the network. One of the characteristics of e-mail is that it is easy to send a one-line message or a hundred-page file to one or a thousand people. You just make an automatic mailing list that contains the addresses of the people you want to reach. Another characteristic of e-mail is that you can reply to any message that arrives in your private electronic mailbox by typing one keystroke ("R" for "reply," on most systems). If you get a message from one person on a mailing list, you can reply privately to that person, or you can reply to everybody on the list. Suddenly, correspondence becomes a group conversation. Private lists continue to proliferate today as a way for individuals to create their own personalized conferencing systems: "roll your own" virtual communities.

The first large list, the first to foster its own culture, ARPANET veterans recall, was SF-LOVERS, a list of ARPA researchers who wanted to participate in public discussions about science fiction. SF-LOVERS started appearing publicly on ARPANET in the late 1970s. Attempts were made to suppress it, because it clearly fell outside even the most liberal interpretation of research-related activities. It is to the credit of the top ARPA managers that they allowed virtual communities to happen, despite pressure to reign in the netheads when they seemed to be having too much fun. The system engineers redesigned the system again and again to keep up with the explosive growth in network communications traffic. The social side of computer networking found its first forum in the HUMAN-NETS e-mail list.

By the time ARPANET was up and running and the different communities were knitting themselves into e-mail lists, the Vietnam War was beginning to politicize ARPA policy. Many of the brightest young researchers weren't as comfortable working for the Department of Defense. At that time, yet another visionary in the private sector came along and was fortunate enough to capture the best and the brightest of the ARPA crew.

In 1969, Peter McCullough, chief executive officer of Xerox, proclaimed the intention to make his company "the architect of information for the future." He initiated the construction of a multimillion-dollar, state-of-the-art, information-processing research facility in California, the Xerox Palo Alto Research Center, known as PARC. To create and manage the Computer Sciences Laboratory, Xerox hired Robert Taylor, formerly of NASA and ARPA. And Taylor hired Alan Kay and a few dozen of the best ARPA luminaries, who had been scattered around the country at different institutions for years.

PARC was hog heaven for the hardware engineers and software programmers who converged on Palo Alto in the early 1970s. These were people who had known each other by reputation, cooperated as colleagues, competed as peers, for almost ten years of ARPA-sponsored work. Here they were, together for the first time in one place as an all-star team, working for a research manager who shared their vision, with a generous budget and the best possible equipment. These were people who, as Alan Kay put it, "were used to dealing lightning with both hands." Many of them had been in their teens and early twenties when they created time-sharing and computer graphics; they were still young enough to accomplish another revolution. They were working for private enterprise now rather than the military, but the goal of the quest remained unchanged when the focus moved to PARC: liberating computer power for nonprogrammers to use to help them think and communicate.

Xerox PARC in the 1970s was the second crusade for the thinking-tool builders. Many of the ideas developed by Engelbart's team at SRI migrated to PARC. At PARC they knew exactly what they wanted to do: they wanted to go beyond time-sharing and create computers powerful, compact, and inexpensive enough to put one on everybody's desk—personal computers. They knew that the cost of computing power fell by half every two years, and that the coming technologies of microchip fabrication, known as integrated circuits, would make personal computers economical in about seven years. They also knew it would take about seven years to design them so people could use them. The PARC team also knew that the cost of another technology, televisionlike display screens, was dropping drastically as well. Cheap computers and cheap screens meant you could design a highly graphic human-computer interface, where people "point and click" at graphic representations instead of typing commands in computer language.

The first personal computer was the Alto, the workstation that the PARC team designed and built for themselves in the early 1970s. At the same time they were building the prototypes for the PCs of the future, the ARPA veterans at PARC didn't want to lose the personal communication connectivity they had enjoyed with time-sharing and ARPANET. So they designed a very high speed network—Ethernet—to link all the Altos in their building. The idea of local area networks (LANs) grew out of Ethernet. All the offices and factories and campuses full of workstations in the 1990s are becoming linked by LANs. PARC researchers also pioneered research into ways that local networks such as PARC's Ethernet could be linked through gateway computers to wider networks such as ARPANET. The technology of "internetworking" that started at ARPA and PARC has been one of the stimulants for the rapid growth of the Net, because it allows all the individually emerging archipelagoes of local networks to link with each other into internetworks.

Throughout the 1970s and the 1980s, the technology of internet-working itself evolved at a rapid rate. The speed with which information can be transmitted through a medium is one fundamental determinant of what kind of information can be transmitted, the value of the information, and who can afford to send or receive it. This is one place where technological leaps in capability transform into economic leaps. When your bits-per-second rate is low and expensive, you can send messages laboriously via telegraph. When your bits-per-second rate is high and inexpensive, you can send books, encyclopedias, entire libraries, in less than a minute. The economics of speed in CMC technology are central to the notion of citizen-accessible computing. If a citizen today can have the telecomputing power only the Pentagon could afford twenty years ago, what will citizens be able to afford in telecommunications power five or ten years into the future?

ARPANET used 56,000-bit-per-second links for over a decade. This is a very high speed compared to the speed of the first personal modems, for example, which sent information at 300 bits per second. In 1987, NSFNET (the successor to ARPANET) moved to communication lines capable of transporting 1.5 million bits per second. By 1992, the NSFNET backbone had moved to 45-million-bit-per-second lines—a seven-hundredfold increase in speed in five years. At that speed, you can send five thousand pages per second, a couple of encyclopedias per minute. The next quantum leap in speed is the gigabit level—billions and hundreds of billions of bits per second; at the multigigabit-per-second level, you are talking about how many Libraries of Congress you can transmit every minute. Gigabit-rate networking is one of the projects of the present NREN testbed, so Libraries-of-Congress-per-minute networking is already in the prototype phase. And research into terabit—trillions of bits per second—networking is well under way. Just as the cost of anything de-pendent on computer power dropped drastically when miniaturization made computers more powerful, the cost of anything that depends on the speed of information transfer is going to drop.

Gross and/or rapid changes in quantity can make for equally discontinuous changes in the quality of a phenomenon, when "emergent behaviors" kick in. When you can transfer the Library of Congress from one place to another in under a minute, the very notion of what it means to have a place called the Library of Congress changes. As it goes digital, that place in Washington, D.C., is virtualizing. I can already get the Library of Congress catalog from my desktop. When I can download the source text itself to my desktop, my sense of where that information resides changes. It's at the other end of my modem line, along with the rest of the Net, which means it is more or less on my desktop.

In terms of population growth, the original ARPANET community numbered around a thousand in 1969. A little over twenty years later, the Internet population is estimated at between five and ten million people. The rate of growth is too rapid for accurate measurements at this point, with worldwide internetworking plugging together all the little and medium-size networks that have been growing over the past decade or so. The total number of connected networks grew from a couple hundred in the early 1980s to over seventy-five hundred by the early 1990s, reaching people in more than seventy-five countries. In the September 1991 issue of Scientific American, then-senator Albert Gore noted an estimate that has been supported by others: for the past five years, Internet alone has been growing in numbers of users at around 10 percent per month.

The hosts on Internet are the individual computer communities. Some hosts, like the WELL, have thousands of users; a few have tens and hundreds of thousands of users. On Internet, in a publicly available document known as an RFC (Request for Comment), is a graph of the rate of growth of Internet hosts for the 1980s (see page 81).

Obviously, these rates of growth have to level off eventually. There aren't enough people in the world to sustain growth rates like that. But cyberspace cartographer John Quarterman, in his article "How Big Is the Matrix?" captured the most important aspect of these growth rates, the obvious implication that this largely invisible subculture is likely to break the surface of the world's awareness, due to sheer size, soon:

In two years, there will be more network users than residents of any state in the United States. In five years there will be more network users than citizens of any single country except India or China. What will happen when McLuhan's global village becomes one of the largest countries in the world? Using two-way communications, not broadcast? And crossing boundaries of space, time, and politics?

By the early 1980s, the bureaucratic and financial demands of running ARPANET had outgrown ARPA. The Net was an intellectual resource now, and scholars and scientists were clamoring to get in on it, even if

RFC 1296   Internet Growth (1981 – 1991)   January
                    Number of Internet Hosts (linear)   1992

Thousands
of Hosts

```
740 ┤                                                          *
720 ┤
700 ┤
680 ┤                                                       •
660 ┤
640 ┤
620 ┤
600 ┤                                                    *
580 ┤
560 ┤
540 ┤
520 ┤                                                 *
500 ┤
480 ┤                                               •
460 ┤
440 ┤
420 ┤                                            •
400 ┤
380 ┤
360 ┤                                        *
340 ┤                                        •
320 ┤
300 ┤                                     *
280 ┤
260 ┤                                   •
240 ┤                                 •
220 ┤
200 ┤                              •
180 ┤                            •
160 ┤
140 ┤                         *
120 ┤                       *
100 ┤
 80 ┤                    * ••
 60 ┤                   •
 40 ┤                *   *
 20 ┤  *     *    *    *   **  ••**••
  0 ┤•• ••••  •••••  ••••••  •••• •• •••••
    └────┬────┬────┬────┬────┬────┬────┬────┬──
       81   82   83   84   85   86   87   88   89   90   91   92
                          Date
```

"*" = data point,   "•" = estimate

they weren't doing weapons-related research. CMC was following the same path of diffusion that computer technology had followed ten to twenty years before: first developed as part of weapons-related research, computers and networks soon proved valuable and then affordable first to scientific researchers outside weapons research, then to big businesses, then to small businesses, and then to citizens. By the early 1980s, scientists outside the most liberal interpretation of military-related research wanted to make use of computer networks.

Science is a communication-dependent enterprise, one of the most universal communications enterprises in the world: If you are a scientist, you make an observation or think up a theory, and you publish it; other scientists can read your observation and theory and test it, then publish the nature and results of their tests. From this process of observation, experimentation, theorization, and communication, scientific knowledge is supposed to emerge. The bottleneck is access to the academy, to the scientific hierarchies that admit novices to circles where their communications can be noticed. In the nineteenth century, an Austrian monk, Gregor Mendel, experimented with sweet peas and discovered the laws of genetics, but he did not have access to the highest scientific journals. The knowledge lay fallow for decades, until it was rediscovered in an obscure journal by biologists who were on the track of the mysteries of genetics. Mendel's experience is worth remembering as scientific discourse moves onto the Net.

If more and more scientific communication moves onto the Net, as it seems to be doing, where anybody who has net access to put forth their equations or their theory along with the academicians, several kinds of results are likely. First, you are as marginalized as Gregor Mendel was if you are a member of neither the academy nor the Net, because that is where all the important attention will be. Second, if you are Gregor Mendel, all you have to do is gain net access in order to participate in the international group conversation of science.

But before the Net grew enough to allow citizen participation, access to the Net enabled scientists in quickly moving fields to have their own specialized versions of the living database that the WELL and Usenet provides other groups; to the degree that the process of science is embedded in group communication, the many-to-many characteristic of virtual communities can both accelerate and democratize access to cutting-edge knowledge. Hence, the pressure from nonmilitary scientific researchers to gain access to the Net in the 1980s.

In 1983, ARPANET split into ARPANET for research and MILNET for military operational use. These were both wide-area backbone networks that communicated among their own backbone nodes at the highest speeds, supporting communities of users that numbered in the hundreds and thousands. When networking began to be built into the kinds of computers most colleges and research laboratories were using, Internet grew explosively. This was, in part, encouraged by ARPA. When computers changed from the old-fashioned batch mode that took punch cards to time-shared multiple-access computing, new ways of operating computers were created. Unix, an operating system for multiple-access computers, was created by programmers at Bell Laboratories for research uses in 1969, the year ARPANET went online.

An operating system is a master control program that handles interactions between human users and computer programs; Unix was designed for programmers of interactive computers who needed to be able to build tools for each other, share those tools, and propagate successful tools throughout the programmer community. Nobody ever dreamed it would become a worldwide standard, used by millions of nonprogrammers. Thus, the unexpected success of Unix, originally a research tool for programmers, as an operating system for use by scientists and students created a uniform set of communication building blocks built into every Unix-using computer. These building blocks came in handy later, when all those Unix machines in colleges and laboratories around the world started calling each other with modems and communicating via high-speed networks. UUCP, a Unix to Unix Copy Program, made it possible for any computer using Unix to automatically dial and share information via modem with any other Unix computer. This was to provide an alternative networking infrastructure for those computers not on Internet.

In 1983, programmers at the University of California, funded by ARPA, created a version of Unix for the new kinds of computers becoming available; the computer codes for communicating with Internet, known as the TCP/IP protocol suite, were built into Berkeley Unix. Now, Unix computers not only could call each other via relatively slow modems, but could encode and decode the packets of data that travel at much higher speeds on Internet. Because public funds had supported its development, this new version of Unix was distributed for the cost of distribution. New companies, like the ARPA-funded Sun Microsystems, sprang up in the mid–1980s and instantly flourished as carriers of Unix and built-in networking. Local networks grew in science departments of colleges all over the world. And the local networks started grouping with larger networks such as ARPANET and MILNET. Another network for scholarly and academic discussions not limited to the sciences, BITNET, sponsored by IBM, started to grow. Huge internal corporate networks grew at DEC and IBM and AT&T.

This network of networks that emerged in the 1980s was called ARPA Internet, then just Internet. The more useful this new tool proved to be, the more people who were not originally authorized to use it wanted to get their hands on it. The computer scientists who were denied access to the Net according to the Defense Department's strict interpretation of "acceptable use" turned to the National Science Foundation (NSF). Now that internetworking was becoming a valuable intellectual resource for scientists, NSF established CSNET, another science-oriented network within Internet, and funded other regional research networks. Nonscientist scholars wanted access to CMC, so BITNET was established by NSF and IBM. Because packet-switching and networking technology was created with tax-supported funding, successive generations of network implemented "acceptable use" policies that ruled out commercial activity; this situation started to change in 1993 as Internet began to privatize.

Time and again, the Net has been widened and the definition of "acceptable use" has expanded as the result of pressure by people who wanted access. The first definition of "acceptable use" limited the Net to DARPA (as ARPA is known now) researchers; that was expanded to include other military- and government-funded scientific researchers, then expanded to the scientific and scholarly communities, and now it is in the process of expanding to the business community. Right now, whether the next and most important extension of the Net community—to the education field and then to all citizens—will happen remains in question. The mid–1990s look like a fork in the road: will the expansion process continue beyond the business community, or will they try to own it all?

The reason the U.S. Congress continues to allocate funds to develop increasingly powerful networks is that it has been told that America is in danger of falling behind, either in supercomputer research or in competitive economic advantage. Educational and citizen uses—and rights of access —are a relatively recent issue. Supercomputer competition, not a recognition of the intrinsic intellectual value of high-speed networking, was the key factor in funding the upgrade of the old ARPANET to a new generation of networking technology.

NSF was also involved in the early 1980s with another experiment in leapfrogging, a high-speed network to interconnect supercomputer centers around the United States. Supercomputers were too expensive to distribute widely, so NSF supported five regional supercomputer centers. By the mid–1980s, supercomputing had moved to the part of the cycle where scientists wanted to use it for non-weapons-related research. High-speed networking was by then a proven technology, and ultra-high-speed networking technologies on the horizon could do for supercomputers what ARPANET did for the first multiple-access computers. NSF initiated the NSFNET project to link the supercomputer centers and their communities of users. The network came online in 1986, and NSFNET became Internet's main backbone. By that point, transmission speeds on the backbone were at the million-bit-per-second level. ARPANET was honorably decommissioned in March 1990.

The process of technology transfer, of handing off the government-developed Internet to private enterprise, has been controversial from the start. In 1987, NSF awarded a contract to manage and upgrade the Internet backbone to Merit Network, Inc., which was running the state educational network in Michigan in partnership with IBM and MCI Communications. By that time, several ARPANET veterans and others had set up small organizations to develop new applications for new network communities, and these companies were not at all happy to hear about the entry of the same old big boys into what had previously been a wide-open frontier.

Like computer technology in the 1950s, CMC technology in the late 1980s had reached the point where it was time to migrate from publicly funded defense research to private businesses and citizens. This is the most critical point in the history of the technology, as the decisions and events of the near future will cast a long shadow into the future. As the Net continues to serve as an intellectual, economic, and perhaps cultural resource to citizens, a kind of knowledge-tide that lifts all boats, should it be the kind of infrastructure project that is properly funded by the national government in the United States, as it is in Japan and France? If this technology is more properly left to the marketplace and private industries, how should the rights of citizens be protected against infringement from those industries, the way those rights are constitutionally protected when the government runs it? How should small start-up companies be protected from unfair competition from today's industry giants? Who shall determine the new rules about privacy, intellectual property, international trade, that accompany the growth of the Net? In the early 1990s, these questions became the topics of heated debate that will continue for years to come.

By the late 1980s, the Net began to outgrow the government's ability to manage. It was time to hand off the wider-access networks to private industry. But serious questions remained about the appropriate way to privatize this publicly funded technology. Is CMC a publishing medium or a communication service or an informal public space? What degree of public regulation is appropriate in an industry in which the citizens' rights to communicate about matters of public interest is staked to the price of access? Now that some of the same commercial outfits that weren't interested in developing the technology twenty years ago are competing for contracts to provide it in the future, what rights do citizens have to determine the way this tool is handed off from the public to the private sector?

At the same time that the Net has once again outgrown its government sponsors, a movement to create an even more powerful and even more inclusive Net has grown into the legislative foundation for the next incarnation of ARPANET-INTERNET-NSFNET, called the National Research and Education Network (NREN). Again, the legislation was heavily influenced by fears of U.S. military and industry losing a competitive edge in supercomputer and networking technologies, in response to a report from the Office of Science and Technology that emphasized the possibility of falling behind in those fields. In the late 1980s, the High Performance Computing Act began its way through Congress. Along the way, the notion of a "national superhighway for information" became attached to the legislation for looking into upgrading Internet, and Senator Albert Gore of Tennessee emerged as the champion of a network that would enable schoolchildren to access the Library of Congress and rural physicians to upload CAT scans to metropolitan medical centers. During congressional hearings, experts such as Robert Kahn, who had been instrumental in creating ARPANET, made a strong case for the utility of a national information infrastructure that would bring the benefits of the Net to elementary schools and libraries as well as to laboratories, universities, and businesses. The High Performance Computing/NREN bill, signed by President Bush, authorized $650 million of new spending by NSF, $388 million by DARPA, and $31 million by the Departments of Commerce's National Institute of Standards and Technology. Five gigabit-network testbeds were set up around the United States. The fundamental research for a vastly faster network technology, capable of sending CAT scans and real-time video, along with Libraries-of-Congress-per-minute of text, got under way. The debate over how much of that money should be allocated for educational and citizens' applications is far from over. At the same time, there is controversy over the institutional transfer of technology from NSF to private corporations. The initial funds necessary to create the technology for a new national information network will be spent, no matter what budget cuts may come in the future. The question of who will run it and who will be allowed to use it is wide open. Again, the terms of "acceptable use" are being challenged by populations of outsiders who want in.

As commercial organizations—including two of the biggest corporations in the world, IBM and AT&T—take over management of the Net from government institutions, who will gain access and who will be denied access? Who will make policy about what users can say or do in the Net? Who will arbitrate disagreements about access or online behavior? This technology was developed with tax money. Should there be a cap on the amount that private companies will be allowed to charge us in the future for using a technology that public dollars were used to develop in the past?

The furor was not limited to Netheads when IBM began staking out territory on the Net. It began to look as if some of the industry giants were planning to become competitors in the same market where, as Internet contractors, they controlled commercial access to the Net. IBM and MCI's venture, ANS, had been managing NSFNET since 1987; in 1991, ANS, a nonprofit corporation, set up a for-profit subsidiary called

ANS CO+RE to sell CMC services. In a December 1991 story in the *New York Times*, headlined "U.S. Said to Play Favorites in Promoting Nationwide Computer Network," technology reporter John Markoff, who broke the story of the Morris Worm, wrote, "Just one week after President Bush signed legislation calling for the creation of a nationwide computer data 'superhighway,' a debate has erupted over whether the government gave an unfair advantage to a joint venture of IBM and MCI that built and manages a key part of the network." Markoff quoted several experts and private competitors who fear ANS could use its position as manager of the NSFnet to make things difficult for competitors who want to connect to the Net.

"People involved in planning for a national data network say it is essential to provide for fair competition, which will lead rival companies to offer creative and entrepreneurial services in the hope of building market share. Without competition, they say, the government will have created a monopoly that has little incentive to innovate," wrote Markoff. He quoted David Farber, one of the pioneers of the original ARPANET and now a computer scientist at the University of Pennsylvania testbed for the high-speed NREN: "This is the first major communication business to be born under the deregulation era. This hasn't happened since the growth of the telephone industry. You want it to be a business that doesn't repeat the errors of the past."

One private contractor who fears competition with ANS CO+RE is William L. Schrader, president of Performance Systems International, Inc., a company in Reston, Virginia, that provides commercial connections to Internet. "But there is no level playing field. It's like taking a federal park and giving it to K mart," Schrader said to Markoff. "It's not right, and it isn't going to stand. As a taxpayer, I think it's disgusting."

Markoff also quoted Mitchell D. Kapor, founder of Lotus and head of the Electronic Frontier Foundation: "Nobody should have an unfair advantage. This is important because we're talking about something that is in its infancy but that one day could be on the order of the personal computer industry."

What will people have to pay, and what will we have to agree to say or not say, in order to both feed information to the Net and take information from it? Pricing determines access. What do the big businesses who want to be the chief Net contractors of the future want to control?

If they control the conduits for information, the fiber-optic networks and high-speed routers, and they also compete to provide commercial services through that conduit, what effect will that have on their smaller competitors? What should be a fair price for them to charge for continuing network services? And in ways might these major players be tempted to restrain mom-and-pop information providers to compete with them as vendors of content? Government and major business leaders are debating these questions now, which is why the 1990s are a time when the voice of citizens counts in determining the shape of the technology's future.

In early 1993, a press release electrified the Net. The National Science Foundation announced that it was turning over three of the most important administrative functions of Internet management—assigning Internet addresses (and thus acting as a gateway and potential chokepoint for determining exactly which sites are granted permission to join the high-speed network), maintaining directory and database services (keeping track of how to locate people and resources), and maintaining information services provided to Internet users (modernization of tools for making use of the Net). The contracts, totaling $12 million, were awarded to Network Solutions (registration services), AT&T (directory and database services), and General Atomics (information services). First, MCI and IBM jump in. Now AT&T. Have the big boys already made their secret deals? Is a pricing structure being constructed hastily, before anybody but a minority of the population even understand the implications of a privatized Internet? There is a troubling sentence in the press release: "Consistent with FNC guidelines on obtaining reasonable cost recovery from users of NREN networks, the NSF has determined that the INTERNIC Information Services provider may charge users beyond the U.S. research and education community for any services provided...."

Gordon Cook, a well-known Net gadfly who publishes a newsletter on the political and policy issues related to the emerging Net, pointed out in a widely quoted flame to the Community Networks e-mail list that the grassroots applications so dear to all the utopian populists are not the primary purpose of NREN:

Date: Wed, 9 Jun 1993 20:11:48 -0700
From: Gordon Cook <cook@PATH.NET>
Subject: Re: A WAR OVER THE FUTURE OF THE
NREN/INTERNET

. . . .Unfortunately a lot of folk never stopped
to read the actual legislation [The High
Performance Computing and Communications Act, 1991.

PL 102-194 "Sec 102 © Network Characteristics

The Network shall (6) have accounting mechanisms
which allow users or groups of users to be charged
for their usage of copyrighted materials available
over the network, and, where appropriate and technically feasible, **for their use** of the network."

Now I'd say that's pointing pretty squarely in
the direction of metered individual bills. Still
happy with what Al Gore has brought you?

The big advocates of NREN have been the federal
agencies who have believed that public funds will
be poured into buying bigger and better bit-pipes
for various HIGH end uses. For this reason not many
of the network insiders have wished to rock the
boat when the bill authorizes $500 million for NREN
from fy [fiscal year 92 through 96. But there is a
huge difference between authorize and appropriate,
and even when appropriated it can be pulled. . . .

The whole thing is hideously complicated.
Unfortunately very few folk have any view of the
WHOLE picture. . . . which leaves the pieces in
charge of the special interests as usual. (After
three years full time on the trail I think that I
DO have an idea of the WHOLE picture.)

I have interested a reporter at the Washington
Post. But so far all his editors do is yawn. And
most reporters have to cover such a broad swath of
technology that they can never find time to educate

```
themselves in how all these pieces should be put
together.
    The grass roots aspect is a bore to the special
interests. There's not enough money there. And as I
tried to say when this list first got started, if
the grass roots thinks it will reap significant
benefits from NREN, it will probably be disillu-
sioned. . . .
```

This might be the beginning of a well-thought-out process of privatizing a technology that long ago outgrew its government sponsors. But key questions remain to be answered if citizens are to be assured that we aren't being bamboozled: Who will have access, what will it cost, and how will disputes over access, cost, or content be arbitrated? The key questions of access, pricing, censorship, and redress of grievances will be answered in practice, in law, in executive order or legislative action, over the next five years, and thus determine the political and economic structure of the Net for decades to come.

What Can You Find on the Net?

The content of ARPANET started to grow rapidly in two directions from the very beginning. Once the Net exists, all you have to do to increase the collective resources of the entire community is to add a valuable resource to your node and allow other Net citizens to access it. Every day, more and more informational and computational resources came online as local nodes added to that part of their resources they shared with the rest of the Net community, and more and more people started communicating with each other in new ways. The key is the way the resources available to any individual user of the Net multiply along with the Net's growth in other dimensions—number of different computers online, speed at which information can be transferred, amount of material transferred from analog to digital form. The bigger and faster the Net grows, the more leverage it gives each individual who can gain access and who knows how to use it.

When the WELL linked to Internet in 1992, more information became available to me than I could handle in a hundred lifetimes. One computer on Internet, for example, carries up-to-the hour versions of digitized satellite radar weather maps. If I have an account on a computer connected to Internet, I can transfer that computer file containing the satellite photo to my desktop. Another program on my desktop computer transforms that computer file into an image. Presto! There, in living color, is a radar profile of the west coast of North America, taken by a satellite a few hours ago; if I download a set of successive photographs, I can step through them on my desktop machine like electronic flipcards and watch a storm front move across the Pacific. You can go to your local computer store and buy commercial software today that will automatically dial a Net host, download to your desktop the latest weather files, and convert them to ready-to-view images.

The Library of Congress card catalog is available and searchable by any Net citizen, as are several hundred card catalogs and periodical collections of libraries around the world. The latest decisions of the Supreme Court are available online, and so is the full text of the annual CIA *World Factbook*. I can use sophisticated search engines on powerful computers to find the lyrics to popular songs. The full text of the Bible, the Torah, and the Koran are available and searchable by keyword. Network technology automatically makes all the machine-to-machine connections between my desktop computer and my Internet host computer, and through the host to any other computer connected to the Net, which means the Library of Congress, every university library catalog on the Net worldwide, the Supreme Court, and other knowledge resources are more or less virtually available to me at all times.

The increasing digitization and availability of information collected by governments at taxpayer expense is another converging force that is pushing the Net toward a critical mass. More and more public and government databases are going online at local and national levels. The coexistence of very large and up-to-date collections of factual information in conjunction with a medium that is also a forum for discussion and debate has important implications for the public sphere. The ability of groups of citizens to debate political issues is amplified enormously by instant, widespread access to facts that could support or refute assertions made in those debates. This kind of citizen-to-citizen discussion, backed up by facts available to all, could grow into the real basis for a possible electronic democracy of the future.

On June 1, 1993, the following notice was posted, copied, and reposted throughout the Net:

THE WHITE HOUSE

Office of Presidential Correspondence

For Immediate Release   June 1, 1993

LETTER FROM THE PRESIDENT AND VICE PRESIDENT
IN ANNOUNCEMENT OF WHITE HOUSE ELECTRONIC MAIL
ACCESS

Dear Friends:
  Part of our commitment to change is to keep
the White House in step with today's changing
technology. As we move ahead into the twenty-first
century, we must have a government that can show
the way and lead by example. Today, we are pleased
to announce that for the first time in history, the
White House will be connected to you via electronic
mail. Electronic mail will bring the Presidency and
this Administration closer and make it more accessible to the people.
  The White House will be connected to the
Internet as well as several on-line commercial
vendors, thus making us more accessible and more in
touch with people across this country. We will not
be alone in this venture. Congress is also getting
involved, and an exciting announcement regarding
electronic mail is expected to come from the House
of Representatives tomorrow.
  Various government agencies also will be taking
part in the near future. Americans Communicating
Electronically is a project developed by several
government agencies to coordinate and improve
access to the nation's educational and information
assets and resources. This will be done through
interactive communications such as electronic mail,

and brought to people who do not have ready access to a computer.

However, we must be realistic about the limitations and expectations of the White House electronic mail system. This experiment is the first-ever e-mail project done on such a large scale. As we work to reinvent government and streamline our processes, the e-mail project can help to put us on the leading edge of progress.

Initially, your e-mail message will be read and receipt immediately acknowledged. A careful count will be taken on the number received as well as the subject of each message. However, the White House is not yet capable of sending back a tailored response via electronic mail. We are hoping this will happen by the end of the year.

A number of response-based programs which allow technology to help us read your message more effectively, and, eventually respond to you electronically in a timely fashion will be tried out as well. These programs will change periodically as we experiment with the best way to handle electronic mail from the public. Since this has never been tried before, it is important to allow for some flexibility in the system in these first stages. We welcome your suggestions.

This is an historic moment in the White House and we look forward to your participation and enthusiasm for this milestone event. We eagerly anticipate the day when electronic mail from the public is an integral and normal part of the White House communications system.

```
            President Clinton       Vice President Gore
PRESIDENT@WHITEHOUSE.GOV
VICE.PRESIDENT@WHITEHOUSE.GOV
```

A few days later, the following was posted to the Net:

UNITED STATES HOUSE OF REPRESENTATIVES
CONSTITUENT ELECTRONIC MAIL SYSTEM

We welcome your inquiry to the House of
Representatives Constituent Electronic Mail System.
Currently, seven Members of the U.S. House of
Representatives have been assigned public
electronic mailboxes that may be accessed by their
constituents.

This effort represents a pilot program that will
be used to assess the impact of electronic mail on
Congressional offices and their mission of serving
the residents of a Congressional District. This
initial project will be expanded to other Members
of Congress, as technical, budgetary and staffing
constraints allow.

Please review the list of participating
Representatives below, and if the Congressional
District in which you reside is listed, follow the
instructions below to begin communicating by
electronic mail with your Representative. If your
Representative is not yet on-line, please be
patient.

U.S. REPRESENTATIVES PARTICIPATING IN THE
CONSTITUENT ELECTRONIC MAIL SYSTEM

Hon. Jay Dickey
4th Congressional District, Arkansas
Rm. 1338 Longworth House Office Building
Washington, DC 20515

Hon. Sam Gejdenson
2nd Congressional District, Connecticut
Rm. 2416 Rayburn House Office Building
Washington, DC 20515

Hon. Newton Gingrich
6th Congressional District, Georgia
Rm. 2428 Rayburn House Office Building
Washington, DC 20515

Hon. George Miller
7th Congressional District, California
Rm. 2205 Rayburn House Office Building
Washington, DC 20515

Hon. Charlie Rose
7th Congressional District, North Carolina
Rm. 2230 Rayburn House Office Building
Washington, DC 20515

Hon. 'Pete' Stark
13th Congressional District, California
Rm. 239 Cannon House Office Building
Washington, DC 20515

Hon. Mel Watt
12th Congressional District, North Carolina
Rm. 1232 Longworth House Office Building
Washington, DC 20515

INSTRUCTIONS FOR CONSTITUENTS

If your Representative is taking part in the pilot project, we encourage you to send a letter or postcard by U.S.Mail to that Representative at the address listed above requesting electronic mail access. In your correspondence, please print your name and INTERNET ADDRESS, followed by your postal (geographical) address. When your Representative receives the letter or postcard, you will receive a reply by electronic mail that will include the Representative's Internet address. After you receive this initial message, you will be able to write your Member of Congress at any time, provided you follow certain guidelines that will be included in that initial message.

We are aware that it is an inconvenience for electronic mail users to be required to send a post card in order to begin communicating with their Representative. However, the primary goal of this pilot program is to allow Members to better serve their CONSTITUENTS, and this initial postal request is the only sure method currently available of verifying that a user is a resident of a particular congressional district.

In addition, constituents who communicate with their Representative by electronic mail should be aware that Members will respond to their messages in the same manner that they respond to most communications from constituents. That is, Members will generally respond to messages by way of the U.S. Postal Service. This method of reply will help to ensure confidentiality, a concern that is of utmost importance to the House of Representatives.

COMMENTS AND SUGGESTIONS

Please feel free to send electronic mail comments about our new service to the Congressional Comment Desk, at

COMMENTS@HR.HOUSE.GOV

We will make every effort to integrate suggestions into forthcoming updates of our system.

Thank you again for contacting the House of Representatives' Constituent Electronic Mail System. We are excited about the possibilities that e-mail has to offer, and will be working hard to bring more Members on-line and to expand our services. We feel that this pilot program is an important first step, and we urge your cooperation and continued interest to make the program a success.

This message will be updated as necessary.

Honorable Charlie Rose (D-NC)
Chairman
Committee on House Administration

A week later, the following message propagated through the Net. Events are moving fast.

GPO ACCESS BILL SIGNED INTO LAW

On June 8, President Clinton signed into law S. 564, the Government Printing Office Electronic Access Bill. It is now P.L. 103-40. A statement released by the President said that "this important step forward in the electronic dissemination of Federal information will provide valuable insights into the most effective means of disseminating all public Government information."

The law establishes in the Government Printing Office a means of enhancing electronic public access to a wide range of federal electronic information. The system will provide online access to the Congressional Record and the Federal Register, and other appropriate publications distributed by the Superintendent of Documents. It will also establish an electronic directory of federal public information stored electronically and an electronic storage facility. The system will be available without charge to depository libraries; other users will be charged approximately the incremental cost of dissemination. The law requires the system to be up and running within one year from the enactment date.

In a press release issued by his office, Sen. Wendell Ford (D-KY) called the law "one more way we can make government more accountable to the American people. This law puts information about the government right at the public's fingertips. Whether they live in a rural community in Eastern Kentucky or the big cities of New York, San Francisco and Chicago, anyone will be able to

access government documents through their home
computer or a local depository library."

In concluding his press release, Sen. Ford
stressed that this law is "the first step to creating across-the-board public access." He believes
that coverage of congressional hearings and committee prints will be made available very soon.

In 1992, Rick Gates, director of library automation at the University
of California at Santa Barbara, started the tradition of Internet Treasure
Hunts. Periodically, Gates posts a list of questions to Usenet, the floating
conference that most Internet sites participate in:

```
* * * * * * * * * * * * * * * * * * * * * * * * * * * * * * * * * * * * * * * * * * * * * * * * * * * * * *
                                 *
                        THE  INTERNET  HUNT
                                 *
                        for January, 1993
                                 *
                (deadline: Midnight PST 1/10/93
                                 *
* * * * * * * * * * * * * * * * * * * * * * * * * * * * * * * * * * * * * * * * * * * * * * * * * * * * * *
```

Welcome to the first Hunt of the New Year. This
Hunt is running a little late due to a small but
tenacious virus (carbon-based variety), that has me
pooped.

This Hunt has a maximum of 43 points (with the
extra credit).

I'm pleased to announce that past Hunts are now
being archived at the Coalition for Networked
Information. Thanks to http://www.cni.org/~craig/
and Paul Evan Peters.

The files are available via anonymous ftp at:

```
ftp.cni.org
```
. . . in

pub/net-guides/i-hunt/

. . . and the readme file should explain exactly
what's there.

I'll also archive files for introductory text,
tips, rules, history, and a list of winners.

I also hope that sometime very soon I'll be able
to post these files to a gopher server somewhere,
for distribution purposes.

Enjoy, you intrepid hunters. I'm going back to bed.

THE RULES

1. There are a total of 12 questions. The first 11
questions count toward your score. I have
personally verified that each of these can be
answered using only the resources of the Net. These
are contrived questions.

2. The last question is the mystery question. I
don't know if there's an answer to this on the
Net. I may or may not have tried to find one.
These questions usually come to me from people
asking for information. This is a real question.

3. Each of these first 10 questions carries a value
in parentheses. This point value is my best guess
on how tough that question is to answer. The scale
is 1 (easy), to 10 (hard). Total points for all
questions is listed at the top of this message.
Extra credit questions are always worth 1, not
because they're easy, but because they're extra
credit.

THE HUNT

1. (7) How does one say "Merry Christmas and a Happy New Year" in Czech?

2. (6) Is the Toyota Motor Corporation connected to the Internet?

3. (3) Hi! I have a new account on a unix machine here, and I HATE the editor I have for my mail. It's called vi. So I found another editor that I can use called emacs. Emacs is supposed to be customizable, but I've managed to screw things up a little. Can you tell me where I can get some advice from more experienced emacs users?

4. (5) Can you get AIDS from kissing?

5. (3) I read in an electronic journal somewhere that a conference was held in Padova, Italy on models of musical signals. I wrote down the name of a contact, 'Giovanni De Poli'. Can you find his e-mail address for me?

6. (2) What is the primary religion in Somalia?

7. (4) I understand that the Net is being put to use distributing information and pictures of missing childrenIf you know how to do it, you can find the answer to each of these questions by using the tools available to every registered user of an Internet node.

8. (4) Where can I find tables listing the nutritive values of different foods?

9. (3) What is the text of the 1st Amendment to the Constitution of the United States?

10. (5) You know, I've gotten a lot of good network information by FTPing files from nnsc.nsf.net. What kind of computer and operating system is nnsc.nsf.net?

Extra Credit. (1) Where can I find the exact time?

If you know how to do it, you can find the answer to each of these questions by using the tools available to every registered user of an Internet node.

Internet provides each registered user with access to three important tools; with this toolkit, a whole range of applications becomes possible. An Internet user who is initiated in the arcane codes of nuts-and-bolts level CMC can use these tools to build more elaborate and personalized tools. If the Internet user just wants to communicate with people and gain access to valuable information without learning computer arcana, these fundamental tools can be masked behind more user-friendly menu systems.

Electronic mail service, the first and most widely used tool, is a set of programs that enables private mail among individuals and groups to be distributed within seconds to any site on the Internet backbone, and within hours to satellite nodes around the world. Access to the programs, including facilities for appending large text files, forwarding messages, and sending one message to all the members of a mailing list, is what makes every Net citizen a publisher as well as a consumer of information. The other two tools are telnet and ftp.

Telnet is a way of issuing a command to your host computer that automatically connects you to another Internet computer. If you have the right password, you can interact with that remote computer in real time, and many computers on the Net make part of their resources available to anybody who uses the password "anonymous"; telnet is how students from around the world participate in MUDs or how I can use a few keystrokes to travel from the WELL to the Library of Congress catalog. "Telnet" is used as a verb on the Net, as in "telnet to well.sf.ca.us for a good time."

The Net's collection of information is not organized like a library or anything else a person would have designed rationally; it's more like something that grew on its own. As new sites join Internet every day, often bringing along large collections of Net-accessible resources, the problem of keeping track of what is out there has spawned new generations of software. One free tool that is spreading through the Net these days, for example, is hytelnet. This program, which your Internet host computer runs, turns the Net into a series of menus you can navigate with the arrow keys on your desktop computer keyboard. The name of the command combines an ancient grail quest in the computer world with the Internet tool for hopping from computer to computer.

The ancient grail quest, known as hypertext, was first proposed by Ted Nelson in the 1960s and first implemented by Engelbart's SRI project, as a linked series of texts that could automatically summon other texts for viewing. When you come across a reference or footnote in one document of a hypertext database, you can point at it and instantly see the source document cited, then go back to the first document, if you wish, or continue to explore links forward, to other documents. The entire library is interconnected in such a scheme. When you expand the linkable database to include video, graphics, and sounds, the medium becomes hypermedia, but the idea of links that jump from document to document remains central.

By means of a simple program that maps the arrow keys on most users' computers to the telnet program, hytelnet turned Internet into a hypertext database of sorts.

When I log into the WELL, give it my password, gain access to the Net, I can type the command "hytelnet" and I will see the following menu. Because the hytelnet software is freely available through the Net, millions of other people can use the same command to use the same service. The first menu looks like this:

```
What is HYTELNET?     <WHATIS>      Up/Down arrows
                                    MOVE
Library catalogs      <SITES1>      Left/Right arrows
                                    SELECT
Other resources       <SITES2>      ? for HELP anytime
Help files for
catalogs              <OP000>
Catalog interfaces    <SYS000>      m returns here
Internet Glossary     <GLOSSARY>    q quits
Telnet tips           <TELNET>
Key-stroke commands   <HELP>
          HYTELNET 6.3 was written by Peter Scott,
               U of Saskatchewan Libraries,
             Saskatoon, Sask, Canada. 1992
          Unix and VMS software by Earl Fogel,
             Computing Services,U of S 1992
```

Keep in mind that this top level can hide nested levels that you could take all day to navigate. When I decided to see what "Other resources" means, I used my down-arrow keys to move the cursor on my computer screen and highlight , then used my right arrow key to see the next menu:

```
<ARC000>    Archie: Archive Server Listing Service
<CWI000>    Campus-wide Information systems
<FUL000>    Databases and bibliographies
<DIS000>    Distributed File Servers
                (Gopher/WAIS/WWW)
<ELB000>    Electronic books
<FEE000>    Fee-Based Services
<FRE000>    FREE-NET systems
<BBS000>    General Bulletin Boards
<HYT000>    HYTELNET On-line versions
<NAS000>    NASA databases
<NET000>    Network Information Services
<DIR000>    Whois/White Pages/Directory Services
<OTH000>    Miscellaneous resources
```

Just for the heck of it, I decided to see what is available in "NASA databases" and got this menu:

```
<NAS013>    Astronomical Data Center
<NAS015>    Coastal Zone Color Scanner Browse
                Facility
<NAS010>    COSMIC Online Information Services
<NAS006>    ENVIROnet (The Space Environment
                Information Service)
<NAS014>    International CEDAR Data Base
<NAS001>    NASA/IPAC Extragalactic Database
<NAS002>    NSSDC Online Data and Information
                Service (NODIS)
<NAS005>    NASA Science Internet (NSI) Online
                Network Data
<NAS003>    NASA Spacelink
<NAS008>    NSSDC-National Space Science Data
                Center
```

```
<NAS009>    Pilot land data system
<NAS007>    PDS (Planetary Data System)
<NAS017>    Space Data and Computing Division
              Information Service
<NAS016>    Standards and Technology Information
              System
```

When you consider that I could go "deeper" or "down" into the NASA files and find days or years of text to read and graphics to view and data to study, or go back "up" a level or two and search the bibliographies online from all the university libraries on the Net, you can see how even a simple two-page menu like this makes it possible at a very crude level to explore and steer my attention through the Net's information resources in a systematic way. Hierarchical menus make it possible to browse through large collections of information and zero in on the specific subcategory you seek. So if new programs can find ways of keeping track of what is on the Net, channel it into the proper categories, and present it to users with menus, then it really doesn't matter that the Net's information resources are expanding so chaotically. The focus of organization in an ever-changing distributed system like the Net turns out to be not in how the information is stored but in how it is found.

The Internet tool ftp stands for "file transfer protocol," and that is a way for the network to move files around the network. I might have an account on the WELL in which I collect files to download to my home computer, while I range around to dozens of other computers on the Net, using ftp to quickly transfer texts, encoded sounds and pictures, and even software for my computer, from various archives on the Net. Other tools that simplify the Net for users turn an index of key resources into a menu and use ftp behind the scenes to move files from computer to computer, while the users select menu items.

The ability to do very high speed transfers from machine to machine multiplies the resources available to each user. Why keep a document stored on your personal computer when it takes only a few seconds to retrieve it from a computer in Düsseldorf or Tallahassee? What is important is that you know where to find that information, or most important, how to find out where to find that information. One popular form of ftp, "anonymous ftp," creates a kind of Net ethic, in which computer communities on the Net are applauded for making material available via ftp for Net citizens who don't have the passwords for those communities. It also decentralizes distribution of information to a degree that stymies all thoughts of central control.

When a newspaper reporter in Houston revealed that Internet sites in Texas were serving as repositories of pornographic pictures-which the sites were providing, along with all the Supreme Court and Library of Congress stuff—the archives of the notorious Usenet newsgroup "alt.sex.pictures" instantly moved to Finland. The Net traffic to Finland jumped significantly overnight. The issue of community standards and dirty pictures is key in questions of censorship of content, but the point here is that the concept of "where" something is kept online is spread all over the Net instead of located in one or two or three places you can pinpoint.

The Net can be used to distribute new Net tools in the form of computer programming code, as well as communications and information services, which means the Net is inherently a bootstrapping medium that constantly changes itself as people discover and invent new tools, and then use the Net to distribute them. When the Net upgrades its own software, the Net is used to distribute the upgrade. IRC, the program that connects Internet users into worldwide real-time chat "channels," started out as an experiment by a programmer in Finland. Multi-User Dungeons originated at a University in England.

Among the original hackers at MIT, the ones who helped invent time-sharing, the hacker ethic was that computer tools ought to be free. The first personal-computer makers were outraged when William Gates, now the richest man in America, started selling BASIC, which PC hobbyists had always passed around for free. The software industry exists now and Microsoft is bigger than General Motors, but the Net continues to grow because of intellectual property that skilled programmers have given to the Net community. Again and again, programmers have created and given to the Net powerful tools that have changed the nature of the Net and expanded its availability. At the grassroots level, in the world of BBSs outside the Net, the key programs that make amateur CMC via modem possible were also distributed for free or at little cost.

It makes sense, even if you plan to profit from a communications medium later, to give away access to the medium in the beginning, when you are trying to build a critical mass. The people who built CMC systems wanted to have a large population of people to communicate with; the value they sought was not the value of metering access to the community, but in the intellectual value, the collective goods, that a community could create together. The tradition of free bootstrapping software is alive and well. Now, tools that act as personal information servants to shield users from the complexities of the Net are becoming available, also free of charge. Like MUDs and IRC and Usenet and public-domain BBS programs, these tools are contributed to the Net community and propagate through the Net itself.

When you begin talking about using your desktop computer to download the actual text of books stored in the Library of Congress, you come up against two barriers. First, only a small fraction of the material in libraries and archives is in machine-readable form, and the process of digitization necessary to make the information available online is no longer prohibitively expensive but remains time-consuming. The Library of Congress is growing far faster than it can be digitized by present-day technology. Clearly, until some breakthrough makes digitization easier, people will have to choose which material is valuable enough to convert to electronic form; even with these obstacles, the amount of data converted from analog to digital form every day is staggering. Telnet to lib.dartmouth.edu and type connect dante at the first prompt if you want full text access to Dante's *Divina Commedia* and hundreds of years of commentary. Or use the Wide Area Information Server to find the lyrics to that song running through your head.

The other barrier to a Net that contains all the text and photos and sounds in the Library of Congress is a less technical and more social issue: intellectual property. A lot of the best books, photos, lyrics, articles, and videos are owned by somebody. How are royalties to be determined and collected in a world where you can copy anything with a keystroke and transfer a library around the world in a minute? Ted Nelson, who coined the term *hypertext*, first dreamed up a scheme in the 1960s, looking forward to the day when this social problem lurking at the heart of computer technology would grow large. Nelson's scheme, called Xanadu, involves a database of all the literature in the world, including anything anybody wants to contribute; readers would be able to have access to documents, and the system would automatically pay from their accounts a tiny amount of money to the original author. The Xanadu project, long notorious as the world's most ancient software project that has yet to produce a public product, is still alive. And the problem still exists.

The amount of information available or potentially available to the Net strictly via public-domain information—that which was created with public funds or for which the original copyrights have expired—is still enormous. And thanks to the efforts of yet another Net crusader and his volunteers around the world, public-domain literature, in full text form, is becoming available. Michael Hart, professor of electronic text at Illinois Benedictine College , is the leader of Project Gutenberg, which aims to add ten thousand volumes of public-domain literature to the Net by the year 2001. They have already digitized and uploaded *Moby-Dick*, *Aesop's Fables, Alice in Wonderland*, the complete works of Shakespeare, The Federalist Papers , Roget's International Thesaurus, The Book of Mormon , and many other works in the public domain. Volunteers around the world use scanning machines to convert printed text into digital form. The library is doubling in size every year.

To find out whether a drug has been approved recently, you can telnet to fdabbs.fda.gov and log in as bbs to connect to an Internet BBS containing up-to-date information on FDA actions and consumer information. There is a menu-style interface to all the weather information for the United States and Canada located at madlab.sprl.umich.edu port 3000. Accurate and up-to-date agricultural information, seismicity reports, water quality information, patent information, genealogical information, and medical, scientific, and scholarly archives are available to any user who knows where they are and has learned the magical incantations necessary to move them from their home archive to his or her desktop. All the arcana and uncertainty make Netsurfing somewhat alchemical. Things change so fast that folklore is the only reliable way to find out what is really new. If you poke around on the Net a little, or buy one of the paper guides to the Net, you will find that there are public lists of public lists of resources. Net citizens and self-proclaimed Net architects take it upon themselves to compile lists of resources, keep the lists updated, and post the lists regularly.

There is, everybody agrees, a firehose of information coming through the Net, and we need to find ways to channel it. It's disorganized, it's coming at a titanic and accelerating rate, and our minds shut down in the face of all the options the Net represents. We need some kind of go-between to mediate between human and network capabilities.

* * *

Answers to the bewildering complexity of the Net are emerging from the Net itself. Archie , a play on the word *archive*, for example, is a file-finder program developed by Peter Deutsch and others at McGill University in Montreal. If you are directly on Internet you can telnet to one of the Archie servers now scattered around the globe. If you don't have a direct Internet connection, but your network can send e-mail to Internet, you can do it by e-mail. The Archie database keeps track of all the files that are added to "anonymous ftp" public-archive sites, and the archive sites continue to update Archie. That means Archie knows about tens of thousands of files spread throughout forty-five countries. If you know the name of a file, or part of the name, you can ask Archie, which will consult its database and send you a list of the exact sites that have files that match that name. I've used Archie to explore the Net. Ask it to find a file that exemplifies the kind of information you are looking for, and then use the list of sites returned by Archie in response to your request as a list of places likely to have other interesting information. Then you can use ftp to browse the indexes of files at those sites.

Don't forget that the computing power of machines attached to the Net is often available, as well as the words or files stored in their memory banks. The computers on the Net can help keep track of the information on the Net, and they can distribute their indexes among one another. The problem of finding enough computing power to build an effective software go-between to control the complexities of the Net becomes far more computation-intensive when you want to search the Net for chunks of text rather than just the names of files. Another Net visionary by the name of Brewster Kahle conceived of a powerful text-finder that will literally hunt through hundreds of databases and libraries on the Net for text that contains specific information. The tool, developed jointly by Kahle and Dow Jones, Thinking Machines, Apple Computer, and KPMC Peat Marwick, is freely available to Net users as WAIS—Wide Area Information Servers. Thinking Machines is a company in Massachusetts that makes extremely powerful computers by networking large numbers of smaller computers; maintaining an enormous index and searching that index very quickly is one of those tasks that you need an extremely powerful computer to do. If you can keep that index on a Thinking Machines computer in Massachusetts, the WAIS program that you use on your Internet host (known as the "client" program that interacts with the WAIS "server" program at Thinking Machines) can make use of the WAIS server's computational speed.

One of the capabilities of the WAIS software is a harbinger of future information-finding software agents that will roam the Net in search of information. This capability is known as relevance feedback. You can ask WAIS to search its databases for information about a subject—say, Japanese gardening. In a few seconds, you will get a list of hundreds or thousands of sources. If you pick out three sources that look interesting because they are about the aesthetics rather than the horticulture of gardening, you can ask WAIS to restrict its search. By this kind of back-and-forth dialogue, you can refine the search.

Other experimental projects, such as the Knowbots project, send off software servants to roam the nets and monitor the streams of information that feed the Net, and the vast pools of online databases, in search of specific information. Vinton Cerf, one of the creators of the original ARPANET, has been working at the Corporation for National Research Initiatives, in Reston, Virginia, creating information-gathering robots. A knowbot is represented on the user's screen as an icon, a graphic symbol. The computer user can program and activate the knowbots by pointing and clicking at the icon and associated menus. Those menus present a series of questions; answering those questions defines a search strategy. The software then travels across the network, using tools like Archie and WAIS and whatever else is available, to zero in on the kind of information specified by the user. Knowbots can make decisions while conducting a search and send clones to search other networks. The first tests of knowbots involve researchers at the National Library of Medicine. The online library includes forty databases and 80 billion bits of information.

One tool I've seen that I wanted to grab for my own use was a program named Rosebud that my friend Steve Cisler, the librarian at Apple Computer, had running for him. Named, I presume, after the key word in *Citizen Kane*, Rosebud is an experimental project sponsored by Apple and Dow Jones. It's a customizable personal newspaper that searches the Net and reports back to you. Rosebud, now known as Applesearch, will be a commercial product.

First, you train knowbot-like agents called reporters. You select a fresh reporter, and say that you want these newswires and those databases searched every twenty-four minutes or twenty-four days, for any reference to *virtual communities*. You can vary the search interval and the reporting interval and construct logical searches based on keywords. You can build your own menus of likely databases and sources you want to choose from. And then you select another fresh reporter and tell it to look for and retrieve any article or news item with the words *electronic democracy* in the title or abstract. After you train as many reporters as you need to keep track of your current hot issues or your constant professional specialty, you turn them loose on the Net. Your reporters take advantage of the Net's resources and use your account numbers to access commercial sources of information, look for only those items in the information flow that match your criterion, and keep their findings organized for you. The next time you open your "newspaper," Rosebud has organized on your computer screen all the reporter's findings into newspaper-style columns, with headlines and subheads if necessary.

Judging from the proliferation of Net tools today, it seems clear that entire ecosystems of Net-spawned information-seeking robots will be circulating through the Net. These entities are formally more akin to robots (*automata* is the precise jargon) than to living creatures, but increasingly, automata are being designed to incorporate biological behaviors. The "worms" that can attack networks, and the "viruses" that pester computer users, are the malevolent side of this trend. Knowbots and Rosebud are the benevolent side. In the environment of a heterogeneous, free-form Net, you are going to find both kinds. How you protect the community from dangers of attack without destroying the openness that makes the community valuable is a social problem, as is the problem of who should pay for access to this increasingly powerful pool of knowledge tools.

Gopher is yet another tool that emerged from the Net, this time from the Campus Wide Information System environment. It is not so much like an agent that runs around and finds what you need, as a knowbot does. Gopher is more like one of those stylized maps that enable people to find their way around subway systems in major cities. Gopher is an intelligent map that can take you anywhere it shows you—all you have to do is point. Now that so many colleges are using Internet protocols to link the many computing resources located on most campuses, students who are not computer-sophisticated must have a way of finding information relevant to their studies. Gopher, developed at the University of Minnesota and named after its mascot, is a way of eliminating the telnetting and ftping a student needs to do to find a resource. Gopher hides the incomprehensible command language by substituting menus and abbreviated commands for the telnet and ftp syntax. The resources that are linked together in such a way, known as gopherspaces, can be located on one part of campus or another, or even on a campus system on the other side of the world. As the gopher tool propagates through the Net, more and more sites add their own documents and indexes to the worldwide gopherspace. Now, with special client software for your host computer, you can literally point at maps of resources and tell your computer to transport you there.

The information available through the Net is not limited to the huge amounts of data that collect in databases and stay there until you find them. The Net is constantly receiving input, and the input sensors are proliferating. The Net is growing via many different, separate streams of information, the way great rivers grow from the accumulation of independent tributaries. As entire networks join Internet, their online libraries become available. As more print-based information is digitized, more information becomes available. And now, the constant and evanescent stuff of the news, the wire-service news feeds from its international correspondents, the latest stock quotes—continuous rivers of information—are available through the Net. Internet will now take you to the door of Dow Jones or other pay-for-information services; you still have to open an account on the pay-for service to have access to it.

The remarkable degree of citizen toolbuilding in the Net, particularly tools that enable wider and wider segments of the population to make use of Net resources, is a de facto argument for keeping a widely accessible Net open for citizen experimentation.

The mechanics of the Net support citizen-created tools for people to talk with one another, as well as tools for enabling people to find information. The biographical files that most Internet users keep on their host computers are usually searchable from a distance, through the "remote finger" command. Several different kinds of electronic white pages and other services help people find other people's addresses. If you locate a user on a remote system who is on his or her host system at the same time you are online to your host system, you can chat in real time, just the two of you, with the talk program; your screen display splits horizontally, so the words you write are displayed above the line and the words the other person types are displayed below the line. You can use Internet Relay Chat to tune in to one of dozens of different channels of chat among Internet users from twenty different countries. You can telnet to a MUD and communicate through the commands available in that imaginary world. You can telnet to one of the medium-size BBS systems that are beginning to emerge on Internet, like the WELL. Or you can participate in the largest conversation of the day, the working anarchy known as Usenet, which is available through Internet but travels outside Internet's boundaries when necessary.

Information and access to information is a complicated matter. Librarians and other specialists have a toolkit and syntax for dealing with well-known problems that people encounter in trying to make sense of large bodies of information. The art and craft of building tools from the Net's resources to help make sense of the Net's resources is well advanced. Human-to-human communication is a more complicated matter. Humans communicate in groups for a variety of reasons. Community might be at the center of those reasons in any society that hopes to endure, but it is not the only reason that groups of people comunicate.

The essence of CMC as a human communication medium is many-to-many capabilities. The idea of a computer conference came from the work Engelbart and others were doing in building the first computer-based thinking tools. The capability of any group to think together over a period of time about a number of distinct, focused topics was the first of several important applications of many-to-many communications to be used. But CMC didn't stop there. This new medium is the result of a transformation of other technologies, accomplished by people who had a purpose different from that which motivated the creators of the enabling technologies. A network that was originally designed to survive a nuclear attack evolved into a citizen's thinking tool, and the structured conversations on the network among people from so many different cultures grew out of national emergency planning. The transformation of many-to-many communications is not complete; the experiments that groups are performing on the Net today will influence the generations of CMC tools that will dominate the Net in the future.

The Net is not only Internet. You could shut down all the hosts on Internet today and millions of people would still find ways to exchange e-mail and newsgroups. The Net is also partially a highly redundant citizen-to-citizen network that grew on its own, using the spinoffs from ARPA research to create something more akin to a fan culture than a military-industrial elite. The parts of the Net that grew out of ARPANET are the mainstream, and definitely the technological leaders, but not the only important tributary that contributed to today's Net. The other two confluent streams are the grassroots movement known as computerized bulletin-board systems (BBSs) that took off in the 1980s, and the history of group conversation systems over the past several decades, culminating in Usenet, the biggest, freest, noisiest one so far.

4

Grassroots Groupminds

"This is like a groupmind!" I remember blurting out something like that when I first visited the physical headquarters of the WELL and met Matthew McClure, the first WELL director, face-to-face. I might have startled him with my fervor, but he didn't disagree. The sensation of personally participating in an ongoing process of group problem-solving—whether the problem is a tick on my daughter's head or an opportunity to help policymakers build a public network—electrified me. The feeling of tapping into this multibrained organism of collective expertise reminds me of the conversion experience the ARPA pioneers describe when they recall their first encounters with interactive computers.

The experience has to do with the way groups of people are using CMC to rediscover the power of cooperation, turning cooperation into a game, a way of life—a merger of knowledge capital, social capital, and communion. The fact that we need computer networks to recapture the sense of cooperative spirit that so many people seemed to lose when we gained all this technology is a painful irony. I'm not so sure myself anymore that tapping away on a keyboard and staring at a screen all day by necessity is "progress" compared to chopping logs and raising beans all day by necessity. While we've been gaining new technologies, we've been losing our sense of community, in many places in the world, and in most cases the technologies have precipitated that loss. But this does not make an effective argument against the premise that people can use computers to cooperate in new ways.

Computer-assisted teleconferencing continued to develop for as long as it did because it worked well for the people who developed it, the think-tank secret elite who spun nuclear war scenarios and the more mundane government bureaucracies who coordinate response to national emergencies. Computer-assisted groupminds were confined to these elites for many years, while the state of computer and network technology caught up with the demands of CMC systems. The computers were expensive, the software was strictly roll-your-own, and the tasks that the tools were used to accomplish were sensitive. Everything written about CMC in this paragraph was also true about computer technology itself thirty years ago.

In combination with a truly grassroots communications medium, however, such as Usenet's millions of reader-contributors and the computer bulletin-board systems that are springing up by the tens of thousands, the same many-to-many communications capabilities of CMC formerly reserved for the elites could catalyze the emergence of a formidable, far more populist kind of social organization. Grassroots groupminds and their impact on the material world could grow into one of the surprise technological issues of the coming decade.

Going back to the beginning of computer conferencing technology is essential if one is to understand where it ought to head in the future. Once again, we find that the new technology took the form it did because the technology's inventors believed that the tools they created should belong to citizens to help us solve problems together. There are other important parallels between the history of many-to-many communication tools and the history of other inspired inventions that made the Net possible. Like the other components of the Net, the facilities for structured group discussions evolved slowly until the convergence of key enabling technologies made explosive growth possible. Like the rest of the Net, access to these tools was originally restricted to government and military planning and research elites, then expanded first to defense-related researchers, then opened to other scientists in non-defense-related fields, and then again expanded to nonscience scholars, and finally, now, the focus of debate is whether and how access can be expanded to include educators, students, and citizens.

One of the pioneers in CMC technology dating back to Engelbart's group at SRI, Jacques Vallee, in his prophetic 1982 book *The Network Revolution*, claims that the first attempt to create a group communication medium was the Berlin crisis and airlift of 1948. An attempt was made to wire together telex machines from a dozen different countries, but with everybody trying to communicate at the same time in different languages, it didn't work out. By 1970, ARPANET was online and new tools were available for accomplishing the same task of geographically distributed, asynchronous, group decision making.

Computer based conferencing, the platform for virtual communities like the Well and others, were inspired and preceded by two way-ahead-of-their-time experiments known as PLATO and EIES. One grew out of education, another out of emergency planning. PLATO was the original distance learning platform, the first virtual community years before the ARPAnet or e-mail was create. PLATO was the software ancestor of several kinds of contemporary computer-mediated conferencing systems. It was the main inspiration for Lotus Notes and one of the contributing streams in the creation of Usenet News. David Woolley, one of PLATO's creators, has published a history of PLATO online, *Plato: The Emergence of Online Community* <http://thinkofit.com/plato/dwplato.htm>.

The PLATO system was designed for Computer-Based Education. But for many people, PLATO's most enduring legacy is the online community spawned by its communication features.

PLATO originated in the early 1960's at the Urbana campus of the University of Illinois. Professor Don Bitzer became interested in using computers for teaching, and with some colleagues founded the Computer-based Education Research Laboratory (CERL). Bitzer, an electrical engineer, collaborated with a few other engineers to design the PLATO hardware. To write the software, he collected a staff of creativ eccentrics ranging from university professors to high school students, few of whom had any computer background. Together they built a system that was at least a decade ahead of its time in many ways. Throughout the 1960's, PLATO remained a small system, supporting only a single classroom of terminals. About 1972, PLATO began a transition to a new generation of mainframes that would eventually support up to one thousand users simultaneously. (Woolley 1994)

Like packet-switching, computer-mediated teleconferencing owes its birth, in part, to nuclear war planning. In the late 1960s, Murray Turoff was working on war games and other kinds of computer simulations for the Institute for Defense Analysis. Some of these games involved connecting several players at once via remote computing systems. As a result of this experience, Turoff started experimenting with computers as a way of mediating a special expert-consulting process developed at RAND, known as the Delphi method. Delphi was a formal method of soliciting anonymous ideas and critiques of those ideas from panels of experts—a combination of brainstorming and opinion polling. It was done by passing a lot of pieces of paper around in a specified order. Turoff started to computerize Delphi and ended up realizing that there were much wider horizons to the business of convening panels of experts to pass messages around via computer.

In the early 1970s, Turoff moved to the U.S. Office of Emergency Preparedness, where his job wasn't related to his continuing interest in teleconferencing via computer. His superiors found out that he was using his computer terminal to experiment with an unauthorized conference system, and there was some bureaucratic friction. But then history intervened in the form of the wage-price freeze of 1971, an action by the Nixon administration that required the overnight construction of a system for rapidly collecting and collating information from geographically dispersed branch offices. Turoff's prototype became an authorized project, and the computerized Delphi experiment turned into the Emergency Management Information System and Reference Index (EMISARI).

Along with parts of Engelbart's NLS (oNLineSystem), EMISARI was the original ancestor of today's CMC groupmind systems. It was used to monitor data from forty regional offices, the IRS, and the State and Treasury departments, and to conduct policy meetings among thirty to one hundred experts to determine how the wage-price regulations should be employed. EMISARI evolved into Resource Interruption Monitoring Systems (RIMS) and was used for years by the Federal Preparedness Agency as a form of geographically distributed decision making and crisis management.

In the process of designing EMISARI, the people who built it and the people who used it began to discover that some of the system's features were far more popular with the online community than were others, even though there was no official emphasis on these features and no obvious connection to the tasks at hand. There was, for example, a feature they simply called "messages." Anyone plugged into the system could leave a message for anyone else on a kind of computerized public blackboard space. As with a blackboard, participants could check their messages later to see if anybody else had appended a reply. Notes and replies proliferated so fast that people began to develop programs for sifting through them. When you create a public blackboard, you make everybody a publisher or broadcaster of text. When you begin to sort the messages, you get into groupmind territory, for what you are structuring is a collective memory for many people to communicate with many others.

Engelbart's Augmentation Research Center in California had been working in parallel since the 1960s, but ARC was a much larger project and grander scheme than EMISARI. When Engelbart gave a famous demonstration that literally changed the worldviews of computer designers in 1968, he used a system that linked people via keyboards and screens, and gave each member of the augmented knowledge workshop the ability to mix voice dialogue and even video windows in real time, while also sending text back and forth. It was all part of an integrated system Engelbart had in mind for turning computers into tools for thinking. That was sixteen years before the Apple Macintosh brought the most basic subset of these tools to consumers; and only a tiny minority of the most sophisticated of the personal computer users in the 1990s have access to multimedia capabilities like those Engelbart demonstrated in 1968.

Turoff's research was sharply focused on one part of the idea of augmentation. The computer conferencing features of NLS were powerful, but there was more work to be done to turn online "journals" and "notebooks" into flexible conferencing systems. Turoff concentrated on structuring text messages into dialogues. ARPA continued to support Engelbart's work. After he completed EMISARI, Turoff moved from the Office of Emergency Preparedness to the New Jersey Institute of Technology, where the National Science Foundation funded him to develop his CMC tool into something scientists, educators, and others could use.

Turoff noted in 1976:

I think the ultimate possibility of computerized conferencing is to provide a way for human groups to exercise a "collective intelligence" capability. The computer as a device to allow a human group to exhibit collective intelligence is a rather new concept. In principle, a group, if successful, would exhibit an intelligence higher than any member. Over the next decades, attempts to design computerized conferencing structures that allow a group to treat a particular complex problem with a single collective brain may well promise more benefit for mankind than all the artificial intelligence work to date.

Turoff's Electronic Information Exchange System (EIES—pronounced "Eyes") became operational in 1976, and it still lives as the lively great-great-grandmother of all virtual communities, now a node on the Net—predating the WELL by almost a decade. It was funded by NSF as "an electronic communication laboratory for use by geographically dispersed research communities." By July 1978, seven trial projects were under way, each part of an established research community of ten to fifty members. The system was set up to collect data on its own operations, in order to test the hypothesis that a teleconferencelike system could enhance the effectiveness of research communities. EIES, like ARPANET, was designed to be a testbed for experimenting with the nature of CMC.

Because it was built to be extensively self-documented and extendable to fit the needs of expert users, EIES, like NLS, wasn't the most user-friendly system. Today's computer conferencing systems, several software generations and decades later, aren't much better in that regard. In terms of usability by nonspecialists, CMC today is where personal computing was before computer graphics and the mouse pointing device made the "point and click" method of operating computers possible. Point-and-click tools that hide the complexities of the Net and get you to the information or people you seek were just beginning to emerge from the research-and-development phase by the early 1990s. The human interface problem aside, once you learn your way around a full-fledged conferencing system, you gain a lot of power. There are some things that can't be simplified to point-and-click. Human communication is the most complex system we know about. As Engelbart often said about NLS: "If ease of use was the only valid criterion, people would stick to tricycles and never try bicycles."

EIES, like ARPANET, was another one of those experiments that never shut themselves down because the experimental subjects just wouldn't let go of them. EIES quickly expanded from pure scientific research communities to legislative and medical researchers. Some of the EIES users concentrated on designing new generations of conferencing systems, based on what they had learned from their EIES participation. In this way EIES was the protocommunity that seeded the Net with CMC designers. Peter and Trudy Johnson-Lenz, for example, worked with Harry Stevens, another early EIES enthusiast, and others to develop a system for the Massachusetts state office of technology called legitec, created with the scripting language built into EIES. And in 1979, Harry

Stevens and others created the Participate conferencing system for a new service called the Source. Stevens was an early advocate of inquiry networking, deliberately harnessing the living database powers of CMC via the architecture of the conferencing system. Participate was designed to structure short discussions, especially around questions and answers, that can later be searched for specific information. Parti on the Source turned out to be another pioneer public virtual community.

The Johnson-Lenzes coined the term *groupware*, which has been taken up by the business-oriented part of the software industry that is selling CMC products to business organizations. But these EIES veterans, based in Lake Oswego, Oregon, continued to pursue for decades the paradoxical goal of using CMC to find not only community but true spiritual communion. They lived on a shoestring for years, put their money into state-of-the-art hardware, programmed their own software, and created a series of specifically tailored CMC communities. Their goal was to combine the best of the soft communication techniques that had emerged from the human potential movement of the 1970s, with the capabilities of CMC. In the late 1980s, I participated in one of their experiments for several months. The Johnson-Lenzes called their community Awaken, and they included a nondenominational but explicitly spiritual dimension to it.

I knew Peter+Trudy, as their online friends know them, for years before I met them in the material world. When we shared a train to Kyoto from Oita, in the southernmost part of Japan, I had the opportunity to talk with them about their role as early CMC enthusiasts. They and their friends around the world had labored for years to use CMC as a means of achieving reconciliation, community, and enhanced communication. Judging by the state of the world today, almost two decades after EIES opened, CMC has yet to make the world a more peaceful place in any perceptible way.

"Is it worth continuing to try?" was the question we had arrived at by the time the train pulled into the last major station before our destination. We continued to talk with each other, but the three of us were looking out the window. It was another medium-large Japanese city with standard postwar architecture, hard to distinguish from any other, but something about the shape of the landscape that framed it was very familiar to me. I had seen that bowl of hills around the city, and that hill toward the center, in so many photographs. It was Hiroshima Station. We rode in silence for some minutes after that.

Utopian hopes for CMC go back to the heady early days of EIES. By 1978, policymakers, artists, long-range planners, and others began to join EIES. Starr Roxanne Hiltz and Turoff published a book that year, *Network Nation*—about a revolution that took more than another decade to break out beyond the small circles of enthusiasts—in which they predicted that the medium wouldn't be limited to a few laboratories and think tanks. They noted some of the well-known advantages and disadvantages of the medium. They forecast that people would use the medium to find others who shared their interests and values. They began the first systematic research of how different kinds of organizations use and fail to use CMC technology.

Another group that was developing CMC in the 1970s was a think tank in California called The Institute for the Future (IFTF), a few blocks away from SRI, that saw itself as a kind of tool shop for think tanks. The application of computer technology to bureaucratic planning was a possible strategic resource and potential growth industry in those days. DARPA and NSF funded a group at IFTF to develop a planning and forecasting tool. Jacques Vallee had worked with the original NLS project at SRI, but he, Roy Amara, Robert Johansen, and their colleagues were concerned about building something a policymaker, rather than a techie, would be able to use. The EIES and NLS systems were designed to explore the capabilities of computer systems as communication tools. But PLANET, the PLAnning NETwork designed by IFTF, was designed for easy use by planners in government and industry—most of whom had no previous computer experience. The command set was ultrasimplified to be operated by a few specially designated keys on a specially built portable telecommunications terminal. PLANET later evolved into Notepad, a private global conferencing system still used by a number of large clients such as Shell Oil. Johansen remains at the Institute for the Future, working on the field now known widely as groupware.

Several different events far beyond these laboratories began to add up in the late 1970s to the spontaneous emergence and rapid growth of grassroots networks in the 1980s. In 1977, programmers for Bell Laboratories created a Unix-to-Unix Copy (UUCP) utility that was shipped along with future versions of the Unix operating system. This utility made it possible for any computer that uses Unix to automatically dial and connect via modem with any other computer using Unix, and exchange files from one computer to another. In an unrelated but convergent development, the Telecomputing Corporation of America opened for business in 1979 out of a host computer in Virginia. CMC was now available to anybody with a modem and the price of access. Reader's Digest bought the company in 1980 and renamed it Source Telecomputing Corporation. By the end of 1982, when I joined, the Source had more than twenty-five thousand subscribers and a growth rate of over one thousand subscribers a month.

My Source membership in 1982 cost me a $100 initiation fee and between $7 and $22 an hour, depending on the time of day. The Source, where many of us experienced conferencing for the first time with Participate, and its competitor, CompuServe, offered computer owners outside the military-industrial elite admission to an electronic community. The Source was absorbed by CompuServe, which now has hundreds of thousands of subscribers worldwide.

The years 1979 and 1980 were particularly crucial in the history of CMC. The large utility-company information services such as the Source and CompuServe began operation, the first MUDs appeared in England, the first BBSs started emerging in an entirely different part of the population, and two programmers in North Carolina began using elaborations of UUCP to exchange more structured messages, messages ordered by topic, into a kind of intercommunity conversation. Different communities that used the time-shared services of different computers on different campuses were able to participate in a kind of abstract community constructed from that structured interchange of messages. The first nodes in what has come to be known as the Usenet began in 1980. Like others before them, they had no idea that it would grow to cover the world.

This was a case of a technology that came from the fringes of the Net and emerged precisely because it was not the mainstream. ARPANET and its successors expanded access to communication and information-finding capabilities, as long as you were affiliated with one of the research institutions that ARPA or NSF authorized for network access. Duke University and the University of North Carolina in 1979 were not on Internet, but they did have UUCP. Graduate students Tom Truscott and James Ellis of Duke, working with graduate student Steve Bellovin of UNC, developed the first version of Usenet News in 1979 and circulated a leaflet about it at the winter 1980 Unix Users' Conference (known as Usenix). By the time of the 1980 summer Usenix conference, the News software was being distributed on computer tape to attendees. The News software, which evolved over the years into three progressively more sophisticated versions, was in the public domain; users were encouraged to copy and distribute the software that enables new computer communities to gain interactive access to all the others.

Usenet

Usenet, meant to represent Unix Users Network, was designed as a forum for discussions about Unix and for Unix troubleshooting. Unix itself was deliberately designed to foster a professional community of programmers who used the Unix toolbox to create new tools that all the other Unix toolbuilders could use. The inventors of Usenet wanted to talk about their tools without having an ARPANET connection. They were surprised at how hungry people were for all kinds of conversations on a worldwide basis, once they caught on to this strange new idea of a conversation in text that floated from campus to campus around the globe. They thought local communities would use it most, but found out that as the network spread, people were more and more interested in participating in conversations on an international scale. The nature of Usenet as we know it today—an anarchic, unkillable, censorship-resistant, aggressively noncommercial, voraciously growing conversation among millions of people in dozens of countries—is largely a result of the way the system was designed.

The fundamental unit of Usenet is the individual posting. Anyone with access to the network can send out a specific, signed, electronic message to the rest of Usenet. The address of the message, however, is not to an individual or even a mailing list, but is the topic of discussion, known as a newsgroup. If I want to contribute to a discussion of the risks of using computers, I compose a message, address it to the "comp.risks" newsgroup, and use the "postnews" software that comes with Usenet to put it in the mail queue. The next time my host computer communicates with another computer via UUCP, that message goes out as electronic mail.

When the next computer in the network gets the message, it checks to see which newsgroups it carries, copies all those messages for its resident newsgroups, and then passes it along to the next site. Each message has a unique identifying number, so each site can discard messages it has received before.

At the receiving end, which could be somebody on the other side of the world, is a computer community that just received an electronic mailbag full of Usenet News from some site. That site subscribes to comp.risks, so your message is stored there for those who regularly read messages from that newsgroup. Instead of putting a separate copy of each new message in each subscriber's electronic mailbox, the way an electronic mailing list propagates, News puts one copy in a file that any user can read. Each user makes use of one of several kinds of software tools available at the host site, known as a news reader. The news reader searches through the local newsgroup database, compares it with each individual user's subscription list, and shows the local users new messages as they arrive, on the user's command.

A person halfway around the world, after reading your posting, can take one of several actions: The person can decide that you are a fool and he or she never wants to see anything you post ever again, and puts your name in what is called a kill file, also known as a bozo filter; the person can decide that he or she has the answer to your question or wants to congratulate you on what you said in your posting, and sends you personal electronic mail; the person can decide to reply publicly by posting a rebuttal. Usenet automatically routes your private e-mail or public reply to the appropriate destination; all the user needs to do is issue a one-keystroke command from a menu. This is a third level of power built into Usenet: not only is it distributed in an informal network, and every person who reads Usenet has the power to post to Usenet, but every person has the means to communicate directly and privately with anyone who states something publicly.

The word *anarchy* is frequently used to describe Usenet, not in the sense of chaotic and disorganized, but in the sense that the whole enterprise of moving all these words from all these people to all these other people is accomplished with no central governing hierarchy on either policy or technical levels. This grew directly out of the way Usenet postings were designed to be passed around the loosely coupled UUCP network.

From the beginning, there was no emphasis on a central organization. All you had to do to join Usenet was to obtain the free software, find a site to feed you News and take your postings, and you were in action. The different newsgroups are arranged according to a branching hierarchy. The main branches (alt, biz, comp, misc, rec, sci, soc, and talk) have their own subbranches. Sites can choose which newsgroups or even which categories of newsgroup it makes available to local users. If your host site is outraged by the content of alt.sex, alt.drugs, or alt.rock-and-roll, it can refuse to carry that newsgroup; other sites will carry the newsgroups that are taboo at yours, however, so there is always an alternate source for any person who is determined to get the information.

The economics of operating Usenet is automatically distributed, another key aspect of the decentralized architecture. If you are a large site and can afford it (like AT&T or Apple), your system administrator arranges to carry some of the communication costs from the smaller sites downstream that get their newsfeeds from your site (for years, Apple's Unix system would automatically call the WELL and transfer Usenet and e-mail, and the WELL fed the stream of messages to smaller local sites). If you weren't from one of the backbone sites that carried more than its share of Usenet traffic, especially in the early years, you paid for your own communication costs when you paid the telephone charges for dialing your Usenet newsfeed site every fifteen minutes or fifteen days.

Growth
The growth of Usenet was biological—slow at first, and then exponential. In 1979, there were 3 sites, passing around approximately 2 articles per day; in 1980, there were 15 sites and 10 articles per day; in 1981 there were 150 sites and 20 articles per day. By 1987 there were 5,000 sites, and the daily postings weighed in at 2.5 million bytes. By 1988, it grew to 11,000 sites and the daily mailbag was more than 4 million bytes. By 1992, Usenet was distributed to more than 2.5 million people and the daily News was up to 35 million bytes—thirty or forty times the number of words in this book.

The Usenet was nurtured in the beginning by a small group of dedicated individuals, some of whom happened to be system administrators at key commercial telecommunications sites. Tom Truscott, a creator of Usenet News, worked at Bell Labs in the summer, and he persuaded them to pick up the telephone charges for calling Duke regularly, collecting Usenet News, and relaying it to other sites. AT&T management benignly neglected to make a fuss about the small but growing amount of telecommunications traffic that the Usenet enthusiasts at Bell Labs were adding to their much larger daily communications traffic. It was a legitimate expense, considering the fact that here was a new communication medium emerging and the research charter of Bell Labs is communications research. Digital Equipment Corporation, the same DEC that made the PDP–1 at the beginning of the era of interactive computing, also picked up some of the costs of relaying Usenet. A few managers with some vision felt it was in the interests of DEC to maintain good relations with the Unix-using community.

At the beginning, there was a kind of quasi-anarchic ruling council known as the backbone cabal, consisting of the system administrators who ran the computers at the sites that were carrying most of the traffic for the UUCP-linked network. Erik Fair, the WELL's man on the Net from the earliest days, now the administrator of Apple's Internet site, always passed along cabal lore to fellow WELLites, but nothing was really secret, despite the mocking name. It was all hashed out endlessly in the appropriate newsgroups. The first major revisions of Usenet software were required by the enormous growth in the number of sites and the amount of messages transferred. Usenix conferences and endless online communications enabled the cabal to continue evolving the software as the system choked on its own success. But the backbone began to disappear when Usenet began to use Internet as well as the ad hoc UUCP network to pass along the electronic mailbag of newsgroup messages. The cabal is a historic artifact. Usenet continues to be ruled by norms, not individuals or organizations. If you violate one of the norms—for example, you blatantly propagate commercial traffic outside one of the specified commercial newsgroups—you'll get a lot of angry e-mail, and people might refuse to give you newsfeeds, but no Usenet cops are going to show up at the door.

Mark Horton plugged the ARPANET mailing lists into Usenet around 1981. The two most popular ARPANET mailing lists, SF-LOVERS and HUMAN-NETS, began to circulate among UUCP-linked as well as ARPANET sites. As more and more Internet sites began to carry Usenet News, this discussion medium with no central control began to gain popularity on the packet-switched networks that also had no central control. Usenet made the whole Internet into a kind of virtual metacommunity, and Internet brought Usenet to ever more sites at ever higher speeds. The powers that be at ARPANET first did not enforce old policies restricting interconnection of Internet with Usenet, and ultimately legitimized Usenet.

Eventually, a high-speed network protocol was created for Internet. That means that a very large number of newsgroups can be maintained at a very small number of sites and are available instantly through the high-speed Internet. By 1992, 60 percent of Usenet traffic was moving through the Net via the instantaneous access protocol and 40 percent still moved via the computer-to-computer slow-speed dial-up grapevine.

Newsgroups collect the comments of people around the world, in a way that enables people to address previous comments and thus conduct a kind of conversation. The conversation is less tightly coupled to serial order than in a computer conferencing system like the WELL, in which each response follows the preceding response in strict order. When you post something to the WELL, others on the WELL can read it instantly. In Usenet, because it used to take so long to distribute individual contributions to interested readers everywhere, the temporal continuity of a WELL-like topic structure wasn't possible. However, people on Usenet make use of automatic tools for "quoting" the responses they are replying to, and newsreaders help people group the responses to similar subtopics (threads) within a newsgroup. When I first started using Usenet, in the mid–1980s, it would take a week for a query or a statement to stir up a round of replies from around the world; the same cycle now takes minutes to hours. It is becoming less like a correspondence and more like a conversation as the Net's transmission speeds increase.

In many newsgroups, a crowd of regulars emerges, and that crowd can be very large in a forum that includes millions of people. Well-known cultures of very different kinds have grown up in different newsgroups. Over time, the ongoing conversations often create communities among the regulars of newsgroups. And other newsgroups are more like battlefields than communities, although they also have their regulars and their norms.

You can get a good idea of what people talk about, and an eye-opening clue to how many of them are talking, by looking at the lists of newsgroups available at the nearest Internet site. The newsgroups are divided into several different types. The kinds that start with the prefix *alt*, for *alternative*, are the most varied and the least controlled. Anybody who can post messages to the rest of Usenet, and who knows how to use the programming tools, can propagate a newsgroup; college freshmen around the world seem to delight in propagating silly newsgroups (e.g., alt.multi-level-marketing.scam.scam.scam). Few sites decide to carry frivolous newsgroups, although the definition of *frivolous* is quite elastic. The biz, comp, misc, rec, soc, sci, and talk (business, computers, miscellaneous, recreation, societies and cultures, science, and general discussion) newsgroup hierarchies have very loose rules about creating new groups. There is a call for discussion, a discussion period, and a vote. If one hundred more people vote for a newsgroup than vote against it, the newsgroup is created.

Hierarchy in the Usenet sense means not a chain of command but a way of simplifying large complex groups of information by branching them as subcategories of fundamental categories. For example, here is how the rec.auto hierarchy works:

```
Introduction to the Rec.Autos newsgroup hierarchy:
rec.autos.tech
is intended for technical discussions of
automobiles, their design, construction, diagnosis,
and service. Other discussions are largely
inappropriate, especially For Sale ads.

rec.autos.sport
is intended for discussion of legal, organized
competition involving automobiles. Technical
discussions are appropriate insofar as they apply
to competition vehicles. Discussion from either of
two viewpoints, spectator and participant, is
encouraged. Arguments about sports cars are largely
inappropriate, as are most other discussions. For
Sale ads are inappropriate unless they are for
competition vehicles and/or equipment. Discussions
of illegal events are marginal; one should probably
avoid advocating breaking the law. (remember, the
FBI reads Usenet!)
```

rec.autos.driving
is intended for discussions related to the driving
of automobiles. Also, if you must discuss 55 vs.
65, or radar detectors, or boneheads, do it here.

rec.autos.vw
is intended for discussion of issues related to the
use and ownership of automobiles manufactured by
Volkswagen (this includes VWs, Audis, Seats, etc.)
It was created on the grounds that the info-vw
mailing list was very successful. It should not be
presumed from the existence of this group that it
is appropriate to create many groups to cover many
different marques; groups specific to individual
marques should only be created on demonstration of
sufficient interest, via some avenue such as a
mailing list.

rec.audio.car
is not properly part of the rec.autos.* hierarchy.
it is, however, the correct place for discussion of
automotive audio equipment, and so is mentioned
here.

alt.autos.antique
is not part of the hierarchy, but of potential
interest to the rec.autos reader; it is intended
for the discussion of older cars (usually more than
25 years old, although this is not a hard-and-fast
rule.)

alt.hotrod
is not part of the hierarchy, but also of potential
interest to the rec.autos reader. it is gatewayed
to the moderated hotrod mailing list, and is for
serious discussion of modifying and developing performance vehicles.

rec.autos
is intended to capture discussion on all other
automotive topics.

The WELL carries about two hundred newsgroups, but there are thousands of newsgroups available around the world. Some of them are local to an organization, a city, a state, or a nation. Some are global. Most are in English, but newsgroups in many other languages are gaining circulation. A Usenet site in the San Francisco Bay area, Netcom, carries a list of newsgroups that is sixty-seven single-spaced pages long. Here is a small sample, a portion of that sixty-seven-page list, in alphabetical order, with very brief descriptions.

alt.3d	Discussion about 3D imaging.
alt.activism	Activities for activists.
alt.alien.visitors	Space creatures ate my modem.
alt.angst	Anxiety in the modern world.
alt.aquaria	The aquarium & related as a hobby.
alt.archery	A newsgroup for people interested in archery.
biz.jobs.	offeredPosition announcements.
comp.ai.vision	Artificial Intelligence Vision Research. (Moderated)
comp.apps.spreadsheets	Spreadsheets on various platforms.
misc.consumers	Consumer interests, product reviews, etc.
misc.emerg-services	Forum for paramedics & other first responders.
misc.entrepreneurs	Discussion on operating a business.
misc.fitness	Physical fitness, exercise, etc.
misc.forsale	Short, tasteful postings about items for sale.
misc.handicap	Items of interest for/about the handicapped.
misc.jobs.resumes	Postings of resumes and "situation wanted."
misc.kids	Children, their behavior and activities.
rec.antiques	Discussing antiques and vintage items.
rec.arts.animation	Discussion of various kinds of animation.
rec.arts.bodyart	Tattoos and body decoration discussions.
rec.arts.books	Books of all genres, and the publishing industry.
rec.arts.erotica	Erotic fiction and verse. (Moderated)
sci.astro	Astronomy discussions and information.
sci.bio.technology	Any topic relating to biotechnology.
sci.engr.chem	All aspects of chemical engineering.
talk.abortion	All sorts of discussions and arguments on abortion.
talk.bizarre	The unusual, bizarre, curious, and often stupid.
talk.environment	Discussion the state of the environment.
talk.origins	Evolution versus creationism (sometimes hot!).
talk.politics.animals	The use and/or abuse of animals.
talk.politics.guns	The politics of firearm ownership and (mis)use.
talk.rape	Discussions on stopping rape; not to be crossposted.

Soc.culture groups capture the truly global favor of Usenet. There are newsgroups for people to discuss the people, culture, and politics of Bulgaria, Canada, the Caribbean, China, Europe, France, Germany, Great Britain, Greece, Hong Kong, India, Iran, Italy, Japan, the Jewish community, Korea, Latin America, Lebanon, Magyar, Mexico, Nepal, the Phillipines...the list continues through dozens more, all the way to Vietnam. Soc. culture.yugoslavia suffered the same fate of the nation of Yugoslavia. Even before armed conflict began making headlines, relations between the Serbian and Croatian factions of the newsgroup started flaming each other.

Postings on Usenet can run from three to three thousand lines. Here is an example, a posting from an authoritative source, about the political impact of Usenet:

```
From: avg@rodan.UU.NET (Vadim Antonov)
   Newsgroups: alt.culture.usenet
   Subject: Re: Usenet leakage into the Real World
   Date: 2 Jul 1992 22:24:35 -0400
   Organization: Berkeley Software Design
In article
<1305hlINNqac@network.ucsd.edu>mark@cs.ucsd.edu
(Mark Anderson) writes:
>
>USENET is not as isolated as some people seem to
think.

Surely. During the coup in Moscow, the information
posted to USENET was used by Voice of America and
CNN and (indirectly) by some other Western
broadcasters and newspapers. In USSR, the USENET
became one of the major information channels--the
conventional phone and telex channels are fairly
clobbered. You even can write an e-mail message to
the Russian Supreme Council. Russian bureaus of
UPI, Frans Press, Associated Press and a dozen of
others get news from Interfax, Agency of Economical
News (Russia) and Russian Information Agency (RIA)
as USENET feed: it works better than faxes.
```

Finally, the current Russian government experts rely on USENET heavily in discussing new legislative proposals with experts and executives from financial and regional groups. USENET works just fine for scientists; there is no reason why it can't be used as fruitfully by governments, mass-media and financial circles.

Vadim Antonov
Berkeley Software Design, Inc.

Here is a request for information, similar to the Experts on the WELL topic. Many postings like this use Usenet as a living database:

Newsgroups: rec.crafts.textiles,alt.sewing
Path: well!uunet!gatech!utkcs2!athena.cas.vanderbilt.edu!vusl
From: vusl@athena.cas.vanderbilt.edu (VU Science Library)
Subject: Social History of Sewing
Organization: Mathematics, Vanderbilt University, Nashville

I am interested in the history of creating clothing. I have seen several books on what clothes of a certain period looked like. I have seen some patterns try to reproduce these clothes.

But what I am interested in is more a social history of sewing. My area of interest here is the years 1066–1500. Who made the clothing the lady of the manor wore? What kind of needles were used? When was the button invented (during the Crusades?)? How did clothing get from the sheep onto the pages of these previously mentioned books on the history of costume? If you know of any books or references along these lines I would appreciate hearing about them. I will be glad to post a summary (if there's any interest!).

Thanks
Carlin
sappenc@ctrvax.vanderbilt.edu

Here's the Usenet as an exotic flea-market:

```
Newsgroups:
uiowa.forsale,misc.forsale,rec.pets,rec.pets.herp
From: bbreffle@icaen.uiowa.edu (Barry Ronald
Breffle)
Subject: Burmese Pythons FOR SALE
Organization: Iowa Computer Aided Engineering
Network, University of Iowa

For Sale

I have several hatchling Burmese pythons for sale.
They are captive bred offspring from a long line of
captive bred. Burmese pythons and are beautiful and
healthy. All are feeding well. They hatched May
'92.

Normal pattern Burmese $100
Green (Patternless) phase Burmese $350

Anyone interested please e-mail:

bbreffle@icaen.uiowa.edu
Barry Breffle
(prices do not include shipping, if required)
```

Constant growth of Usenet means that newsgroups are constantly admitting newcomers. The value of any knowledge-based virtual community derives from the quality of conversation and the expertise of the pool of contributors. People in newsgroups that exchange serious information, tired of the same questions repeatedly asked by newcomers, started compiling and posting FAQs—lists of frequently asked questions. The volunteer editor of a FAQ reposts the latest version to the newsgroup every two weeks or two months, depending on the amount of traffic in the newsgroup. An entire newsgroup is devoted to periodic repostings of FAQs on a panoply of subjects.

Compiling, updating, and republishing a FAQ serves the immediate purpose of preventing the discussion from choking on reiteration of the same old stuff, but FAQs very quickly turn into a unique kind of resource of their own—collectively compiled and verified textbooks on the ten (or forty or one hundred) most important things a beginner ought to know about Unix or pedigreed dogs or Afghani culture or radio scanners or buying a bicycle.

FAQs usually are compiled by the kind of people who like to organize things. Usenet newsgroups are often archived, so anyone with ftp access to the Net can search through them, extract the most frequent questions and the best answers that emerged from the newsgroup, and organize them into a kind of online primer for the newcomer. Thus, the FAQ document keeps the conversation from bogging, provides a structure for a collective database on the subject of the conversation, and serves as an attraction and welcome to people who might want to join the subculture served by the newsgroup.

FAQs are a distilled form of Usenet. A few key bytes from all the millions discarded daily are selected for archival. Sites all over Internet dedicate large amounts of their computer storage to keeping universally accessible resources, such as archives of FAQs. The FAQ becomes a dynamically updated part of the Net's information resource, although it emerged from the informal conversational flow of newsgroups. Here are two examples of the tables of contents of two popular FAQs—a sparse sample from a population of hundreds of different FAQs:

```
FAQs  ABOUT AVIATION
Q1:   How is rec.aviation organized?
Q2:   I'd like to learn to fly. How do I do it, how
      much does it cost, how long does it take?
Q3:   I want to buy a headset. What should I buy?
Q4:   OK, what about a portable intercom?
Q5:   Tell me about mail-order.
Q6:   I'm a private pilot. How should I log time in
      instrument conditions?
Q7:   Tell me about DUATS on-line weather
      briefings.
Q8:   Tell me about BITNET access and the aviation-
      digest list.
Q9:   How do I start a brand-new thread of
      articles?
Q10:  I'm a non-U.S. licensed private pilot. Can I
      fly in the U.S.?
```

Q11: What about hang-gliding? Ultralights?

Q12: Where can I get a copy of public-domain
      flight planning software and other good stuff
      on the net?

Q13: I'm considering buying an airplane. How much
      will it cost?

Q14: Can I use my cellular telephone in an
      airplane?

Q15: Can I use a radio, either a broadcast or
      aviation receiver, in an aircraft?

Q16: I have a physical disability and would like
      to learn to fly. How?

Q17: What are the alternatives for taking an FAA
      written examination?

Q18: Are slips with flaps prohibited in certain
      Cessnas?

FAQS ABOUT DOGS
introduction
getting-a-dog
new-puppy
new-dog
health-care
medical-info
training
behavior
working
service
AKC-titles
resources

Here is an example from a FAQ about cats that illustrates the extremely
fine level of detail many of the FAQs have grown to include. They are, in
effect, collectively written textbooks consisting of lore:

10. "Cat Grass."

Cats benefit from some vegetable matter in their
diet. When devouring prey, the intestines, along

with anything in them, will also be eaten. Many
owners grow some grass for their cats to munch on,
both for a healthy diet, and to distract them from
other household plants!

In general, seeds that are OK to grow and give to
your cats (but do not use treated seeds,
identifiable by a dyed red, blue or awful green
color): oats (cheap, easy, big), wheat (not
wheatgrass) Japanese barnyard millet, bluegrass,
fescue, rye (but beware of ergot, which is a fungal
infection and produces LSD-like chemicals),
ryegrass (annual ryegrass is cheap and easy to
grow, but small), alfalfa sprouts or bean sprouts
in SMALL amounts (these have anti-protein compounds
that reduce the protein value of other things fed
to the animal (or human!).

Seeds that are NOT okay: sorghum or sudangrass,
which have cyanogenic glycosides, and can cause
cyanide poisoning. These are commonly found in bird
seed and look like smallish white, yellow,
orangish, or reddish BB's, or the shiny black,
yellow or straw colored glumes may be intact.

Usenet is a place for conversation or publication, like a giant coffee-
house with a thousand rooms; it is also a worldwide digital version of
the Speaker's Corner in London's Hyde Park, an unedited collection of
letters to the editor, a floating flea market, a huge vanity publisher, and
a coalition of every odd special-interest group in the world. It is a mass
medium because any piece of information put onto the Net has a potential worldwide reach of millions. But it differs from conventional mass
media in several respects. Every individual who has the ability to read a
Usenet posting has the ability to reply or to create a new posting. In television, newspapers, magazines, films, and radio, a small number of people have the power to determine which information should be made
available to the mass audience. In Usenet, every member of the audience
is also potentially a publisher. Students at universities in Taiwan who had

Usenet access and telephone links to relatives in China became a network of correspondents during the 1989 Tiananmen Square incident.

Some newsgroups contain digitally encoded sounds and pictures. Right now, it is possible to use easily-downloaded software tools to convert a scanned photograph or a digitized sound into a series of alphabetic characters. That set of characters can be posted to the Net like any other message, and people who have the software to decode it can turn it into an image or a sound that can be displayed or played on their desktop machines. Nothing you can do in the online universe feels so much like alchemy as connecting to the Net, performing the proper incantations, and watching a fresh satellite weather map of the Pacific pop up in full color on your screen. New standards for exchanging multimedia information, and tricks for compressing complex audiovisual information into easily communicated packages via Internet, will make this multimedia aspect of Usenet even more powerful in the coming years. Think of the impact that one amateur photojournalist had when he videotaped the Rodney King beating by the Los Angeles Police Department. Think of what the impact will be when anybody, anywhere with access to a cheap digital videocamera of the future will be able to upload eyewitness reports to the multimedia Citizen's Reporting Network of the future.

Usenet is an enormous volunteer effort. The people who created it did so voluntarily and put the software into the public domain. The growing megabytes of content are contributed by volunteers. The combination of free expression, lack of central control, many-to-many communication access, and volunteer effort has created a new kind of social organization. Much of this growth has benefitted from the way it has taken place outside the public eye. The first outbreaks of Usenet hysteria in the traditional mass media are beginning to break out. The existence of newsgroups that contain explicit sexual material, either text, graphics, or sounds, is something that is very hard to explain to conservative taxpayers, and the existence of such lurid corners of the Usenet is rarely revealed in the context of the very wide range of valuable information available through the same medium. Usenet libertarians argue that "community standards" is built into the architecture. If your local group does not want to carry a newsgroup, or wants to block access to Usenet by certain users, it is possible to do so. It is much harder for any locality to stop multiple other sites elsewhere in the world from carrying the same material.

Usenet is arguably the world's largest conversation. But it isn't the only grassroots network in the world. Other conversations, tens and hundreds of thousands of them, are taking place in the most local variation of virtual community technology—the BBS culture.

Grassroots: BBS Culture

If a BBS (computer Bulletin Board System) isn't a democratizing technology, there is no such thing. For less than the cost of a shotgun, a BBS turns an ordinary person anywhere in the world into a publisher, an eyewitness reporter, an advocate, an organizer, a student or teacher, and potential participant in a worldwide citizen-to-citizen conversation. The technology of personal telecommunications and the rich, diverse BBS culture that is growing on every continent today were created by citizens, not doomsday weapon designers or corporate researchers.

Like real grassroots, BBSs grow from the ground up, are self-propagating, and are difficult to eradicate. All the high-speed, government-financed internets in the world could turn to lime Jell-O tomorrow and the BBS community would continue to thrive, along with the parts of Usenet that don't propagate via Internet but are passed from computer to computer via modem. Increasingly, the BBSs are linked to the rest of the Net via gateways, but, by their nature, they are not dependent on the Net. There is no way to stamp out the BBS subcultures, unless you shut down the telephone system or go back to the 1970s and un-invent the microprocessor.

A BBS is a personal computer, not necessarily an expensive one, running inexpensive BBS software, plugged into an ordinary telephone line via a small electronic device called a modem. Reliable modems cost less than $100, and the price is dropping. Attach a modem to your computer, plug the modem into your telephone, create a name for your BBS, post the telephone number on a few existing BBSs, and you're in the virtual community business. People call your BBS number and leave private messages or public information. I know a fellow in Colorado Springs, Colonel Dave Hughes, who uses his BBS to fight city hall. I know a fellow in Zushi, Japan, Mayor Kichiro Tomino, who used to fight city hall and now runs the mayor's office via BBS. In the former Soviet Union, BBSs proved to be a potent political tool as well.

A BBS is also a kind of toolkit for creating different kinds of subcultures. You can use a BBS to organize a movement, run a business, coordinate a political campaign, find an audience for your art or political rants or religious sermons, and assemble with like-minded souls to discuss matters of mutual interest. You can let the callers create the place themselves, or you can run it like your own private fiefdom.

Much BBS culture is mundane or puerile or esoteric. It's a raw, unmediated alternative to mass-media culture. Few of the tens of thousands of BBS operators (known as sysops) are interested in how the mass media define reality. BBSs have something in common with "zines," the small-circulation, homemade, grassroots magazines that grew out of the "fanzines" of science-fiction enthusiasts. Zine publishers and BBS sysops are both channels for the direct manifestation of popular culture, unedited, often unpolished, sometimes offensive to traditional sensibilities.

Sysops are more interested in how the people who communicate in clusters of ten to one hundred via the tens of thousands of BBSs around the world define their own realities. (*Boardwatch* magazine estimates that sixty-thousand BBSs existed in the United States alone by 1993.) These communities are small specks in a virtual universe full of much larger groups. But there are so many of them. And they are beginning to organize collectively. One BBS is a community of one hundred. Fifty thousand BBSs represent up to half a million people—who can spread the word very quickly. Just ask the FCC, which is deluged with mail every time somebody floats the rumor about a proposed modem tax.

Ward Christensen and Randy Suess had no way of knowing in 1978 that they were creating a potent political and educational tool as well as a new medium for community-building. At first, they merely wanted to transfer microcomputer programs from place to place via the telephone system. Christensen started to lay the foundations for the grassroots telecommunications culture in 1977, when he created and released to the public domain a microcomputer program called MODEM. MODEM allowed two microcomputers in different locations to use a telephone line to exchange files.

People at both ends had to perform arcane synchronized rituals in order to make MODEM work. First, the human operators at each end of the line had to make voice contact, and then they would put the telephone headsets into an acoustic coupler, a device the size of a shoebox that would link their telephones with the computer; the acoustic coupler communicated with the computer via a modem (MOdulator-DEModulator) that would turn the electronic impulses coming out of the computer into the audio tones that could travel over the telephone network, as well as convert incoming audio tones into electronic impulses. Once their computers were communicating with one another, the operators had to issue commands to transfer the file. That's a long way from the kind of automated communication afforded by electronic mail or networks like ARPANET. But it was a start.

In 1979, Keith Peterson and Ward Christensen released a new version of the software that would perform error correction, a bit of hobbyist high technology that made it possible to transmit files without error, even on noisy telephone lines. Error-corrected transmission is important when sending computer programs such as MODEM itself, because such transmission errors can render the program unusable at the receiving end. They called their new microcomputer file transfer protocol XMODEM. Although 1979 was almost as long ago as the Jurassic age in terms of contemporary technology, the original XMODEM protocol is still the way millions of personal computer users transfer files. Because of the large number of different kinds of computers it has been transferred to, Christensen believes it is "the single most modified program in computing history."

The act of putting that software into the public domain at the very beginning of the era of hobbyist telecommunications technology had a profound effect on BBS culture. Not only did Christensen give away a tool that would make BBSs valuable (by allowing them to act as publishing houses for public-domain software that could be uploaded and downloaded), he prevented anybody from trying to establish exclusive ownership of the tool.

Christensen and others were interested in storing and forwarding text messages as well as transferring files. In 1978, Christensen and Randy Suess created Computer Bulletin Board System (CBBS). It all started, according to Christensen, on January 16, 1978, a very snowy day in Chicago, when he decided to do the software, and Suess decided to do the hardware, for a simple microcomputer communication system. The November 1978 issue of Byte magazine, a publication that had heralded the microelectronics and microcomputer revolutions, published "Hobbyist

Computerized Bulletin Boards," by Christensen and Suess. Not only did these pioneers create a new technology, they immediately told everybody else how to do it. A whole new way of using personal computers became available; new territories beckoned those early adopters of PC technology who were tired of games and graphics and databases.

In 1989, when Christensen recalled the original chain of events in a posting to Chinet, a Chicago-area conferencing system, he noted: "XMODEM was born of the necessity of transferring files mostly between Randy and myself, at some means faster than mailing cassettes (if we'd lived less than the 30 miles apart we did, XMODEM might not have been born). CBBS was born of the conditions, 'all the pieces are there, it is snowing like @#$%, lets hack.'"

In 1979, CBBS went online to the public in Chicago, enabling individuals to read and write messages to and from many other individuals, like a standard bulletin board in the nonvirtual world, where people tack up notices of community interest on a piece of corkboard in a public place. Modems were expensive and slow, and messages weren't structured in terms of topics or conferences, but people were using their PCs and their telephones to communicate, and that in itself was exciting for the first cadres of enthusiasts. Equally important was the fact that neither the communications nor the computer companies had any idea what people like Christensen were up to.

In 1979, the BBS community was restricted almost exclusively to microcomputer hobbyists, and their interests included all kinds of questions—as long as the questions had something to do with how to make personal computers work. People who used the technology to talk about pets and politics and religion would come later. There was one significant exception, however: the CommuniTree BBS in Santa Cruz, California, went online in 1978, paralleling Christensen and Suess's efforts in Chicago. I stumbled onto CommuniTree myself when I first started BBS-hopping, and what I found there impressed me enough to save some of the postings for ten years.

CommuniTree, starting with its name, was specifically focused on the notion of using BBSs to build community, at a time when most other BBSers were still more interested in the technology itself. The Tree was still active in 1982–1983, when I first started exploring the online world. The item that caught my interest enough to print and file it had to do with some people who were designing a new kind of community based on spiritual practice of a nontheological nature. They called it ORIGINS.

ORIGINS started in the "create your own religion" discussion area. In the midst of an overcrowded northern California marketplace for high-priced, highly organized enlightenment for sale or rent, I liked their declaration that "ORIGINS has no leaders, no official existence, nothing for sale. Because it started in an open computer conference, no one knows who all the creators are." The central tenets of the movement were "practices"—actions to be remembered and undertaken in everyday life in the material world. The kind of world the originators of ORIGINS had in mind is wryly evident in the practices its adherents promised to do every day: "Leverage a favor, Ask for help and get it, Use charisma, Finish a job, Use magic, Observe yourself, Share Grace."

I often wondered what had become of them. At the First Conference on Cyberspace in 1990 in Austin, Texas, I ran into somebody who remembered. The CommuniTree BBS had a chance of being the seed for an entire network, but according to one observer who participated in its heyday, Allucquere Rosanne Stone, it fell victim to a problem that continues to plague the BBS community—people who use BBSs as an arena for acting out antisocial impulses. "The students, at first mostly boys and with the linguistic proclivities of pubescent males, discovered the Tree's phone number and wasted no time in logging onto the conferences," Stone recalled, in her presentation to the Austin conference.

They appeared uninspired by the relatively intellectual and spiritual air of the ongoing debates, and proceeded to express their dissatisfaction in ways appropriate to their age, sex, and language abilities. Within a short time the Tree was jammed with obscene and scatological messages. There was no easy way to monitor them as they arrived, and no easy way to remove them once they were in the system. . . .

Within a few months, the Tree had expired, choked to death with what one participant called 'the consequences of freedom of expression.' During the years of its operation, however, several young participants took the lessons and implications of such a community away with them, and proceeded to write their own systems. Within a few years there was a proliferation of on-line virtual communities of somewhat less visionary character but vastly superior message-handling capability. . . .

The visionary character of CommuniTree's electronic ontology proved an obstacle to the Tree's survival. Ensuring privacy in all aspects of the Tree's structure and enabling unlimited access to all conferences did not work in a context of increasing availability of terminals to young men who did not necessarily share the Tree gods' ideas of what counted as community. As one Tree veteran put it, 'The barbarian hordes mowed us down.' Thus, in practice, surveillance and control proved necessary adjuncts to maintaining order in the virtual community.

CommuniTree's focus on social and spiritual matters was an exception for the era. The first generations of BBSers were the home brewers who had a lot of technical knowledge about how their medium worked. People in a few cities began to set up BBSs. The prices for modems in the early 1980s were high—$500 or more for anything faster than a glacially slow 300 bits per second (most adults can read faster than that). Home-brew telecommunications was still a province for hands-on hobbyists who could debug their own software and configure their own hardware. Then Tom Jennings came along.

Jennings, a programmer for a small computer software company in Boston, started using an acoustic coupler to call up CBBS in 1980 and 1981. When he moved to San Francisco in 1983, Jennings found himself with a few weeks of leisure before he had to start working again, so he decided to write a BBS program. Jennings had Fido BBS #1 online by December 1983.

Jennings and his partner-in-home-brew-networking, Tim Pozar, and I spent an afternoon in 1991 talking about the origins and evolution of FidoNet. Pozar and I had met via the WELL, and I was curious about the history of home-brew BBS networks, so Pozar and Jennings shoe-horned into my minuscule and densely packed office at *Whole Earth Review* to explain how it had all happened. You can tell from ten feet away that Jennings is not a conventional programmer or conventional anything. The day we talked, his hair was purple, and he had a number of metal appliances piercing his leather jacket, his ears, and his nose. He's a skateboarder, a gay activist, and an anarchist who hates the idea of suppressing any kind of free expression of ideas.

The name "Fido" went back to an incident at a small company that Jennings worked for in the late 1980s. The company computer belonged to Jennings; it was a mongrel collection of different parts, "including a ten-billion amp power supply and a fan that would blow it away from the wall," Jennings recalled. One night, drinking beer after work, somebody wrote "Fido" on a business card and taped it to the machine. The name migrated to the BBS. The nose-thumbing informality of the name of the BBS was a harbinger of the cultural flavor of the virtual community that began to grow around it.

From the beginning, Jennings wanted to run an extremely loose ship, in which the people who used the BBS would determine the norms. On the first version of Fido, Jennings had included a free-for-all area called "anarchy." "I said to the users that they could do anything they wanted," Jennings told me. "I've maintained that attitude for eight years now, and I have never had problems running BBSs. It's the fascist control freaks who have the troubles. I think if you make it clear that the callers are doing the policing—even to put it in those terms disgusts me—if the callers are determining the content, they can provide the feedback to the assholes."

Jennings asserts that Fido sysops remain "viciously independent." To this day, the philosophy shared by most Fido sysops is usually stated in these words: "Thou shalt not offend; thou shalt not be easily offended." An attitude like that just asks for people who have problems with authority to test the sysop's level of tolerance. Flames—outbursts of angry personal attacks—are not unknown events on Fido boards. Scatological invasions such as the one that shut down CommuniTree are not unknown. The signal-to-noise ratio on a Fido system can be low, especially in comparison with scholarly electronic mailing lists; other Fido neighborhoods are as congenial and intellectually stimulating as you are likely to find anywhere on the Net. Fido is raw, uncut, street-level telecom. And as William Gibson wrote in Neuromancer, the book that gave us the word *cyberspace*, "the street finds its own uses for technology."

Fido started to propagate when a Fido user from Baltimore persuaded Jennings to help him make a version that was compatible with another brand of computer. In January 1984, Fido #2 started operating in Baltimore. Fidos began proliferating rapidly at that point because the software for running your own Fido system was one of the files that callers could transfer (download) from Fido BBSs: the technology was self-propagating. Jennings recalls that Fido software accounted for about 10 percent of the software downloaded at that time. By the end of 1984, several dozen Fidos were operating.

Jennings has an unusual price structure for those who want to obtain a copy of Fido and put themselves in the BBS business: "For a hundred and ninety-nine bucks, my current price, I'll sell you the commercial package to use in your business. For forty dollars, I'll sell you the *same* package as a hobbyist. And for forty you can download it. Just don't ask me many questions. You pick where you want to be on the tier. If you want to be upscale and official, you can mail me two hundred bucks and what you'll get is your own credibility in your own head. I don't tell people that. Actually, I do tell people that and they do it anyway." The BBS business wasn't Jennings's highest priority. He had a grander plan. If he could home-brew self-propagating BBS software, could he home-brew an entire *network*?

"I had this bug in my head," Jennings recalled, "from years and years before that, about having a network of BBSs that all dialed each other toll-free, local call to local call, all the way across the country. It sounds great for about five minutes, until you realize how many thousands of calls it would take to get across the country. You'd need full saturation, a BBS every twenty miles."

The idea wouldn't go away, even though the dozens of Fidos that existed at the time were far from the continental network required to make Jennings's scheme feasible. So he calculated what long distance calls in the middle of the night might cost in relation to the amount of material that could be transferred. By 1985, personal computer modems capable of transmitting 1,200 bits per second were becoming affordable. At that time, he figured it would cost roughly twenty-five cents to send three single-spaced pages of text across the continent. "So you don't need to hop across the country," Jennings realized. "You just direct dial, and you do it in the middle of the night when the rates are cheapest."

That was the beginning of National Fido Hour. Between 1:00 and 2:00 a.m., Fido BBSs shut down for dial-in users, and the BBSs call each other. Jennings gave each BBS a unique node number, and people were able to send mail to each other from any node of the network; the network would forward messages according to the node numbers attached to them, and nodes would keep track of the telephone numbers of other nodes via a nodelist that was also distributed by Jennings via e-mail. As nodes began to cluster in major cities, Jennings upgraded the system to include local gateways. Instead of making seventeen calls to St. Louis, a Baltimore Fido could make one call to St. Louis, and the St. Louis gateway would redistribute in the local area.

One characteristic of networks is that events at local nodes can quickly ripple out to the entire group. In 1985 and 1986, several developments, some coming from Jennings, some originating from sysops and users at the nodes, began to expand the growth of Fidonet, as it was coming to be known. A fellow in Dallas came up with a scheme to ride on Fidomail, called Echomail, a tool that made something more like computer conferencing possible. Fido boards at the beginning distributed mail to one another, but other than the newsletter Jennings sent out with the nodelists and e-mail, there was no distributed conferencing system. Echomail made that possible. By 1986, several hundred Fido sysops showed up at the first Fido users convention, now known as Fidocon, in Colorado Springs. By late 1986, network growth and use started exploding.

By the end of 1986, there were about one thousand nodes. Estimating conservatively at ten users per node, that meant about ten thousand people were on the network. All the telephone bills were paid by the sysops, who also had total control of whether to make usage of that board free or commercial. By 1991, there were over ten thousand nodes, with a conservative estimate of one hundred thousand Fidonet users. When the connectivity issues began to get interesting—there were gateways to Europe, Australia, and Asia by 1991—Tim Pozar began working on the ultimate connection.

"I joined the WELL and I had seen the conferences there and the Usenet newsgroups that came there, so I had always known there was another world to connect to," Pozar explained. Around 1986 and 1987, Pozar started working, via Fidonet, with programmers in Florida and Wisconsin, on a scheme to convert Fido electronic messages to a form that could be read by other networks. "I also worked with Ken Harrington at SRI on mapping Fidonet onto Internet. He was excited about the idea of being able to make the Internet accessible by ordinary citizens. He helped us with a lot of the monetary and administrative bullshit." That was probably a key element in the success of the venture. SRI was the latest incarnation of Stanford Research Institute, where the Department of Defense had funded the original ARPANET's first Network Information Center in the late 1960s. By the late 1980s, Net techies at SRI still had a lot of pull.

Pozar set up the first FidoNet-Internet gateway at the radio station in San Francisco where he worked as a technician. By 1991, there were forty gateways around the world. Internet's worldwide nodes communicate with each other at very high speeds, so if you can use the Rube-Goldbergesque National Fido Hour scheme to get a message into

Internet at one node, it will pop up at the speed of light on another Internet node in Australia or Amsterdam, where it reverts to the old late-night-relay style of distribution.

There are many different kinds of Fido boards, and many different boards outside the Fido cosmos. Like Usenet, the sheer variety of BBSs gives the newcomer a glimpse at the dizzying varieties of subcultures that are popping up all over. Most boards are free and don't require a registration procedure, so it is possible to log onto one board, find its list of other boards, and spend an evening hopping from one board to another.

The best way to get a sense of what people talk about on BBSs is to see for yourself. Even looking at the introductory menus of different boards can reveal something about the diversity of the BBS world. Here is a glimpse of a BBS that attracted me because of its name. BBSs are used by people of every political stripe. The far right, the far left, pagans and Presbyterians, activists and publicists, have BBSs. The COMBAT ARMS BBS is one example of what is out there. You can make some good guesses about the nature of the community a BBS nourishes by browsing the menus of information and discussion available.

The log-in banner of COMBAT ARMS announces, among other things:

```
\\\:       PLEASE. . . Use real names only!       :\\\
\\\:                                               :\\\
\\\: This BBS is geared toward firearms, law,      :\\\
\\\:           aviation and science.               :\\\
```

```
IF YOU WISH TO ANONOMOUSLY [ sic] REPORT A CRIME,
USE THE FIRST NAME OF "CRIME", A LAST NAME OF
"REPORT" AND USE THE PASSWORD "CRIMETIP" WHEN YOU
LOG IN. THEN LEAVE YOUR CRIME REPORT.
\\\:  If you want a reward (if available), sign
your crime report with a unique 9 digit number. You
can safely use your Social Security number if you
wish. It will remain confidential.
```

Some of the regular discussions ("echoes," in Fidospeke) in the menu of COMBAT ARMS attracted my attention. There are echoes for questions and answers to and from law enforcement personnel, for discussions of the civil war, questions and answers about firearms and home-schooling, civil liberties and real estate, setting up a BBS and participating in search and rescue operations. This BBS appears to be something of a soapbox for the sysop, who includes an extensive collection of essays and texts for free downloading. Here are a few of the bulletins available.

```
            \\\\\Combat Arms BBS Bulletin Menu
\\\\\
\\\\\\\\\
\\\\\  1-What the Combat Arms BBS is all about.
\\\\\  5-Getting ready for a disaster.
\\\\\  6-Bay Area legislators to contact to let them
know you are
\\\\\  opposed to gun control moves on their part.
\\\\\  7-Information on ballistics for police
officers (& others).
\\\\\  8-Here is a list of gun related BBS systems
nationwide!
\\\\\  9-Some of the events that preceded the
American
\\\\\  Revolutionary War. Read this and LEARN. Most
people do not understand this!
\\\\\  10-How to hunt for wild pigs in California.
This applies to
\\\\\\  most all other states as well (except the
regulations)
\\\\\\11-Here is the text from the California gun
ban that explains
\\\\\  which guns are banned. It went into effect on
January 1, 1990.
\\\\\\12-How to qualify for an M1 Garand and receive
it direct from
\\\\\  the U.S. Army. This is the Director of
Civilian Marks-
\\\\\  manship (D.C.M.) program.
```

\\\\\ 14-B.A.T.F. explanation of "straw purchases" of firearms. It is
\\\\\ important that all dealers and customers understand this.
\\\\\ 15-What to know what an "assault rifle" really is? Here is a
\\\\\ report by Dr. Edward C. Ezell from the Smithsonian
\\\\\ Institution to Congressman Dingell on the subject. This is very
\\\\\ valuable information for researchers and those shooters
\\\\\ who need technical information for the ignorant media reporters. This may be downloaded as EZELL.ZIP.
\\\\\ 16-Tips on the proper display of the American Flag.
\\\\\ 17-Results of UCLA study on condoms. Some they tested are NO good whatsoever and will not keep you safe from AIDS.
\\\\\ 18-The news summary for the Gulf War from January 18th through March 3rd. This bulletin is 231,808 bytes long.
\\\\\ 19-How to get upgraded to a higher access level on this BBS.
\\\\\ 21-Excellent article on Springfield Armory's 1911-A1 pistols.
\\\\\ Please be sure to read this before buying one.
\\\\\ 24-How to write an article and upload it as a message on the
\\\\\ Combat Arms BBS. This method generally works on other
\\\\\ bulletin boards as well.
\\\\\ 26-This is the actual text of the Supreme Court ruling in the
\\\\\ classic case of U.S. versus Miller. Also

```
included are your
\\\\\ SysOp's comments as well as those of a
pro-gun attorney.
37-How to make a long distance call when your regu-
lar long distance carrier is inoperative. This is
very, very useful info.
\\\\\ 33-The entirety of Patrick Henry's famous
"Give me Liberty
\\\\\ or give me death!" speech of March, 1775.
Read this and
\\\\\ ponder America's present political situation.
\\\\\ 42-Are you seriously interested in the sci-
ence of ballistics?
\\\\\ If so, here is some information on a graduate
program in the
\\\\\ field of ballistics at Drexel University in
Pennsylvania.
\\\\\ I would consider providing scholarship money
to any user
\\\\\ Level 10 or higher) who later enrolls in this
program.
```

Note menu item 19. This is a common feature of BBSs. The BBS is
open to anybody who wants to call in. You have to stick around for a
while, perhaps meet the sysop in person, to be granted access to more
restricted discussions that take place among an inner circle in the same
BBS.

In one telephone call, it is possible to BBS-hop from survivalists to the-
ologians. It didn't take me long to discover there isn't enough time in the
day to keep up with what is happening in religious BBSs of the San
Francisco Bay area. Some are connected with real-life congregations,
others are free-form and come in sixteen shades of unorthodox. The role
of communications media in shaping religion has been central since the
time of the Epistles, and perhaps the most important change in organized
religion to take place in the twentieth century has been the advent of television congregations. Mass-market religion in the style of television
evangelists is thoroughly a product of the old broadcast paradigm that

has dominated institutions in recent decades. The grassroots dynamism within the world's major religions is an unusually promising environment for a many-to-many paradigm, where coreligionists can find each other, stay in touch between services, and even commune in traditional ways via nontraditional media.

The Catholic Information Network (CIN) has four nodes in the bay area and six others around the country; CIN message areas include a main area, prayer, ecumen, "Ask Father," Bible, ethics, and homeschooling. LDSnet, a sixteen-node national network for Church of Jesus Christ Latter Day Saints (Mormon) believers, has two nodes in Colorado that are located in churches. CompuPal BBS message area provides access to several Christian Fido echos, an online Bible search program, and a Bible text available for downloading. NewLife Christian Network includes around thirty-five active BBSs nationwide and includes echos for Christian media, creationism, spiritual warfare, and sports. There is also the Orthodox Christian BBS, Corpus Christi BBS, the Computers for Christ network of about thirty nodes in the United States, Canada, and England, AgapeNet, and Christian Fellowship Net. This is a sample, not an exhaustive listing, of the Christian BBSs available in just the San Francisco Bay area. Like Deadheads and computer programmers, people with strong religious beliefs are members of communities who want to stay in touch with one another between face-to-face communions. There's a lot more to the BBS culture than cyberpunks and computer nerds.

Christian BBSs are prominent, but far from the only denomination available within my area code. Keshernet is a Jewish network (*Kesher* means "connect" in Hebrew) of different Jewish FidoNet echoes, including Judaica, Interfaith, and Jewish Genealogy. Body Dharma online devotes message areas to the entire spectrum of Eastern, Western, and pagan traditions. Zen Connection is a Fido board. PODS, the Pagan/Occult Distribution Network, carries interfaith information as well as Goddess spirituality information. There are boards such as Bay Area Skeptic for people who are skeptical about religion. Or dozens of BBSs like the Temple of the Screaming Electron if you want to step entirely off the scale.

BBSs devoted to health and medical discussions also abound. Body Dharma, in addition to spiritual material, offers resources and discussion areas in medical, disability, and alternative therapies. ADAnet is a

Fidonet-wide echo that includes message areas for epilepsy, multiple sclerosis, muscular dystrophy, and post-polio syndrome. Sponsored by the Disability Law Foundation, ADAnet makes information available to employers who need information about the Americans with Disability Act of 1991. The Grateful Med BBS carries medical and alternative health echoes, including echoes devoted to biomedical engineering and search and rescue medicine. Blink Connection BBS is a forum for exchanging information in support of blind and visually impaired computer users (who can use print-to-voice and large-print technologies to "read" BBS text). There is an AIDS Info BBS, as well.

Earthquakes are a bay area special interest, but BBSs devoted to disaster preparedness are nationwide. In the bay area, there is the Public Seismic Network, a four-node BBS network spread between Menlo Park, San Jose, Pasadena, and Memphis, Tennessee; U.S. Geological Survey volunteers staff the Menlo Park node. Rising Storm BBS is oriented toward general emergency preparation and survival, including message areas in self-sufficiency, self-defense, law and order, firearms, and civil liberties. Rising Storm is the California node of Survnet, a small survivalist network that includes information and discussion about survival politics as well as survival techniques. SALEMDUG is a BBS for state, local, and FEMA (Federal Emergency Management Administration) workers.

And, of course, there's always sex. Kinky Komputer was one of the first BBSs in the San Francisco Bay area, a mostly straight sex-oriented BBS that was going full swing, so to speak, when Tom Jennings arrived in the area and started boardsurfing. A communications medium that allows people to make connections without revealing their true name, age, gender, or physical appearance is certain to evolve erotic variants. Some sex BBSs are all talk and little action—playgrounds for sex fantasies with strangers who don't know where to find you. Other sex BBSs are more like pickup bars than theaters. Some sex BBSs ask participants to fill out detailed sex questionnaires. And in most sex BBSs, the place always seemed to be filled with manly men and womanly women and no end of people who have no apparent inhibitions—at least in this medium—about describing their sexual preferences in precise detail.

Although my research into BBSs has been confined to the San Francisco region, most BBSs contain lists of other BBSs in other parts of the world.

If you find one special-interest BBS, they usually have a list of others. A BBS known as Linkages leads to dozens of African-American BBSs. There is an entire network of MUFON (Mutual UFO Network) boards that all point to each other. There are networks of boards devoted to recovery from substance abuse or sexual or physical abuse. I've also found BBSs for fat people (THE BIG BOARD, associated with the National Association for Fat Acceptance), photographers, Trekkies (there are many BBSs for *Star Trek* fans, including the splinter groups of fans who are convinced that Spock and Kirk are secretly lovers—known as K/S enthusiasts), veterans, Zionists, white supremacists, environmentalists, feminists, libertarians, animal rights activists, Asian-Americans. When you walk down the street in your city or town, it is likely that at least one of the people you see every day is a BBSer.

From the WELL to the world's largest conversation to the wild and woolly reaches of BBSdom, the universe of virtual communities seems to grow larger and larger as one's imagination stretches to accommodate the knowledge of what is happening right now. Discovering the existence and depth of this worldwide subculture is a little like discovering a previously unknown continent, teeming with unfamiliar forms of life.

5

Multi-User Dungeons and Alternate Identities

Your character, Buffy Mojo, is crawling through a maze of tunnels in the dungeon of her archenemy's castle. The walls are dank, the lighting is dim, the silence is ominous. A spell has turned Buffy's only ally into a toad. Your hands feel clammy on the keyboard; your heartbeat seems too loud. If Buffy runs into the wrong character down here, your persona will die, and hundreds of hours of work you put into constructing her will have been wasted. More than just your imaginary character is at stake. Buffy's fate will influence the virtual lives of other characters who represent real friends in the material world. You are in a MUD, along with tens of thousands of others around the world who build fantasy worlds in the Net.

Welcome to the wild side of cyberspace culture, where magic is real and identity is a fluid. MUD stands for Multi-User Dungeons—imaginary worlds in computer databases where people use words and programming languages to improvise melodramas, build worlds and all the objects in them, solve puzzles, invent amusements and tools, compete for prestige and power, gain wisdom, seek revenge, indulge greed and lust and violent impulses. You can find disembodied sex in some MUDs. In the right kind of MUD, you can even kill—or die.

It all started on a computer in a university in England in 1980. By July 1992, there were more than 170 different multi-user games on Internet, using nineteen different world-building languages. The most popular worlds have thousands of users. Richard Bartle, one of the fathers of MUDding, estimated one hundred thousand past and present MUDders worldwide by 1992. MUD researcher Pavel Curtis estimates twenty thousand active MUDders in 1992. The MUDding population now is far smaller than the populations of other parts of the Net, but it is growing fast, and spawning new forms at an impressive rate.

MUDs are living laboratories for studying the first-level impacts of virtual communities—the impacts on our psyches, on our thoughts and feelings as individuals. And our attempts to analyze the second-level impacts of phenomena like MUDs on our real-life relationships and communities lead to fundamental questions about social values in an age when so many of our human relationships are mediated by communications technology.

"What is the matter with these people?" is a question that many people ask when they first learn about MUDding. "Don't they have lives?" This is the most serious question that emerges from the early history of the medium—is this a dangerous form of addiction? The strongest case for the possibility that CMC might present grave social dangers as well as opportunities stems from the documented instances of MUDders who spend most of their waking lives in their alternate worlds. The question of communication addiction isn't as simple as it seems at first. One of my guides to the MUD universe, herself a student of the phenomenon, is Amy Bruckman of MIT's Media Lab. She put it this way: "How do we feel about tens of thousands of college students spending their time and government-sponsored resources to chase virtual dragons? To answer this question, you have to dive in and explore assumptions about what is a meaningful way to spend one's time. What are the value judgments implicit in various answers to that question?"

First, it is necessary to look at the fascination, the allure, the reasons why people use the medium so enthusiastically, even obsessively. What are the unique features of this medium that appeal to people psychologically, and what does that say about people's psychological needs? I believe the answer lies in the changing notions of identity that were precipitated by previous communications media. Some people are primed for the kind of communication saturation that MUDs offer because of the communication-saturated environments that have occupied their attention since birth. MUDs are part of the latest phase in a long sequence of mental changes brought about by the invention and widespread use of symbolic tools.

Previous communications media dissolved ancient barriers of time and space that had separated people, and in the process changed the way people thought; first, alphabetic language and then printing technology created a kind of community memory, a stored groupmind accessible to many, not just to the bards and priests who had been the keepers of collective knowledge in the era of oral cultures. The nature of the individual psyche changed when it became possible for so many people outside the priesthood to take advantage of the collected knowledge of the culture. Literate people think differently from people in nonliterate or postliterate cultures, and they think of themselves differently. The telegraph, telephone, radio, and television, as Marshall McLuhan pointed out, turned everywhere and every time into here and now. An ordinary person today with a coin and access to a telephone booth commands powers over time and space that the potentates of antiquity never dared covet. People who routinely accept such power as part of their reality think of themselves in a certain way. Like previous historical changes, such as the transformation from people who thought of themselves as subjects of royalty to people who thought of themselves as citizens of democracy, this one has started at the fringes and is working its way toward the center.

Similar to the way previous media dissolved social boundaries related to time and space, the latest computer-mediated communications media seem to dissolve boundaries of *identity* as well. One of the things that we "McLuhan's children" around the world who grew up with television and direct-dialing seem to be doing with our time, via Minitel in Paris and commercial computer chat services in Japan, England, and the United States, as well as intercontinental Internet zones like MUDs, is *pretending to be somebody else*, or even pretending to be several different people at the same time.

I know a respectable computer scientist who spends hours as an imaginary ensign aboard a virtual starship full of other real people around the world who pretend they are characters in a Star Trek adventure. I have three or four personae myself, in different virtual communities around the Net. I know a person who spends hours of his day as a fantasy character who resembles "a cross between Thorin Oakenshield and the Little Prince," and is an architect and educator and bit of a magician aboard an imaginary space colony: By day, David is an energy economist in Boulder, Colorado, father of three; at night, he's Spark of Cyberion City—a place where I'm known only as Pollenator.

Some people seem to use these depersonalized modes of communication to get very personal with each other. For these people, at the right times, CMC is a way to connect with another human being. But the authenticity of human relationships is always in question in cyberspace, because of the masking and distancing of the medium, in a way that it is not in question in real life. Masks and self-disclosures are part of the grammar of cyberspace, the way quick cuts and intense images are part of the grammar of television. The grammar of CMC media involves a syntax of identity play: new identities, false identities, multiple identities, exploratory identities, are available in different manifestations of the medium.

Once inside a MUD, you can be a man or a woman or something else entirely. You can be a hive identity. The Net that to others represents access to the Library of Congress or political debates or scientific data or idle chat is, to MUDders, just the road they have to travel to get to the virtual places where their other identities dwell.

Identity is the first thing you create in a MUD. You have to decide the name of your alternate identity—what MUDders call your character. And you have to describe who this character is, for the benefit of the other people who inhabit the same MUD. By creating your identity, you help create a world. Your character's role and the roles of the others who play with you are part of the architecture of belief that upholds for everybody in the MUD the illusion of being a wizard in a castle or a navigator aboard a starship: the roles give people new stages on which to exercise new identities, and their new identities affirm the reality of the scenario.

In MUDs, as in the WELL, participants can communicate with each other through a number of public and private channels: MUD dwellers can send each other private e-mail that is stored in the recipients electronic mailbox to be read and replied to at the recipient's leisure; they can page each other in different parts of the MUD with person-to-person chat, like a person-to-person telephone call; they can "say," "whisper," and "pose" to anybody else in the same room—a form of group chat that uses the boundaries of metaphorical rooms as social boundaries; they can turn on or off special-interest CB channels for other semipublic conversations across different parts of the MUD that take place while you are talking and emoting in a specific place. It's dizzying at first, like learning a new kind of communication gymnastics.

The use of poses as well as words to convey meaning gives MUDs an odd but definitely useful kind of disembodied body language. Posing (also known as emoting) can be used in polite, informal conversation, in more structured discourse, and in that radically informal behavior known as tinysex. If you are a character named "hivemind," and you give the command "emote leaps onstage," everybody else in the same room sees the message "hivemind leaps onstage" on their computer screens. It adds a new dimension to your communications. Instead of replying to a statement, you can smirk. Instead of leaving the room, you can disappear in a cloud of iridescent, bubble-gum-flavored bubbles. Emoting seems awkward and artificial at first, but once you get the hang of it, poses give you some added control over the atmosphere in which a conversation takes place—a taste of the all-important context that is often missing from words alone.

A MUD is communications soup in real time, with a flavor of improvisatory theater. Unlike computer conferencing systems or bulletin boards, people's social interactions are in different varieties of real-time chat mode, not the kind of bulletin-board style communication you can find on BBSs or places like the WELL. MUDs are very much about who is in the place at the same time and how they interact. It's more of a hangout than a publication, more like a game board than a bulletin board.

In MUDs, however, unlike computer conferencing systems or ordinary chat services, participants also create objects with powers, such as magic carpets that transport their owners to secret parts of the kingdom. Other participants can buy or steal those carpets; people can gain power to make even more useful carpets, but only after amassing sufficient knowledge of the MUDs' lore as well as formal mastery of the MUDs' world-building languages and meeting certain challenges. There are quests and trials by fire. In some worlds, the only way to gain the most potent secrets on the road to extraordinary powers is to kill another character or cast a crippling spell. In other worlds, a majority of the other MUD-ders have to agree that you have built something worth keeping for public use before you can gain wizard powers.

There are worlds where you have to look out for a dagger in the back, and worlds in which building something together rather than dueling to the death is the acceptable mode of discourse. Gaining the power to modify the environment in which the game takes place is a primary goal for newcomers in both the "adventure" and "social" MUDs. When you log off the WELL, all you leave are the words you have posted. When you log off a MUD, many of the dwellings you have built, the cities you have constructed, the tools and toys and weapons you have created, can be explored or used by other people.

The communities that have arisen in MUDworlds are distinctly different from places like the WELL or the vast electronic chatauqua of Usenet or the innumerable town halls and pool parlors of small BBSs. In a MUD, you are communicating with other people elsewhere on the Net, via your characters, but you are also playing a role and learning your way around a world where knowledge of how that world works can translate into power over the other inhabitants. People who have traded enough hours of their lives to become "wizzes" (the informal, gender-neutral term for wizards, MUD experts who have earned special powers), for example, can gain the power of invisibility, which gives them the ability to spy on other conversations. One notorious trick in less reputable corners of the MUD universe is to talk somebody into going into a dark corner of a MUD for some tinysex—dirty talking via computer screen, within character for the MUD, along with explicit posing—a dark corner where some invisible wizzes are hiding. The misuse of wiz-level "snoop" powers is a recurrent theme of debate in the parts of Usenet where MUDders debate.

Net.sleazing, as the practice of aggressively soliciting mutual narrative stimulation is known, is an unsavory but perennially popular behavior in MUDland. Possibly the nastiest trick to pull on a newcomer to MUD culture is to talk him (most MUDders are males, including many who present themselves as females) into tinysex, which you clandestinely record in a text file and consequently post to the worldwide Usenet discussion of MUDlife. It's akin to seducing someone, videotaping the encounter, and putting out copies for free at the neighborhood video store. There are MUDs in which outright orgiastic scenarios are the dominant reality. There are MUDs that are as chaste as classrooms, but sex talk definitely has a place in the MUD universe.

Tinysex, net.sleazing and gender deception are aspects of MUDs and CMC worth examining, but it's a mistake to stereotype the very broad range of MUD behavior with images of its most sophomoric elements. It pays to keep in mind that most of the most notorious offenders are in fact sophomores in colleges in Indianapolis and Helsinki. The single largest category of MUDders are college students, age seventeen to twenty-three, and the particular uses they find for this technology—identity play and sexual innuendo—reflect the preoccupations of that population. But not all undergraduate MUDders are immature, nor are all MUDders undergraduates. For many, a MUD is a place where they feel more comfortable in some ways than they do in the real world. Here's how Amy Bruckman describes the place she likes to spend her time:

It is 3:30a.m. EST, and I am talking to my friend Tao in my quarters aboard the Federation Starship the USS *Yorktown*. Actually, I am in Massachusetts and Tao is in South Carolina. We are logged onto a Multi-User Simulation Environment (MUSE) based on a Star Trek theme. At this moment, there are thirty-six people logged on from all over the world. My character name is Mara. Anything I say or do is seen by Tao, since he is in the same room; anything which is announced is seen by all thirty-six people logged on. Our private conversation—about gender roles and the ways female characters are swarmed with attention—is interwoven with a public conversation filled with computational puns and Star Trek references.

Amy is describing an intellectual, ironic, media-savvy place, where multileveled metaphors, puns, wordplay, and clever programming are the coin of the realm. Trek-MUSE is modeled on the roles played in the television series "Star Trek—The Next Generation." By contrast, if you entered the original MUD1, created in 1979 and 1980 by Roy Trubshaw and Richard Bartle, then students at the University of Essex, England, this is what you would see:

You are stood on a narrow road between The Land and whence you came. To the north and south are the small foothills of a pair of majestic mountains, with a large wall running round. To the west the road continues, where in the distance you can see a thatched cottage opposite an ancient cemetery. The way out is to the east, where a shroud of mist covers the secret pass by which you entered The Land.

The Land is a place where cunning can be essential to life, and the friendship of a wizard a shortcut to prosperity. It's a place where your character can lose its life if you aren't careful where you tell it to go. You'll need a shield and a sword if you want to last long, and if you happen upon an object or being, you better think twice about what you intend to do with it.

By typing commands, traveling around, getting bearings, gaining knowledge, making friends, and demonstrating your own contributions to the collective enterprise, you can gain enough knowledge and power from your wanderings in a MUD to be able to build additions to the fantasy world yourself and make life interesting for the people who come to play there. The wizzes are only the junior grade of the MUD illuminati. The people who attain the senior grade of MUD freemasonry by starting their own MUD, with all due hubris, are known as gods. Wizzes make life interesting for players, and gods are the ultimate arbiters.

But to the hardest-core MUDders, the traditional online epithet "Get a life" is more the issue. When you are putting in seventy or eighty hours a week on your fantasy character, you don't have much time left for a healthy social life. If you are a college student, as the majority of MUDders are, MUDding for seventy hours a week can be as destructive to the course of your life as chemical dependency. Computer scientist Pavel Curtis created an experimental MUD, LambdaMOO, on his workstation at Xerox Corporation's renowned Palo Alto Research Center. At a panel discussion in Berkeley, California, Curtis had this to say about the addictive potential of MUDding:

I am concerned about the degree to which people find virtual communities enchanting. We have people who use LambdaMOO who are not in control of their usage who are, I believe, seriously and clinically addicted. . . .These people aren't addicted to playing video games. It wouldn't do the same thing for them. They're communication addicted. They're addicted to being able to go out and find people twenty-four hours a day and have interesting conversations with them. We're talking about people who spend up to seventy hours a week connected and active on a MUD. Seventy hours a week, while they're trying to put themselves through school at Cambridge. I'm talking about a fellow who's supposed to be at home in Cambridge to see his family for the holidays, missed his train by five hours, phoned his parents, lied about why he was late, got on the next train, got home at 12:30 in the morning, didn't go home, went to a terminal room at Cambridge University and MUDded for another two hours. He arrived home at 2:30 in the morning to find the police and some panicked parents, and then began to wonder if maybe he wasn't in control.

These are very enticing places for a segment of the community. And it's not like the kinds of addictions that we've dealt with as a society in the past. If they're out of control, I think that's a problem. But if someone is spending a large portion of their time being social with people who live thousands of miles away, you can't say that they've turned inward. They aren't shunning society. They're actively seeking it. They're probably doing it more actively than anyone around them. It's a whole new ballgame. That's what I'm saying about virtual societies.

Amy Bruckman used the rich social worlds she discovered in her favorite MUDs as the subject of her MIT graduate studies of the psychological and social significance of MUD culture. In 1992, Bruckman wrote about MUDs as "Identity Workshops." In 1993, she instigated the creation of MediaMOO, the Media Lab's version of a MUD—one designed to become a serious adjunct to scientific conferences. Bruckman's 1992 study dealt with the question of what it was about the MUDs that addicts people. Like Pavel Curtis, Amy Bruckman touched on the problems of judging hastily whether prolonged MUDding is good or bad for a particular person in a particular situation. In her paper, Bruckman cites the case of a MUDder of her acquaintance who managed to maintain a B average as an undergraduate, hold down a part-time job, and still find time to MUD for seventy hours a week or more. This person met his responsibilities in life, so whose cultural police are going to tell him he's an addict who needs help?

One of Bruckman's mentors, MIT professor Dr. Sherry Turkle, wrote something about the behavior of young, compulsive computer programmers that seems to offer a key to understanding MUDding's addictive potential. Turkle focused on the notion of *mastery* as a crucial missing element in the lives of some of these young people:

The issue of mastery has an important role in the development of each individual. For the developing child, there is a point, usually at the start of the school years, when mastery takes on a privileged, central role. It becomes the key to autonomy, to the growth of confidence in one's ability to move beyond the world of parents to the world of peers. Later, when adolescence begins, with new sexual pressures and new social demands from peers and parents, mastery can provide respite. The safe microworlds the child master has built—the microworlds of sports, chess, cars, literature, or mathematical expertise—can become places of escape. Most children use these platforms from which to test the difficult waters of adolescence. They move out at their own pace. But for some the issues that arise during adolescence are so threatening that the safe place is never abandoned. Sexuality is too threatening to be embraced. Intimacy with other people is unpredictable to the point of being intolerable. As we grow up, we forge our identities by building on the last place in psychological development where we felt safe. As a result, many people come to define themselves in terms of competence, in terms of what they can control.

Pride in one's ability to master a medium is a positive thing. But if the sense of self becomes defined in terms of those things over which one can exert perfect control, the world of safe things becomes severely limited—because those things tend to be things, not people. Mastery can cease to be a growing force in individual development and take on another face. It becomes a way of masking fears about the self and the complexities of the world beyond. People can become trapped.

Knowledge of MUDlore and skill at communicating with people to help you achieve your ends, and the ability to create places and puzzles for others to explore, are a form of mastery, a way for people who might lack social status in their real-world community to gain status through their MUD skills in their alternate community. For people whose lives are controlled by parents or professors or bosses, there is a certain attraction to a world in which mastery and the admiration of peers is available to anyone with imagination and intellectual curiosity.

In one family I met in a MUD, the father tutors his kids in programming, science, and the sheer art of having literate fantasies. In fact, the education these children are getting is taking place in small part in Cyberion City, a special MUD where such educational experiments are encouraged. For this family, is MUDding an addiction or a model of the way education ought to take place? This question can be generalized to the use of other CMC media in other social contexts. You have to examine the way a person uses the medium, and the way that use of the technology affects the person's behavior, thoughts, and relationships with other people, before you can begin to determine whether an eighty-hour-a-week MUDder is an addict or a virtuoso.

You can have different identities in several different kinds of places. I am represented by a character known as Pollenator in Cyberion City and Funhead in WELLMUSE. When I use the "look" command to examine Spark in Cyberion City, his identity description informs me of his resemblance to Thorin Oakenshield:

```
look Spark
You see a cross between Thorin Oakenshield and the
Little Prince. Always smiling and whistling. Mostly
tunes that are 600 years old by now.
Carrying:
Spark's hoverboard (#41221vI)
The Enlightened Creator (#1255v)
mg
flame
apple
```

Looking at any of the objects that Spark carries would reveal further descriptions, perhaps even instructions on how to use them. In MUDworlds, description is the same as creation. MUDs are evidence that text still has its powers, even in this highly visual era. When you weave text into the kind of interactive landscape that computer models provide, you can build a kind of magic into the environment. Amy Bruckman remembers that the first object she created in a MUD was a plate of pasta that "squirmed uneasily" whenever anyone in the room mentioned the word *hungry*. Even if Amy's character wasn't there in the MUD at the time, everyone in the room of the MUD where she left the plate of pasta would see on their screens, on utterance of the word *hungry* in public conversation, the message that "the plate of spaghetti squirms uneasily." It makes for a very different kind of context for communication when you have sentient bowls of spaghetti lying around, waiting to enter the conversation. Watching other people's reactions to the objects you create adds to the excitement of MUDding.

The first object I created in a MUD was a magic camera I learned to create in a self-guided wizardry class in a virtual university within the MUD. I could put the camera in my room and it would report to me, wherever else I might be wandering, any activity that took place in my absence. Jetboy in Cyberion City has an antique phonograph in his parlor; if you invoke the command "play phonograph," thereafter, every thirty seconds, the name of a new tune from Jetboy's extensive collection of Hawaiian classics will be announced in the middle of whatever else is happening.

The roots of MUDs are deep in that part of human nature that delights in storytelling and playing "let's pretend." Brenda Laurel, in *Computers As Theater*, claims that the strong identification players feel with artificial characters in a computer database is an example of the same human capacity for *mimesis* to which Aristotle attributed the soul-changing (and, thus, society-changing) power of drama.

Richard Bartle, cocreator of the first MUD, the first of the MUD gods, has his own version of the mimesis theory. In 1990, he wrote:

MUAs [Multi-User Adventures] can exert an influence over a large number of these players out of all proportion to that of either a chatline or game alone. MUAs have an emotional hold over their players which stems from the players' ability to project themselves onto their game personae, feeling as if the things which happen to the game personae are happening directly to the players themselves.

The first MUD was a Multi-User *Dungeon*, modeled on a Tolkienesque domain of dwarves and treasure, warriors and wizards, swordplay and magic, known as "the Land." Second-generation MUDs encompassed different metaphors. And now we have third-, fourth-, and fifth-generation variants. A MUSE is a Multi-User *Simulation Environment*, one of a variety of MUDs in which all players, not just wizards, are granted powers to shape the environment itself; MUSEcode also conveys the ability to build automata, computer simulations that can model real phenomena, which has both scientific and educational implications.

Narrative is the stuff of which MUDworlds are made. Everyone and everything and every place has a story. Every object in a MUD, from your character's identity to the chair your character is sitting in, has a written description that is revealed when you choose to look at the object. The story is known in MUDspeke as "the description." If you have the authorization to do so, you could create a small brown mouse or purple mountain range or whatever else words can describe. Although the MUD worlds are fantasies, with no more tangible reality than the settings and characters in a novel or a soap opera, the people I've met in real life who live in MUDlands testify passionately that the feelings they have about their characters and worlds are real to them, and often quite intense.

In a conversation with the author in 1992, Richard Bartle said:

Losing your persona in a game is absolutely terrible. It's the worst thing that can happen to you and people really get put up about it. They usually say they're gutted. "Gutted" is the word players use because it's about the only one that describes about how awful it is. It's not as if "Oh dear, I've lost my persona" in the same way you may say "I've lost my shoe." It's not even "Oh dear, I've lost my persona" in the same way as "I've lost my pet hamster." It's more as "Oh dear, I've just died. That's me they've just killed!" It's not "Oh, I've lost all that work and all that time and effort." It's "I've just *died*, this is terrible! Oh my God, I'm *dead*! Empty!"

In some MUDs, you can reincarnate your character; in others, death is irrevocable.

My first adventure in a MUD—actually, in a MUSE—was a space colony/science museum. I had heard about Cyberion City from a WELLite I had met in a rather serious business-oriented private conference; he discovered that I was interested in virtual communities, so he told me in e-mail that there was a place on the Net where he and his ten-year-old son were helping build a space colony. My friend, a man I had never met face-to-face, known as Kline in the WELL and Spark in Cyberion City, told me that some knowledgeable people who had utopian faith in the potential of cyberspace as an educational medium had chartered a new kind of computer conferencing system explicitly as a virtual community.

Aslan and Moulton, the first wizards I encountered in a MUD, were the helpful variety of wiz. It could have been an altogether different experience if I had appeared, unsponsored, in a hardcore hack-and-slash world, and attracted the attention of a foul-tempered wiz or god before I could afford a shield. I can see now that I was lucky to have chosen Cyberion City. This was before Pollenator existed, before I devoted a moment's thought to the idea of creating the right name for the identity I was going to assume in a whole new world. I was, as they say in some of the rougher neighborhoods of the MUD universe, a "clueless newbie," a bit of public-school jargon that found its way into MUDspeke via the original MUD's British origins.

Moulton, one of the three directors of MicroMUSE, was there to show me around the first time I arrived at the arrival gate. This is how Cyberion City looked to me, the first time I visited:

```
------------------------------------------------------
------------------------------------------------------

Welcome to MicroMUSE! We are hosted at
chezmoto.ai.mit.edu, port 4201.

------------------------------------------------------
------------------------------------------------------

REMINDER: Read 'NEWS' regularly to keep up on
changes and additions to the server. New commands
will be listed in 'news' with details provided in
'help'. For more information, new players should
type: help getting started

------------------------------------------------------
------------------------------------------------------

Cyberion City Main Transporter Receiving Station
The bright outlines of the Cyberion City
Transporter Station slowly come into focus. You
have been beamed up here (at considerable expense)
from one of the Earth Transporter Stations. You are
among the adventurous and moderately wealthy few
```

who have decided to visit (and perhaps dwell) in
Cyberion City, the largest space city in the solar
system. You are welcomed by the transporter
attendant, who gives directions to all newcomers to
this space city.

Contents:
Attendant
Obvious exits:
Out

Welcome to MicroMUSE, your name is Guest1

attendant says "Welcome, Guest, to Cyberion City."
attendant says "Feel free to contact any Official
for aid."
attendant says "Be sure to use our extensive
on-line help command."
attendant says "I hope you enjoy your stay."
The attendant smiles at you.
You step down off of the MTRS platform.

Main Transporter Lobby

This room has high, vaulted ceilings and white
walls. The thick, black carpet makes no sound
beneath your feet. You are just inside the
Transporter Lobby, where Visitors arrive from
Earth. To one side is an Information Desk. A door
leads to the Tours office, and another leads Out
into Cyberion City proper. A Public Relations Dept.
Intercom stands in the center of the floor; type
'look Intercom' for instructions.

Contents:
Spark
Spark's helper, the Firefly
koosh
Mymosh
Ramandu
Intercom
TourBot

```
Obvious exits:
Information Tours<T>Out
```

Sparks says "Hi!"

You say "Hi"

Spark says "You wouldn't be Howard, would you?"

You say "yep. got here!"

Spark says "All right!"

Spark says "Wait a sec"

You say "Now what?"

Your wrist communicator quietly announces "Take a flight on a Dragon to the fabled planet of Pernth, home of the DragonRiders of Pern! Dragon flights depart from Section 0—Arc 7 in the Teleportation and Transportation Center. Go there and 'beckon dragon' for a free discovery flight to Pernth."

Spark says "I think Aslan would like to say hi, and he said he has to leave soon."

Aslan has arrived.

While you're not looking, Aslan appears.

Spark says "Would you like to say hello?"

Spark says "Darn wizards:)"

Aslan says "Hello, Howard. Nice to meet you!"

You say "Hello!"

Guest5 has arrived.

Guest5 leaves the Main Transporter Facility.

Guest5 has left.

Aslan says "Perhaps you would prefer a character with a name other than Guest1?"

You say "I gotta think about that. Name is a big thing. Right now, I'm trying to figure out where I am.;-)"

Aslan says "Okay:)"

Aslan says "Well, I need to run. Glad you could make it, and Spark will show you around, I guess."

You say "See you later."

Spark says "I'd recommend staying a guest for a

```
bit. For one thing, you're wearing a sign that says
"Be courteous, I'm a guest" "
Aslan waves.
Spark says "Bye!"
While you're not looking, Aslan disappears.
Aslan goes home.
Aslan has left.
Spark waves
You say "What do you mean, "Spark waves?" How do
you do that"?
Spark says "If you type a colon instead of a
quote, like in that case ":waves," we all see your
character adopt that pose.
:waves
Guest1 waves.
```

In the snippet of a MicroMUSE session quoted above, you see that the computer announces whenever someone enters the same space you occupy. Whenever anyone enters or leaves a space, a message is sent to the screen of everyone whose character is in that space. So it matters who is in the place you do your talking, and that means you have to look around and see who is there. Since Cyberion City and the MicroMUSE planets beyond it consist of many hundreds of interconnected spaces, you can find both highly populated areas (like the main arrival area) or private areas (like citizens' homes).

When people enter or leave or talk or emote, everyone in the same room knows it. Or if a magical object in the room or the room itself has been programmed to react to certain words or behaviors, everybody in the same room knows it. The public announcement that broke into my conversation with Spark was on the public channel, a kind of systemwide CB. A number of channels are available, and anyone can create private channels for themselves and their friends or work groups. You can turn channels on and off, and you can create private places where you can be sure a conversation isn't overheard—unless a wizard is "snooping" on you.

It took me hours of wandering around Cyberion City to get an idea of the scope of the place. As a new citizen, Pollenator, my character, was granted enough credits to buy a dwelling in one of the housing districts. Moulton, who seemed to be one of the wizzes in charge (except here they call them citizens, builders, and administrators instead of newbies, wizzes, and gods), showed me how to issue the commands that would create ("dig") a few rooms for me to entertain guests and work on projects. There is a set of self-paced tutorials in Cyberion City University, and an online glossary of commands, but the way you learn, everybody tells you, is by asking others. The metaphor of this MUD is a learning colony, where everyone teaches everyone else. Cyberion City's charter warns you when you enter that there are children there and educators and librarians and people having fun, and anybody who abuses the rules of polite communication is likely to have his or her character removed. After the rough-and-tumble of the WELL or Usenet or a serious adventure-style MUD, it's an altogether different feeling trying to find your way around a new place where the locals all seem to go out of their way to show you around.

While I was looking around and making myself at home, I met a few other characters. One friend I've never met in the material world is Eri, a librarian from North Carolina who has a wicked sense of humor: a sign on the floor of Eri's dwelling in Cyberion City says "Caution, black hole." If you make the mistake of looking in the black hole, you fall into the basement, where you discover that the look command only gets you the message "The basement is dark." Then you try a bunch of commands, and you get the message "Say the magic word." And if you say "shazam" or "abracadabra," you get the message "Say the magic word your mommy taught you." When you say "Please," Eri's black hole lets you back into her living room.

Moulton taught me how to make objects with MUSE code—an enterprise that is frustratingly arcane to a nonprogrammer like me. Teenage kids looking for something to do with their curious minds seem to find MUSE code hypnotically fascinating. One of the great rewards in a social MUD comes from creating a tool or a toy or a little astonishment that others want to adopt or buy or copy. If you are female-presenting, male wizards sometimes give you power objects that can be very useful in getting from place to place or shielding yourself from some kinds of attack.

While he showed me how to become one of the world-builders of Cyberion City, I asked Moulton how he got into the MUSE business.

Moulton, also known as Barry Kort, had a twenty-year career as a network planner for Bell Laboratories, NASA's space station, and MITRE, a top software think tank. In the late 1980s, Kort felt compelled to do something about the state of the world. He decided to concentrate on education, an area where he thought his expertise might help. Science education, in particular, is something our society needs badly and is sadly lacking. He knew that high-capacity networking technology, together with a means of making computer models and simulations, had a tremendous and almost totally unrealized educational potential. He stumbled onto the MUDs and became convinced that he could transform the MUD technology into something with greater social value than just a hack-and-slash game. At one of these MUDs he met Stan Lim, at the time a senior at California State University accomplished in systems design. They started planning a new kind of MUD.

Kort retired as a network planner several years ago. He devotes part of his time as a volunteer at Boston's Computer Museum and the rest of his time to building MicroMUSE, the computer universe in which Cyberion City is growing (along with other planets and colonies). He has the use of some computing hardware and Internet connections at MIT's Artificial Intelligence laboratory, and an office at the Cambridge computer consulting firm of Bolt, Beranek, and Newman—where the first computer networks were born twenty years ago.

Kort's self-study of educational theory led him to the work of the Swiss educational psychologist Jean Piaget, who spent decades directly observing how children play. That people spend so many hours of their lives in MUDs, often neglecting their other duties, was, to Kort, evidence of the power locked into the medium—just look at the trouble people take to learn the esoteric MUD codes. Piaget said that children seem to learn about the world by exploring it and playing with it—that play is a powerful form of learning—and that by shaping the way the environment invites discovery, people can design some of this power into traditional curricula. Piagetians believe that children can gain more understanding in faster time out of the same material if it is presented as a world to explore rather than as a package of information to be learned by rote.

"I knew that if we could create a suitable play space," Kort told me during one of our world-building sessions, "children would learn at remarkable rates, and they would learn a wide range of skills and subject matter." Kort was also interested in community-building. Education could also be the focus of an online intentional community.

Kort and Lim modeled the organizational charter of MicroMUSE, the simulation environment in which Cyberion City exists, on Children's Television Workshop—as a nonprofit, noncommercial enterprise dedicated to harnessing the inherent educational power of networks. The charter—required reading for prospective citizens—sets forth a democratic but definite standard of behavior, and the personal commitment the MicroMUSE architects brought into the venture set the tone for the new kind of MUD. Instead of battlefields, there is a science museum where kids can play with computer simulations that teach scientific principles, a tutored or self-tutored curriculum in MUSEcode at the university, playgrounds, magical kingdoms, even spaceports where you can embark on spacecraft bound for other planets in the MUSE.

Cyberion City and the larger MicroMUSE universe grew to more than two thousand registered citizens from all over the world. Citizens are free without restriction to build one hundred objects. If they want to build more, they are asked to build something of public value. The science center, museum, university, shopping mall, entertainment section, rain forest, Yellowstone Park, and planetarium were built by citizens who became Builders.

The traditional, or adventure, MUDs in their many forms all depend on a structured game in which a fixed number of "experience" points gain initiation to higher levels of power and prestige. In the bloodiest of the worlds spawned by MUD1 from University of Essex and its descendants, beheading new, inexperienced players as a way of gaining experience points is frowned on but not outlawed. In some worlds, nothing is frowned on. It can be like participating in a roll-your-own slasher movie.

If MUDs were nothing more than a way of participating in vicarious violence and other antisocial behavior, the question of how to deal with them on campuses and tax-supported networks would be easier to answer. But the evolution of MUDs began to branch when people began exploring less lurid modes of interaction using the same technology. The genre of social MUDs, where there might or might not be hierarchies of power but where there are no fixed goals or point systems, and murder is not possible, emerged when James Aspnes of Carnegie-Mellon

University created TinyMUD in 1988. It spawned a variety of different worlds and new MUD languages based on egalitarian and nonviolent values. When every citizen, not just wizards, gained the power to build the game, and there was no longer a gain in killing or stealing, a new variety of MUD enthusiast emerged.

In response to a question from Amy Bruckman about where these ideals came from—deliberate design on his part, or from the members of the first TinyMUD community?—Aspnes offered a revealing reply:

Most adventure-style games and earlier MUDs had some sort of scoring system which translated into rank and often special privileges; I didn't want such a system not because of any strong egalitarian ideals (although I think that there are good egalitarian arguments against it) but because I wanted the game to be open-ended, and any scoring system would have the problem that eventually each player would hit the maximum rank or level of advancement and have to either abandon the game as finished or come up with new reasons to play it. This approach attracted people who liked everybody being equal and drove away people who didn't like a game where you didn't score points and beat out other players (I did put in a "score" command early on since almost everybody tried it, but most players soon realized that it was a joke). I think that this effect created a kind of natural selection which eventually led to the current egalitarian ideals. I like the egalitarianism, but it wasn't my original goal.

Bruckman treated Aspnes's reply as "a confirmation of Langdon Winner's assertion that artifacts have politics. The change in the software encouraged different styles of interaction, and attracted a different type of person. The ethics of the community *emerged*. The design of the software was a strong factor in shaping what emerged."

Richard Bartle doesn't have a lot to say about the use of MUDs as social tools, but he has strong opinions about MUDs as games. In conversation with the author, he emphasized repeatedly that the real juice of MUDding as he first conceived it is removed if you remove the possibility that a character will die. People might use it as a social toy or a theatrical device, but in Bartle's opinion, it isn't a game if you can't die. The evolution of MUDs forked into two paths over the issue, and each fork—the adventure and the social varieties of MUD—can be expected to develop further.

* * *

When you are not just communicating, but building virtual objects in virtual buildings in virtual kingdoms, you are also taking up much more space in a computer database. MUDs bring two things to the computers that host them—increased telecommunications traffic from everywhere and increased use of computer memory. One of the most famous of the nonviolent MUDs, Islandia, a TinyMUD at the University of California at Berkeley, grew to more than 3,000 players, of which more than 1,500 were active, and the database had expanded to 14,900 rooms. The combination of the potential for addiction and the drain on local computer system resources led to a ban on MUDding at Amherst University in 1992. The increase in telecommunications traffic was the official reason for the Australian ban on MUDS. The Australian regional network that connects to Internet must use a satellite to move information to backbone sites on other continents; NASA, which pays half the bill, asked the Australian network to find ways to cut back on the growth of traffic. MUDs were an extremely low priority on the network administration's list of "acceptable uses" for Internet.

The prevalence of gender play in MUDs is one factor that leads more traditionally minded authorities to discourage MUDding on campus computers. Gender deception and the presence of impostors is nothing new in cyberspace. Richard Bartle told me the tale of "Sue," who had captivated so many minds and hearts in the first MUD, in the early 1980s:

Sue lived in South Wales, which is some distance away from the rest of the MUD-playing community, long phone calls away. And Sue got all the way up to game administrator level, "Arch Witch." She used to write letters to everybody, great long old-fashioned letters on paper. She enclosed photographs. She's quite good-looking. As far as we were concerned, Sue was a female. One of our other wizzes fell quite heavily in love with Sue and sent photographs and gifts and so on, flowers, and he even proposed marriage. Then Sue started behaving out of character. And all of a sudden Sue said she was going to Sweden to be an au pair and that was that. We never heard any more, so we thought something seemed suspicious here.

So a group of the wizzies put together facts from Sue's letters, like her father ran some kind of a factory and you know she lives in South Wales and we've got the address that we write to, and went around—I wasn't there—but they went around to see Sue, knocked on the door, this woman opens the door. "Hello, we've come to see Sue." The woman says, "I think you better come in. Unfortunately, Sue's name is Steve and he's been arrested for defrauding the Department of Transport. He's presently in prison. I'm his wife."

The possibility of an electronic impostor invading people's most intimate lives is inherent in the technology. More than a few people out there want to be impostors. If you count the *messageries rose* in Paris, along with the electronic chat services and BBS worldwide, the population of online gender-switchers numbers in the hundreds of thousands. A very few can carry their deceptions far enough to turn an entire virtual community inside out.

"The Strange Case of the Electronic Lover," by Lindsy Van Gelder, a cautionary tale for all who venture into virtual communities, was published in Ms. magazine in October 1985—when the WELL was six months old.

Van Gelder had been exploring the worlds of online communications, and happened upon the CB channel on CompuServe. CompuServe is a national commercial information service that provides access to electronic mail, conferences, and a chat service modeled on the audio citizens' band radio channels of the 1970s. In 1985, CompuServe already had more than one hundred thousand subscribers—at prices three to five times higher than what the WELL was charging. One CB regular Van Gelder met, Joan, was a celebrity on CompuServe. After Van Gelder encountered Joan in a wide-open, public chat session, she engaged her in private chat. She learned that Joan was a neuropsychologist, in her late twenties, living in New York, who had been disfigured, crippled, and left mute by an automobile accident at the hands of a drunken driver. Joan's mentor had given her a computer, modem, and subscription to CompuServe, where Joan instantly blossomed.

Not only was Joan a source of wit and warmth to the hundreds of people who participated in CompuServe CB in the late 1980s, Van Gelder reported, quoting many of Joan's friends, she had a kind of online charisma. Joan connected with people in a special way, achieved intimacy rapidly, and gave much valuable advice and support to many others, especially disabled women. She changed people's lives. So it was a shock to the CB community when Joan was unmasked as someone who in real life, IRL, was neither disabled, disfigured, mute, nor female. Joan was a New York psychiatrist, Alex, who had become obsessed with his own experiments in being treated as a female and participating in female friendships.

The sense of outrage that followed the revelation of Joan's identity came first from the direct assault on personal relationships between Joan and others, friendships that had achieved deep intimacy based on utter deception. But the indirect assault on the sense of trust essential to any group that thinks of itself as a community, was another betrayal. Van Gelder put it this way: "Even those who barely knew Joan felt implicated—and somehow betrayed—by Alex's deception. Many of us online believe that we're a utopian community of the future, and Alex's experiment proved to us all that technology is no shield against deceit. We lost our innocence, if not our faith." Van Gelder quoted another woman, one of Joan's best friends, who agreed to the interview only because "although I think this is a wonderful medium, it's a dangerous one, and it poses more danger to women than men. Men in this society are more predisposed to pulling these kinds of con games, and women are predisposed to giving people the benefit of the doubt."

Personally, I think the fundamental understanding that CMC is "no shield against deceit" is a necessary immunization for the larger, uninitiated populations who are homesteading cyberspace today. The presence of skilled imposters in every virtual community is information that must disseminate formally and informally before the online population can develop a collective immune system to identity predation. People who join virtual communities today are rarely given any set of formal rules for the finer points of online relationships—like the possibility of identity deception. The best response from the online world would be to formulate norms and spread them around so that newcomers can be aware of the darker possibilities of making friends you can't see.

Although the technology of CMC provides the instrument of deception, the special importance we place on gender roles and the prevalence of swindlers in a population are both rooted in social questions that extend far beyond the technology that brings them into focus. The opportunity for deception, however, is designed into the medium. Cyberspace explorers ignore that fact at their peril.

Nearly a decade has passed since Van Gelder's article, and more than a decade has passed since Sue of MUD1, and gender deception occurs often enough in MUDS that female-presenting characters usually are assumed to be lying until they can prove otherwise. Pavel Curtis made his own educated guess, in a 1992 paper, about the reasons for the persistence of gender-switching in MUDS:

It appears that the great majority of players are male and the vast majority of them choose to present themselves as such. Some males, however, taking advantages of the relative rarity of females in MUDs, present themselves as female and thus stand out to some degree. Some use this distinction just for the fun of deceiving others, some of these going so far as to try to entice male-presenting players into sexually-explicit discussions and interactions. This is such a widely-noticed phenomenon, in fact, that one is advised by the common wisdom to assume that any flirtatious female-presenting players are, in real life, males. Such players are often subject to ostracism based on this assumption.

Some MUD players have suggested to me that such transvestite flirts are perhaps acting out their own (latent or otherwise) homosexual urges or fantasies, taking advantage of the perfect safety of the MUD situation to see how it feels to approach other men. While I have had no personal experience talking to such players, let alone the opportunity to delve into their motivations, the idea strikes me as plausible given the other ways in which MUD anonymity seems to free people from their inhibitions.

Other males present themselves as female more out of curiosity than as an attempt at deception; to some degree, they are interested in seeing "how the other half lives," what it feels like to be perceived as female in a community. From what I can tell, they can be quite successful at this.

Female-presenting players have told me that they are frequently subject both to harassment and to special treatment. One reported seeing two newcomers arrive at the same time, one male-presenting and one femalepresenting. The other players in the room struck up conversations with the putative female and offered to show her around but completely ignored the putative male, who was left to his own devices. In addition, probably due mostly to the number of female-presenting males one hears about, many female players report that they are frequently (and sometimes quite aggressively) challenged to "prove" that they are, in fact, female. To the best of my knowledge, male-presenting players are rarely if ever so challenged.

True-life romances, sometimes at the intercontinental level, are no rarity in MUDding circles. Even online marriages, with or without corresponding corporeal ceremonies, are nothing new. There are people in different parts of the world who are married to each other today because they met and fell in love in a MUD before they met face-to-face. The technology that can serve to deceive can also serve to connect.

Why do people pretend they are characters in a television program? Perhaps the most well known "fan culture" in the material world is the international, intergenerational cult of Star Trek enthusiasts—"trekkies." They have newsletters and fanzines and conventions. They were even mocked on "Saturday Night Live" when William Shatner, the actor who played Captain Kirk of the original *Starship Enterprise*, told an audience of Trekkies at a fictional convention to "get a life."

One honest answer to the question "Don't these people have lives?" is that most people don't have a terribly glamorous life. They work, they subsist, they are lonely or afraid or shy or unattractive or feel that they are unattractive. Or they are simply different. The phenomenon of fandom is evidence that not everyone can have a life as "having a life" is defined by the mainstream, and some people just go out and try to build an alternate life. In the Deadhead freemasonry, this failure to conform to normal cultural expectations is embraced in a similar way as "misfit power." By what criteria does one judge whether a fan culture is constructive community-building or pathological escapism, and who does the judging? These questions are the subject of lively debate among students of a discipline known as reader-response theory.

Amy Bruckman pointed me to the phenomenon of fan culture when I was looking for reasons that so many people are attracted to MUDding, some of them obsessively so. In her master's thesis, "Identity Workshops," Bruckman cites the work of Henry Jenkins, a student of fan culture, as one key to understanding hard-core MUD culture and its appeal today:

Why are these fictional worlds so popular? Fans of *Star Trek* attend conventions, write stories and novels, make videos, and write folk songs about the *Star Trek* world. In *Textual Poachers, Television Fans and Participatory Culture*, Henry Jenkins analyzes fan culture with an emphasis on fan reading and writing practices. Like MUDs, the world of fandom is an alternative reality that many participants find more compelling than their mundane lives. The conclusion of *Textual Poachers* is called "'In My Weekend-Only World...': Reconsidering Fandom," and begins with this epigraph from a fan writer:

In these warm convention halls
In an hour of make-believe
In these warm convention halls
My mind is free to think
And feels so deeply
An intimacy never found
Inside their silent walls
In a year or more
Of what they call reality.
In my weekend-only world,
That they call make-believe,
Are those who share
The visions that I see.
In their real-time life
That they tell me is real,
The things they care about
Aren't real to me.

Jenkins writes about the fan folk song "Weekend-Only World" that it "expresses the fans' recognition that fandom offers not so much an escape from reality as an alternative reality whose values may be more humane and democratic than those held by mundane society." The author of the song "gains power and identity from the time she spends within fan culture; fandom allows her to maintain her sanity in the face of the indignity and alienation of everyday life."

"Jenkins' claims here are strong," Bruckman points out, "and I do not know whether they are true for fandom or whether they translate to the world of MUDding. However, it is important to recognize that when one makes statements about what is a constructive use of another person's time, one is making a value judgment. Such judgments often masquerade as 'taste,' and their political and ethical nature can be obscured." Another way of saying this is that many of the highbrows of Elizabethan England would have died laughing if they knew that vulgar, nerdy Shakespeare would be remembered as great literature centuries later; who is to say MUDs and other alien suburbs of fandom are not as legitimate as Elizabethan theater? We remember Shakespeare because of the quality of his insight and his use of English, not because his contemporaries considered him to be a "great artist" or "in good taste."

Another social commentator, looking more broadly at the way communication technologies have been changing human psychology, uses the term "technologies of social saturation" as a kind of media-driven change in the pace of our interpersonal lives. Kenneth J. Gergen, in *The Saturated Self: Dilemmas of Identity in Contemporary Life*, makes a case that modern communication media expose the average person to the "opinions, values, and lifestyles of others." It is self-evident that many of us communicate with many more people every day, via telephone, fax, and e-mail, than our great-grandparents communicated with in a month, year, or lifetime. According to Gergen, social saturation is an effect of internalizing parts of more people than any humans have ever internalized before. Our selves have become "populated" by many others, Gergen claims.

I didn't know whether Kenneth Gergen ever heard of MUDs, but one passage he wrote stood out as another clue to what MUDs might be reflecting about changes in human personality:

In the process of social saturation the numbers, varieties, and intensities of relationship increasingly crowd the days. A full appreciation of the magnitude of cultural change, and its probable intensification in future decades, requires that one focus first on the technological context. For in large measure, an array of techno-logical innovations has led us to an enormous proliferation of relationships. . . .

In an important sense, as social saturation proceeds we become pastiches, imitative assemblages of each other. In memory we carry others' patterns of being with us. If the conditions are favorable, we can place these patterns into action. Each of us becomes the other, a representative, or a replacement. To put it more broadly, as the century has progressed selves have become increasingly populated with the character of others. We are not one, or a few, but like Walt Whitman, we "contain multitudes." We appear to each other as single identities, unified, of whole cloth. However, with social saturation, each of us comes to harbor a vast population of hidden potentials— to be a blues singer, a gypsy, an aristocrat, a criminal. All the selves lie latent, and under the right conditions may spring to life.

In MUDs, those latent selves are liberated by technology. And boy, do they "spring to life."

Extrapolating the future of MUDs from today's applications of the technology is hazardous business because the medium is in such creative flux. The social and adventure MUDs are the ancestor species. Nobody can predict what variations and mutations of this technology will emerge downstream a few generations hence.

In the summer of 1992, Xerox PARC, where Pavel Curtis initiated the LambdaMOO experiment, began the Jupiter project—a multimedia, eventually intercontinental MUD, meant to be a working tool for designers of virtual workplaces of the future.

Curtis is currently involved in adapting the LambdaMOO server for use as an international teleconferencing and image database system for astronomers. This would enable scientists to give online presentations to their colleagues around the world, complete with slides and illustrations automatically displayed on the participants' workstations. "The same approach could be used to create on-line meeting places for workers in other disciplines, as well as for other non-scientific communities," wrote Curtis. "I do not believe that we are the only researchers planning such facilities. In the near future (a few years at most), I expect such specialized virtual realities to be commonplace, an accepted part of at least the academic community."

Another idea guiding research at PARC is to use virtual reality to help break down the geographical barriers of a large building, of people increasingly working from their homes, by adding digital voice to MUDs. When two people are in the same virtual room, their audio channels are connected.

Xerox PARC, where personal computers and local networks were invented in the 1970s, has a sister research facility in Cambridge, England, that fits into this grand scheme for a future virtual multimedia office linking Xerox researchers worldwide. When I visited EuroPARC in Cambridge in 1992, I got a taste of what it's like to extend the networld into the video range. My guide for the day, Paul Dourish, a computer scientist from Scotland, is a Deadhead Nethead, so we had two overlapping freemasonries to chat about while I acclimated myself to what was happening. In his office, Paul sat in front of a large screen, with several windows open to documents and to the Net. And to his left of that large screen was another screen, only slightly smaller, that showed a video image. At the moment we came in, it showed the image of the laboratory's common room, one floor below ours. Above the video monitor was a camera lens.

About a minute into my conversation with Dourish, we heard a squeaking sound, like a very old wooden door creaking open. He explained that it was the most commonly used of a number of sounds EuroPARC researchers had available to signal that somebody was peeking at them.

"It's important to put something as invasive as a video technology in your office under social control," Dourish explained, calling up a menu of communications options on his computer display. I saw a list of people. There were little checks next to some of the names.

"I can select, from the roster of people who have technical access, which people I give permission to peek at me," Dourish continued. "Peeking" means that the authorized person can look into your office, with your permission, at will, for a two-second glance. It's the equivalent of peeking into your open office door to see if you are occupied or open for conversation. He showed me the menu where he chose the squeaky door as a means of reminding him that somebody was peeking. And he showed me the ultimate social control of the technology on the corner of his desk—a lens cap.

The next time the camera squeaked at us, Dourish looked over at the monitor below the camera and started talking to it. The scene on his video monitor switched from a long shot of the common room to a close-up of a young woman. They talked about a document they were working on. While they talked, they also looked at the document on their computer screens. Paul introduced me. I looked at the video camera and smiled and said hello. I could see her face as I was talking to her. Their conversation about a certain paragraph in their document took about thirty seconds. Then they signed off and Paul turned back to me. The scene on his video monitor went back to the common room.

Every ten minutes, there was another sound, a clicking sound like a camera shutter. That was the slo-scan camera that transmitted a still image across the Atlantic Ocean and the North American continent to the sister Xerox laboratory in Palo Alto. These still images were the first stage in what would ultimately be a full video link.

The idea of the common room changes when you know who is in there. One premise behind going to the trouble of adding a video channel to group communication is that it can stimulate the kind of informal, serendipitous conversation that takes place in the hallway or at the coffee machine, but in such a way that the informal space extends to wherever your colleagues are located. In a sense, they are trying to synthesize what sociologist Ray Oldenburg calls "informal public spaces." Another recent Xerox experiment linked a wall-sized monitor in a common room in the Palo Alto laboratory with a common room in a sister laboratory in Oregon. People in Oregon could walk down the hall in the material world, notice on the monitor that you are in the California half of the common room, and engage you in conversation.

I didn't see the video wall experiment, but computer pundit John Barlow saw a demonstration. We are both interested in the possibility of adding video to computer conferencing. Part of that ontological untrustworthiness of cyberspace is the lack of body language and facial expression. Misunderstandings that tangle group communications and sour personal relationships online might be avoided if you could add a raised eyebrow or a playful tone of voice to the online vocabulary. Barlow told me that he found himself somewhat disappointed in that hope. Something seemed missing. Barlow told the computer scientist who was giving him the demonstration about his disappointment. The researcher, a native of India, smiled and told him that what the video does not transmit is "the prana," the life force, literally the breath of the other people. Judging from the way other group communication media have proved to be double-edged, it would be prudent to assume that adding video to CMC will bring both advantages and disadvantages when trying to achieve communication among groups of people.

The idea of Project Jupiter that grew out of the multimedia MUD Curtis described is a common space where you can extend your informal space, with voice, text, and video all mixed together in a virtual office space; the MUD structure gives the different communication channels coherence in the form of an architectural metaphor. With the ability to build your own spaces within the MUD, it is possible to create "rooms" specifically for certain projects; you can keep reference materials there, communicate with colleagues on a virtual whiteboard, drop in for informal chats. You can move your character around a map of the MUD space, and make real-life voice contact with anyone in the same virtual space, while retaining the ability to put words and graphics up on the common MUD room space. PARC researchers are attempting to accomplish several goals with this project. At the same time, they are designing a mental model of cyberspace, experimenting with ways to use cyberspace as an augmentation of a material office, as well as mixing several different media together, and using these tools as they build them, in the bootstrapped research tradition, in their own daily work.

The first multimedia MUDs are beginning to appear. The first ones I heard about, in Scandinavia, require a powerful graphics workstation and a high-speed connection to Internet. Now you can steer your character through a visual model of a dungeon or a space colony, or even create your own visible worlds and share them with other participants. The advent of multimedia MUDding is too recent to have a significant body of observations to evaluate. Now people who can express themselves visually, using computer tools for manipulating graphic language, can add a new element to the worlds that were formerly limited to text. Text-only worlds will continue to thrive, considering how much easier it is to construct an entire civilization with words than with graphics, but it remains to be seen whether multimedia MUDs will thrive as a medium in their own right.

Amy Bruckman, after finishing her "Identity Workshops" research, extended her professional exploration of the MUD medium by creating, with colleagues at MIT's Media Lab, MediaMOO, yet another kind of serious-communication MUD. Bruckman noticed another area in her life where a communications medium with some MUD characteristics could serve a serious purpose, yet retain the fun and informality of a MUD—

the virtual communities that exist around special areas of interest or professional disciplines. Scientists or scholars or specialists from the private sector meet for face-to-face conferences and conventions once or twice a year, read the same journals and electronic journals, and correspond with one another, but there is a lack of daily, informal continuity to these communities of interest that span continents. Why not design a MUD to continue the kind of informal conversation that makes conferences so important to scientific communication? The "professional virtual community" that Bruckman and colleague Mitchel Resnick had in mind was the community of people like themselves—media researchers.

MediaMOO was announced in 1993. In the abstract for an oral presentation, Bruckman and Resnick spoke of the relationship between the MUD design and the social goals of the project:

MediaMOO is a virtual version of MIT's Media Laboratory.... The developers have deliberately chosen not to build the entire Media Lab, but to construct just the public corridors, stairwells, elevators, and a few interesting public places. It is up to the community of users to create the rest. This is not a practical limitation, but a deliberate design decision. The act of collaborating on building a shared world creates a basis for interaction and community.

Visitors to a conference share not just a set of interests, but also a place and a set of activities. Interaction is generated as much by the latter two as the former:

Person A: Can you tell me how to get to Ballroom A?
Person B: I'm headed that way now. It's up this way.
Person A: Thanks!
Person B: I see you're at Company X....
Person C: Is this seat taken?
Person D: No, it isn't.
Person C: I'm surprised the room is so packed.
Person D: Well, Y is a really good speaker....

A text-based virtual environment can provide both a shared place (the virtual world), and a shared set of activities (exploring and extending the virtual world). Like at a coffee break at a conference, there is a social convention that it is appropriate to strike up a conversation with strangers simply based on their name tags. In most MU*s, characters are anonymous; there is no way to match the real world person to the virtual one. On MediaMOO, a character can either be anonymous or reliably identified with the person's real world name. Additionally, users are encouraged to wear a description of their research interests. More information is provided than a name tag, and it is provided more discreetly—the person is not notified that you looked at their research interests, and you are therefore free to decide whether or not to use that information as a basis to strike up a conversation.

The architects of MediaMOO decided to have an inaugural ball on inauguration evening, January 20, 1993. A week before, at Amy Bruckman's invitation, I showed up early and designed a few of the men's costumes for the festivities. First, I had to learn my way to the wardrobe off the main ballroom, which was located two floors above the roof of the real-life Media Lab. In places, the topology of MediaMoo replicates the real hallways of the material Media Lab building, and in places, like the ballroom, MediaMOO just builds its own cyberspace extension. Once I learned the path to the ballroom, Amy showed me the incantation I would need to create costumes. Each costume thus created could be added to the rack. When sixty-seven MediaMOO inaugural ball participants attended from five countries, they were invited to go to the wardrobe, give the "search" command, and wear one of the costumes. I was one of several costume designers, contributing a green on orange double-breasted paisley dinner jacket, a minimicro velcro tuxedo, and a loincloth of many colors.

Besides my costume, others who attended the ball could see my real name, the fact that I am writing about virtual communities, and my home e-mail address. Although it opened with a party, and the atmosphere is informal, MediaMOO consists of people who are studying virtual communities. In that context, meeting someone "socially" at an event like an inaugural ball has implications for everyone's intellectual and professional life.

Whenever people find something in a new communication medium so attractive that it becomes the focus of obsessive behavior, several questions arise: What is it about the way people are today, and the way we interact, that leaves so many people vulnerable to communication addiction? What responsibility do institutions such as universities have to regulate the online behavior of obsessive users, and what rights do students have to protect them from invasion of privacy? By what criteria should obsessive use be determined? I do not know the answers to questions about the value of MUDding, but I do know that the questions are broad ones, addressing key ambivalences that people have about personal identity and interpersonal relationships in the information age.

6

Real-time Tribes

Thousands of people in Australia, Austria, Canada, Denmark, Finland, France, Germany, Israel, Italy, Japan, Korea, Mexico, the Netherlands, New Zealand, Norway, Spain, Sweden, Switzerland, the United Kingdom, and the United States are joined together at this moment in a cross-cultural grab bag of written conversations known as Internet Relay Chat (IRC). IRC has enabled a global subculture to construct itself from three fundamental elements: artificial but stable identities, quick wit, and the use of words to construct an imagined shared context for conversation. For a student of virtual communities, IRC is an opportunity to observe a critical experiment-in-progress: What are the minimum elements of communication necessary for a group of people to cocreate a sense of community? What kinds of cultures emerge when you remove from human discourse all cultural artifacts except written words?

An artificial but stable identity means that you can never be certain about the flesh- person behind an IRC nickname, but you can be reasonably certain that the person you communicate with today under a specific nickname is the same one who used that nickname yesterday. There's nothing to stop anybody from getting a new nickname and creating a new identity, but both the old and the new nicknames have to be unique. The stability of nicknames is one of the few formally structured social requirements in IRCland; an automatic "Nickserv" program ensures that nobody can use a nickname ("nick") that has been registered by someone else. Quick wit is necessary because rapidity of response becomes important in this written medium in the same way it is important in face-to-face conversation. IRC is a dynamic form of communication: new comments appear at the bottom of your screen as you watch, and older comments scroll off the top of your screen. Somewhere in the world, a human being has typed those words on a keyboard, no more than a couple seconds ago; if you know the right words to say in response, you can leap into the conversation and make that person and others around the world laugh out loud, grow angry, feel lustful.

Perhaps one attraction of IRC is that the conversation literally continues to move up your screen as you watch. You can treat IRC as a spectator sport, never venturing into the flow. Or you can show the IRC tribe how fast you are with a well-worded rejoinder by keeping up with other participants in a rapid interweaving of cleverly linked comments. IRC is a stream. Many people who work for long hours in front of computer workstations—college students, computer programmers—leave a small "window" on their computer screens tuned in to IRC while they go about their day's work. They have their own automated programs, known as bots, to greet newcomers and say goodbye to people who leave. When they see something interesting going on, from the corner of their eye, they jump in.

The initial absence and subsequent reconstruction of social context is the third fundamental element that IRC enthusiasts use to build their subculture. Without facial expressions, tone of voice, body language, clothing, shared physical environment, or any other contextual cues that signal the physical presence of participants in a social group, IRC participants use words alone to reconstruct contexts in their own image, adding imagined actions (such as "Howard smiles ironically" or "Howard takes offense and it looks like he's going to punch you in the nose") as metadescriptions to the running dialogue. These virtual actions are typographically set apart from words meant as straight dialogue. The "actions" in IRCland are the same as "poses" or "emoting" in MUDs, and serve a similar purpose. They add a modifier to the strict definitions of words, indicating intention, mood, or other contextual cues.

Those thousands of people tuned into IRC at any one time are divided into hundreds of "channels" that Internet users can "join" or "leave" at any time; like Usenet newsgroups, the channels operating at any one time include a rich variety of topics, from the scholarly to the obscene. Farflung business groups, task forces of technical experts, and scholars also use IRC to do real work. I have participated in IRC discussions of electronic publishing, organized by the participants in an electronic mailing list who wanted to add a real-time dimension to our collegial relationship. This variation of CMC wasn't invented specifically for real work, however. IRC was invented as a means of playing with communication, and that remains its most popular use.

IRC is what you get when you strip away everything that normally allows people to understand the unspoken shared assumptions that surround and support their communications, and thus render invisible most of the web of socially mediated definitions that tells us what words and behaviors are supposed to mean in our societies. You can't see people when you are computer-chatting with them; you can't even ascertain their true identities, and you are unlikely ever to run into them on the material plane or recognize them if you do. Chat systems lack the community memory of a BBS or conferencing system or MUD, where there is some record of what was said or done in your absence. Although words are written and broadcast (and thus can be electronically captured, duplicated, and redistributed by others), they aren't formally stored by the chat system. The discourse is ephemeral.

Despite the anonymity and ephemeral nature of their communications, IRC habituees become addicted, form close friendships, fall in love. There is even a Usenet newsgroup—alt.irc.recovery—for IRC addicts and former addicts to testify, support, and debate each other. You sense, even from a brief visit to IRCland, that many of these people have built a kind of community that they would defend as passionately as the most committed WELLite, habitual mailing-list participant, Usenet veteran, or accomplished MUDder.

Chat systems that enable one person to send typed words directly to the screen of another person who is logged onto the same system date back to the first time-sharing computers of the 1960s. In this regard, they are probably the oldest form of CMC, predating electronic mail. By storing electronic messages in a private computer mailbox until the recipient logs in and reads it, electronic mail differentiated itself from existing chat programs that required both participants to be logged into the computer at the same time. But the need for a kind of direct conversational form of CMC continued to flourish as asynchronous many-to-many written media emerged. The CB service on CompuServe is probably the oldest, continuously operating, commercial chat service in the world. Minitel's messageries in France are into their second decade of a wildly popular, national, government-supported, written-word chat system. Fujitsu's

Habitat combines a cartoonland graphical representation of participants and their environment with a synchronous chat system. IRC is Internet's pioneering multi-user chat system. IRC is the corner pub, the caf,, the common room—the "great good place" of the Net.

Most computers connected to Internet run a program called "talk" that enables people on different host computers to communicate screen-to-screen simultaneously. If I suspect that a person I know is online at a different site, I can issue a chat request through Internet. If that person is logged in, even if the computer is on the other side of the world, my chat request will go directly to the recipient's screen for immediate attention (rather than going to an e-mailbox for later attention). If the recipient agrees to chat, we can communicate by typing to each other's screens in real time. I see my words on the bottom half of the screen, and the other person's words on the top. It's the only conversational medium in which both participants can talk and listen simultaneously, which can be liberating for typographically loquacious types who are likely to be found online. But "talk" involves only one-to-one communication.

In 1988, Jarkko Oikarinen at the University of Oulu, Finland, wrote the original IRC program, a multi-user, synchronous communications tool designed to work over Internet. First it was tested on a local community of twenty users and then installed throughout the Finnish national network and ultimately the Scandinavian portion of Internet. IRC—the software needed to access the medium, as well as word of its attractions—propagated throughout the wider Internet by the end of 1988. By the early 1990s, there were hundreds of channels and thousands of people chatting across the Net, twenty-four hours a day. Eventually, scientists and scholars began to get the word that IRC was a way to convene informal discussions among geographically distant colleagues, but the continuing popularity of IRC appears to be primarily a function of its appeal as a psychological and intellectual playground.

Why should taxpayers support anyone's playground? It's a good question, and it goes to the heart of the current debate over privatization of the Net. It pays to keep in mind a bit of history when addressing this question, however, because playgrounds have played a critically important role in the evolution of computer technology. The very earliest creators of interactive computing also created the enormously popular Spacewar game in the early 1960s, which turned expensive research computers into powerful versions of what would come to be known in the 1970s as video games. At top computer science research centers, the very people who were supposed to be creating the next generation of computer technology were staying up late to blast each other with proton torpedoes on primitive graphic display screens. Note that most attempts to eliminate Spacewar from computer centers failed. When administrators shut down Spacewar activities at their centers, they found that programmer productivity went down instead of up. Spacewar lived on despite bureaucratic opposition because its enthusiasts were also their research projects' best programmers.

The government-sponsored researchers who built the first ARPANET started using government resources to exchange e-mail about science fiction. ARPA administrators wisely invested in building even more powerful CMC systems when the SF-LOVERS list began to eat up more and more of the communication capacity of the system. In computer technology, playgrounds often are where real innovations emerge. Those who would characterize IRC as a frighteningly cerebral and mechanically dehumanized form of interaction that has no conceivable socially redeeming value would do well to recall the cases of Spacewar and SF-LOVERS.

IRC does not fit well with conventional theories of human communication because CMC technology makes possible something that human communicators could not do previously—a geographically dispersed group of people now can use the written word as a conversational medium. So much of what scientists and scholars know about human communication involves physical presence or even potential physical presence, both totally absent from IRC. The telephone has more physical presence, more of a direct sense of the living being behind the words. Words, and the elegance of expression and timing that accompany their use, exist in a purely disembodied state in IRC.

Subcultures based on chat programs constitute a rich, uncharted domain for social research. Like Amy Bruckman, who opened the phenomenon of MUDs as a legitimate topic of media research, and Marc Smith, who investigated online cultures from the perspective of sociology, Elizabeth M. Reid was a graduate student who found her way to the Net and realized that cyberspace is a living laboratory for some of the hottest theoretical controversies in her discipline, history. "Electropolis:

Communication and Community on Internet Relay Chat" was Reid's honors thesis in 1991 for the University of Melbourne. The full text was widely circulated through the Net. Reid's central thesis is that "IRC is essentially a *playground*. Within its domain people are free to experiment with different forms of communication and self-representation." From that communication playground, Reid claims, IRC habituees have evolved rules, rituals, and communication styles that qualify them as a real culture according to criteria defined by prominent social scientists.

Reid's thesis derives from IRC's reversal of the role of social context in shaping conversation and community. In the material world, social conventions are built into houses and schools and offices, signaled by modes of dress and codes of etiquette, posture, accent, tone of voice, and hundreds of other symbolic cues that let people guess accurately how to behave in a particular social situation or society. People learn how to adjust their behavior to conform with a learned mental model of conventional behavior. Until the era of electric communications media, almost all the cues people used to ascertain social context in communications were more physical than verbal. In IRC, however, participants react to a world stripped of nonverbal context by re-creating the context that has been lost. They do this by using written words to describe how they *would* act and how the environment would appear in a shared mental model of a wholly constructed world. People can "swoon" or "charge to the rescue" or "look askance," and they can do it from horseback, the back of a limo, or the far side of the moon.

Reid's theory is that IRC participants use the lack of context and geographical separation to create alternative communities, with written-word versions of several of the essential tools face-to-face communities use to encourage solidarity: "Both positive and negative methods of sustaining community are developed on IRC. Computer-mediated rewards and punishments are developed, and complex rituals have evolved to keep users within the IRC 'fold' and to regulate the use of authority." The main taboo is using a computer hack or other subterfuge to adopt the nickname of another user. Reid cited heartfelt "confessions" on a Usenet newsgroup devoted to IRC enthusiasts as the example of an expiation ritual for a subculture member who has committed its ultimate taboo. Reid noted that channel operators (chanops) who administer individual channels, and IRC operators (opers) who voluntarily keep the

IRC service running on the Net, have special powers that can affect users. Chanops can kick people off a channel; opers can ban people logging in from specific Internet sites from participating in IRC. But these powers are never used without explanation, even though there is no official governing body that requires such explanation.

Violating the sanctity of nicknames is a taboo because it attacks one of the fundamental forces that holds the IRC culture together—a minimum certainty about the identity of all participants in discourse. According to Reid, "The uniqueness of names, their consistent use, and respect for—and expectation of—their integrity, is crucial to the development of online communities." Public confession, Reid points out, is a ritual that reaffirms the taboo and allows the confessor to rejoin the fold. Explanation messages for chanops and opers are voluntary rituals that constrain the power of authorities while upholding loyalty to the hierarchy of power that maintains IRC's minimum of social order.

These aspects of IRC behavior noted by Reid fit several characteristics of culture as defined by contemporary anthropologist Clifford Geertz. Culture, according to Geertz, is "a set of control mechanisms—plans, recipes, rules, instructions (what computer engineers call 'programs')—for the governing of behavior." Referring to Geertz's definition, Reid concludes, "In this sense the users of IRC constitute a culture, a community," because they have devised elaborate social mechanisms for addressing the problems posed by the medium.

Taboos and expiations are negative social control mechanisms. The IRC culture's most powerful positive mechanism for maintaining solidarity is peer recognition. The ability to use words to create context by describing imagined actions and environments is one key to high social status in IRC culture. Those people who are most skilled at creating the illusions of shared context (and thus those who most strongly uphold the elements of the imagined community) are those who are most rewarded with words of recognition and expressions of affection by their peers. Like a relative newcomer to a pub or other informal public space, you know you've arrived in the social hierarchy of an IRC channel when the regulars begin to greet you heartily when you arrive, instead of sending you the kind of canned greetings that bots provide. Personal attention is a currency in IRC: everyone is on stage who wants to be, everyone is the audience, and everyone is a critic.

The notion of mastery that Sherry Turkle and Amy Bruckman mention in regard to the popularity of MUDs among college students generalizes to IRC. The written composition of poses to accompany actions requires creativity, quick thinking, imagination, and either a literary sensibility or the style of a stand-up comedian. Many IRC participants, like many MUDders, are undergraduates. Some, who might not find their skills of quick description and witty rejoinder—a combination of applied day-dreaming and advanced bull session—fully appreciated in other parts of their lives, find that they are higher in the IRC social hierarchy. The regulars in an IRC channel might be the first "in-group" that ever accepted some of these people socially.

During informal monitoring of the alt.irc.recovery newsgroups, I noticed frequent confessions that constant IRC use led chat addicts to spend less time with physical friends in the immediate geographic neighborhood; in the long run, this reclusiveness led to loneliness even more acute when they weren't logged onto the one community in which things went smoothly. Like the question of MUD addiction, any question about proper ways to use a communications medium leads to deeper questions about what our society considers to be proper ways to spend time. If a lonely person chooses to spend many hours a day in an imaginary society, typing witticisms with strangers on other continents, is that good or bad? By what authority should any person or institution have the right to intervene in such cases?

The lack of systematic observations of real case histories, beyond the anecdotal evidence of Usenet, makes any conclusions about the dangers of IRC addiction premature. Enough people think IRC is dangerous to their emotional health to keep an online support group alive; that constitutes evidence that a social problem might exist. We need to learn more about the dimensions of the problem. The serious questions about the possible negative effects of this medium sharpen the need for serious scientific attention to the social dimensions of cyberspace. Banning MUDs or IRC activity is one natural bureaucratic impulse in response to tales of addiction. Do we need to create a new kind of online cultural policing mechanism in response to this problem, or would effective prevention and treatment of obsessive communication behavior, on a case-by-case basis, be a wiser strategy?

   The most popular continuing IRC channels are +hottub, an ongoing flirtation space, mostly heterosexual, and +gblf (gays, bisexuals, lesbians, and friends). Sexy chat and chat about sex, net.sleazing and gender-switching, are as well known in the IRC community as they are in MUDland. And just as there are by now dozens of cases of MUDders who met in a fantasy world and eventually married, although they lived on different continents when they met, there are similar cases in IRC where informal chat led eventually to matrimony. I spotted this electronic wedding notice in a Usenet discussion of IRC, formatted electronically to simulate the more traditional kind of announcement:

```
In deference to the circumstances of their meeting,
          Karl "poptart" Kleinpaste
                      and
          Deborah "KarlsGirl" Brown
   are pleased to announce to the IRC community
                their engagement,
               which became a fact on
            the evening of 7 August 1992.
         A wedding is planned for May 1993,
      its location being anyone's guess just now,
          following Miss Brown's graduation from
   Case Western Reserve University School of Law.
           The couple will be residing in
                Pittsburgh, Pennsylvania
                     thereafter.
```

I sent e-mail to Karl "poptart" Kleinpaste, asking about the circumstances, and he replied:

```
About 4 months ago, Debbie was looking for someone
to chat with, scanning through a /names list. She
said hi to me because (as she said later) I had a
"cute, non-scary" nickname. We chatted a little bit
just casually then and for a few days, then it
became a pretty much every-day occurrence. We had a
lot in common, and after a month or so, I invited
her to visit me here in Pittsburgh. (She lives in
```

Cleveland.) She came down for the first time over
Memorial Day weekend. We've managed to spend every
weekend since together, alternating which one of us
travels to the other's city, as well as continuing
to talk daily in IRC or, more recently, on the
phone. We went out for a special dinner last
evening, I asked her to marry me, and she said
yes. We'll be getting married in May of next year,
probably.

We're waiting until next year due to logistics;
she's entering her 3rd and last year of law school.
But now she's shifting her plans to take the
Pennsylvania bar instead of the Ohio bar, and will
be looking for a position with a Pittsburgh firm.

Just goes to show, and contrary to the opinions of
many, relationships that start in IRC really can
work out after all . . .

Love and matrimony—net.romances—might represent one of the
more socially attractive examples of IRC as a communications medium.
Other examples are less positive. Sara Kiesler and others who have studied the social effects of CMC in business groups have noted that the lack
of social context cues encourages both positive and negative disinhibi-
tion. Normally shy people react by speaking up, and people who would
never shout at others or hurl insults in a physical gathering sometimes
behave that way online. Reid notes that regulars on IRC channels tend
to be uninhibited about self-disclosure, discussing serious problems in
their real lives with their online friends. Such channels are self-regulating
in the sense that newcomers who take advantage of this openness and
trust by insulting others can be "killed" by the chanops. And IRC
includes a mechanism for countering the insularity of established channels with cliques of regulars who define the criteria for membership. Any
IRC user can create a new channel, and thus become a chanop, at any
time. There are private channels, as well, but the majority of traffic these
days is in the public channels.

Antisocial behavior is not rare in IRC. Racist and homophobic out-breaks are regular events. Hostile individuals can program their bots to flood a channel by sending out a stream of characters to IRC. It's very annoying when you are devoting part of your desktop computer screen and part of your attention to a conversation on an IRC channel and someone's bot somewhere in the world starts sending profanities or scriptures or dictionaries or gibberish to everyone else's screen. The same lack of social feedback that lowers inhibitions enough to promote self-disclosure among groups of people can also lower inhibitions enough for individuals to disrupt those groups and sometimes tear the delicate fabric of trust that has been carefully woven over months of conversation among disembodied strangers.

Reid points out that IRC is a global cultural phenomenon, with high potential for citizen-to-citizen communication across national and ideological boundaries:

It is not uncommon for IRC channels to contain no two people from the same country. With the encouragement of intimacy between users and the tendency for conventional social mores to be ignored on IRC, it becomes possible for people to investigate the differences between their cultures. No matter on how superficial a level that might be, the encouragement of what can only be called friendship between people of disparate cultural backgrounds helps to destroy any sense of intolerance that each may have for the other's culture and to foster a sense of cross-cultural community.

Just as the stories of addiction are evidence of a social problem that deserves closer attention, the possibility of a new tool for fostering cross-cultural understanding is worth a closer look as well.

The most widely cited instance of cross-cultural dialogue on IRC is the use of the medium during the Gulf War. An Internet link had been set up in Kuwait before the Iraqi invasion, and the link stayed up for a week after radio and television broadcasts ceased. Kuwaiti students used IRC for eyewitness reports, and so did Israelis. According to Reid, "I am told that users from the two countries often interacted with very few disagreements and mostly with sympathy for each other's position and outlook." There has been some discussion of the role of the Net in the Gulf War, via Usenet.

```
From: frechett@spot.Colorado.EDU (-$SIRunaway
Daemon$SI-)
Subject: Re: IRC Folk History
```

The channel at the time was called +report. It was
moderated by a bot first run by lynx and then by
myself. Basically it was a moderated channel and a
number of people around the world would come onto
the channel and listen. If someone had something to
report then they would change their nickname to
something like NBC or CBS or AP. etc. . .
representing some news reporting agency. (Just
people listening to the news though, not real
representatives of that agency) Those people would
get chanop and could report the news as it came
in.

One of the notable things I recall was an Israeli
on the channel (was in the Wall Street Journal too
I believe) who had a terminal in the sealed room
and would talk about an incoming scud alert and
then would come back a few minutes later typing at
us from in the sealed room.

I also recall one of the Isreali's [sic mentioning
to us when he heard one of the first scuds hit
that he heard Isreali jets scrambling and flying
west. This was a bit of information I never did
hear through CNN, AP or the network news.

A little research on the Net led me to the archives where the logs of the
Gulf War IRC sessions are kept. Reading through a transcript certainly
re-creates that feeling of news hunger that surrounds the fog of war during the early hours of a major conflict. Here are a few selected excerpts
from the IRC channel that preceded the +report channel. Ironically, these
remarks took place among participants in the +peace channel:

```
IRC CHANNEL +peace
IRC Log started Thu Jan 17 01:03
<umfonta6> bombsd are droppiong in baghdad
```

<hstanley> jeesh
<spamgod> am i getting through?
<CaptainJ> CNN HAS THE SCOOP!
#Breeze# has CNN on
<Arkie> this channel name is fairly oxymorninical [sic.
<spam> koala* 20 minutes since first attack
<spamgod> thanks
<hstanley> who's in baghdad here?
<Mark> scoop? hah!
<umfonta6> bombs are happening
<Mosiah> bombs hitting the net!
<CaptainJ> 2 major explosions–1 near major comm center.
<umfonta6> phones are going down
<stealth> Attack started at 2:30am baghdad time.
<Lipstick> I dont think bagdahd is on the net $SI
<BOY> No arab countrys on the net..
<Datawolf> hold for net diagnostic..
<Phaedrus> welost the finnish d00ds
<Faustus> ANYBODY FROM ISRAEL HERE?
<stealth> Boy and Ely are on from israel.
<<BOY> Fau: i'm FROM ISRAEL!
<stealth Got your gas mask ready, Boy?
<CaptainJ AA-fire still going up-very random (CNN)
<BOY> steal: yes .. and we just finished silling the house from gas. .
<Alexander> WAR!!!!!!!!!!!!!!!!!!!!!! WAR!!!!!!!!!!!!!!!!!!
!!!! WAR!!!!!!!!!!!!!!!!!!!!!! WAR!!!!!!!!!!!!!!!!!!!!!!
WAR!!!!!!!!!!!!!!!!!!!!!! WAR!!!!!!!!!!!!!!!!!!!!!! WAR!!!
!!!!!!!!!!!!!!!!!
#Hamlet# The liberation of Kuwait has begun
<Bertin> Hallo bardo Willkommen in +peace. Hallo chris Willkommen
in +peace.
<<Will> u guys lets please keep this channel english only

Like MUDs, IRC has the potential to develop into a more serious
communications medium. Can chat be a tool as well as a toy? Jupiter
and MediaMOO are attempts to create MUDs without the dragons, substituting informal discourse among intellectual colleagues for symbolic

combat between imaginary adventurers. In IRC, the equivalent to taking away the dragons would be for colleagues who share a specific interest to meet on an IRC channel at a specified time every day or every week for the kind of interaction that is best done synchronously—brainstorming is the primary example of the kind of group interaction IRC could facilitate, if used adroitly.

At the point where groups in academia or private enterprise start using MUDs and IRC channels as communication tools, the way they started using word processing in the 1970s and e-mail in the 1980s, these CMC playgrounds converge on the discipline known as computer-supported cooperative work (CSCW). CSCW has been the focus of international, interdisciplinary conferences, scholarly journals, and corporate consultants for the past several years. It's part of a movement among many information systems specialists in the business world to embrace the notion of groupware—a term first coined by hard-core CMC revolutionaries.

Computer-supported cooperative *play*, however, is an online dimension in its own right.

Habitat: Computer-Mediated Play

When I first encountered the phrase "computer-supported cooperative play" in a scientific paper from the Kyoto Institute of Technology, several ideas that had been floating around in my head began to fit together. CSCW is promising, but it is a strictly utilitarian perspective. If industrial civilization has a taboo so engrained in the culture that few even recognize it as a taboo, *play* may be it. Play is somehow not quite proper behavior if you aren't an infant or a professional athlete. People are expected to spend their time "constructively." Working, educating oneself, parenting, even organized commercial recreation such as watching television or taking an elaborately planned vacation, are considered constructive. Playing around, however, is not considered constructive. Yet the history of CMC reveals that people often use the new medium to do just that. And some educational psychologists, most notably Jean Piaget, claim that play is the way humans learn best.

Atsuya Yoshida and Jun Kakuta, of the Department of Information Technology at the Kyoto Institute of Technology, proposed the term "computer-supported cooperative play" in their study "People Who Live in an On-line Virtual World":

We would name the Habitat type of communication as a playful communication. Historically, we have the example of the playful communication such as a wall painting in a cave and a drumming behavior to neighboring villages at a festival, while Indian's signal fire and military flag signals are the examples of task-oriented communications. Playful communication could be a key concept in the next generation human interface architecture and the Habitat presents a good model for the study of the concept of playful communication, that is, computer supported cooperative play.

The Habitat that Yoshida and Kakuta discussed as an example of an online community devoted to cooperative play is a project of the Japanese computer-aerospace-electronics giant Fujitsu. Fujitsu's Habitat is based on an older, pioneering, graphical virtual community first developed by Lucasfilm Games and an early commercial online service in America, QuantumLink Communications. I observed the Japanese version of Habitat when I visited Fujitsu's research-and-development facility in Kawasaki, but my first encounter with Habitat's original architects took place years earlier. In Austin, Texas, in 1990, at the First Conference on Cyberspace, I met the two programmers who created the first large-scale, multi-user, commercial virtual playground.

In their address to the conference, and the paper they later published, "The Lessons of Lucasfilm's Habitat," Chip Morningstar and F. Randall Farmer recounted their experience as the designers and managers of a virtual community that used computer graphics as well as words to support an online society of tens of thousands. Much of that conference in Austin was devoted to discussions of virtual-reality environments in which people wear special goggles and gloves to experience the illusion of sensory immersion in the virtual world via three-dimensional computer graphics. Randy Farmer and Chip Morningstar stood out in that high-tech crowd because the cyberspace they had created used a very inexpensive home computer, often called a toy computer, and a cartoon-like two-dimensional representation to create their kind of virtual world. Farmer and Morningstar had one kind of experience that the 3-D graphics enthusiasts did not have, however—the system they had designed, Habitat, had been used by tens of thousands of people.

In the early 1980s, LucasArts Entertainment began a series of ambitious research ventures through the Lucasfilm Games division.

Morningstar and Farmer were handed the tempting and vexing task of designing a graphic virtual community for a large population that was using computationally puny Commodore–64 computers. Before the Macintosh came along in 1984, the Commodore–64 was the world's most popular home computer. The "64" stood for the 64 thousand bytes of main memory. Today's desktop computers use millions of bytes of main memory, which is why the C–64 is considered a toy. But Lucasfilm Games had made a business deal with QuantumLink Communications, an online service that connected C–64 users via modems.

Morningstar and Farmer were given the design constraints of a population of users numbering in the tens of thousands, hundreds of whom would be online at any one time, each of whom would have a laughably small amount of communication bandwidth and home computers that were barely more intelligent than hand-held calculators. Within these constraints, they created a graphical chat system that enabled tens of thousands of participants to play games, build societies, engage in politics, fight and even "kill" each other, start religions, wage wars, fall in love, get married, and create markets and economies. The central meta-lesson the system designers had learned from Habitat was that "detailed central planning is impossible; don't even try." Create the tools for users to build their own society, Morningstar and Farmer concluded, and let the users tell you what they want to do, because that is what the users of an online communication system will do, no matter how hard you try to structure some other purpose into the tool.

The C–64 computers acted as the front end to the Habitat system. When you logged onto the service, the front end would create an animated computer graphic model of Habitat on your screen. The user interacts with the Habitat world by moving around a joystick, and by means of a cartoonlike representation known as an Avatar. Avatars are mostly, although not exclusively, humanoid, and have heads and bodies that can move around the space depicted on the screen. The Avatars of multiple users are visible on the screen, as well as external objects and parts of the environment, like coins or guns or trees. The thousands of individual users were linked to far more powerful computers that constituted the back end to the Habitat system. The back end kept track of who was where and which objects were lying around—the "world model." When you type something on your keyboard, the back end takes the message from your desktop computer and displays it to anyone else who is in the same region of Habitat by means of a speech balloon that appears above your Avatar's head. If you pick up or drop an object, the back end moves the object in everyone else's world model.

One thing that Avatars, unlike IRC users, can do in a real-time chat is use gestures such as nodding and eye movement to indicate unspoken feedback while others are speaking. In normal conversation, these phatic utterances and gestures are an important if invisible part of navigating from topic to topic or understanding unspoken nuances. The conversation does seem more alive in a sense, when you can move your eyes toward someone's Avatar when it says something interesting. Besides moving their heads and changing their facial expressions, Avatars can move from place to place and pick up, put down, and manipulate objects. Dozens of classes of objects, including examples such as Tokens, act as Habitat currency, a Change-o-matic for changing an Avatar's gender, a club, gun, or knife for protection in some of the rougher neighborhoods, drugs to cure wounds.

Habitat was designed with a spatial metaphor in mind. Each user can see a region of Habitat at one time on the screen. The Avatar can move to one of four adjacent regions from any region by moving through a door, or use a teleport booth or device to move instantly to a distant region. Habitat was designed to hold twenty thousand regions. Each user was given a private region, known as Turf, to store objects, hide out, and invite guests.

Morningstar and Farmer reported that their software engineering backgrounds led them to think of the design of Habitat in terms of central planning. For twenty thousand Avatars, there had to be twenty thousand houses, clustered into towns and cities. Thoroughfares, wilderness areas, and shopping centers were needed. "We, attempting to play the role of omniscient central planners, were swamped," the world-designers reported. When the issue of entertainment and recreation facilities— activities that would presumably keep Habitat users coming back for more—arose, the designers explicitly rejected the game structure used by the first MUDs, with experience points and hierarchical grades and wizard powers:

The idea behind our world was precisely that it did not come with a fixed set of objectives for its inhabitants, but rather provided a broad palette of possible

activities from which the players could choose, driven by their own internal incli-
nations. It was our intent to provide a variety of possible experiences, ranging
from events with established rules and goals (a treasure hunt, for example) to
activities propelled by the players' personal motivations (starting a business, running the newspaper) to completely free-form, purely existential activities (hang-
ing out with friends and conversing).

After putting weeks into designing and building highly structured
treasure hunts for the first Habitat users, Morningstar and Farmer began
to understand that the users themselves would use the tools they provided to create activities unplanned or unsuspected by the system's original designers:

Again and again we found that activities based on often unconscious assumptions about player behavior had completely unexpected outcomes (when they
were not simply outright failures). It was clear that we were not in control. The
more people we involved in something, the less in control we were. We could
influence things, we could set up interesting situations, we could provide opportunities for things to happen, but we could not dictate the outcome.... Propelled
by these experiences, we shifted into a style of operations in which we let the
players themselves drive the direction of the design. This proved far more effective. Instead of trying to push the community in the direction we thought it
should go, an exercise rather like herding mice, we tried to observe what people
were doing and aid them in it. We became facilitators as much as we were designers and implementors. This often meant adding new features and new regions to
the system at a frantic pace, but almost all of what we added was used and appreciated since it was well matched to people's needs and desires.

Avatars can die in Habitat, and weapons are allowed in certain areas
because the designers "felt that players should be able to materially affect
each other in ways that went beyond simply talking, ways that required
real moral choices to be made by the participants. We recognized the age
old story-teller's dictum that conflict is the essence of drama." In
Habitat, death means that the Avatar is teleported to his or her home
region, head in hands, divested of all possessions carried at the time of
death. In many MUDs, death is equally impermanent. Morningstar and
Farmer echoed MUD1 designer Richard Bartle's observations about the
way people took even imaginary online death seriously: "Nevertheless,
the death metaphor had a profound effect on people's perceptions."

Because the designers imposed very few rules on Avatar social behavior, Habitat players were forced into social debates. One core issue
regarded the ontological status of Avatars. Is an Avatar a personal projection of the player, entitled to be treated respectfully? Or is an Avatar

no more real than a video game character? Polls of the population revealed it to be about equally split on the issue. The arguments were brought into focus when a group of players, out to make a point, started using their freedom to shoot many other Avatars. Two interesting results emerged from the great debate about gunplay that ensued. First, the players decided to outlaw guns in cities but leave them legal outside city limits. That decision led to online elections for a sheriff, because you are obliged to enforce a law once you make one. The other intriguing result was the founding of the Order of the Holy Walnut, the first Habitat church. The founder, a Greek Orthodox priest in real life, required his disciples not to carry weapons or steal. "His church became quite popular," Morningstar and Farmer noted, "and he became a very highly respected member of the Habitat community."

The designers built the elements of an economy into Habitat, which is even more interesting given that they are now employed by American Information Exchange (Amix), a company that is creating an online knowledge marketplace where contractors and clients can exchange information, graphics, and software for real money. In Habitat, there were Tokens, which your Avatar could earn by spending time in Habitat to supplement the 2,000 it was given when it was "hatched." You could buy a new head for your Avatar, or various objects that are useful in Habitat, from automatic online vending machines. An interesting situation occurred one night when some users learned that a Vendroid in one region was inadvertently selling Dolls for 75 Tokens, and a Pawn Machine in another region was redeeming Dolls for 100 Tokens. Worse, the same Vendroid was selling Crystal Balls for 18,000 Tokens and the Pawn Machine was redeeming them for 30,000 Tokens.

When the designers were offline, a couple of users invested all their money in Dolls and shuttled between the machines until they could afford to trade in Crystal Balls. The next morning, when Morningstar and Farmer logged on, their monitoring programs told them that the money supply in the Habitat database had quintupled overnight! When they tracked down the entrepreneurs and fixed the bug, they found that the users didn't want to give the money back. The powers that be decided not to force the issue, and conviviality was not only restored but boosted when the newly rich players then used their amassed Tokens to underwrite a series of games for the other players on the system.

By 1991, when Morningstar and Farmer reported on their experience, the North American version of Habitat, called Club Caribe, had been running on QuantumLink for almost two years, and sustained a population of some fifteen thousand users. By 1993, QuantumLink had become America On-Line, a Macintosh-oriented commercial online service, and the number of active C–64 users had dwindled. In 1993, Farmer reported to me via e-mail that "Club Caribe is still up and running on QuantumLink, the ever-shrinking Commodore–64 corner of America On-line. CC is completely managed by the customers themselves. There are only a few thousand QuantumLink customers remaining, and some hundreds of them remain active in Club Caribe."

The experiences of Habitat's designers should be required reading for anyone involved in the design or management of commercial online systems. One of the earliest companies to heed Morningstar and Farmer's advice was Fujitsu, which bought Habitat from Lucasfilm Games and redesigned it to use in Japan. Instead of the computationally antique C–64s, Fujitsu adapted Habitat for its new personal media hardware, the FM Towns, a computer that includes a CD-ROM drive—a mechanism for storing and retrieving large amounts of sound and/or images. This machine is a prototype for the multimedia desktop devices that Fujitsu and other companies are planning for the world market in the late 1990s.

The complex graphics capabilities necessary to make any on-screen depiction look more realistic than a crude cartoon figure was far beyond the capabilities of the C–64 and other early personal computers. But the graphics and information-shuffling capabilities of next-generation personal computers—the much-ballyhooed multimedia revolution that combines sound, text, graphics, and video on one affordable unit—have taken an unusually long time to get off the ground. In many ways, like the very first personal computers, the multimedia machines that Fujitsu, Apple, and others are preparing for market are a solution looking for problems to solve. The idea of connecting multimedia capabilities with an online audience, building on the pioneering work of Habitat, made sense to Fujitsu's managers. The push to ultra-high-speed fiber-optic communication in Japan by NTT, Fujitsu, and others, and the continuing evolution of personal computers, was creating a need for real applications that could demonstrate to people who are already information-

and technology-saturated that they need to use all the new capabilities available to them. On the scale that these companies operate, buying Habitat, converting it for use on a new computer, and setting up a new online service was a cost-effective research-and-development strategy.

In March 1992, I visited Fujitsu's research-and-development center in Kawasaki, outside Tokyo. Their researchers asked me questions about the online world as I saw it, and they showed me Fujitsu Habitat as they had implemented it. Fujitsu Habitat started operation in February 1990, using the Fujitsu-owned NIFTY-serve network to connect FM-Towns owners with modems to the central computer (the software for Habitat has since been translated to other popular Japanese computers). NIFTY-serve is a commercial service that provides e-mail, chat, and other online services to about 360,000 Japanese users. By April 1992, the virtual community of Populopolis—the official name for Fujitsu Habitat's society—had a total population of 6,200. By the standards of mass media, those figures aren't large enough to be visible. By virtual community standards, Populopolis took two years to reach a population that required seven years for the WELL.

I believe that Fujitsu managers are on their way to discovering, as did Morningstar and Farmer, that the Habitat users themselves, given sufficient tools and freedom, will create their own culture. The multimedia machines are still a small minority of personal computer sales, even in Japan. According to e-mail from Farmer in 1993, "Fujitsu Habitat is still growing daily, with over 7,000 customers currently registered. About 10% of these are 'highly active' customers, making up the core of the community. The Macintosh frontend software shipped in March, 1993 in Japan, and, as with the previously released FMTowns, FMR, and PC–9801 compatible versions, the new version should cause a sharp increase in new customer registration. Fujitsu is currently considering an American version."

Some of the most interesting questions had to do with whether or not Habitat showed any potential for a more sophisticated, more finely tuned, more technically powerful version in the future. User behavior is always important in the Japanese research-and-development cycle. Early prototypes of many kinds of different consumer devices traditionally are made available to Japanese consumers, and only those devices that succeed well at home are considered for the world market. Prototypes and proof of concept are another important fixture in the Japanese consumer electronics research-and-development culture. The seven-thousand-and-growing population of Populopolis is a commercial and cultural laboratory for experimenting with cyberspace design—Japanese style. The highly visual nature of Japanese communications is sometimes mentioned as one reason why the text-only nature of the Net is not well suited to the wider Japanese population. Given the tools and the freedom to use them, the citizens of Populopolis have a crack at designing a more visually oriented online culture.

Atsuya Yoshida and Jun Kakuta from the Kyoto Institute of Technology, supported by Fujitsu, formally investigated Habitat "users' social and behavioral characteristics in an on-line virtual world." They chose to investigate the social structure of the system by selecting a novice user of e-mail and chat in Japanese University NETwork (JUNET), a male graduate student of information technology, twenty-four years old, and introducing him to Fujitsu Habitat. For the eighty-one days they observed their experimental subject, "Mr. T.," Yoshida and Kakuta reported that

Mr. T. showed magnificent social adaptation to the visual network society of Populopolis. From March 16, 1993, when the experimental observation was started, the daily access time increased rapidly. We would call this phenomenon 'addiction.' Mr. T. smoothly got into the network group and became active to join an on-line election of a president of the town-block association and an on-line discussion about Osaka dialect, and also joined an off-line meeting at an early stage.

Yoshida and Kakuta also observed that Mr. T. and other Habitat users "showed the tendency to use the language specific to themselves, such as special sign language and terms which could not be understandable for the person without knowing the networks and Populopolis." Part of this special sign language was the use of emoticons, or typographic conventions to denote smiling or frowning. The Net version of the smiley face consists of a colon, a dash, and a close-parenthesis symbol that looks like a face if you turn your head sideways: :-) but the Fujitsu Habitat version looks more like an abstract facial representation: (^—^). Analysis of conversations in Populopolis revealed that 45 percent of the total number of utterances contained sign language.

Nonverbal context is particularly important in Japan, where gesture, posture, and tone of voice convey overtones and references that are clearly understood within a formal and well-understood set of contextual references.

Accents and dialects are particularly important—one phenomenon uncovered by the researchers was that Japanese users who are fluent in the Osaka dialect are underrepresented on Habitat in comparison to their numbers on NIFTY-serve; something about the Habitat online culture inhibits the use of Osaka dialect expressions—itself a matter of some online discussion. This invisible and perhaps partially ineffable component of Japanese spoken communication is sometimes called *kansei*, which can be only loosely translated as an intuitive, partially aesthetic, sense of rightness about the contextual elements in a conversation.

Yoshida and Kakuta emphasize that "Habitat users seemed to have rich electronic kansei to transmit and receive the social-emotional information by coded symbols." They specifically compare the human interface in communications technologies to the notion of kansei. My friend Joichi Ito, a pioneering young networker in Japan and America, also emphasizes the need for understanding kansei when evaluating communications in Japan, even online—especially online, where many of the acutely important social cues are missing. If there is an ideal place to torture-test the notion that adding graphic representations that can emulate facial expressions and body language can re-create context—kansei— Fujitsu Habitat is it.

Kansei might turn out to be an important term all over the Net, as an aid to evaluating the advantages and disadvantages of each Net tool in different situations. The Net is increasingly a multicultural forum—the only multicultural forum of any scope. To focus on developments in the United States is wise, because that is where the Net began, and where many technical and social innovations continue to emerge. But to do so exclusively is to miss the big picture: the Net is happening to the whole world. Because of the sharp focus on communications and information technologies at the highest levels of Japan's industrial policymakers, the question of Japan and the Net is perhaps the most important critical uncertainty in the shaping of tomorrow's Worldnet.

7

Japan and the Net

Izumi Aizu reached through the Net and transported me bodily to Japan. Our friendship started when an American friend of mine made a request via e-mail: Would I be interested in traveling to Japan, all expenses paid, to talk to Japanese technologists about the future of virtual communities? A Japanese friend of my American friend had organized a conference of Japanese researchers to discuss a vision of telecommunications culture they called the Hypernetwork Society. The offer sounded too good to be true, but that didn't stop me from saying I was interested.

The next day, I received a telephone call from Izumi Aizu, who assured me that it wasn't a fantasy. The day after our telephone conversation, we started planning the visit in earnest, via e-mail. The third day of this unexpected turn of events brought e-mail from Katsura Hattori. Hattori-san introduced himself as the science and technology editor of *Asahi Shimbun*—the second largest newspaper in Japan. He had read my previous books, and when he heard from Aizu-san that I was planning to be in Tokyo, he offered his services.

Aizu, Hattori, and I quickly discovered via e-mail that we shared some important common history, values, and interests that drew us together despite the geographic and cultural boundaries that separated us. We were all baby boomers who had participated in the political protests and cultural upheavals of the late 1960s, and we were professional communicators who spent our time trying to help the different worlds of science, citizenry, government, and industry understand the implications of new technologies. Most important, we were all believers in the potential of computer networking to help us build a better world for our children.

Aizu-san and Hattori-san literally opened a whole new world to me. I ended up visiting small virtual communities far from Tokyo, meeting a regional governor and a small-town mayor who both use CMC as part of their government, participating in social gatherings of enthusiasts from two different Japanese conferencing systems. Those face-to-face gatherings had the same kind of zeitgeist—or perhaps *kansei* would be a better word—as the WELL face-to-face gatherings I know so well. That feeling of strong but ineffable kinship that cut through other social barriers led me to investigate those communities more deeply, online and in person. My exploration of the Japanese online culture over the last three years has revealed both similarities and differences between Japanese and American virtual communities.

I've spent about a month in Japan in two visits. My electronic correspondence now includes half a dozen friends I met during my trips. I've stayed with Izumi Aizu and his family in their Tokyo home—a rare experience for an American visitor—and he has stayed with me and my family in the United States. We've become social interpreters for one another, translating the fine points of Japanese and American cultural codes that aren't written in books. Because of the deep cultural differences that lurk between the surface similarities, I would never have understood 1 percent of what happened to me as an American in Japan, nor would the doors have been opened for me there, without Izumi Aizu's assistance. Through him, I met several colleagues whose friendships also have endured. I never would have known him or any of the other Japanese virtual communitarians if we had not met and grown to know each other in cyberspace.

Although my travels and observations of the real communities behind the virtual communities in different parts of the world have been unsystematic and cursory—it would take many years to visit and get to know people from any more than a handful of virtual communities—I think some of the similarities that surfaced are worth attention, at the level of what scientists call anecdotal evidence.

Similarities are easier to detect because they pop out at you when the background is mostly unfamiliar. The *differences* between virtual communities based in different cultures are far more difficult to tease out. For that information, I have to rely on my native guides and on the informants they introduce to me. My travels with Izumi Aizu around rural Japan brought me into direct contact with key virtual communities, and many of the places we visited together, online and in real life, revealed possible similarities between American and Japanese cybercultures. These observations were mostly at the grassroots level.

The researchers and research managers I met, men at the highest levels of Japan's telecommunications companies, shared one important characteristic with their counterparts in large American and European telecommunications companies I've visited—they seemed generally unaware of the impending collision or convergence between the social revolutions at the grassroots of CMC and the high-tech communications infrastructure the big companies were installing in Japan. The telecommunications policymakers at NTT (Nippon Telephone and Telegraph), Fujitsu, and other mainstays of Japan's communications industry seem to be waking up very quickly, however, given President Clinton's plans to build a national information infrastructure in America. Ideas can move much more quickly from the fringes to the center in Japan, especially technology-related ideas. Japanese leaders, like American technology managers, find themselves forced to look beyond their piece of technological turf or the perimeter of their profit centers, to consider the larger system, the *infrastructure*—the social changes as well as the hardware and software involved in creating a national or international highway of the mind.

Through Aizu, I met Jeff Shapard, the cofounder of TWICS, a pioneering virtual community in Tokyo that draws half its participants from Japanese residents of the Tokyo area, and half from Tokyo's non-Japanese population, including a large American expatriate contingent. Shapard introduced me to his partner, Joichi Ito, a fast-moving, bicultural young fellow who became my friend in the United States as well as Japan. Just as Aizu and Hattori introduced me to some similarities among virtual communities at the grassroots, my ongoing dialogue with Shapard and Ito helped me perceive the significant differences between Japanese and American online cultures—and the significant cultural challenge that the worldwide Network poses to Japan's society and its planners.

In the early 1980s, Aizu and Ito were among the first people in Japan to explore the use of computers as communications media, at around the same time that U.S. pioneers such as Hiltz and Turoff, Dave Hughes, Lisa Carlson, and Peter and Trudy Johnson-Lenz were using EIES and the Source to talk about the social networks that could be grown by means of CMC networks. Izumi Aizu had been looking for a tool for social change for a long time. As a self-employed consultant and college dropout, he also needed something to give him social networking leverage.

Because entry into a top university, preferably the University of Tokyo, is overwhelmingly the most important criterion for career success in Japan, Aizu's deliberately deciding not to take the entrance examinations was a far more radical act than it would have been in the United States. Aizu was a networker in the social sense of seeking and following up social contacts to support his business, by necessity, because the lack of a traditional college-corporation network means he constantly has to build his own support networks.

"I was sixteen in 1968 and I was seriously affected by the student protests in America and Paris and Tokyo," Aizu told me the first night I was in Tokyo. Japanese houses, with their paper walls, generally are colder than American homes, so we sat up late that night, around the *hori-gotatsu*, a pit in the floor with a foot warmer at the bottom. Sitting with a lap blanket and our legs in the *hori-gotatsu*, sipping tea, talking about the values and decisions that had shaped our lives, is an experience I'll never forget. The environment was so alien, yet the conversation was so familiar. "I started to read more books that weren't on the school reading list. I started to question the meaning of life. Why should I take all these pains and go through exam hell to do something that didn't mean anything to me?" Aizu continued.

His mother supported him at first, during a period when he read voraciously. At age twenty, he went to work at a printing company. A few years later, he moved to an advertising agency as a printing specialist, and that led to his work translating sales manuals into English. By the time he was twenty-eight, the first personal computers were available in Japan. He found that the PC manuals in Japanese left a lot to be desired, so he helped start a company, High Technology Communications, in 1983, and produced what turned out to be a successful guidebook to the first Apple computers used in Japan. Then he started experimenting with using an old-fashioned acoustic modem to send text to a phototypesetting machine. He became a charter member of the Computer Press Association and joined the Source. Finding that the technical writer's forum on the Source was moribund, Aizu decided to liven it up again. After conversation came back to life in the forum, due to his transpacific verbal prodding, Aizu announced that he was coming to the United States— would any other modem-using technical writers like to meet him?

By the time the WELL started, in 1985, Aizu had begun to meet some of the key members of the then-small society of CMC enthusiasts. His history wasn't too different from my own. I didn't drop out of college, but becoming a freelance writer at twenty-two was my way of dropping out to find my own kind of meaning in life. Like Aizu, I became personally and professionally drawn into the world of personal computers and then into the world of CMC. Like Aizu, I felt that CMC had reawakened my interest in social change in a way that personal computers by themselves had not. But Aizu had been drawn directly into the use of CMC as a political tool (around the time I was just beginning to find my way around the WELL), because of events in his hometown of Zushi.

In Japan, the place you are born and raised is exceptionally important. Joichi Ito told me that in Kyoto there is an old stone with the names of twenty-four generations of his family engraved on it. That's where he is going to go. It's his spiritual home. For Izumi Aizu, that place-based loyalty was focused on Zushi, a seaside town outside Yokohama, where he was raised. Before World War II, the city limits included the very large Ikego forest, which took up one-eighth of the city. It had been preserved for a long time because an enormous underground ammunition depot for the Japanese navy existed underneath it. After World War II, it served the same purpose for the U.S. Navy. Since you don't want strangers walking around ammunition dumps, both the Japanese and U.S. military authorities had kept the area free of human interference. In 1983, when the ammunition depot was moved, the Japanese government announced they would build one thousand housing units in the Ikego forest, for American military personnel. The Japanese government and construction industry and the U.S. military were formidable foes, but the citizens of Zushi decided to fight to preserve the forest. They elected a young mayor, Mr. Kiichiro Tomino, who was one of the leaders of the grassroots movement.

"Mr. Tomino went to the same school I had attended, although he was nine years older than me. We had mutual friends, and when he heard that I was involved in computer networking, he asked me if I could use these computer networks to find international support for the anti-development campaign," Aizu recalled, the day we made the two-hour drive from Tokyo to Zushi. Turning to his modem to find people, Aizu made contact with Lisa Carlson and Frank Burns, who were starting their Metanetwork system, and met them face-to-face in Washington, D.C. As a result of that meeting, Aizu used the Metanetwork to distribute a plea for support from the people of Zushi. They appealed specifically for people to distribute the message to as many different countries as possible. More than one thousand replies came in over a period of months, from people in more than fifty countries. The message posted on Metanet had propagated through the BBSs of the world and via the networks of environmental activists—and this was in 1985, before the Net's most explosive period of growth.

When I met Mayor Tomino in his office at Zushi City Hall in 1992, he acknowledged that the computer conferencing campaign played a major part in the citizens' grassroots movement. City hall for this town of fifty thousand, a middle-class seaside resort community, includes a row of Macintosh computers in a common room on the ground floor, where citizens who do not have home computers can communicate directly with city officials. Tomino created a municipal conferencing system. "People think that ordinary citizens have little power against big institutions," Tomino told me, when I asked him what he had in mind when he helped set up Zushi's online system, "and I want to show them that citizens can help city government solve problems that involve all of us." With the positive experience of the Ikego forest movement behind them, several hundred citizens took up the mayor's invitation and used online discussions to help redesign the city library system. "The citizens here are trying to prove that they can decide their own fate by themselves. That's what the United States taught us years ago. Your military occupation policy to democratize Japan was very successful," Tomino told me, smiling.

In the early 1980s, some of the people who had been finding each other through computer conferencing began to embrace the idea of networking as a social movement as well as a way of using computers to communicate. Although the late 1980s turned the idea of networking into a new name for an old form of using social relationships to advance one's professional ambitions, the early promoters were driven far more by revolutionary zeal than profit motive. Izumi Aizu was influenced by CMC evangelists, Jessica Lipnack and Jeffrey Stamps, who were known in the online world as "J. and J." Lipnack and Stamps published a book about their ideas, *Networking, People Connecting with People, Linking Ideas and Resources* , in 1982. "They could have been writing it about me," Izumi Aizu exclaimed when he recalled their early influence.

As a self-selected outsider from the mainstream of Japan Inc., and a grassroots organizer, Aizu had the respect of the alternative culture. His business experience and his understanding of CMC technology, however, brought him the support of some influential insiders in the Japanese power structure. After his first visits to the United States and online explorations via the Source, Aizu wrote and distributed in Japan a report on the state of CMC and its potential. At that time, most Japanese citizens who were knowledgeable about the use of modems thought of them as a way to access information in a big database; Aizu's report concentrated on the human networking that could piggyback on computer networks. That report quickly became popular in several different circles in Japan. Computer enthusiasts saw the first road map to a whole new territory. A few of the most visionary planners in Japan's communications companies began to pay attention.

Aizu was becoming a bridge person, linking Japan and America, grassroots and corporate planners, citizens and technologies. He decided to specialize professionally as well as avocationally in combining the social and technical sides of networking and computer conferencing. He found financial backers and opened an enterprise he confidently named the Institute for Networking Design.

Hard on the heels of his successful application of CMC to both grassroots activism and municipal government, Aizu became involved in the design of a virtual community and computer network for an entire prefecture—a region of 1.25 million people spread over more than six thousand square kilometers. This time, one of the most enthusiastic supporters of the virtual community was the prefectural governor. The speech that first brought me to Japan was to be introduced by Governor Hiramatsu. The morning after my first late night in Tokyo, in the spring of 1990, I boarded an All-Nippon Airlines flight with Izumi Aizu for Oita prefecture, on the southernmost island of Kyushu. Anyplace you go in Japan that requires an hour-and-a-half plane flight from Tokyo is indeed remote from the main metropolitan centers. I remember that culture shock was still ahead of my jet lag when I arrived at the conference center on Oita's Beppu Bay.

The conference I was invited to address was attended by researchers from Japan Inc.'s biggest names in technology, but the local organizers were all members of a virtual community known as COARA, based in

Oita. After the first Hypernetwork conference was over, toward the end of my first week in Japan, I went out for an evening of food, drink, and merriment with about thirty COARA members who had just successfully completed the weeks of hard work necessary to make a conference like this successful. Neither Aizu nor one of my other regular interpreters was able to join us. I don't speak any Japanese, and few people in our party spoke any English. I was treated as an honored guest, of course, and those who could speak some English did their best to inform me about what was happening. I can still feel the amazement that came over me as I realized that although I didn't understand a word they were saying, I recognized the emotional tone of the COARA gathering. It reminded me of nothing so much as the WELL's monthly parties. Here were people who seemed to know each other well, delighted in each other's company, had a rich set of mutual experiences to draw them together despite gender, class, occupational, and geographic differences. They talked and talked and talked.

Oita was as far from home as I had ever been in my life. I never expected to see it again. Two years later, I was invited back, along with John Barlow, Robert Johansen, and Peter and Trudy Johnson-Lenz. The idea of using CMC as a tool for social change on a grand scale as well as at the grassroots level was becoming popular with Japanese communications technology planners, and COARA was becoming known as a social experiment. This time, COARA members greeted me like a long-lost relative. During my second visit, they had a party that ran late into the night, every night of the conference. They had a *karaoke* bar set up in the conference center—a microphone and videodisk setup that plays backup music and displays lyrics on the screen, so people can take turns singing solos.

Karaoke is an important new part of Japanese professional life. People in Japan who work together all day in offices often go out together at night as a group to a favorite karaoke bar, where they drink many diluted scotch-and-waters and cut loose a little bit from the formal solidarity of corporate life by singing badly and laughing about it. COARA members seem never to tire of taking turns singing, which is interesting given that they are most accustomed to interacting strictly by means of mute letters on a computer screen. There is indeed something funny about watching someone whose serious arguments you have been read-

ing for months step up to the microphone and do an Elvis imperson-
ation. It puts more of the person back in the online persona you have
modeled in your mind. They insisted that I sing "I Left My Heart In San
Francisco."

After the second Hypernetwork conference, I stayed around with the
COARA people for a couple of days after the other participants had left.
We traveled together to the village of Yufuin, site of famous hot springs.
We took the waters and relaxed after the days of formal speeches and
informal but no less important social networking. I asked the COARA
members I had met, one by one, how their virtual community had come
into being and how it had affected their lives. Izumi Aizu acted as an
interpreter in both directions during both the formal and the informal
parts of my visit.

COARA, I learned, had been designed originally as a kind of database
for a small group of local business people to provide local information
about business, transportation, weather, and other civic matters, but a
series of events led the founders to redesign it into a full-blown conferencing system. One of the historical roots of the strong feeling of community that emerged is the fact that COARA started out as a series of
face-to-face meetings among citizens who wanted a shared information
resource they could tap into via their modems, but who weren't quite
sure what it was they wanted. One early event that steered COARA
toward community was the involvement of Izumi Aizu. Mr. Toru Ono, a
computer enthusiast and owner of an electrical contracting company in
Oita, who wanted to start a community information system, had read
Aizu's report. Ono telephoned Aizu in Tokyo and asked him to consider
helping them design the system.

COARA was one of several experiments that started in 1985, a water-
shed year for grassroots telecommunications in Japan because the
Japanese telecommunications industry was deregulated. Before that, it
was bureaucratically difficult and expensive for ordinary citizens to use
modems. There was a lot of talk in the wake of deregulation about "new
media." Mr. Ono was interested in what he had heard about BBSs and
other CMC systems. Many of the "new media" experiments that were
springing up were modeled on the old broadcast paradigm of putting a
lot of information into a central source and then allowing people to contact it remotely. Aizu had been one of the few voices for taking a more

person-to-person, network-oriented approach, because he had observed in the United States that people wanted to use CMC primarily to connect with each other, and only secondarily to download information.

One COARA person who took the excursion to Beppu was Yukitsugu Fujino, a young computer science student who had been actively involved with Mr. Ono in founding the service in 1985. At the beginning, Fujino was looking for nothing more than a database to help him catalog his personal library of more than twenty-thousand books. When he began reading about PC networking, Fujino, Ono, and about a dozen other people met in Oita in 1985 with local government officials to discuss buying a computer to use as a kind of community database and public computing resource. It turned out that the Oita regional government had a computer that could be used. Fujino and Ono worked together to create database software. The first information they put up for public use was a train timetable for Oita. The thirty founding COARA members decided that they wanted to put in more information, but they weren't sure what kind of information would attract more usage, so they created a simple public forum to communicate about it. People started to communicate informally. Then something happened that seemed to precipitate the evolution of a community.

More than a dozen COARA members I interviewed mentioned that the community really began with the advent of online autobiographical reports from a high-school student named Masaharu Baba, a very skilled computer programmer. "But when he started writing online about what it was like to be a high-school boy," Fujino told me, "COARA became much more interesting. Hearing about the real life of a high-school student was more exciting than publishing a lot of dry information. People started to log on more regularly to find out what was going to happen, and to talk about it with each other. We began to realize the value of people-to-people interaction. We decided we wanted to be able to write more personally."

Fujino created an informal public discussion area, a virtual café, called Café COARA, without asking permission from anyone. This isn't the way things are done in Japan ordinarily, but everyone involved agreed that it was good. At that point, Aizu became involved, and they rewrote the software, added more modems and incoming telephone lines, and set up a regional conferencing system at about the same time the WELL was starting up in the San Francisco region and TWICS was starting in Tokyo. The Oita Junior Chamber of Commerce became involved because they thought a new information service could be useful to small-business operators. The online population began to grow.

The kinds of people I got to know from COARA's core group seemed to me more diverse in several ways than traditional Japanese social groups, and the individual members confirmed that when I asked. For one thing, the community appeared to cut across class and professional lines. Ono-san is the owner of an important industry in Oita. Fujino-san was a salesman in a construction company. A prominent member of the community, Mr. Masato Kubaki, who eventually visited me in California, is a pottery teacher at the local university. Several housewives, whose children are grown and out of the nest, and whose husbands have not yet retired, became the social organizers of the face-to-face events. The presence—the very vocal presence—of so many women was also unusual for Japanese society, where many activities are gender-segregated. The usual boundaries of profession, class, age, and gender appeared to be significantly looser in COARA than in other Japanese social groups.

Like the WELL, some of the use and some of the myth of COARA is its courtship function. When people can watch two members of their group meet and marry, it seems more like a real community—and Fujino-san was one of the community's founders. Fujino-san and his wife met and courted via COARA, and their wedding was one of the early bonding events of the community. One of the younger women in COARA told me that joining COARA gave her a much larger range of choice when it came to meeting eligible young men in a socially acceptable way. Young women in Japan usually meet their future husbands through introductions by family members or by employers. COARA was both liberating, in that it enabled people whose families or employers might not know each other to meet in a properly chaperoned manner. If it is true that older housewives and younger working women can use CMC in Japan to transcend traditional constraints on their social behavior, then the new medium poses a potentially formidable threat to gender relations—one of the mainstays of Japan's core social structure.

One of the most energetic members of the thirty to fifty people who always can be counted on to show up for a COARA event is a housewife who started learning to use a computer for word processing. "Although after I found COARA," Mieko Nagano told me, "I learned that the computer can do more than word processing. It can help me interact with people's minds and hearts." Just as the autobiography of a high-school student turned out to be fascinating to the mostly older community, the strongly stated point of view of a housewife with grown children turned out to win attention by the mostly male COARA population. Her husband, in his fifties, works in the Nippon steel manufacturing plant in Oita. Husband and wife logged on daily for about an hour each. When I asked him what continued to attract him to COARA, he told me: "See those sick forests outside of town? The ones where all the trees die are where they planted just one kind of tree. The forests that survive and do well are the ones where many kinds of trees grow. I think it is like that with people. I enjoy many different opinions. It keeps my mind healthy."

Not everyone in any society enjoys many different opinions, and in that sense, the strongest similarity between the WELL and COARA—the willingness of the online population to tolerate wide diversity of opinion—might turn out to be a limiting factor of the medium's growth. The present state of porosity between the boundaries of different online groups on the Net might be an artifact of the early stages of the medium —fragmentation, hierarchization, rigidifying social boundaries, and single-niche colonies of people who share intolerances could become prevalent in the future.

I spoke with young professionals—an insurance salesman, an employee of an auto leasing firm, a city hall employee involved in the department of education—who had left Oita for college in one of the larger cities, and had started using COARA to stay in touch with people in Oita while they were gone. When they returned to their hometown, as many college graduates do, they still had connections to the social life that had been going on in their absence. I talked to another couple who were passionate about COARA's parenting conference. I told them that I understood them exactly when they emphasized how important the support and advice from other COARA parents had been when their child ran a fever that temporarily puzzled the doctors. Another woman, a housewife in her fifties, told me that she received a very detailed personal reply from Governor Hiramatsu when she sent him electronic mail about government compensation for typhoon damage, and that im-pressed her enough to get more involved in the online discussions of local politics.

When Governor Hiramatsu became a COARA member in 1986, and began talking with other community members about the medium's potential, COARA experienced another period of rapid growth in its population and expansion of its vision—and considerable excitement among the community members. This was not just an honorary membership. The governor actually participated in online discussions, actually replied to electronic mail.

"Governor Hiramatsu is a very interesting person," Aizu told me, before I met the governor in Oita. He explained that Hiramatsu had been a powerful member of MITI —Japan's influential Ministry of International Trade and Industry—and had been one of the planners of Japan's success in computers in the 1970s. Like his American counterparts at ARPA, Hiramatsu was known as a technology manager who found breakthrough projects and supported them, rather than trying to advance technology through top-down design. After leaving MITI, he returned to his home province to fulfill his vision of high-tech economic development that would not make the mistakes of overcentralizing industry and destroying the natural environment. He was one of the architects of the Technopolis vision of technology-linked regional economic development. As governor of Oita, a resource-rich, largely rural province far from the centers of power, he had an opportunity to start from scratch. Beppu Bay, where the city of Oita is located, is a rich source of seafood and includes some still-unspoiled coastline. The countryside is agricultural, with some local crafts and light industry.

Hiramatsu's vision, as he explained it when I interviewed him in 1990, was to "find harmony between this special environment and the high-growth, typically high-tech industries we want to attract to this area. We want to make sure these high-tech businesses do not weaken the agriculture and fishery businesses and the natural beauty of the region. The third element of this vision is to provide education and skill training, so the high-tech companies can transfer their technology to local industries." To do that, Hiramatsu had believed from the beginning, it would be necessary to overcome the centralization of information as well as population and industry in Tokyo. The Oita region would have to create its own information pool. When COARA came along, Hiramatsu jumped right in. He attended the face-to-face get-togethers as well as the online forums. He pushed the idea of involving ordinary citizens as well as the captains of industry and local business people and the natural constituents among the younger computer enthusiasts. He particularly advised an outreach effort to involve more women.

With Hiramatsu's support and vision, and the continuing growth of the COARA population into the hundreds and then thousands, it became possible to upgrade the system's hardware and software to accommodate the users' needs. Many more online forums, to discuss books, restaurants, entertainment, parenting, local politics, art, and philosophy, began to open. A core of COARA members started having monthly face-to-face gatherings. They began to think of themselves as a community. Another key member of the community was drawn into COARA from far-away Tokyo. Shumpei Kumon, a distinguished scholar and adviser to high government officials, had become very interested in the role that information technologies might play in the larger social transformation he foresaw. COARA turned into a conversion experience as well as a source of direct observations to test his theories. The Hypernetwork vision that emerged from the collective enterprise of COARA and its founders, Governor Hiramatsu's office, and Izumi Aizu was given a strong intellectual framework by Kumon, whose theories gave form to their collectively evolving vision of CMC-assisted social change.

Shumpei Kumon, who is always addressed in Japan with the honorific "sensei," because he was once a professor at the all-important University of Tokyo, is a maverick of a different kind. In his fifties, he looks every bit the modern Japanese government adviser that he is, but he started out as an orthodox leftist in the 1960s. He lost faith in the left and began looking at the way civilizations like the United States and Japan and those that had gone before had managed the large-scale transformations triggered by technology. He became a professor, and his colleagues introduced him to some of the brightest, most open-minded members of Japan's powerful Liberal Democratic Party (LDP). When he realized that the time was not ripe to achieve deep political reform, Kumon concentrated on developing his theories in history, economics, and cybernetics. He was coming to see Japanese-American political and economic relations in the 1990s as the linchpin of a social transformation triggered by new information technologies.

In Kumon's framework, the three most important stages in the history of human civilization are most usefully seen in terms of the social games that governed those civilizations' sources of power: first the Prestige Game, then the Wealth Game, and finally the Wisdom Game. The Prestige Game was triggered by militarization, the use of force and the threat of force to gain and maintain power over other actors. The idea of nationhood came along and the use of force was abstracted on a higher level, in which national economic and cultural power challenged raw military power for importance. The industrial revolution made possible the most recent era in which technologically produced wealth rather than either prestige or military power alone became the most important marker in the world's highest-level social games. The older games continue to exist, but the center of attention moves from royal courts to national elections to virtual, transnational, communication-mediated relationships as the system evolves.

The current trigger for a transition to a new stage, in Kumon's theory, is the world telecommunications network, and the next game will involve information, knowledge, and folklore-sharing cooperatives around the world that will challenge the primacy of traditional wealth the way industrial wealth challenged the primacy of military and national power and prestige. Today's virtual communities, Kumon came to understand firsthand, offer a small-scale model of a society in which people communicate in a way that creates collective wealth. A kind of wealth that includes the existence of Parenting conferences is more than a cold-blooded exchange of information, hence his characterization of the coming social framework as the Wisdom Game, in which the source of power is "consensus-formation through information and knowledge sharing." He saw it working on a regional level. Would it scale up? For a student of history, the temptation to seize a social lever, once his intellectual exploration led him to discover it, was very great.

Kumon decided to make a move almost as radical as Aizu's decision to drop out of the college examinations—he decided to leave his professorship and devote himself to studying the economic and sociological consequences of the computer networks that came to enthrall him. But he intended to do more than study. Along with activists such as Aizu and Hiramatsu, he had an opportunity to demonstrate in real life the social potential of networks he had been writing about in his books. He cofounded an institute, GLOCOM, devoted to the study and implementation of the Wisdom Game. I met with Kumon and his colleagues in

Oita and in Tokyo on both my trips to Japan, and they have visited me in the United States.

Kumon's interest in economic and social change had led him to learn the basics of computer technology with the eyes of a beginner. When he understood the power of networks, he wrote books and articles about Japan as a "network society" in a social sense, which it is in many ways, with its overlapping circles of formal and informal association that weave Japanese social, professional, political, and cultural institutions together. But the whole world is not as racially and historically homogeneous as Japan. One chief criticism of Japanese culture as a model for other societies is that the social networks in diverse societies such as the United States and other parts of the world lack the shared ethnic and historical context that strongly guides people's social communications in Japan. When he came across the computer concept of "emulation," Kumon believed he had found the solution to the most vexing problem in his theory—the way Japanese and American cultural approaches are integrated in a global context.

Emulation in computers is an answer to the translation problems caused by the great diversity in computer hardware. Because a computer can simulate the operations of any machine, it is possible to write a program that causes a computer from one manufacturer to behave the way a computer from a different manufacturer behaves. Each computer contributes a portion of its resources to emulating another computer, which means that data and programs in a network environment can be shared, thus enriching the network's computational collective goods.

Could cultural co-emulation be an effective social metaphor for finding ways for Japanese and American sensibilities to meet on the Net? "The best way for Japan and other nations of the world to deal with the information age is to co-emulate other's civilizational components that each lacks and that seem to cope with the demands of this new phase of modernization," Aizu and Kumon wrote—which explains why I was invited to Oita in 1990, and why Barlow, Johansen, and Johnson-Lenz were invited to join me there in 1993. Recent efforts to put this cultural co-emulation theory to the test have led to meetings between Kumon's GLOCOM Institute and Mitch Kapor of the Electronic Frontier Foundation, to Izumi Aizu's continuing presence on the WELL, to GLOCOM jumping the political hurdles to become an Internet site, and to a stream of young Japanese CMC enthusiasts who make sure to visit those of us in the United States whom they met when we were their guests in Japan.

The Hypernetwork Society was the vision that led Japanese communications researchers to begin gathering every other year in Oita. Although Kumon and Aizu spent most of their time physically in Tokyo, the developing vision remained rooted in COARA. Their vision of COARA as a testbed for future international communities was supported by the core members in Oita, who were hungry to communicate with people in other parts of the world. If CMC could help local people cut across social boundaries that normally separated them in rural Japan, it made sense that citizen-to-citizen communication could help overcome some of the national differences that lead to conflict. One thing I didn't understand until I visited Japan in person is that while Japan is important to Americans and America, America is almost all-important to Japanese and Japan.

With Japan seen as a dangerous economic competitor by many in the United States, and a strong, vocal contingent of Japan bashers who see Japan as an outright enemy of the United States, ordinary people in Japan seem frustrated by what they learn from their own media about what is going on in the United States, and what American news media seem to be telling Americans. The citizens I met in Oita were eager to use CMC to bypass the mass media and communicate directly with their counterparts—the housewives and professionals in Santa Monica and elsewhere—to show that there is more to Japan than the picture painted by the American media.

When COARA members first wanted to expand the community to include more people from the villages and agricultural regions, the telecommunications costs for long-distance modem calls made that impossible. Governor Hiramatsu, however, decided in 1990 that it would be good for Oita prefecture, good for his Technopolis vision, and good for COARA to sponsor the first government-supported free regional packet-switching network in the world. Special routers were located in key cities, and the prefecture and city governments paid for the installation of a network that would enable people in twelve other cities and towns to make an inexpensive local call to connect to COARA and other information services. Ultimately, COARA was also linked across the Pacific, to Santa Monica's PEN (Public Electronic Network) system.

Not only the countryside, but other parts of the world, became parts of the plan: members of PEN and COARA eventually were able to communicate in a shared forum. By the time they started inviting CMC evangelists from around the world, COARA had become more than a successful experiment—it was a testbed for the idea of citizens' movements and regional governments working cooperatively to create virtual communities.

In 1992, Governor Hiramatsu addressed a small invitational forum of technology developers, including Apple Computer's John Sculley, and top managers from NEC and other Japanese companies:

I see the toyonokuni network as being an "information road." Just as the automobile society wasn't built on the development of motor vehicles alone, it also required a network of roads. I think the true information society will require this kind of social infrastructure as an essential building block. As a rural area, Oita prefecture does not attract a great deal of private sector commercial investment; that's why I judged it necessary to allocate government funds to provide a service which I believe will be regarded as a social necessity in the future.

Since Oita, a paradigm example of a mature virtual community, was the first place I visited in Japan after my first night in Tokyo, I was in for a shock when I visited telecommunications research centers in Kyoto and Tokyo. Although I had met a provincial governor and a mayor of a small city who were well aware and actively involved in many-to-many communications media, I discovered that the higher-level research managers in Japan's telecommunications companies were just as uninformed as American telecommunications managers regarding the explosive grassroots growth of the Net. Like American and European telecom managers, they were interested enough to listen to my tales of grassroots culture-building. It was as if I were telling them that a colony from another planet had found a way to occupy the telephone network.

The odd irony of this nearly global ignorance of the person-to-person potential of CMC among telecommunications managers is that the technologies they are very good at creating—the ultra-high bandwidth fiber-optic networks, wireless communicators, digital video compressors—have the potential to amplify the power of today's grassroots experiments by orders of magnitude. Japanese researchers in electronics and computer technology had decades to develop their body of collective knowledge and accumulate expertise. Those who would learn how to build virtual communities in Japan were discouraged until the mid–1980s. In Japan, because it was illegal to use a modem until 1985, only a few pioneers began to dabble in Netsurfing before that. If the pattern in Japan repeats the evolution of new technologies in America, those few intrepid pioneers who started using modems when you had to pay a hefty fee to an unsympathetic government ministry will end up influencing the shape of Japan's Net culture as it catches up. The hundreds of thousands of Japanese Netheads today will diffuse what they have learned to those who will follow the pioneers. NTT has committed itself to delivering broadband fiber-optic cable to every home in Japan by the year 2015.

At the same time that Japan's industrial planners are building on the hardware of telecommunications as the core of their strategy for the twenty-first century, Japanese students are not on Internet in the same growing numbers as the Americans or Europeans, because government policy makes it very difficult to get an Internet account. The main data-communications link between Japan's networks and the worldwide Internet is a relatively slow, relatively low-capacity channel. Japan's powers -that-be have always exercised strict control over citizen communications with the outside. That control is directly challenged by the prospect of widespread access to a high-bandwidth international network. This conflict could be the fulcrum for major changes in the entire culture in the near future.

Herein lies the dilemma. Japan's continuing economic success depends on continuing success in technological research and development, and, increasingly, access to information about what your colleagues are doing and what is happening in different but related fields is the key to scientific or technological success. To open the Net to its citizens might be necessary to continue to compete; that same simple act of letting people drink what they choose from the Net's great gushers will inevitably change both Japanese culture and Net culture. Whether Japan joins in the Net in a big way is an extremely important question that has not, until very recently, attracted much attention at the highest levels of Japanese or American decision making. The race to build the most successful fiber-optic networks, high-definition televisions, or hand-held wireless communicators is more concrete, more easily understood. The need to keep up with the evolution of a worldwide intellectual communication medium is more abstract, but no less vital to an innovation-dependent economy like Japan's. A collision or a convergence seems likely very soon.

COARA was the first of several virtual communities I came to know in Japan, but I learned that there was an even older one. Before I left the United States, I obtained an account on the TWICS system in Tokyo and started introducing myself to members of that community. I had heard a great deal about Jeff Shapard and Joichi Ito, cofounders of TWICS, and people on the system seemed to be arguing and communing in ways that reminded me of the WELL. When the time came, after a few weeks of discussion about virtual communities as they looked from both sides of the Pacific, the TWICS people I had met decided to hold one of their monthly meetings to coincide with my visit.

The TWICS office in Tokyo is right downtown, in the office of its parent organization. The night I showed up I met most of the people I had already met online, plus about thirty others. Eventually, we traveled en masse via subway to a raucous underground sushi parlor where the management had a section reserved for them regularly. One force that keeps virtual communities in Japan from coalescing quickly is that Japanese homes are small, so people do most of their socializing and entertaining in their version of "third places." This virtual community liked to crowd together around a few tables in a working-class restaurant, and eat, drink beer, and talk, for four or five hours at a time. Before we went out to socialize, we gathered in a meeting room in the TWICS office building so I could talk with them as a group about their virtual community, and so they could ask me questions about the other communities I had visited.

Jeffrey Shapard somehow wandered from his native Montana in 1981 and ended up in Japan. He became an English teacher, "stumbled into electronic networking in 1984," he said, and has been involved "nonstop and more than full-time in this medium ever since. Some have described me as a raving mad lunatic obsessive workaholic passionate believer in a solution looking for problems to solve," he added, wryly. It makes sense that a Tokyo resident with a Montana accent and an interest in CMC would be a perfect partner for a young Japanese with the sensibilities of an American teenager. Joichi Ito got Shapard involved in a project aimed at providing opportunities for continuing education and international communication, sponsored by the International Education Center, where the TWICS office is now located. They built a small BBS, in the days when that wasn't easy, one of the first half-dozen such experiments at the time. From the start, TWICS had a strong purpose determined by its mission: "We were oriented more toward people and communication rather than data and information. From the beginning, we made it clear we wanted something more than just another place to talk about computers and exchange software."

In 1985, TWICS became a multi-user system and "we discovered that conferencing was what we were really doing." Before COARA or the WELL opened as a regional conferencing system, TWICS was up and running. In 1986, they upgraded their system hardware and found a way to plug into the rest of the world, albeit at slower-than-Internet speeds. International telecommunications companies often provide cheap data communications during their normally slower hours, and these commercial data services enable systems like the early WELL and TWICS to provide cheap communication costs to reach their system. In 1988, Shapard and Ito attended the Electronic Networking Association conference in Philadelphia, where Shapard met John S. Quarterman, cartographer of the Net (which he calls "The Matrix"). That opened Shapard's eyes: "I felt like we had been living in some electronic version of the Middle Ages, building little villages off in remote regions, trying to figure out ways for people to get to us and for us to have routes to our neighbors, thinking we were really doing something new and hot, and then discovering China, with a vast, complex, and ancient civilization." After that, TWICS found a way to get a full Usenet feed.

The people who had joined TWICS before it became a full conferencing system were able to participate, through the original BBS, in designing the shape of their virtual community. Shapard proposed that the metaphor of their place would be very important in determining what kind of place it would be, and, through a process of community design, created the metaphorical electronic island called Beejima: "Since we wanted to build a place where people would feel like they were members of something more than just another information service, we decided to use the metaphor of a community as the basic organizing principle for the new computer conferencing system we were going to install. The image of Beejima was a friendly little island community in the electronic seas of Japan, close to Tokyo but accessible from anywhere, a Japanese system modeled on Japanese context, with an international and multi-cultural outlook."

The questions that the TWICS members asked me, after they told me about themselves, began to surface some similarities with other online systems. In fact, the first question touched off a discussion among the TWICS people that could have been a word-for-word transcript of a discussion on the WELL or CIX. I was asked: "Do people in other virtual communities think that words on a computer screen are capable of hurting people?" I said that I personally felt that to be the case, but that others raise the argument that it is really a matter of choice when it comes to determining how you feel about what a stranger might have typed on one computer and sent to another computer via modem. One fellow, an American who participated in a lot of Usenet discussions as well as TWICS (which may explain his attitude), volunteered: "All you have to do is turn off the computer. If you don't like a BBS because people are argumentative, log into a different BBS." A Japanese woman stood up and said that some people do feel that you can be hurt, and maybe that means that only "the thick-skinned stay around."

That familiar discussion veered into another familiar discussion about how easy it is for misunderstandings to become conflicts because of the lack of social cues. "How do you avert your eyes online, how do you bow?" was the way one TWICS member put it (all-important nonverbal components of polite Japanese conversation). Another TWICS member replied that CMC is attractive precisely because it is different from every-day life. "Why duplicate the face-to-face world in a new medium? It isn't polite to communicate with three people at the same time in physical conversation, but you can do that online." The ensuing discussion reminded me of what Elizabeth Reid said about the community-building function of creating a shared imagined context for a virtual community.

Then it came down to the nature of community, as these discussions always do. So Jeff Shapard stood up at the blackboard and asked the TWICS members to name as many attributes of community as they could come up with. Some of the responses were "shared taboos," "a common forum for social interaction," "a means of banding together against a common threat," "shared culture," "familiarity and respect," "mutual sustenance," "shared joy and pain," "rites of passage." As it turned out, the Beejima face-to-face meeting I attended was a rite of passage for the

TWICS community. Jeff Shapard stood up before the group and delivered a speech that brought tears to his eyes and a few others: after twelve years in Japan and nine years with TWICS, he was returning to the United States.

Not until I too returned did I meet Joichi Ito, the other founder of TWICS, a person whose name comes up no matter whom you talk with about the history of CMC in Japan. His business brings him close enough to my location for us to meet face-to-face once in a while. I learned that he was born in Kyoto, one of the most conservative Japanese cities in terms of tradition—it was the capital for a thousand years before a little fishing village called Edo grew up to become Tokyo. His mother was from a ruling-class family going back eighteen generations. His father was from an old merchant-class family. Both families disowned them when they married because of the contradiction of such a marriage. "Now they like us again," says Ito. His mother and father moved to the United States when he was three, so Joichi was brought up mostly in the suburbs of Detroit when Detroit was going through a financial crisis precipitated by the success of Japanese automobile imports. He and his sister spent summer vacations with his grandmother who "indoctrinated us with the values of traditional Japan." When he was fourteen he moved back to Japan, where he attended Nishimachi International School and later the American School in Japan "and learned Tokyo street language, street smarts, and computers."

As a teenager in the early 1980s, Joichi discovered computer networking as a "means of communicating with people beyond the confines of a high-school reality. Computer networking expanded greatly my understanding of society as I dealt on a day-to-day-level with classes, Judo, varsity wrestling, girlfriends, and stupid teachers." He got so involved with a group of people he met on the Source that he and others from different parts of the world traveled to Toledo to meet each other face-to-face at the wedding of two group members. He remembers how most of his online friends were shocked with the physical evidence of how young he was, despite his cultural sophistication.

Ito was a bit of a hacker in his younger days, so he found ways to keep down his communication costs while sampling online cultures around the world. He even discovered the original MUD, MUD1, at the University of Essex in England; MUD1's founder, Richard Bartle, still remembers the one early enthusiast who logged on all the way from Japan. Ito remembers the night he sat in his room in Tokyo and wept because his MUD character had been killed. Later, he attended Tufts and the University of Chicago, but like Izumi Aizu, he felt the cultural and professional opportunities in computer networking in Japan were more important, so he dropped out in his senior year to work part-time with the Metasystems Design Group, start a virtual community in Tokyo with Jeff Shapard, and work nights as a deejay in nightclubs.

In 1985, at nineteen, Ito found himself back in Japan to develop and distribute the Japanese version of Caucus, one of the leading computer conferencing software packages. "At the same time," he recalled in conversations with the author, "I produced nightclub events trying to create cultural and artistic synergy between contradictory cultures, something that I had learned to do since my childhood." He currently works as a negotiator for problematic U.S./Japan negotiations for American and Japanese companies, develops and coordinates Pan-Pacific technical and cultural projects, and is a member of Japan's Ministry of Post and Telecom's Computer Networking Subcommittee of the New Media Committee. If anybody understands the challenges Japan and the Net pose for each other, particularly among the younger generation now in their twenties, it's Joichi Ito. He believes that most Japanese underestimate the potential for social change inherent in new communications technologies simply because Japanese culture has evolved such a sophisticated mechanism for resisting externally imposed change.

"Japanese culture doesn't change and since it's so comfortable with the fact that it doesn't change and it's so secure with the absolute core of Japanese culture, it's very comfortable changing on the surface," Ito explained. I had asked him about the impending collision of values and technology that seemed likely as the Net grows in Japan.

The cultural immune system reacts at a much higher level in America. Americans stay away from dangerous things. Whereas the Japanese immune system is so well adapted to change, they can talk about hypernetworking or about cyberspace or robotics. They don't think that it's really going to bother them. When punk rock came into Japan and you could bump into a punk kid who wore a "fuck off and die" button on his shirt, that looks pretty rebellious, there was still a significant difference. You bump into him on the street, he's going to say "excuse me, I'm sorry." And that doesn't change, you see. But I have a feeling that computer networking and the global culture right now could change the

Japanese system for the first time in thousands of years. A lot of people don't get it yet. So you'll see a reaction coming, a kind of allergic reaction in Japan that no one's ever seen before in Japan. I think we'll see the day that happens.

Ito believes that several of the cliches about why Japanese citizens might not embrace cyberculture have a basis in reality. For example, Japanese are reluctant to debate in an argumentative sense in public forums. The Net could learn something from Japanese conversational etiquette, and Japanese Netheads are going to have to learn something about the virtues of public debate. "Debate is not a part of the culture," Ito claims. "Litigation is rare, group therapy doesn't work well," he points out, adding, "I think it is difficult to get Japanese to relax in front of people and thus it may be difficult to get a sense of community in a group of invisible strangers unless they have something significant in common such as being outcast from society in some way, or sharing a strong common interest, or common physical location."

"I know it is difficult for Japanese to participate in the Net culture as it exists today," says Ito. "It wasn't designed for the Japanese. I just don't know what is going to happen when the next generation network Nintendo game with all of the quirks, aesthetics, communication needs, and timing of Japanese culture designed in is developed and deployed with the high-bandwidth networks the big companies are planning." The Japanese written language, with its ideographic calligraphy, is an important part of the visual culture in Japan that resists the starkness of alphabetic characters on screens. The experiments at NTT, Fujitsu, and elsewhere on highly visual media may take an interesting turn when communication on the Net includes a more visual element. This may be a place where Japanese communication aesthetics might take a leadership position. "I think the Japanese will make their own version of online communication media and the Net will grow to include it," says Ito. "I think that the product of such a fusion may be the greatest transmission of Japanese culture to the West yet. Americans have begun to use Japanese quality control techniques in their business management. Imagine what might happen when the West begins to use communication tools based on Japanese/Eastern ways of communicating."

8

Télématique and *Messageries Roses*: A Tale of Two Virtual Communities

A year and a half after I met Izumi Aizu and Katsura Hattori from Tokyo, I met Lionel Lumbroso and Annick Morel from Paris, who also became my friends, interpreters, and guides to their charming city. My encounters with French online culture helped me see a few more outlines of the Net's global nature. Japan's own versions of Net culture first showed me how much bigger than its American origins the Net has become, and how far from English-speaking or culturally American discourse virtual communities have traveled. My explorations of France's two different virtual cities have surfaced another theme that seems to recur everywhere I've looked—big institutions often think of CMC as a kind of database, a way of broadcasting information on screens to large populations who spend their time interacting with information, but populations of citizens almost always use CMC to communicate with each other in new ways unforeseen by the system's original designers. People everywhere seem more interested in communicating with each other than with databases.

The first of Paris's two virtual cities I encountered was CalvaCom, the oldest surviving enclave of French virtual communitarians who use systems like the WELL or COARA to attempt a relatively high level of discourse and conviviality. The other virtual city is much larger—the six million Minitel users who created by themselves an enormously lucrative chat culture in an information system that was originally designed to be a telephone directory and database. The way small-scale virtual communities have failed to catch on among the personal computer users of France, and the way the Minitel-using population subverted the medium to uses not envisioned in the planning of the multi-billion-dollar system, are key case histories for future virtual community designers on local or national scale. Although my four visits to Paris and the interviews I conducted there can only touch on the most prominent landmarks of French online culture, the importance of France's ten-year Teletel project, the world's largest national CMC network, is another critical uncertainty in the evolution of Worldnet, too important to be left out of anyone's mental model of the Net.

I found my Parisian friends the same way Izumi Aizu had found me—through mutual friends on the Net. I had heard of the Minitel and the notorious *messageries roses*—the "pink" sex-chat services that overloaded the entire French national network during their first surge of popularity. I couldn't believe that sex chat of the most unsubtle kind is the most important French contribution to Worldnet. It wasn't easy at first to find virtual communities in France from my location in California—they didn't show themselves prominently on Usenet or MUDs or IRC. I was curious about other kinds of CMC in France, but didn't have any direct contacts at first. The Net led me through two intermediate steps, the Electronic Networking Association and a member of it who lived in Paris, to Lumbroso and Morel, two Parisians who had been active members of the oldest virtual community in Paris.

CalvaCom is a dial-up system like the WELL that connects personal computer users into group discussions via their modems and a central computer. This is now a technical minority in France, because the Minitel terminals distributed for free by the French government plug directly into the telephone system without a computer or modem. CalvaCom's population of several thousand is equivalent to that of the WELL or COARA or TWICS a few years back, although the original system, known first as Calvados, went into operation before any of the other pioneering virtual communities I had visited. CalvaCom was already in existence when France Telecom, the government-operated telecommunications company, decided to give away millions of Minitel terminals to French citizens in a conscious effort to bring the population into the information age all at once.

I had met Annick Morel face-to-face on a previous visit to Paris, but Lionel Lumbroso and I exchanged e-mail about twice a week for several months before we met. I had seen him in my mind's eye as a portly fellow in his mid-fifties and was shocked to discover he was slim and in his late thirties. We found that we shared the same history, values, and concerns that I had found in common with Aizu and Hattori.

In 1968, as a college war protester and counterculture activist myself, I remember feeling that the students who were challenging the French government on the streets of Paris and the Japanese students challenging their own authorities in Tokyo were, in some sense, members of the same global cohort as I and my American companions were. We were all saying, in our own ways, that the injustices of the old ways of doing things were not going to get us through the rest of the century. When I met Aizu and Hattori, they told me that they had felt exactly the same way back then; and here we were, more than two decades later, intersecting in cyberspace, excited about a new tool for making the world work better than it does. Lumbroso, Morel, and I went through an almost identical conversation at first; just like my first encounter with my Tokyo friends, we talked late into the night from the moment we first met face-to-face in Paris, like old cronies who hadn't seen each other in years.

Lionel Lumbroso lives in an apartment on one of those hidden Parisian blocks of high-ceilinged apartments arranged around a little private square off the main street, behind a wooden door, long ago converted from the stables of Napoleonic officers. Lumbroso's living room, where much of the offline socializing for CalvaCom takes place, and the bistro around the corner that specializes in steak tartare, are the images I see in my mind's eye when I think of CalvaCom.

Lumbroso was one of the founders of Calvados, in the early 1980s. In the late 1970s, Lumbroso started working as an interpreter in technical fields, which led to some interest in computers. In 1981, he met an American woman, Gena, who later became his wife. Through Gena he became involved with Steve Plummer, the dean of students at the American University of Paris. Plummer and another partner wanted to give personal computer users remote access to advanced programming languages. At that time, most PC users in France used the Apple II, a laughably puny antique by today's standards, with modems that transmitted information at 300 bits per second. But they had high hopes that the hardware would become more powerful in the future and they would have a growing business.

Plummer and his partner needed a technically knowledgeable Parisian. Lumbroso came along, took a crash course in computers, and started to create an online system from scratch, in time for a big computer show. At that time, Apple was just establishing Apple France, and the fellow who took charge of Apple France, Jean-Louis Gassée, thought the Calvados system could become important for Apple users. Apple and the American University were supporting him to create something entirely new.

Lumbroso wrote programming code, he went out to visit Apple dealers, he met with the business managers. "I was a jack of all trades. It was quite exciting," Lumbroso recalled, ten years later. "At the time we started, in 1982–83, Minitel was still an experiment confined to one suburb of Paris, Velizy, where France Télécom was testing the idea. Our models at Calvados were the big American online services. The Source was big at that time; CompuServe was not that big yet."

It started out as a community of Apple users and Apple dealers, and people still exchanged information about Apple computers and argued about different kinds of Apple software, but they also started chatting, in groups of twenty or thirty, for no particular purpose other than to make each other fall off the chair laughing, every day. "We would shoot phrases at each other, carry on multiple conversations. All the fun came from the mingling of different conversations. You could see the transcript on your screen. We would do it for hours on end." The word began to get around the French Apple community, and by 1985, Calvados had grown to about three thousand users, and income was about $100,000 a month. In 1986, Steve Plummer found $2 million to finance the system outside the American University. They bought more powerful hardware, rewrote the software, and targeted the service not just to Apple II users but to all PC users.

They designed the new version of their online service, which they renamed CalvaCom, using the metaphor of different "cities" to represent different forums. The Macintosh city, The PC city, and the Atari city were the major discussion areas. Like the first BBSs in the United States, CalvaCom was still frequented mostly by computer enthusiasts or people in the computer business, talking mostly about computing. "We deliberately created cities that weren't linked to computer-related topics," Lumbroso recalled. "For example, one we called 'free expression.'" It was a catchall term for arguments about political issues, discussions about cinema or video, philosophy—whatever people wanted to talk about in a forum. A forum was different from the group chat service that was still popular when CalvaCom started; in a chat, there is no record or structure to the conversation, but in a forum, there is a structured record of comments that are all supposed to be related to a specific topic—a conferencing system.

One of Lumbroso's strategies for keeping their service lively and growing was to identify those users that were the most active, the most stimulating, and hire them as *animateurs*—the paid equivalent of the WELL's hosts. That is where he met Annick Morel, who also helped me meet the architects of Télématique, as well as the sysops of pink chat services. I asked Lumbroso what the most vexing social problems had been, from his position. "The conflict between the need to keep the atmosphere convivial, and the temptation to censor people," he replied.

For a couple of years, Lumbroso noted, there has been a vocal group of people online in the Macintosh city who hate the products of Microsoft, and whenever people in public forums try to exchange information about how to use Microsoft products, the discussions are derailed by familiar, tiresome tirades about the evils of Microsoft. "I think that online is a stage for some people who don't have opportunities to express themselves in real life." Whenever a system manager tries to curb expressions that probably drive away all but the thick-skinned, the system seems to get embroiled in a debate about censorship and the free expression of ideas. I've seen the same debates on the WELL and on TWICS, and according to Lumbroso, they continue on Calvacom.

In recent years, since he has not been working for CalvaCom, Lumbroso has cut back on his online time. He and Gena have two young children they didn't have when he started, which now take up his time, and he told me that he has grown weary of the constant argument online. He said that, after the exchange of information, wisecracks, and casual humor, argument was the single most frequent online activity. I described the WELL's and COARA's Parenting conference, and he said that nothing resembling that kind of community existed on CalvaCom, although a core group of CalvaCom users met socially. Funny chat was common. Brainstorming was uncommon. Barn raising was unheard of.

Nina Popravka, a computer professional who chose Calvados instead of Minitel because of the quality of the technical conversation, showed up at Lumbroso's house, together with several other old friends who had met through CalvaCom. She came into our conversation when Lumbroso and I were talking about the kind of communion represented by a Parenting conference in America or Japan, and why it isn't common on either CalvaCom or the larger Minitel services. Popravka theorized that there really isn't a market for communion-type CMC services, or they would have proliferated on Minitel. "In France," she insisted, "people put fences between their houses. They don't want to socialize with their neighbors. If they want to meet with their friends, they go to a café." Truly, if a city can be said to remain rich in the kind of informal public spaces that Oldenburg called "great good places," it's Paris.

Perhaps the public conviviality that Paris is famous for is the real thing that others seek, and for which they find only a substitute, a simulacrum, in virtual communities. The question naturally arises, as Popravka pointed out, whether the communion kind of virtual community has the same potential in a place where people commune in the still-vital heart of their city, or whether the suburbanized, urban-decayed, paved, and malled environment of modern America is a necessary condition for the proliferation of virtual communities. Certainly, that is the implication of the theories of the French philosopher and social critic Baudrillard, who sees electronic communication as part of the whole web of hyperrealistic illusion we've turned to, in our technologically stimulated flight from the breakdown of human communities.

Two other CalvaCom users I met at Lumbroso's house, Jean-Marc and Jean-David, reminded me of very similar young men I had met in the United States and Japan. They became interested in computers at age eleven or twelve, started exploring online systems with their modems, and found ways to use those systems without paying any bills—"cracking" the system. One day, one of them made a verbal slip in a public forum, revealing that he wasn't the person he had led CalvaCom to believe he was. Lumbroso, on discovering that this fellow and a friend had cracked the system, instinctively made the brilliant move of giving them free accounts and putting them in charge of system security.

A young woman who now works for the trendy alternative French television channel Canal Plus, Chine Lanzmann, was another legendary animateur from Calvacom. She was notorious in France for having written an erotic autobiography of a high-school girl, and found that she had both a talent and a weakness for keeping an online group chat session going. "Finally, I realized it was taking up too many hours of my real life.

It was an addiction. I quit cold turkey." I learned more about chat addiction on Minitel when I tracked down the person responsible for loosing the chat hack on the rest of the French online world.

Something much larger than CalvaCom came along in the middle of that community's evolution—Minitel. It's no mystery why modem dial-up services for PC users in Paris did not grow explosively, when the government was handing out free terminals (with built-in modems) by the millions. And Minitel was part of something even larger, a French national information technology policy specifically formulated to leap into the CMC era on a national level. And that national information technology policy was based on a vision that emerged from a study conducted by the nation's best scholars. The most amazing part of this futuristic vision is that it all started in the 1970s and that the driving force was a notoriously bad telephone system.

From *Télématique* to Pink Messages: The Surprises of Minitel

Only 60 percent of French households were equipped with telephones in 1968. The distribution of telephone lines was closer to third world countries than a nation that made its own nuclear weapons. The state of French telecommunications was seen as a national crisis. The French government has a long history of taking direct action to guide the development of the arts and sciences. The word *dirigiste* refers specifically to a political regime like the French government, which actively promotes, regulates, controls, and influences cultural or technological developments deemed vital to the public good. In the early 1970s, the Direction Générale des Télécommunications (DGT) was charged with creating a plan to modernize the telephone system.

By the mid–1970s, French industries were frightened of IBM and worried about the British experiments in videotext—the (failed) experiment in selling information services to British subjects via their television screens and telephone touchpads. French intellectuals and scientists were beginning to write about the significance of the coming information age. Pressure was mounting on the government and industry to do something more than modernize an antiquated telephone system. The DGT obtained a superministerial budget in 1975 to develop a megaproject. In 1978, Simon Nora and Alain Minc submitted a decisive report, requested by the president of the French Republic, Valery Giscard d'Estaing, on "the computerization of society."

The Nora-Minc report, as it is still known, was bold in its forecasts: "A massive social computerization will take place in the future, flowing through society like electricity.... The debate will focus on interconnectability.... The breakdown of power will be determined between the people who create networks and those who control the satellites...." The report concluded that the advent of cheap computers and powerful global communications media was leading to "an uncertain society, the place of uncountable decentralized conflicts, a computerized society in which values will be object of numerous rivalries stemming from uncertain causes, bringing an infinite amount of lateral communication." To continue to compete in the first rank of nations, Nora and Minc exhorted, France would have to mount a full-scale national effort in the new field they named *Télématique* (merging the French words *Télécommunications* and *informatique*). They didn't fail to note that "*Télématique*, unlike electricity, does not carry an inert current, but rather information, that is to say, power" and that "mastering the network is therefore an essential goal. This requires that its framework be conceived in the spirit of a public service."

The cost of distributing the paper directory for the new, upgraded, expanded French telephone system was becoming a significant factor. The DGT estimated twenty thousand tons of paper needed by 1979, and one hundred thousand tons annually by 1985. The notion of a national videotex system to replace the paper telephone book provided one more crucial but unexpected trigger for the creation of the Télétel system, the massive overall project of connecting computer centers all over the country into a high-speed data communication network. By the summer of 1980, the DGT was able to demonstrate a Télétel test in the Presidential Palace. The first experiments in electronic directory services began in Saint-Malo.

Soon thereafter, one of those decentralized conflicts and numerous rivalries began to break out: the privately owned newspapers reacted quite strongly to the idea of distributing words on screens instead of sheets of paper. Some of the newspaper owners denounced the whole idea: *Le Monde*, on September 27, predicted that *Télématique* was "digging the grave of the written press." Other newspapers decided to get into the Télétel business themselves. In the summer of 1981, the crucial experiment took place. Twenty-five hundred households in Velizy were equipped with electronic decoders that would enable them to use approximately twenty different services on their home television screens. By the fall of 1981, three key municipal projects were set up around the country. The one in Strasbourg, Grétel, was sponsored by a newspaper, *Derniéres Nouvelles d'Alsace*. Grétel, according to Minitel mythology, is where users hacked the database service to enable themselves to communicate in real time.

In early 1992, I caught up with Michel Landaret, the man responsible for Grétel, when he was changing airplane flights at San Francisco International Airport. We talked for about an hour in the quietest cocktail lounge we could find. He confirmed that the first chat system was a user's hack:

We were running an experiment with a very small number of users, to determine whether professional associations and institutions would use data banks. The DGT had not focused on Minitel's communication functions. What happened with Grétel altered the users' relationship to the service in a crucial way. We had only a few dozen users who called into the service. For research purposes, we monitored their usage. We could see how people new to the system could get confused and enter a series of ineffective commands. So we designed a system to communicate with those users by sending a message directly to their screen, and receive messages back from them, to help them learn how to use the system. One of our users just cracked that part of the system and used it to talk with friends. As soon as we found out what was happening, we made improvements on the service and made it a legitimate part of the system. They loved it.

Six months later, the system was totaling seven hundred hours of connection time per day, compared to the total of one hundred to three hundred in the Velizy experiment, where people had access to information but not person-to-person communications. When I next visited Paris, I followed leads provided by Landaret and my other friends who had been involved in French telecommunications, and talked with some of the people who were involved in the fateful decision to adopt the chat services that surfaced in Grétel to the national Minitel system. Landaret, however, had more to say about the significance of what they had learned over the past ten years.

"Because our system was set up to study the way people use these services," Landaret explained. As the system evolved, it became a very loosely coupled collection of different information services and communications forums. Many people stayed in only one or two different domains, Landaret and his colleagues discovered, but a small number of people seemed to move ideas very swiftly from one group to another. "We found that we could feed a small piece of deliberately false information to one of these people, and it spread throughout all the different groups, to as many as four thousand people within two days." The public and private communication channels, in the hands of a core group of cross-pollinators, served to distribute certain kinds of ephemeral information very quickly.

Landaret confirmed what many have noted about CMC—that it breaks down certain traditional social barriers. He cited an early user, an eighty-five-year-old woman who took great pleasure in talking with very young people: "Nobody knew she was eighty-five, and when we interviewed her, she said she would never address in public any of the young men she conversed with online." He talked about a lonely young man who found the only social life he had ever known in chat sessions, and who plunged into depression when access was cut off due to nonpayment. Landaret became most serious when he began talking about the way their research turned up the potential for addiction from the very earliest days of the medium.

"In 30 days, there are 720 hours. How many hours would you say our first addict spent online in 30 days?" Landaret asked me. I figured that a truly obsessive user could devote about half that time to chatting online, given time for meals and normal sleep.

"520 hours," he finally declared grimly.

"What is the maximum number of hours that a single person can spend in front of a terminal without leaving it to drink, eat, or sleep?" was Landaret's next question. I guessed a few hours, five or six maximum.

"The maximum we recorded was seventy-four. What do you think the maximum bill for a period of two months might be?" I guessed $1,000 or more. Landaret came back with another stunning figure—more than $25,000.

Indeed, when Minitel terminals were distributed and the *messageries*, as the chat services are called, became popular, there were abundant tales of chat addicts, but that phase was short-lived, for the most part, because the people who spent all their money and credit lost their access to the expensive services. People still get into trouble with Minitel addiction, but the ability to continue to pay high monthly bills is a limiting factor that isn't built into inexpensive systems such as BBSs or Internet.

The most obvious factor contributing to Minitel's success was the government's decision to distribute small terminals free to the population. Each unit included a small screen, a small keyboard, and a telecommunications connection that required nothing more complicated than plugging the unit into a standard telephone jack. The major opposition force in French society, the newspapers, reached an accommodation with the DGT; newspaper owners accepted the opening of online information services other than telephone directories, and the DGT financed the foundation of services for daily newspapers and magazines. This deal turned out to have an unexpected twist in 1986, when a national student strike was organized through the messaging service of the newspaper *Libération.*

I talked with Henri de Maublanc, one of the former executives for France Télécom, the government-owned telecommunications company that administers Télétel. Maublanc now operates one of the most successful (nonpink) *messagerie* services. He told me that the whole fuss about Minitel replacing newspapers was an illusion that only a few within France Télécom recognized at the time. The Minitel screens are tiny and fuzzy, and people will prefer reading their newspapers the traditional way until future mass-produced screens can rival their readability. "By 1984, a few people like me and others thought that videotext is not the point of this network. The point is to know what kind of service through the network and screen we can provide that is competitive with their other sources of information." They started with stock exchange information and designed all kinds of services for providing other timely information. Then the infectious notion of the *messagerie* came out of Strasbourg. Maublanc and his colleagues designed the user interface of systemwide chat service and presented the idea to France Télécom.

According to Maublanc, when he tried to explain to the architects of the Teletelsystem that their giant distributed database could best be sold as a communications system, "they said I was crazy, it would never work, the entire idea is to deliver good information, not to deliver chat lines. In fact, it turned out that as soon as we opened communication services, they very quickly became the largest ones."

Maublanc and others I queried pointed to one key economic factor that unleashed the potential in the convergence of chat services and a national telecommunications infrastructure. France Télécom started the kiosque system in 1984 that enabled the national telephone company to take over individual billing for different services, collecting money from users via telephone bills and paying out to service providers, for a percentage of revenues. The sex-chat services quickly became the most popular and most controversial of these new, unexpected uses people were finding for Télétel. By the summer of 1986, there were more than one thousand different services. In 1985–1987, as the number of terminals in use reached into the millions, chat services drove Minitel usage to initial success—crashing the entire system at least once because so many people were trying to type at each other at the same time.

At their peak, the messaging services, the chat lines, represented about 4 million hours a month, according to Maublanc, and have dropped since then to about 1.5 million hours per month. "And in my opinion, about a million of those hours every month are through the chat services that create 'false persons.'" The "false persons," to whom Maublanc attributes the decline of popularity in chat services, are the animateurs that the sex-chat services hired to keep conversations going. Almost all of the animateurs are young men whose job is to pretend they are young women.

My friend Annick knew a young fellow named Denis, an actor whose day job was to pretend to be several women at a time, via Minitel, from 8:00 p.m. to 2:00 a.m., three days a week, plus all weekend from 8:00 p.m. to 4:00 a.m. for thirty francs an hour. I met Denis at Annick's house, and he used her Minitel terminal to show me what he did for all those hours. He explained that it was a fun job for an actor, to try to create four or five different women at once, and keep up four or five conversations with credulous men, preventing them from guessing the duplicity as long as possible. Denis was cynically gleeful about his performance: "This fool still believes I'm a woman!"

Even the people who aren't paid to pretend to be someone else are obviously pretending to be somewhat different from their real-life identity. Like the usual sex BBSs everywhere else, every man is a stud, every woman is a beauty. The conversation level, to put it mildly, is direct. Here is a very brief excerpt, with translations, of the kind of dialogue that characterizes a pink messagerie:

JF: Jeune fille = young girl or young woman
JH: Jeune homme: young man
H: Homme: man
F: femme = woman
CH: cherche: looking for
BCBG: Yuppy

                LISTE DE TOUS LES CONNECTES
            (list of all people connected)

1 JF PLUTOT AUTORIT. POUR JF DOCIL (rather authoritarian young
girl looking for docile girl)
2 RAYMOND
3 AMANDIN
4 FRANCK95 (95 means the area where he lives)
5 ALAIN
6 *TENDRE CH.F.COMPLICE (tender man looking for
woman same type)
14 COQUINE (naughty)
15 LEZE 74
(* = pseudo certifi, registered pseudo nobody else
can use)
                Suite de la liste Suite
            (list continued, type Continued)

Les connect{s de votre r{gion R + Envoi (To get
the list of people connected from the same area as
yours, type R + Return)

            Changer de pseudo P + Envoi
        (To change your pseudo :P + Return)
        Guide G + Envoi (Guide : G + Return)

(What happens now is that someone has sent a
message to Denis, who pretended to be Elodie, a
twenty-three-year-old girl living in the 16th
arrondissement of Paris.)
***

Message pour vous (message for you) de H TENDRE PR
FEMME TENDRE
(from tender man looking for tender woman)
***
TU AS ENVIE DE FAIRE L AMOUR?
(Do you feel like making love?)
--Votre response------sinon RETOUR--(Your answer—If
not, Return)
tout de suite comme ca en fin d' apres midi sans se
connaitre?
(Right away, at this time of the day, without
knowing each other?)
Message pour vous de BOSTON 87 H
***
EXCITEE
(Excited)
--Votre response------si non RETOUR--
oui mon chou
(yes, darling)
Message pour vous de BEL H 36ANS CH F AU TEL DE
QUAL
***
QUE RECHERCHEZ VOUS? SI JE NE SUIS PAS INDISCRET
What are you looking for? if I' m not too indiscreet
to ask you?)
VOTRE-REPONSE—(Vous lui avez dit:GUIDE)
vous n' etes pas indiscret tres cher je recherche
une compagnie pour le moment apres on verra
(You' re not indiscreet, my dear, I' m looking for
some company for the moment, and I' ll see what I' ll
do afterwards)

And that's about it. As Denis explained the way he saw it, it was a case
of intermittent reinforcement, the same quirk of human behavior that
makes slot machines work. "If you maybe try five hundred times, you
might actually get laid" was the way he put it. Those are very low odds,
but when you compare them with the odds of making actual sexual

contact with another person if you are home alone, it's enough reality to keep people wading through all the fantasy. More important, noted Denis, was that most people, in his opinion, were in it for nothing but the fantasy. It was a chance to step out of their normal identity and be superman or a beautiful woman and say all the things that they only think about in their most secret fantasies. You are a nobody at work. You have to fight a commute to work and back. You are lonely, or you are married. Indulging in an hour of sex chat is a crude but effective way of creating a different self.

Watching Denis in action was like watching the theories of sociologist Erving Goffman come to life. In his *Presentation of Self in Every Day Life*, which long predated the age of *Télématique*, Goffman theorized that people are always onstage in a sense, always creating a persona that they project to one audience or another. Much of our lives, seen from Goffman's perspective, consist of constructing responses in public that paint a certain public persona, and taking actions that live up to the image of the persona we present. Denis was what you get if you combine McLuhan and Goffman and plunk them down in the regular working population. *Messageries* are a particularly successful variety of the participatory soap operas of CMC that include MUDs and IRC.

The unpredicted economic success of the chat services set off another one of those clashes of values that the Nora-Minc reportedly had warned about. A small medical service decided to call their service <SM> for "Service Medical," but so many Minitel users confused this with the acronym for *sadomasochism* that the service was flooded with kinky queries. The churches and many citizens looked on in horror as the explicit services began plastering Paris with huge erotic posters advertising their Minitel access numbers. The minister responsible for DGT publicly responded to calls for censorship on the grounds of moral pollution (one prominent figure called the *messageries* "electronic urinals") by saying that "the postman does not open envelopes." Electronic messages were considered private communications between sender and receiver, and thus sacrosanct. The guardians of traditional morality put pressure on other political fronts, succeeding in passing taxes on the sex-chat services. In October 1991, as the controversy continued to rage, a Harris France opinion poll showed that 89 percent of the French people polled were against banning the *messageries roses*.

Andrew Feenberg, himself a CMC pioneer, points out that the uproar over the sexual content of the first popular services in the new medium is nothing new. In his article "From Information to Communication: The French Experience with Videotext," he writes:

> Curiously, those who introduced the telephone a century ago fought a similar battle with users over the definition of the instrument. The parallel is instructive. At first the telephone was compared to the telegraph, and advertised primarily as an aid to commerce. Early resistance to social uses of the telephone was widespread and an attempt was made to define it as a serious instrument of business.... In France erotic connotations clustered around these early social uses of the telephone. It was worrisome that outsiders could intrude in the home while the husband and father were away at work.... So concerned was the phone company for the virtue of its female operators that it replaced them at night with males, presumably proof against temptation.

Sex chat might prove to be a passing phase. Sex is the first thing people often do with a new medium. It is common folk wisdom in the video industry that the VCR boom was initially fueled primarily by x-rated videos. The deeper underlying point, Feenberg claims, is that the emergence of chat services was the outcome of a clash of values concerning the use of a new technology: "Télétel was caught up in a dispute over which sort of modern experience would be projected technologically through domestic computing. The definition of interactivity in terms of a rationalistic technical code encountered immediate resistance from users, who redirected the emphasis away from the distribution of information toward anonymous human communication and fantastic encounters."

Feenberg's ultimate point is that this user rebellion irrevocably changed the way large information infrastructure projects can be conceived: "But beyond the particulars of this example, a larger picture looms. In every case, the human dimension of communication technology only emerges gradually from behind the cultural assumptions of those who originate it...."

The challenge now confronting France, after more than a decade of this experiment, has some of the same elements of the challenge that faces Japan. Because of Japanese restrictions on their own telecommunications market, they were late to develop; now they are faced with the growth of Internet and the cultural conflicts that full Internet access would precipitate. France closely guards against cultural intrusion, as in its *dirigiste* attempts to control the French language through the Academie.

Fear of American competition and distrust of the Internet experiment colored the decisions that went into the original Télétel design. The tiny screens and almost unworkable keyboards of the millions of Minitels now in use are clearly inadequate in the age of high-bandwidth communications and powerful desktop computers. Will France redesign its user interface, and thus leap forward again, or will it be chained to the investment in crude terminals that was revolutionary ten years ago? And if France leaps ahead with a user interface to what has already proved to be a successful national network, will that French network wall itself off from the Net, the way it has done in the past? Or will it join the Net and give it more of a French flavor—and, inevitably, discover that the Net has changed French culture, in ways that are not all pleasant?

Other national experiments are brewing. Singapore is in the process of implementing a national telecommunications plan, as is Taiwan. What will happen when these authoritarian governments meet the same challenges—to hook up to the Net and benefit from the new kind of wealth it makes possible, and at the same time accept unpredictable cultural changes that accompany the introduction of the new medium? But for now, the more immediate comparison lies just across the channel.

Virtual Communities in England

A friend in England sent me a newsclipping about an unusual fellow named Dave Winder who was part of a London-area virtual community known as CIX. I sent e-mail to the postmaster at CIX (a standard e-mail address that gets you an answer from the system operator) and began an electronic correspondence with Winder. Soon, a British virtual community, a whole new set of friends with a whole new, distinctly un-American outlook, came tumbling out of cyberspace, acting like every other virtual communitarian I've met thus far.

Dave Winder's story was an unusual one to start with—a crippling disease had changed his life, and the virtual community he found online turned out to be a way out of the psychological depression that had engulfed him. I ended up staying with Winder and his friends on two different visits to England and participated online in their public and private conferences for months, before and between physical visits. Again, we seemed to have a peculiar running start on our relationship, from the weeks and months of online discussion that preceded our first face-to-face meeting. The CIX gatherings I attended had a familiar feel. People began to tell me stories about their online adventures that sounded remarkably similar to stories I had heard in California and Japan and France.

Dave Winder and his friends went through a high-speed version of what has become a familiar evolutionary cycle: disparate characters meet online, find that they can discover depths of communication and deep personal disclosures with each other online, form equally intense friendships offline, and when the inevitable conflict occurs, it is sharp and schismatic, spawning splinter subgroups.

I met with Dave Winder and four of the core members of Herestoby (pronounced "Here's Toby"), a virtual community within CompuLink Information Exchange, or CIX, that coalesced around Winder's online personality and soon started meeting physically at Winder's place. I took the train for an hour out of London to Surrey, and walked a few blocks, following e-mailed directions, to Winder's apartment. Even though he had prepared me for his unusual appearance, he was still quite a sight. There was the hefty electric wheelchair, of course, modified to go faster than the legal limit. There was also the black bandanna with white skull print motif that covered his head, the motorcycle jacket and chains, the wraparound shades even indoors, the body piercings. A gentle-voiced if bawdy-tongued fellow, he seemed to have gone through morbidity and black humor about his physical condition and popped out on the other side, into pure theater. Later, I watched him turn on the television, turn the sound way down, and keep half a dozen people in stitches with his dark-humored running commentary, late into the night. Online, he has created a persona to match—known to most of the seven thousand members of CIX as Dwinder and notorious in the wilder neighborhoods of Usenet, such as talk.bizarre, for a more consciously outrageous persona known as Wavy Davey.

The Herestoby group were as motley in person as any WELL or TWICS crew. There were the nerds, the rebels, the cosmopolites, all in one intense cluster. They were from all over England—several regularly drove for hours for the face-to-face gatherings. They were from different class backgrounds. They had different accents—the way people speak out loud is an important cultural identifier in England, and it's striking to be in a small group that exhibits so many different regional accents. They didn't have accents when they met, of course, because of the contextual filtering of text. Adding voice to communications in England is equivalent to adding body language and facial expressions to communications in Japan.

Despite their more obvious differences, they were all either professionally or avocationally wrapped up in computers—computer graphics, computer software, computer journalism. Toby is a programmer and software designer whose new program, a world simulation game, was the main object of excitement when I arrived the first time. Pat, a single mother from the North, is a computer journalist. Matthew is a more cosmopolitan, patrician, British public school type, who was fluent in French and had been a CalvaCom member. Peter talked a lot and reminded me of Blair Newman in that way. He asked where I was staying and I named a hotel. "I stayed in a hotel once," he replied. Their ages range from early twenties to late thirties; more than fifteen years separate the oldest and youngest. Pat was the only woman in the group. By the time we had worked through a couple pints at the pub together, they had inducted me into the family—they even decided to grant me online access to their private conference.

The other thing they had in common was the sense of having found something new and precious—the magical, intensely personal, deeply emotional bonds that the medium had enabled them to forge among themselves. They had questions, the way the TWICSters had questions, about whether people in other parts of the world formed similar bonds, about whether people got into fierce arguments and ended up posting private e-mail in public forums, and whether other people argued about that. We were discovering together that our experiences in virtual communities created a strong shared context in themselves. The Herestoby crowd were all eager to tell how it felt to find others who could reach out to them emotionally as well as intellectually, through their computer screens. We piled into two cars and drove back to London and then across town to a pub where one of their friends was playing in a band. After the pub closed, they drove back to Dave's and talked until dawn. They made me beg to be allowed to crawl off to the guest bedroom at

3:00 a.m. These people party harder than even the COARA crowd—they even do karaoke. Perhaps one of the unintended side effects of CMC is that the Net is a vector for the spread of singing off-key in bars.

A few years ago, Dave Winder was, in almost every way, a different person. At twenty-four, he was a hard-driving, money-motivated businessman, developing land around horse-racing tracks. "We were a three-car family, I worked sixteen hours a day, seven days a week," Winder recalls with an inexplicable grin. "Then I got encephalitis. I spent a year in the hospital, and when I came out my legs were paralyzed and my left arm was paralyzed. My eyes were painfully sensitive. The brain damage scrambled my perceptions. I couldn't read, write, count, or remember my address or telephone number."

A neuropsychologist thought that simple computer drawing programs might give Winder a way to find out if he could "get my brain working again." He started out with simple tracing exercises. "It was something I could be left alone to do." When it started to work, he found he could teach himself to read again, using the "Janet and John" books well known to preschoolers in Britain. Then he started using a word processor, with a spelling checker that forced him through a menu of choices and thus gradually helped him remember how to spell.

After nine months of work, he could read and write, and hold conversations. In 1989, a friend gave Winder a modem. He joined Prestel, a data-communication service similar to CompuServe. Prestel is one of the surviving remnants of the British attempt to leap into the videotext age— the same experiment that partially triggered the French effort in *Télématique*. The data-communication service for delivering modem users to libraries of information or discussion forums is particularly important in Britain because British Telecom charges by message units that take into account the distance of the call and the amount of time metered. It makes using modems more expensive if the service you are trying to reach isn't in your immediate neighborhood. One of the general results of this policy is that those people who belong to communities like CIX use special software, known as offline readers, that log onto the service and quickly download all the e-mail and new responses in public forums, then quickly logs off the service. Offline reader users can then read and write without the meter running; the software then logs on again automatically, delivers replies to e-mail, and inserts responses in the proper places in public topics.

"Then I heard about CIX," he recalls, grinning even more broadly, "which I was told was more of a community than the forums I found on Prestel."Frank and Sylvia Thornley started the BBS called the CompuLink Information Exchange in 1985, the same year COARA and the WELL started. Most BBSs in England at the time were like most BBSs in the early days in the States—strictly oriented toward downloading software for specific computers, and talking about those computers. CIX started out with an orientation to many-to-many discussion. The Thornleys used a full-blown conferencing system known as COSY that predates the PicoSpan software that the WELL uses and the Caucus software that TWICS uses.

One interesting characteristic of CIX had a powerful influence on the way the community has developed. On the WELL, you have to ask WELL management to start a private conference for you, or you have to prove that your conference idea is worthwhile before they will create a public conference. On CIX, any CIXen, as they call themselves, can start a conference at any time. They can start closed conferences with restricted membership or public conferences or closed and confidential conferences with restricted membership and that don't show up on any public lists.

The first time he logged onto CIX, Winder jumped right into the community. "I saw something that a fellow wrote about the Amiga computer, and I disagreed with him. So I challenged him online. My first night out."

It was a difficult time. Winder's personality had changed along with so much else. He could no longer work at his former profession. His marriage was on the rocks. His disease was so serious that none of his doctors could assure him he would live more than another five years. The social side of CIX came along and "sucked me right in," he says. He started spending hours online, hours writing responses. Soon, he began moderating conferences. He had found more than something to do, and a new way to meet people. A new persona started constructing itself online, and a new Dave Winder seemed to be coming together offline. His online persona was distinctive: flamboyant, argumentative, unafraid of personal disclosure, often outrageously funny. Offline, he had transformed from the three-piece-suit-wearing businessman, through the long phase of hospital gowns and pajamas, directly to heavy-metal motorcycle gear.

He found one very close friend, Kevin Hall, who was often the only other person logged into CIX at 3:00 a.m. Hall invited Winder to join a small group of fellows in their closed and confidential conference—Herestoby. The name was a joke, referring to one of the founders, Toby. Each of the six young men who made up the original group was approaching a crisis in his life just when the group started experimenting with talking about their deepest feelings in a private forum. Dave Winder's health was the most acute problem. Then Toby was devastated when his best friend ran off with his girl. His online friends encouraged him to talk about his feelings with them instead of indulging in self-destructive behavior. That triggered a period of weeks in which people went beyond extending emotional support to make revealing confessions about their own inner lives.

Pat joined the group because one of the originals thought she would be an addition to their enterprise—the collaborative construction of a social arrangement that was more like a group heart than a group mind. Their communications were centered on feelings; their communication protocol was to break taboos against self-disclosure. "We had been involved in a very intense discussion about sex when Pat joined. Pretty personal stuff. And here was this woman joining six men. We didn't know what to expect. As it happened, she was fine. We decided at that point to close the group at seven people."

The initial bonding among the group took place entirely online. They didn't decide to meet face-to-face for six months. Everybody turned up at Dave Winder's place, nervous at first. "We were quaking in our boots because none of us knew what to expect," Winder recalled. "We were actually worried that meeting face-to-face would blow the whole thing apart." But the first get-together quickly became congenial, if not raucous. And then came New Year's Eve 1991, when one of the most beloved members of the group, Kevin Hall, died in a motorcycle accident.

The online funeral of Kevin Hall was a rite of passage for all of CIX, a time when the original members of the group felt closest to each other. My first visit was at the end of that period. In the four months between then and my second visit, the Herestoby group broke out in conflict.

Harsh words were exchanged in public conferences among former intimate friends, private e-mail was posted publicly, rival private and public conferences were started. Several months after the shock of the group's breakup, a little more than a year after it started, the various factions began speaking to one another again. With the schism, the idea of creating a small, private place for a small group of friends to share personal experiences and offer support and help solve problems seems to have spread to other parts of CIX.

I wasn't able to visit them personally, but I also corresponded with many others in England involved in spreading the word about CMC: the city of Manchester is experimenting with an electronic city hall, similar to PEN; a group of young radicals in Oxford and London are setting up "fast breeder BBSs" linked into an alternate culture youth network throughout Europe. Greenet is an important partner of Econet and Peacenet and others in the Association for Progressive Communications; Geonet; Geonet is providing conferencing for nonprofits, CompuMentor style. Commercial Internet sites began to appear in England in 1993, and CIX joined Internet. The British contingent on Internet is already a strong presence. I've received e-mail pointers to networks in Africa and South America. A new mailing list for community networks started in 1993 on Internet, and within a day, people who had been building community networks in Finland, Germany, Colorado, and dozens of other sites surfaced.

Connectivity between networks is achieving a critical mass around the world—the means of jacking in are becoming more affordable every day, and the expertise needed to set up networks is diffusing rapidly. Many countries will soon face the conflict that Japanese and French telecommunications planners must address: to refuse to join the Net in its widest sense and face being left behind, or to join the Net and face social upheaval.

9

Electronic Frontiers and Online Activists

"Ben Franklin would have been the first owner of an Apple computer. Thomas Jefferson would have written the Declaration of Independence on an IBM PC. But Tom Paine would have published *Common Sense* on a computer bulletin board," Dave Hughes insists. If you want to talk about grassroots activism, Hughes is a good place to start. He's an old infantryman: you don't always wait for headquarters to give you permission to cobble something together in the real world; if it might save your ass, you just do it.

In real life, Dave Hughes is a West Point graduate who commanded combat troops in Korea and Vietnam. He looks like the kind of officer the troops would call "the old man." Since he retired from the military and decided to use technology to change the world, Hughes has been acting out an ongoing online melodrama of his own devising. The scenario: Hughes rides into town—and "town" can be an actual small town on the prairie, or a hearing room on Capitol Hill, or the political structure of his hometown, Colorado Springs. He meets the locals, who are frustrated by the old ways of doing things. Hughes takes out his laptop, plugs it into the nearest telephone, reveals the scope and power of the Net, and enlightens the crowd. He tempts them into putting their hands on the keyboard, and they're hooked. When Hughes rides out of town, the town is on the Net.

Installments of Dave Hughes's stories of electronic political pioneering in America have proliferated by way of his online proclamations, manifestos, and seminars on a dozen different public-access CMC networks for more than a decade. Dave's modus operandi is straightforward and uncomplicated: First he brags shamelessly about what he is going to do,

then he does it, and then he shows everyone else how to duplicate his
feats. Then he brags shamelessly some more. If you want the hard information about how to put your own system together, you have to listen
to his stories.

I first ran into Dave Hughes during my first session online to the
Source in 1982–1983. I saved his 1983 self-introduction to the online
world because I had a hunch this electronic vanity publishing business
might be important some day:

Hello.
    I am "Sourcevoid" Dave. Dave Hughes otherwise.

    I was born in Colorado, descended from stubborn
Welshmen who were never too loyal to the king,
which is probably why I am content being a maverick
of sorts, with a Welsh imagination.

    I live in Historic Old Colorado City at the base
of 14, 114 foot Pike's Peak.

    I work out of my 1894 Electronic Cottage with a
variety of microcomputer and telecommunications
tools. . . .

    I am a happily married middle-aged family man
who has seen enough of Big Government, Big Wars,
Big Industry, Big Political Causes--either of the
left or right--to now prefer to operate a small
business out of a small house, in a small
neighborhood, working with small organizations,
using a small computer to make it all possible.

Hughes is a believer in teleports—communities like his own, where
people can enjoy a small-town atmosphere and work from their homes
by using computers and modems. When it looked as if the Colorado
Springs city council was going to make a decision that would effectively
prohibit telecommuting from his home in nearby Old Colorado City,
Hughes went into action.

"The city planners of Colorado Springs decided to tighten the ordinance that regulates working out of the home," Hughes recalls. "I was
the only person to stand up in front of the planning commission and

testify against the ordinance; the planners tabled the matter for thirty days. I then brought the text of the ordinance home with me and put it on my BBS."

Hughes sent letters to the editors of his two local papers, inviting people to dial into his BBS and read the ordinance. Two hundred and fifty callers above the normal traffic level for his BBS called within the next ten days. What Hughes did not realize at the time was that many of those callers worked in large high-tech plants, and they downloaded, printed, copied, and circulated hundreds of copies of the ordinance throughout the city. At the next city council meeting, more than 175 citizens, representing every part of the political spectrum, showed up to protest the ordinance. It was defeated. Hughes pointed out that "ordinarily, the effort needed to get involved with local politics is enormous. But the economy of effort that computers provided made it possible for me to mobilize opinion."

Hughes made his next foray into online activism in Colorado Springs because he wanted to find a way of letting local vendors air their complaints that they had been shut out of bidding on the county computer contract for fourteen years. The press dialed in to Hughes's BBS, asked questions online, and confronted the county commissioners with the complaints and the facts they had compiled.

"It got so hot that county staff members were reading from BBS printouts at the podium during formal meetings," Hughes recalled when I interviewed him in 1988. "In the end," he added, "the commissioners knuckled under, went to bid, the whole inefficient and incestuous system was exposed, and today there is a whole new approach to information management in the county."

For his next venture into BBS politics, Hughes invited a candidate for city council to post his views on Hughes's BBS and to respond to questions from voters. The candidate was elected, and the councilman continued to use the BBS to communicate with his constituents during his tenure on the council.

Dave tries a lot of things, and when something works, he pushes the pedal to the metal. Next, he prodded Colorado Springs to create a City Council Telecommunications Policy Advisory Committee, which does its business on the city's new BBS; the committee is proposing recommendations on how to make elected officials publicly accessible online.

Penrose Public Library in Colorado Springs, working with the city, now has City Hall Online, which includes all agendas, announcements, and minutes of meetings. Then Hughes decided to see what he could do for candidates on a countywide scale: "I used my personal computer to dial into the county clerk's computer and download the entire registration list of all the voters in my precinct. Now anyone can dial me and go into the world's first political precinct BBS." Then he told his local branch of the Democratic party that he could put 100 percent of the voters in every one of the 120 precincts of the county on a public BBS. The cost would be nominal, considering that his county normally charges $800 to print out their list.

It isn't hard to imagine the light bulbs going on in their heads when Frank and Reggie Odasz, educators and activists from Montana, came to Hughes in the late 1980s with some ideas about hooking up inexpensive BBS systems in rural Montana schoolhouses, to help overcome the educational isolation of some of the widest open spaces in America. They called their project Big Sky Telegraph. Dave had spent enough time and money in his retirement, learning how to operate the equipment that linked his electronic cottage with his worldwide constituency. He knew how to cobble together BBS systems from the cheapest hardware, and how to get it to work with the telecommunications system. And he was burning to demonstrate how his "great equalizers" could revitalize real communities.

Frank and Reggie Odasz were computer-literate change agents who were eager to use the kind of technology they had encountered on Hughes's own online system to enhance educational resources and other aspects of life in rural Montana. They had in mind practical ways of helping real people with down-to-earth problems, and they also had big dreams. Like Hughes, Frank and Reggie Odasz felt that they had found something more than a communication tool with CMC. It was, to them, a means of trying to fulfill their hopes of improving their community. It was part of a new way of thinking that technology made possible. CMC technology was the means to the end of enhancing human relationships in a rural area where long distances made traditional face-to-face community-building more difficult. The possibility of using CMC to extend all kinds of Montana citizens' power to build relationships with each other was the feature of virtual communities that drew together the principals of Big Sky Telegraph.

This idea of many-to-many communications as a framework for collective goods is a powerful one that many who are familiar with previous communication revolutions are often slow to grasp. Most people think of mass media as one-to-many media, in which the mass represents a large population of consumers, who pay to be fed information by the few who profit from their control of that information conduit: the broadcast paradigm. For years, educators and political activists have not taken advantage of the power inherent in CMC networks because they failed to take advantage of the power of a many-to-many or network paradigm.

In terms of the high expectations of a microchip revolution in our badly ailing schools, computer education was a failure in the 1980s. One reason dispersal of personal computers to schoolrooms failed to check the deterioration of traditional public education in the media age was that the computers were so often seen as just another channel for transferring knowledge from the teachers to the students (broadcast paradigm) rather than providing an environment in which the students can explore and learn together (network paradigm). Only a very few pioneers in the early 1980s thought of plugging their schoolroom computer into a telephone line, and few could have afforded the online resources available at the time.

To Frank Odasz, CMC wasn't just a shift from the broadcast paradigm of educational technology to a network paradigm, it was a consciousness shift on the part of the people who took to the technology. As he told researcher Willard Uncapher:

It's more a consciousness thing than anything else. And I'm in the business of teaching new ways, new levels of thinking, new levels of intellectual interaction.... When I e-mail with Dave, or when I e-mail with you, that is more consciousness than any other single thing. So we are not just computer networking, when you and I share comments back and forth. It's in a context that to me is much more a consciousness thing. It's literally, as I have said tongue in cheek before, working as an electronic analogy for telepathy. I don't even think that's right. I think it's something more. I think, in a sense, it is shared consciousness.

In the 1980s, Frank Odasz and his wife, Reggie, worked in rural Montana as educators who were determined to improve the living conditions for their community by "thinking globally and acting locally," as Buckminster Fuller advised. They were enthusiastic about the educational potential of computer technology, especially the kind of CMC technology they had seen through Chariot, the conferencing system Dave

Hughes and his partner Louis Jaffe ran in Old Colorado City as a successor to Dave's original "Rogers' Bar" BBS.

Frank and Reggie Odasz had been looking for ways to use new technologies to improve the communication problems inherent in an area where very small schools are spread out over a large amount of countryside. Teachers are on their own, without the kind of personal as well as pragmatic support network that is available even in impoverished urban schools. Communication costs are high in that part of the country, and transportation costs are even higher. The Big Hole Valley, part of the territory included in Big Sky Telegraph, has the longest school-bus route in the United States.

When Frank Odasz talked about his hopes for using something like Chariot to encourage resource-sharing among the schools, Dave Hughes pointed out that they were already ahead of the game because so many rural schools probably had old computers sitting around from the first failed computer revolution in education, when everybody thought computer literacy was a great idea and many school districts purchased computers. Indeed, they did.

In the early 1980s, the only affordable computers were pathetically underpowered compared to what is available today, which severely limited their usefulness. The initial computer literacy grants that purchased the computers, however, usually did not include training and continuing support, so most of the computers were never used. And those teachers who did learn how to use the machines had trouble sifting out the few examples of genuinely useful educational software from the large amount of crap. Many schools abandoned the attempt, but few threw away the old Apple IIs or Ataris or Commodore–64s.

Although none of the old computers in storage rooms all over Montana could hold a candle to the kinds of graphics and simulation that are available on today's computers, Dave Hughes knew that they are all perfectly serviceable terminals for a telecommunications network. You don't need fancy graphics or a color screen to run simple terminal software. Even one-room schoolhouses usually have a telephone line. The modem —the piece of hardware that plugs the PC and the network together— used to cost $500 or more; now they cost $50. So the actual physical infrastructure for most of what Frank and Reggie envisioned for Big Sky Telegraph (BST) was already in place when they got together with Dave Hughes.

Hughes just happened to know the right things to say and used the Net to discover the right people to say it to at U.S. West—the regional telephone company for both Colorado and Montana. Frank and Reggie Odasz knew the *where* (rural Montana) and the *who* (schoolteachers, students, local change agents, and ranchers) of Big Sky; the rural teachers they trained to use the technology provided the what; and Dave Hughes came along with the *how*. They obtained two grants, of approximately $50,000 each, to equip and train rural teachers to communicate with a central BBS and information database.

Students of CMC are fortunate that social scientist Annenberg School of Communications "Rural Grassroots Telecommunications," reflects the most important aspects of BST: it was a rural, populist effort, rather than an urban, top-down design.

Uncapher went to the Big Hole Valley, in the heart of BST territory, for two weeks, after BST had been operating for a short time. He interviewed the teachers, ranchers, local social activists, Hughes, and Frank and Reggie Odasz. This was not strictly a study of CMC technology, but a study of the social changes that were triggered, or failed to be triggered, by introducing the technology to a largely nontechnological part of American society.

Uncapher declared his intention to observe the impact of CMC technology in the context of the community the technology was entering. His thesis was that you can't predict the way people will use communications technologies without knowing something about the social, economic, political, and cultural circumstances of the specific environments in which the technologies are introduced. Uncapher hypothesized that the skills necessary to use the new technologies and the inspiration to adapt them to new uses would be unevenly distributed in each community. Some groups would lack the skills, some groups would resist the changes, and the reasons for those reactions would be rooted not in technology but in local culture, economics, and politics.

Western Montana offered an interesting mix of people for observations to test such a thesis. There were the teachers, mostly women; the ranchers who supported the schools through taxes, controlled the school board, and were traditionally conservative about newfangled technology; and the students, who were far away from the world's centers of learning. There were also environmental groups, domestic violence support groups, and other nonprofit organizations who might also make good use of CMC, if somebody could show them how. The organization most important to the early success of BST, as it turned out, was the Women's Resource Center in Dillon, where the vital ingredient of a highly motivated population of early adopters was found.

According to Uncapher, Hughes sought to broaden Frank and Reggie Odasz's involvement with the wider community. "While Frank Odasz had come up with the idea, and had apparently discussed it with some of the rural teachers, Dave Hughes sought to involve the broader community in an effort of rural self-development," says Uncapher. "His idea was not to bring specific ideas to the area (other than interactive telecommunications), but to provide an augmented means by which the rural communities could acquire and exchange their own ideas and resources, beginning with the rural teachers. The Big Sky Telegraph represented an extension, thereby, of his own online efforts."

Big Sky Telegraph went online January 1, 1988, at Western Montana College. As Uncapher had hypothesized, it appeared at the beginning that some existing groups in the community resisted the technology—the ranchers, for example—and other groups seized the technology as a way to alter their own status in the community. The Women's Resource Center, for example, was the nexus of a widespread community of interest that lacked the resources to get together often in the same physical place. The center's mission was to find ways to retrain and help women who were having a rough time—victims of physical abuse, unskilled women who were divorced late in life, single mothers without child support—who needed ways to climb out of their predicaments.

Teaching computer skills to some of these women was a good idea, Jody Webster, director of the center, noted, for reasons related to their sense of themselves. Could this be an example of the "change in consciousness" that Frank Odasz was trying to describe? Jody Webster, as quoted by Uncapher, put it this way: "Some of it is attitude. All your skills aren't the physical skills, like typing or shoveling. A lot of it is attitudinal skills, communication skills: how to ask for a raise, or how to ask for a job or not to ask for a raise; the fact that you need to sell yourself; the difference between self-esteem and conceit."

Through Big Sky, women across western Montana were given an opportunity to teach and support each other emotionally as well as a way to impart skills. "The Women's Resource Center ... would get funding, often project by project, primarily to aid the women in the region to get new jobs, to learn new self-esteem, and to protect women and their rights;" Uncapher reported. "In fact, to a great extent the use of the Telegraph took off first in the general community in the hands of women, and the kinds of issues this center addressed revealed why. Indeed, most of the rural teachers were women.... When I visited a woman who ran her connection to Big Sky Telegraph from the Lima Stop 'n Shop gas station, which she and her husband ran near the Idaho border, it turned out that the computer had been loaned to them by the Women's Resource Center."

Frank Odasz, in an article about BST, also mentions the same woman at the truckstop, although he has a slightly different name for the gas station: "Sue Roden, the woman in Lima, was able to learn computer skills from the Gas 'n Snacks truckstop between fillups. When she got stuck on Lesson 2, a trucker named Windy looked over her shoulder and got her going again." You can bet that as soon as Frank told Dave about Sue and Windy, the story started spreading through the Net.

Hughes and Odasz knew enough about the power of citizen-to-citizen (lateral) communications to set up common discussion areas and BBSs as well as databases of information and software. There is power in the broadcast paradigm when you can give people access to large bodies of useful information, such as agricultural and meteorological data that can be critically important in the real lives of Montana rural populations. But the community-building power comes from the living database that the participants create and use together informally as they help each other solve problems, one to one and many to many. The web of human relationships that can grow along with the database is where the potential for cultural and political change can be found.

By 1991, the success of the system enabled BST to meet goals of getting online "forty rural schools, including ten Native American schools, twelve rural public libraries, twelve rural economic development offices or chambers of commerce, twelve women's centers, twelve Soil Conservation Service or County Extension offices, five handicapped organizations, and five rural hospitals," according to Frank Odasz.

Besides the local connections that formed the core and real-life community of BST in western Montana, Hughes and his net-weaving cohorts were plugging places like the Big Hole Valley into the vast rich turmoil of the Net. First, they established a connection with FidoNet, and through FidoNet's gateway, to Internet. Then they looked for ways to take advantage of more direct Internet connections at universities. Dave is the kind of guy who will walk into the county commissioner's office or MIT or the Pentagon and shake down everybody he can find in the cause of an educational crusade. He found a lot of sympathetic Netheads at key power points, as he always does. As he was wiring BST to the world, Dave Hughes also was zeroing in on the kind of distance-education prestigidation he could brag about on the Net: connecting a professor at MIT's Plasma Fusion Laboratory to the BST to develop a course on chaos theory for gifted science students in rural Montana.

After Big Sky was working, and bright kids in Montana were learning physics from MIT professors, Hughes and Frank Odasz started doing demonstrations for another kind of community in that part of the country. Hughes brought a color laptop computer and a modem; all he needed was a telephone line. Hughes has always insisted on including ways for people to create and share graphics as well as text online. He had the notion that the Assiniboine, Gros Ventre, Crow, and Blackfoot who gathered around his computer might be interested in the way the graphics software would enable them to create and transmit text in their native alphabets.

As he had done with the teachers and change agents at BST, Dave encouraged his audience to get their hands on the equipment as soon as possible and teach each other how to use it. After his performance, Dave turned the computer and software over to the graphic artists among the assembled Native Americans and challenged them to create one of their tribal designs on the computer screen and upload it to BST.

By 1990, one of the groups who were inspired by Hughes's first demonstration had opened the Native American Share-Art gallery on the Russell Country BBS in Hobson, Montana. The idea was to make people outside the immediate geographic area aware of tribal culture, and to generate income for tribal artists. The artists used graphics software to create tribal designs that could be viewed on a computer screen. People could dial in to Russell Country BBS and view different designs; for a small fee, dial-up BBS users could download the designs and display them.

Their motivation behind these projects, as Hughes explained it online in 1990, was to "use telecommunications to help Native Americans learn the skills and knowledge they will need, by getting them first to be the teachers of the rest of us about their culture, and in their preferred modes (graphic art, storytelling, native language expression) rather than just feed the white man's view of the world into them by satellite educational feeds, or impose upon them only white man's ascii text."

Dave Hughes and Frank Odasz certainly weren't, and never claimed to be, the first to teach Native Americans to use telecommunications. John Mohawk and AInet (American Indian Network), and other ventures by American Indians to use networking, were also happening. But Hughes was a kind of Johnny Appleseed. It's far easier to operate a well-set-up BBS or network than to set one up. Dave's strategy has always been to come to town, dazzle them with possibilities, show them how to do it on their own, and move on.

Although he believed in working at the local level, Hughes, who had once written a major policy speech for Secretary of Defense McNamara, always showed up in online debates on national and international telecom policy. In 1991, when then-senator Albert Gore began talking about government sponsorship of a National Research and Education Network, Dave started spending as much time online in D.C. as in Dillon.

The budget for a National Research and Education Network to link scholars, scientists, government workers, students, and business people into a national high speed information superhighway was built into the High Performance Computing Act of 1991. There was only one problem, as far as Hughes was concerned: if NREN was going to be a superhighway, there were no on and off ramps for elementary and secondary (K–12) schools. Hughes and others insisted that unless it provided for a truly broad-based educational component, with affordable access by the already-impoverished public schools, NREN could lead to even greater gaps between the information-rich and the information-poor. Dave started haunting hearings on the Hill. He and his cohorts were heard; 1992 amendments to the bill made provisions for the beginnings of K–12 access.

As Dave puts it, in his own inimitable online style:

```
It's ramp-up time in America, for telecom. And
education is going to ride the wave—with all kinds
of fools, charlatans, gold-counting houses, clowns,
```

```
trying to get on their boards.
Its going to be messy. Just like America.
But as they say on Walden Pond.
Surf's up.
```

Dave Hughes is a formidable spokesman and activist. But he's far from the only one. Online education has been pioneered by Paul Levenson's Connect Ed since 1985, and by Andrew Feenberg and others at the Western Behavioral Sciences Institute before that. Entire networks, such as the Institute for Global Communications, use CMC as a political tool. There are municipalities such as Cleveland, Ohio, and Santa Monica, California, where citizens are using CMC to set the political agenda. And organizations such as the Electronic Frontier Foundation are forming committees in defense of the political freedoms previously enjoyed in cyberspace that now are threatened by powerful political interests.

The Birth of the Electronic Frontier Foundation

Fear of hackers in a virtual community is a little like fear of pyromaniacs in a rice-paper city. The goal of every hacker is to attain the system powers granted only to the person who knows the system password, and that includes the power to erase all records of previous conversations, all current e-mail, everything in everybody's private file area. Most hackers just want to explore. Others are vandals.

In an ecology of communities like the WELL, the idea of the managers of the system inviting known hackers to join the system, even temporarily, puts the WELL into a double bind. Yes, they were endangering the security of the WELL's technical and human system. But this system had a long history of avoiding censorship or heavy-handed social management, almost at any cost. If the WELL could be said to be committed to one thing above all, it would be social experimentation. And most of the WELL population understood the difference between a kid out for a joyride on his modem and more serious cases of electronic thieves or vandals. Then *Harper's* magazine offered WELL management a social experiment they couldn't refuse.

The magazine's editors had invited John P. Barlow, Mitch Kapor, Cliff Stoll (author of *The Cuckoo's Egg*, a best-seller about the successful hunt for a KGB-sponsored ring of German hackers), Stewart Brand, Kevin Kelly (one of the founders of the WELL), Dave Hughes, and a number of other cyberspace debaters from the WELL and beyond to meet in a private conference on the WELL with several of the young fellows who hack into other people's computer systems.

I remember the night the chain of events began. None of us could have known at the time that it would involve the FBI and Secret Service and grow into the founding of the Electronic Frontier Foundation. But it did have a kind of western, frontier feel to it from the beginning.

John Barlow recalled the event in his article "Crime and Puzzlement":

So me and my sidekick Howard, we was sitting out in front of the 40 Rod Saloon one evening when he all of a sudden says, "Lookee here. What do you reckon?" I look up and there's these two strangers riding into town. They're young and got kind of a restless, bored way about 'em. A person don't need both eyes to see they mean trouble. . . .

Well that wasn't quite how it went. Actually, Howard and I were floating blind as cave fish in the electronic barrens of the WELL, so the whole incident passed as words on a display screen:

Howard: Interesting couple of newusers just signed on. One calls himself acid and the other's optik.
Barlow: Hmmm. What are their real names?
Howard: Check their finger files.

When you see a name you don't recognize, you can read that person's online biography, or "finger file." That's where the person's real name is supposed to be found on systems like the WELL.

With monikers like these, the young crackers were coming online in full sneer. Barlow is a computer journalist, pundit, third-generation cattle rancher, and former power in the Wyoming Republican party, whose main claim to fame was his history as lyricist for the Grateful Dead. The hackers were not impressed. He could have been the lyricist for Guy Lombardo for all they cared. The cocky young hackers were making a point of getting off on the wrong foot with all the old fogeys *Harper's* had invited to debate them.

At one point, Acid Phreak compared cracking computer systems to walking into a building where the door was unlocked. Barlow responded by saying he kept the door to his house unlocked, and Acid challenged

Barlow to e-mail his address to him. Barlow replied in the Harper's conference:

```
"Acid. My house is at 372 North Franklin Street in
Pinedale, Wyoming. If you're heading north on
Franklin, you go about two blocks off the main drag
before you run into a hay meadow on the left. I've
got the last house before the field. The computer
is always on . . . And is that really what you
mean? Are you merely just the kind of little sneak
that goes around looking for easy places to vio-
late? You disappoint me, pal. For all your James
Dean-on-Silicon rhetoric, you're not a cyberpunk.
You're just a punk."
```

The next day, Phiber Optik posted Barlow's credit history in the *Harper's* conference. He had hacked TRW, the private company that stores the key details of everybody's credit history in online computer systems that are supposed to be secure.

The arguments continued, the WELL conference ended, and the *Harper's* editors started cutting down the hundreds of pages of online rhetoric to paper-publishable size. Before the article was published, however, *Harper's* took Optik, Acid, and Barlow to dinner in Manhattan. As Barlow noted at the time, "They looked to be as dangerous as ducks." They didn't exactly become immediate friends after meeting face-to-face, but Barlow and the crackers did find some common ground—a commitment to individual liberty as a core value.

Cut back to Pinedale: "And, as I became less their adversary and more their scoutmaster," Barlow recalled when he told his story, first online and then in print, "I began to get 'conference calls' in which six or eight of them would crack pay phones all over New York and simultaneously land on my line in Wyoming.... On January 24, 1990, a platoon of Secret Service agents entered the apartment which Acid Phreak shares with his mother and 12-year-old sister. The latter was the only person home when they burst through the door with guns drawn. They managed to hold her at bay for about half an hour until their quarry happened home."

Among the others arrested was Craig Neidorf, whose crime was to publish sections of an allegedly purloined document in Phrack, an online newsletter he distributed electronically. Another related raid resulted in the arrest and confiscation of all the business equipment of Steve Jackson, whose Austin company published a fictional board game that law enforcement officials were convinced was a computer crime manual. The news was all over the Net. Law had come to cyberspace in a big way, and they were busting all the wrong people. More frighteningly, they were arresting people just for the crime of disseminating information, and they were doing it on a nationally coordinated basis.

Acid and a few other young men across the United States were part of the now-notorious Operation Sun Devil, involving more than 150 federal agents, local and state law enforcement agencies, and the security arms of three or four regional telephone companies. It all had to do with the illegal electronic possession of a document that turned out to be publicly available for less than $100. The plot already was sinister enough when Barlow got his call from Agent Baxter of the FBI. Baxter, who operated out of an office in Rock Springs, Wyoming, one hundred miles away from Pinedale, wanted to get together with Barlow as soon as possible to talk about some kind of mysterious—at least to him—conspiracy to steal the trade secrets of Apple Computer.

A word of explanation is always in order when discussing high-tech crimes, because many involve theft or vandalism of intangible property such as private credit records, electronic free speech, or proprietary software. Apple computers all include in their essential hardware something known as a ROM chip that contains, encoded in noneraseable circuits, the special characteristics that make an Apple computer an Apple computer. The ROM code, therefore, is indeed a valuable trade secret to Apple; although it is stored in a chip, ROM code is computer software that can be distributed via disk or even transmitted over networks. If you knew that code, you could make your own ROMs and bootleg Apple computers. Well-known figures in the PC industry had been receiving unsolicited computer disks containing pieces of that code, accompanied by a manifesto by some group that called itself the NuPrometheus League. (Barlow swears that Agent Baxter repeatedly pronounced it the "New Prosthesis League.")

Agent Baxter's puzzlement was the heart of the encounter between him and Barlow. Not only Agent Baxter, but his sources of information, seemed exceedingly unclear about the nature of whatever it was they were supposed to be investigating. It turned out that Barlow had been contacted by the FBI because his name was on the roster of an annual private gathering called the Hackers' Conference. Baxter reported that he had been informed that the Hackers' Conference was an underground organization of computer outlaws that was probably part of the same grand conspiracy as the NuPrometheus League.

Hacker used to mean something different from what it means now. Steven Levy's 1984 book *Hackers: Heroes of the Computer Revolution* was about the unorthodox young programmers who created in the 1960s and 1970s the kind of computer technology that nonprogrammers used in the 1980s and 1990s. Although they kept odd hours and weren't fashion plates, and although they weren't averse to solving lock-picking puzzles, the original hackers were toolmakers, not burglars.

The first Hackers' Conference was a gathering of the traditional kind of hacker, not the system cracker that the mass media have since identified with the word *hacker*. I've attended enough Hackers' Conferences myself to know they are innocent events that celebrate the best in what used to be known as Yankee ingenuity, more like Nerdstocks than saboteur summits. Something seems weirdly and dishearteningly wrong when the FBI is investigating the kind of people that gave America whatever it retains of a competitive edge in the PC business.

That wasn't the only thing Baxter was unclear about. John Draper, known since the 1970s as Captain Crunch, is old enough to be Acid Phreak's father, but he still claims respect and notoriety as the original "phone phreak" who actually predated computer crackers. He's still a (legitimate) computer programmer (who created, among other things, the first word processor for IBM's first personal computer). Crunch, as he is known these days, is an amiable and unorthodox fellow who mostly stays in his apartment and writes programs. Baxter told Barlow, who probably had to physically restrain himself from the kind of involuntary laughter that spews beverages on people's shirts, that Draper was "the CEO of Autodesk, Inc., an important Star Wars contractor." And Draper was suspected of having "Soviet contacts."

Just about everything Baxter told Barlow was wrong, and Barlow knew it. There was a wacky near-miss element to the way Baxter was wrong. It was true that Draper had once worked at Autodesk as a programmer, but that was as close to being the CEO of Autodesk that he ever got; the real CEO of Autodesk, John Walker, definitely was on the Hackers' Conference list of attendees himself. Autodesk makes computer-aided design software for personal computers and was in the process of developing a cyberspace toolkit for architects and designers, but it was hardly a top-secret defense contractor. John Draper did have some Russian programmer friends, but by 1990, the Evil Empire was in the throes of disintegration.

Baxter's story was hilariously misinformed enough to make anybody worry about how well the FBI is doing against the real techno-criminals, the nuclear terrorists and large-scale data thieves. So Barlow sat Baxter down at a computer, showed him what computer source code looked like, demonstrated e-mail, and downloaded a file from the WELL. Baxter, Barlow reported, "took to rubbing his face with both hands, peering up over his fingertips and alternating 'It sure is something, isn't it?' with statements such as 'Whooo-ee.'"

There was controversy on the WELL about Barlow's online recollections of his candid conversations with Agent Baxter. The most radical faction in the online discussion insisted that Barlow was acting as an informant for the FBI. Barlow's point was that if everybody in law enforcement was acting on completely erroneous information about cyberspace technology, travesties of justice were inevitable.

Another person on the Hackers' Conference roster, who had actually received some of the purloined ROM code, unsolicited, and properly reported it to the authorities, was Mitchell Kapor. Kapor had cofounded Lotus Development Corporation, one of the first and most successful software companies of the PC era, and had codesigned Lotus 1–2–3, one of the most successful PC programs of all time. He had sold the company years ago for multiple tens of millions of dollars, and the WELL was one of the places he now could be found, talking about software design, intellectual property, and civil liberties in cyberspace. He, too, was concerned with the Sun Devil arrests and what that might mean for the perhaps short-lived liberties presently enjoyed in cyberspace. He too, had been contacted by the FBI.

In late spring 1991, while he was flying in his jet cross-country, Kapor realized he was almost directly over Barlow's ranch. He had been following Barlow's reports on the WELL; they had met in person for the first time at a WELL party—introduced, as a matter of fact, by Blair Newman. Kapor called Barlow from his jet and asked Barlow if he was interested in a drop-in visit.

Kapor landed, he and Barlow started talking about the Sun Devil arrests, the NuPrometheus affair, the recent state of high aggressiveness by federal law enforcement authorities in cyberspace, and law enforcement's correspondingly high state of puzzlement about what was really going on in the world of high-tech communications. They founded the Electronic Frontier Foundation (EFF) that afternoon in Barlow's Pinedale kitchen.

Within a few days, Kapor had put Barlow in touch with the distinguished constitutional law firm that had made it possible for the *New York Times* to publish the Pentagon Papers. Kapor, concerned about the nature of the Sun Devil arrests and what they signaled for civil liberties in cyberspace, offered to support the costs of legal defense. Acid Phreak, Phiber Optik, and their buddy Scorpion were represented by Rabinowitz, Boudin, Standard, Krinsky, and Lieberman.

Within days of the Pinedale meeting, Steve Wozniak, cofounder of Apple Computer, and John Gilmore, Unix telecommunications wizard and one of the first employees of the enormously successful Sun Microsystems, offered to match Kapor's initial contributions. A board of directors was recruited that included, among others, WELL founder Stewart Brand. The EFF endowment was intended from the beginning to be a great deal more than a defense fund.

The EFF founders saw, as the first reporters from the mass media did not, that Sun Devil was not just a hacker bust. The EFF founders agreed that there was a good chance that the future of American democracy could be strongly influenced by the judicial and legislative structures beginning to emerge from cyberspace. The reasons the EFF helped defend Acid, Optik, and Scorpion as well as Neidorf and Jackson had to do with the assumptions made by the Secret Service about what they could and could not do to citizens. "The Electronic Frontier Foundation will fund, conduct, and support legal efforts to demonstrate that the

Secret Service has exercised prior restraint on publications, limited free speech, conducted improper seizure of equipment and data, used undue force, and generally conducted itself in a fashion which is arbitrary, oppressive, and unconstitutional," Barlow declared in an early manifesto. "In addition, we will work with the Computer Professionals for Social Responsibility and other organizations to convey to both the public and the policy-makers metaphors which will illuminate the more general stake in liberating Cyberspace."

System cracking is serious business. Someday, some data vandal is going to do real damage to something important, like a 911 response system, or air traffic control, or medical records. But Acid Phreak and his buddies weren't the culprits. And the way they were busted sent a chill down the spine of every sysop of every one of the forty to fifty sixty thousand BBSs in America.

The legal defense team blew a fatal hole in the Sun Devil prosecution when an expert who happened to monitor the public EFF conference on the WELL offered a key piece of expert knowledge: the document that was so highly valued that hundreds of law enforcement officers were protecting it on behalf of a large corporation could be obtained legally from the publications department of that corporation for an amount that would merit something more akin to a petty theft misdemeanor charge than a guns-drawn raid. The problem soon turned out to be one of education: not even the deep pockets of the EFF founders and the best legal expertise they could buy could be effective against a system in which very few people involved in enforcing the law or defending suspects understood the kind of place—cyberspace—in which the alleged crimes took place.

It wasn't just the legal system that had been taken by surprise. New social and civil rights and responsibilities, utterly untested by case law, have been emerging from CMC technology, along with the online cultures that have been growing in it. To most citizens and lawmakers in 1990, online newsletters and ROM code and the constitutional implications of computer networks were remote and incomprehensible issues. In that atmosphere of confusion and ignorance, most people thought the EFF was defending hackers, period; the rights of electronic speech and assembly that the EFF founders were so concerned about were invisible to the majority of the population. Someone had to do a better job of explaining to citizens that they were in danger of losing rights they didn't know they possessed.

***

The EFF began its public outreach via a conference on the WELL, inviting both the prosecutors and the defendants in the Sun Devil busts to engage in a dialogue with cryptographers, criminologists, hackers, crackers, and attorneys about the kind of law enforcement that is proper and improper in cyberspace. The Computers, Freedom, and Privacy conference was organized independently by some of the people who had participated in the EFF's online discussions on the WELL and the EFF's node on the Net, bringing the former online and courtroom opponents together face-to-face.

By early 1992, the EFF had opened a national office in Cambridge, Massachusetts, where ex-WELL director Cliff Figallo became the first EFF director, and an office in Washington, D.C., to spearhead lobbying efforts. They hired a legal director and a publications director. They began holding press conferences, attending congressional hearings, publishing online and mailing paper pamphlets, and seeking members via the Net. By the end of 1992, however, tension emerged between the Cambridge office, where the educational and community-building efforts were focused, and the Washington, D.C. office, where the litigation support and political lobbying efforts were based. The EFF board, deciding that the organization should focus its energy on lobbying and legal support, closed its Cambridge office in 1993. By that time, the Computers, Freedom, and Privacy conference and other allied organizations, such as Computer Professionals for Social Responsibility, were in position to pick up the outreach and community-building tasks that the EFF was no longer supporting.

At the end of January 1993, the Steve Jackson case came to a dramatic climax. The EFF and Steve Jackson Games had filed suit against the Secret Service. Jackson's publishing business, almost two years later, had not recovered from the confiscation of computer equipment belonging to Steve Jackson Games. We followed the trial on the Net. Shari Steele from the EFF's legal team relayed news from the site of the trial in Austin to the Net:

Hi everybody.

I really don't have much time to write, but I just witnessed one of the most dramatic courtroom events. The judge in the Steve Jackson Games trial just spent 15 minutes straight reprimanding Agent Timothy Foley of the United States Secret Service for the behavior of the United States regarding the raid and subsequent investigation of Steve Jackson Games. He asked Foley, in random order (some of this is quotes, some is paraphrasing because I couldn't write fast enough):

How long would it have taken you to find out what type of business Steve Jackson Games does? One hour? In any investigation prior to March 1st (the day of the raid) was there any evidence that implicated Steve Jackson or Steve Jackson Games, other than Blankenship's presence? You had a request from the owner to give the computers and disks back. You knew a lawyer was called. Why couldn't a copy of the information contained on the disks be given within a matter of days? How long would it have taken to copy all disks? 24 hours? Who indicated that Steve Jackson was running some kind of illegal activity? Since the equipment was not accessed at the Secret Service office in Chicago after March 27, 1990, why wasn't the equipment released on March 28th? Did you or anyone else do any investigation after March 1st into the nature of Mr. Jackson and his business? You say that Coutorie told you it was a game company. You had the owner standing right in front of you on March 2nd. Is it your testimony that the first time that you realized that he was a publisher and had business records on the machine was when this suit was filed?

The government was so shaken, they rested their case, never even calling Barbara Golden or any of their other witnesses to the stand. Closing arguments are set for this afternoon. It truly was a day that every lawyer dreams about. The judge told the Secret Service that they had been very wrong. I'll try to give a full report later. Shari

The verdict came in on March 12, 1993, a significant legal victory for Steve Jackson Games and the EFF, although certainly not the last battle in this struggle. The judge awarded damages of $1,000 per plaintiff under the Electronic Communications Privacy Act and, under the Privacy Protection Act, awarded Steve Jackson Games $42,259 for lost profits and out-of-pocket costs of $8,781. The method in which law enforcement authorities had seized Jackson's computers was ruled to be an unlawful search and seizure of a publisher.

It remains to be seen whether the online civil libertarians can build a broad-based movement beyond the ranks of the early adapters and whether even a well-organized grassroots movement can stand up to the kind of money and power at stake in this debate. But at least the battle over fundamental civil rights in cyberspace has been joined, and organizations like the EFF, Computer Professionals for Social Responsibility, and Computers, Freedom, and Privacy are beginning to proliferate. If these organizations succeed in gaining supporters outside the circles of technically knowledgeable enthusiasts, citizens might gain powerful leverage at a crucial time. There comes a time when small bands of dedicated activists need wide support; in cyberspace, that time has arrived.

The online community has a responsibility to the freedom it enjoys, and if it wants to continue to enjoy that freedom, more people must take an active part in educating the nontechnical population about several important distinctions that are lost in the blitz of tabloid journalism. Most important, people in cyberspace are citizens, not criminals, nor do the citizens tolerate the criminals among them; however, law enforcement agencies have a commitment to constitutional protections of individual rights, and any breach of those rights in the pursuit of criminals threatens the freedoms of other citizens' rights to free speech and assembly.

The constitutional government of the United States has proved to be a flexible instrument for two centuries, but cyberspace is very new and we are moving into it quickly. Any freedoms we lose now are unlikely to be regained later. The act of simply extending the Bill of Rights to that portion of cyberspace within U.S. jurisdiction would have an enormously liberating impact on the application of CMC to positive social purposes everywhere in the world.

Grassroots and Global: CMC Activists

Are virtual communities just computerized enclaves, intellectual ivory towers? The answer must lie in the real world, where people try to use the technology for the purpose of addressing social problems. Nonprofit organizations on the neighborhood, city, and regional levels, and non-governmental organizations (NGOs) on the global level, can be seen as modern manifestations of what the enlightenment philosophers of democracy would have called "civil society." The ideal of building what one pioneer, Howard Frederick, calls a "global civil society" is one clear vision of a democratic use of CMC. Nonprofits and NGOs that use CMC effectively are concrete evidence of ways this technology can be used for humanitarian purposes.

Nonprofits and NGOs are organizationally well-suited to benefit from the leverage offered by CMC technology and the people power inherent in virtual communities. These groups feed people, find them medical care, cure blindness, free political prisoners, organize disaster relief, find shelter for the homeless—tasks as deep into human nonvirtual reality as you can get. The people who accomplish this work suffer from underfunding, overwork, and poor communications. Any leverage they can gain, especially if it is affordable, will pay off in human lives saved, human suffering alleviated.

Nonprofit organizations and volunteer action groups dealing with environmentalism, civil rights, physical and sexual abuse, suicide prevention, substance abuse, homelessness, public health issues, and all the other people problems in modern society that aren't addressed adequately by the government, the justice system, or the private sector generally operate on a shoestring, with volunteer labor. Few of them have people with enough computer expertise to set up a mailing list database or an e-mail network, so they end up spending five times as much money by paying a service or misusing volunteers to do their mailings.

Dan Ben-Horin tapped the social consciousness of experts on the WELL, matching computer-literate mentors with nonprofit organizations. The scheme worked so well that it turned into a well-funded nonprofit organization itself—CompuMentor. Here is the story of the birth of CompuMentor, in Ben-Horin's own words:

The CompuMentor project began four and a half years ago when I couldn't get my new 24-pin printer to print envelopes without smudging. I had just started logging onto the WELL, so I posted my printer question in the IBM conference. The answers I received were not only informal but also profuse, open-hearted, full-spirited. The proverbial thought balloon instantly appeared. These computerites on the WELL wanted to share their skills.

I had recently spent more than four years as ad director of Media Alliance, of San Francisco, where I had started a technical assistance facility called Computer Alliance. Computer Alliance offered training to nonprofit groups and individuals who traveled to Fort Mason in San Francisco for instruction. From various conversations with nonprofit organizations, as well as my own experience as a fledgling computerist, I knew how easy it is to take a great class and then forget a crucial part of the lesson on the drive home.

My own learning had really commenced when my next-door neighbor expressed a willingness to help me whenever I needed him. And I needed him frequently. Now, here on the WELL was a whole community of helpful electronic next-door neighbors. Of course, few nonprofit organizations are online with their personal computers. Was there a way to connect the online computer guides with the nonprofit organizations that needed guidance? I sent a flier ('Do you need computer help?') to thirty nonprofit organizations, eighteen of which responded, 'You betcha and how.' Then, on the WELL, I started asking folks if they wanted to adopt a nonprofit organization. A dozen folks said they were willing to visit nonprofit organizations as computer mentors. In addition, two dozen more said they would be glad to handle phone queries. One WELLbeing suggested we call the project ENERT—for Emergency Nerd Response Team— but we opted for the more bland CompuMentor.

By December 1990, CompuMentor had set up 968 matches with 446 nonprofit organizations, from a database of 668 volunteer mentors. A few examples of the kinds of organizations CompuMentor helped set up include DES Action of San Francisco, California Rural Legal Assistance, St. Anthony's Dining room, and Women's Refuge in Berkeley. Compu-Mentor has gone national since then and continues to secure funding from charitable foundations that know leverage when they see it.

Environmental activists have been among the most successful of the early adapters of CMC technology. Among the first online environmental activists was Don White, director of Earth Trust, a worldwide non-profit organization that concentrates on international wildlife protection and environmental problems that "fall between the cracks of local and national environmental movements." According to White, "Recent Earth-Trust programs include shutting down Korea's illegal whaling operations, expeditions to South America to save Amazon wildlife, acoustic and communications research on whales and dolphins, and ground-breaking work against deep-sea gillnetting fleets."

EarthTrust is an extremely low-overhead transnational organization that exists almost entirely as a network of volunteers scattered around the globe. Some volunteers are in cities where national governments can be lobbied; many are in remote locations where they can verify "ground truth" about logging, mining, fishing operations, and toxic waste disposal. EarthTrust provides its branch offices with inexpensive personal computers, printers, modems, and accounts with MCImail, a global electronic mail service. Each basic electronic workstation costs less than $1,000. The professionals in the field and those in the offices can coordinate communications inexpensively.

Environmental scientists and activists are dispersed throughout the world, generally don't have the money to travel to international conferences, and are compartmentalized into academic institutions and disciplines. The uses of electronic mailing lists and grassroots computer networks began to spread through the scientific and scholarly parts of the ecoactivist grapevine through the late 1980s. Just as virtual communities emerged in part as a means of fulfilling the hunger for community felt by symbolic analysts, the explosive growth in electronic mailing lists covering environmental subjects has served as a vehicle for informal multidisciplinary discussions among those who want to focus on real-world problems rather than on the borders between nations or academic departments.

By 1992, there were enough online environmentalist efforts to support the publication of a popular guidebook to CMC as a tool for environmental activism, *Ecolinking: Everyone's Guide to Online Environmental Organization*. *Ecolinking* is a combination of CompuMentor-in-a-book that instructs activists in the arcana of going online, and a directory that lists the key information about different BBSs and networks that already exist.

Among the subjects of FidoNet echoes (ongoing, BBS-network-based, international computer conferences on specific subjects), *Ecolinking* lists hazardous waste management, Indian affairs, sustainable agriculture, global environmental issues, health physics, geography, hunger, radiation safety, Native American NewsMagazine, Native American Controversy, and technology education, as well as other interest areas.

The struggle for preservation of the earth's biodiversity, which is threatened on a massive scale by human destruction of old-growth ecosystems, is an environmental-political issue that requires the concerted efforts of a number of different disciplines and nationalities. Ecologists, ethologists, biologists, anthropologists, activists around the world, have been using parts of the Net to coordinate scientific and political efforts. *Ecolinking* notes the example of Aldo de Moor, a fourth-year information management student in the Netherlands who created the Rain Forest Network Bulletin on BITNET as an online think tank for evaluating ecological action plans from both scientific and political perspectives—an incubator for potential environmental solutions.

The importance of BITNET is its reach throughout the world's research establishments. Originally funded by NSF and implemented by IBM, BITNET (Because It's Time Network) links more than two thousand academic and research organizations worldwide, in thirty-eight countries, mostly through automatic Listservs, electronic mailing lists that automatically move written discussions around to those who subscribe; the latest rounds of every discussion show up in the sub-scribers' electronic mailboxes, and the subscribers can send responses around to the rest of the list by replying to the e-mail. The European version of BITNET is called EARN (European Academic Research Network), which begat PLEARN, the Polish network that sprang up the moment communism crumbled.

BITNET mailing lists are gatewayed to the Internet. This means that this "invisible college" already has tremendous reach in the scholarly and scientific world across national as well as disciplinary boundaries. The dozens of BITNET mailing lists, from Agroforestry to Weather Spotters (and including such forums as the Brineshrimp Discussion List, the National Birding Hotline Cooperative, the Genomic-Organization Bulletin Board, and the Dendrochronology Forum), have created a web of inter-disciplinary communications and a worldwide forum for sharing knowl-edge about environmental issues among tens of thousands of experts.

The increasing "networkability" of the nonprofits and NGOs that are springing up around the world, specifically in the area of environmental action and peacework, is what gave birth to the largest and most effec-tive activist network in the world, the Institute for Global Communica-tions, which includes EcoNet, PeaceNet, GreenNet, ConflictNet, and others worldwide.

The NGO movement represents another example of the kinds of organizations that global voice telecommunications made possible in the first place, and which have the potential to thrive in a CMC networked world. Just as nonprofit organizations focus on those social problems that fall between the cracks of local or regional institutions, public and private, NGOs address the issues that national and international institu-tions, public and private, don't seem to address. The Red Cross is the paradigm example. Amnesty International is a contemporary example of an NGO that has had real impact.

Howard Frederick, present news director of the Institute for Global Communications, believes that NGOs are the global equivalent to the institutions of civil society that the first theoreticians of modern democ-racy envisioned. In an online discussion that took place via a BITNET Listserv (and which was compiled into a book by MIT Press), Frederick asserted:

The concept of civil society arose with John Locke, the English philosopher and political theorist. It implied a defense of human society at the national level against the power of the state and the inequalities of the marketplace. For Locke, civil society was that part of civilization—from the family and the church to cultural life and education—that was outside of the control of government or market but was increasingly marginalized by them. Locke saw the importance of social movements to protect the public sphere from these commercial and governmental interests.

Frederick pointed out in our online discussions that big money and powerful political interests have "pushed civil society to the edge," leaving those who would constitute such a culture with no communications media of their own. Frederick believes that CMC has changed the balance of power for NGOs on the global level, the way Dave Hughes believes CMC changes the balance of power for citizens on the community level:

The development of communications technologies has vastly transformed the capacity of global civil society to build coalitions and networks. In times past, communication transaction clusters formed among nation-states, colonial empires, regional economies and alliances—for example, medieval Europe, the Arab world, China and Japan, West African kingdoms, the Caribbean slave and sugar economies. Today new and equally powerful forces have emerged on the world stage—the rain forest protection movement, the human rights movement, the campaign against the arms trade, alternative news agencies, and planetary computer networks.

NGOs, according to Frederick and others, face a severe political problem that arises from the concentration of ownership of global communication media in the hands of a very small number of people. He cited Ben Bagdikian's often-quoted prediction that by the turn of the century "five to ten corporate giants will control most of the world's important newspapers, magazines, books, broadcast stations, movies, recordings and videocassettes." These new media lords are not likely to donate the use of their networks for the kinds of information that NGOs tend to disseminate. Yet rapid and wide dissemination of information is vitally important to grassroots organizing around global problems.

The activist solution to this dilemma has been to create alternate planetary information networks. The Institute for Global Communications (IGC), then, was conceived as a kind of virtual community for NGOs, an enabling technology for the continued growth of global civil society. Again, the distributed nature of the telecommunications network, coupled with the availability of affordable computers, made it possible to piggyback an alternate network on the mainstream infrastructure.

In 1982, an environmental organization in California, the Farallones Institute, with seed money from Apple Computer and the San Francisco Foundation, created EcoNet to facilitate discussion and activism on behalf of worldwide environmental protection, restoration, and sustainability. In 1984, PeaceNet was created by Ark Communications Institute, the Center for Innovative Diplomacy, Community Data Processing, and the Foundation for the Arts of Peace. In 1987, PeaceNet and EcoNet joined together as part of IGC. In 1990, ConflictNet, a network dedicated to supporting dispute mediation and nonviolent conflict resolution, joined IGC.

IGC worked with local partners to establish sister networks in Sweden, Canada, Brazil, Nicaragua, and Australia. Eventually, GlasNet in the former Soviet Union affiliated with IGC. In 1990, the different member organizations formed the Association for Progressive Communications (APC) to coordinate what had become a global network of activist networks. By 1992, APC networks connected more than fifteen thousand subscribers in ninety countries.

APC networks experienced a radical surge in activity during the Gulf War. As the most highly news-managed war of the media age, the Gulf War created a hunger for alternative sources of information, a hunger that was met by the kinds of alternatives offered by APC. During the attempted coup in the Soviet Union in 1990, Russian "APC partners used telephone circuits to circumvent official control," according to Frederick. "Normally, the outdated Russian telephone system require hordes of operators to connect international calls by hand and callers must compete fiercely for phone lines. But the APC partner networks found other routes for data flow. While the usual link with Moscow is over international phone lines, APC technicians also rigged a link over a more tortuous route. That plan saw Soviet news dispatches gathered through a loose network of personal computer bulletin board systems in Moscow and Leningrad. The dispatches which were sent by local phone calls to the Baltic states, then to NordNet Sweden, and then to London-based GreenNet, which maintains an open link with the rest of the APC."

To those of us who had the Net's window on the world during the major international political crises of the past several years, the pictures we were able to piece together of what actually might be happening turned out to be considerably more diverse than the one obtainable from the other media available through conventional channels—the newspaper, radio, and television. Within hours of the crucial events in China in 1989 and Russia in 1991, the Net became a global backchannel for all kinds of information that never made it into the mass media. People with cellular telephones report via satellite to people with computers and modems, and within minutes, witnesses on the spot can report what they see and hear to millions of others. Imagine how this might work ten years from now, when digital, battery-operated minicams are as ubiquitous as telephones, and people can feed digitized images as well as words to the Net.

Information and disinformation about breaking events are pretty raw on the Net. That's the point. You don't know what to think of any particular bit of information, how to gauge its credibility, and nobody tells you what to think about it, other than what you know from previous encounters, about the reliability of the source. You never really know how to gauge the credibility of the nightly news or the morning paper, either, but most of us just accept what we see on television or read in the paper.

With the Net, during times of crisis, you can get more information, of extremely varying quality, than you can get from conventional media. Most important, you get unmediated news that fills in the important blank spots in the pictures presented by the mass media. You can even participate, if only as an onlooker. During the Gulf War, we on the WELL were spellbound readers of reports relayed via BITNET to Internet by an Israeli researcher, who was in a sealed room with his family, under missile attack. We asked him questions in the WELL's many-to-many public conference that were sent to him, and his answers returned, via Internet e-mail.

None of the evidence for political uses of the Net thus far presented is earthshaking in terms of how much power it has now to influence events. But the somewhat different roles of the Net in Tiananmen Square, the Soviet coup, and the Gulf War, represent harbingers of political upheavals to come. In February 1993, General Magic, a company created by the key architects of Apple's Macintosh computer, revealed their plans to market a technology for a whole new kind of "personal intelligent communicator." A box the size of a checkbook with a small screen, sty-lus, and cellular telephone will enable a person anywhere in the world to scribble a message on the screen and tap the screen with the stylus, send-ing it to anyone with a reachable e-mail address or fax machine. The same device doubles as a cellular phone. Apple, AT&T, Matsushita, Philips, Sony, and others have already announced their plans to license this technology. When the price drops to $25, what will that do to the mass media's monopoly on news? What kinds of Tiananmen Squares or Rodney King incidents will emerge from this extension of cyberspace?

Access to alternate forms of information and, most important, the power to reach others with your own alternatives to the official view of events, are, by their nature, political phenomena. Changes in forms and degrees of access to information are indicators of changes in forms and degrees of power among different groups. The reach of the Net, like the reach of television, extends to the urbanized parts of the entire world (and, increasingly, to far-flung but telecom-linked rural outposts). Not only can each node rebroadcast or originate content to the rest of the Net, but even the puniest computers can process that content in a vari-ety of ways after it comes in to the home node from the Net and before it goes out again. Inexpensive computers can copy and process and com-municate information, and when you make PCs independent processing nodes in the already existing telecommunications network, a new kind of system emerges.

Cities in Cyberspace

If electronic democracy is the theory, Santa Monica's Public Electronic Network (PEN) is a vivid example of the practice. And the PEN Action Group's SHWASHLOCK proposal is a classic case history, illustrating how citizens can agree on a common problem, use their collective resources to propose a solution, and convince the city's official govern-ment to help put the solution into practice. It's also an example of how the nonvirtual realities of modern cities can be influenced in concrete ways by the focused use of virtual communities. The scale of the exam-ple is small, and the city is one of the wealthier enclaves in the world, but SHWASHLOCK is what scientists call an "existence proof" for theories of virtual civil society-building.

The name of the proposal is an acronym for "SHowers, WASHing machines, LOCKers," the three elements that PEN members, including several homeless participants, agreed that homeless job-seekers most needed. Having determined that they wanted to address in some way what a Santa Monica Chamber of Commerce survey pinpointed as "the city's number-one problem"—homelessness—PEN members formed an action group that began having face-to-face meetings long with their ongoing virtual meetings. In August 1989, an artist, Bruria Finkel, posted her idea for providing a needed service. Homeless people cannot effectively seek employment without a place to shower in the morning and a free laundry service to help make them presentable, as well as a secure place to store personal belongings. And no city or nonprofit services provided those key elements.

The PEN Action Group discovered that hot showers in public parks were not open until noon, and nonprofit service agencies were reluctant to set up lockers because they didn't want to police their contents. Online with service providers and city officials, the Action Group found no clear consensus on how to implement what all agreed to be a promising new service. PEN enthusiast Michele Wittig, a psychology professor, proposed forming a group to directly address the homelessness issue. Existing social service providers weren't happy with the prospect of this new online group competing for shrinking social service budgets, so the SHWASHLOCK advocates decided to raise funds for an existing agency, which agreed to administer a laundry voucher system. Another obstacle was overcome when a city council member introduced the Action Group to a locker manufacturer who agreed to donate lockers to the city on a trial basis.

In July 1990, the Santa Monica city council, responding to the PEN Action Group's formal proposal, allocated $150,000 to install lockers and showers under the Santa Monica pier, and agreed to open public showers elsewhere at 6:00 a.m. The homeless members of the Action Group continued to ask for some kind of job bank as well, to provide job leads. PEN members decided to try to grow a network: a PEN terminal was donated to a homeless drop-in center already staffed by job counselors, and two graduate students earned course credits for finding job listings. PEN was doing what it was designed to do: enabling citizens to discuss their own agendas, surface problems of mutual concern, cooperatively design solutions, and make the ideas work in the city's official government.

Santa Monica is an exceptional city in terms of local citizen interest, stemming from the renter's rights movement in the early 1980s. The citizens' organizations that helped pass a historically stringent rent-control ordinance also helped elect a city council that was publicly committed to opening up the government to wider citizen participation. The city council, inspired by the way an American company had helped a Japanese city use CMC to resist destruction of a local forest, hired the same American company to help them design a municipal CMC system. Metasystems Design Group (MDG), the Alexandria, Virginia, company that helped Santa Monica set up the Caucus computer conferencing software, is well aware of the culture-altering potential of CMC technology and deliberately blends organizational development work with CMC systems engineering.

MDG's Lisa Carlson was one of the early true believers in social transformation via networking; she practices what she preaches to the extent that it is hard to find any significant CMC system in the world that doesn't have a contribution from her. Another partner in MDG, Frank Burns, was Colonel Burns of the U.S. Army's delta force in the early 1980s, when I first met him at a conference on education and consciousness. He explained to me that the largest educational institution in the world, the U.S. Army,, needed to find out if it could learn anything from the human potential movement. Before he retired to become a toolmaker for electronic activists, Burns came up with the army's highly successful recruitment slogan, "Be All That You Can Be."

If you can convince the army to model itself after Esalen, even in a tiny way, you probably have some knack for facilitating changes in organizations. MDG has always coupled an awareness of the community with its knowledge of CMC tools. CMC was seen by the city and by MDG as a tool to increase citizen participation in local government. The specific changes that they hoped would come about were not designed into the system, for they were supposed to emerge from the CMC-augmented community itself. Four years later, those who started the system began to realize what they should have designed into the system, which those who replicate their efforts ought to take into account—the common problem in cyberspace of the hijacking of discussions by a vociferous minority.

PEN was launched in 1989. Ken Phillips, director of the Information Systems Department in Santa Monica City Hall, was the systems instigator and chief architect. When the city wouldn't pay for his plan, he obtained donations of $350,000 worth of hardware from Hewlett-Packard and $20,000 worth of software from MDG. The city distributed free accounts to city residents who would register for the service. Personal computers at home, terminals at work, and the dozens of public terminals provided to libraries, schools, and city buildings enable Santa Monicans to read information provided by the city, exchange e-mail with other citizens or city hall officials, and participate in public conferences. The police department runs the Crimewatch conference. "Planning" is a forum for discussions of land use, zoning, and development; "Environment" is where air quality, water pollution, and recycling programs are discussed; "Santa Monica" covers rent control, community events, and information about city boards and commissions.

Other forums allow discussion of topics far afield from municipal concerns. MDG, well aware of Oldenburg's ideas about informal public spaces, made sure there was enough virtual common space for people to create their own formal and informal discussions in addition to following the ones established by the system's organizers. MDG knew from experience with other organizations that you have to be careful not to structure a citizen participation system too elaborately in advance, that it is important to give the people who use the system both the tools and the power to change the structure of discussion as well as its content.

Giving the power of expression to citizens and connecting their forum to city officials does not guarantee that all projects will turn out as positively as SHWASHLOCK. Pamela Varley, a casewriter for Harvard's Kennedy School of Government, wrote a full case study of PEN, a version of which was published in MIT's *Technology Review* in 1991. Varley quoted several enthusiasts who acknowledged the real excitement they found in using the system. Don Paschal, who was homeless when he started using the system, used one of the phrases online activists often use: "It's been a great equalizer." People did seem to talk across social barriers. But violent disagreements broke out and spread, according to other informants. "PEN's egalitarianism, however," wrote Varley, "also makes the system vulnerable to abuse. PENners quickly discover that they must contend with people who feel entitled to hector mercilessly those with whom they disagree." She quoted PEN's Ken Phillips saying that it was like trying to hold a meeting while "allowing somebody to stand in a corner and shout."

Women had trouble online with a small number of men who would badger all females as soon as they joined the system, with public and private unwanted attention, innuendo, and violence fantasies that used the initials of women on PEN. A support group, PEN Femmes, emerged and immediately made a point of welcoming women and encouraging them to participate. As women became more visible online, harassment subsided, according to Varley.

Varley noted that "PEN's biggest disappointment has been the domination of its conference discussions by a small number of users. More than 3,000 people are signed up for PEN, but only 500 to 600 log on each month and most never add any comments to the conference discussion. PENners talk about the '50 hard core' users whose names appear again and again in the conference discussions." Varley quoted Phillips as saying, "I recommend to people that if they're going to do a system like this that they start with a group of community leaders, and let them set the tone of the system."

WELLite Kathleen Creighton also spent some time exploring PEN and interviewing PEN members in 1992 about what did and what did not work about the system. Creighton's informants agreed with Varley's, that some people had more time on their hands to harangue city officials online, and those with the worst manners had a powerfully negative impact on the process of communication between citizens and city officials. "Folks' expectations were very high and they counted on a dialogue with city employees," Creighton reported. "Except that city employees don't like being criticized or being held accountable. So users would ask the city folks questions, or PEN staff questions (which is just as bad) and not get any answers. So people got pissed off. Then they realized there was no penalty for being assholes (there isn't because the feeling is that the City of Santa Monica is barred from restricting speech—well, that's the feeling of *some*). And the powers that be told Ken Phillips years ago he couldn't have moderators."

Valuable lessons derived from the PEN experience: People want a means of communicating more than they want access to information; make databases of useful information available, but emphasize citizen-to-citizen communication as well. Citizens can put items on the city agenda, but if you plan to involve city officials, make clear to everyone what can and cannot be accomplished through this medium in terms of changing city policies, and set up some rules of polite communication within a framework of free speech. Free speech does not mean that anyone has to listen to vile personal attacks. Having both moderated forums and totally unmoderated forums for hot subjects is one technique for maintaining a place for reasoned discourse without stifling free expression. The people who use the system can design these rules, but if the PEN experience has anything to teach, it is that citizens can't hope to work with city hall without a flame-free zone for such discussions.

Another manifestation of municipal online systems is the Free-Net concept, pioneered in Cleveland and spreading outward from the American heartland. Cleveland Free-Net and the National Public Telecomputing Network movement grew out of a 1984 research project conducted at Case Western Reserve University. Dr. Tom Grundner, then associated with the university's Department of Family Medicine, tested the applicability of CMC to the delivery of community health information. With a single telephone line, he set up a BBS known as St. Silicon's Hospital, where citizens could pose their questions to a board of public health experts and receive answers within twenty-four hours. The popularity of the project attracted financial support from AT&T and the Ohio Bell Company, which funded a larger project.

Grundner designed a full-scale CMC system as a community information resource for fields far beyond public health alone. The governor of Ohio opened Free-Net in July 1986. The first phase of the experiment attracted seven thousand registered users and more than five hundred calls a day. In 1989, a new system opened, offering access via forty-eight telephone lines, including a connection to Case Western Reserve University's fiber-optic network and, eventually, Internet. People from anywhere in the world can read Free-Net discussions, although only citizens of the Free-Net municipality can participate actively. In 1987, the Youngstown FreeNet went online. In 1990, TriState Online in Cincinnati, the Heartland FreeNet in Peoria, Illinois, and the Medina County FreeNet, a rural system, went online.

In 1989, the participating organizations decided to create the National Public Telecomputing Network (NPTN), modeled after the National

Public Radio and Public Broadcasting Systems in the United States—user-supported, community-based, alternative media. Although the system itself is funded by citizens and by nonprofit funding sources, the core idea of NPTN is that access to the network by citizens should be free. Again, if this combination of organizational vision and CMC technology continues to succeed, yet another approach to building an online civil society could spread beyond the early adapters.

The direction of CMC technology might take a different turn, however. The transition from a government-sponsored, taxpayer-supported, relatively unrestricted public forum to a privately owned and provided medium has accelerated recently, and this transition might render moot many of the fantasies of today's true believers in electronic democracy and global online culture. When the telecommunications networks becomes powerful enough to transmit high-fidelity sound and video as well as text, the nature of the Net—and the industry that controls it—might change dramatically.

Events of the spring and summer of 1993, when entertainment conglomerates, software companies, and telephone companies started jumping into bed with each other promiscuously, may have signalled the beginning of the end of the freewheeling frontier era of Net history. April and May saw a flurry of top-level agreements among the biggest communications and entertainment companies in the world. Every week in June seemed to feature a new bombshell. During a period of a few months, the big players that had been maneuvering behind the scenes for years went public with announcements of complex, interlocking alliances. The results of these deals will influence powerfully the shape of the Net in the late 1990s.

Nobody is sure yet who the winners and losers will be, or even where the most successful markets will turn out to be, but the nature of these interindustry alliances and the announced intentions of the partners paint a picture of what Big Money sees in the Net today: a better-than-ever conduit for delivering prepackaged entertainment to the home tomorrow. Everything that has been discussed in this book seems to be missing from that picture.

Will the enormously lucrative home video and television markets finance the many-to-many communications infrastructure that educators and activists dream about? Or will it all be pay-per-view, with little or no room for community networks and virtual communities?

In the late spring of 1993, U.S. West, one of the Regional Bell Operating Companies, announced their intention to invest $2.5 billion in Time-Warner Inc., the world's largest entertainment company, toward the goal of creating advanced cable and information networks. Time-Warner announced another partnership a few weeks later with Silicon Graphics Company to create computer-switched "video on demand." Suddenly, the most highly touted implication of these high-tech business partnerships was the miraculous ability to download tonight's video rental instead of walking a block and a half to the video rental store.

More than technology has been changing: the nature of the partnerships that emerged in early 1993 could be signs of a major shift in the structures of many traditional businesses, triggered by the shifts in our modes of communication made possible by the new technologies. IBM and Apple joined forces in a partnership that would have been unthinkable a few years ago; the IBM-Apple joint venture, Kaleida Labs, has been developing multimedia software to merge text, sound, graphics, and video in next-generation PCs. Kaleida in turn made deals with Motorola to provide microchips, and with Scientific Atlanta, a firm that makes decoders for cable television systems. Scientific Atlanta also has a partnership with Time-Warner.

The buzzphrase about these new digital channels slated to emerge from these alliances was not "virtual community," but "five hundred television channels." Newspapers started concentrating on the plans that many companies announced to put the control system for the Net connection in the cable box atop the television set—the "battle for the set-top." A reporter for the *San Francisco Chronicle* described these business alliances under the headline, "Future TV Will Shop for You and Talk for You," and began the article this way: "Imagine a television that talks to you, enables you to communicate with the kids who go to bed before you get home, and that helps you select a movie." Will set-top Net boxes bring the mass audiences into many-to-many contact? Or will grassroots conviviality be marginalized by high production values?

The information highways, as many print and broadcast journalists began to describe them, were suddenly seen as ever-more-effective conduits for broadcasting more of the same old stuff to more people, with most interactivity limited to channel selection. *Time* and *Newsweek* magazines both did cover stories on information superhighways. Neither of the major newsmagazines mentioned the potential for many-to-many communications between citizens.

The most powerful alliance was disclosed in June 1993. Microsoft, the company started by home-brew PC hobbyist Bill Gates, dominates the PC software market. Tele-Communications Inc. is the world's largest cable television company. On June 13, John Markoff reported on the first page of the *New York Times* that Time-Warner, Microsoft, and Tele-Communications Inc. were forming a joint venture that, in Markoff's words, "would combine the worlds of computing and television and perhaps shape how much of popular culture is delivered." Markoff quoted James F. Moore, an expert consultant: "This has tremendous economic and social importance; it is the gateway for popular culture.... This is the substitute for newspapers and magazines and catalogs and movies, and that gives it enormous economic potential for those who control the gateway."

The day after Kaleida announced their deal with Scientific Atlanta to develop set-top controllers, Microsoft announced a deal with Intel Corporation, the world's largest chip maker, and General Instrument, a manufacturer of cable converters. Telecommunications industry pundits began speculating that the future Net was going to be a hybrid of cable company conduits, telephone company money, and entertainment company content.

The largest chip maker in the world, the largest personal computer software vendor in the world, the largest entertainment company in the world, the largest cable television company in the world, the largest computer hardware manufacturers in the world—the Net these players are building doesn't seem to be the same Net the grassroots pioneers predicted back in the "good old days" on the electronic frontier. It is possible that the leaders of one or more of these institutions will have the vision to recognize that they are in the business of selling the customers to each other, as well as the business of selling them CDs and videos. But those who are used to thinking of CMC as a largely anarchic, dirt-cheap, uncensored forum, dominated by amateurs and enthusiasts, will have to learn a new way of thinking.

Electronic democracy is far from inevitable, despite the variety of hopeful examples you can find if you look for them. There are those who believe the whole idea is a cruel illusion, and their warnings are worth consideration—especially by the most enthusiastic promoters of CMC activism. The next chapter looks more closely at criticisms of the notion of electronic democracy.

10

Disinformocracy

Virtual communities could help citizens revitalize democracy, or they could be luring us into an attractively packaged substitute for democratic discourse. A few true believers in electronic democracy have had their say. It's time to hear from the other side. We owe it to ourselves and future generations to look closely at what the enthusiasts fail to tell us, and to listen attentively to what the skeptics fear.

For example, the rural BBSs and networks of nonprofit organizations represent only part of the picture of the nascent CMC industry. Consider another case history: Prodigy, the service that IBM and Sears spent a reported $1 billion to launch, is advertised on prime-time television as an information-age wonder for the whole family. For a flat monthly fee, Prodigy users can play games, make airplane reservations, send electronic mail to one another (although not to other networks), and discuss issues in public forums. In exchange for the low fees and the wide variety of services, users receive a ribbon of advertising matter at the bottom of their screens.

Prodigy's approach represents an alternate branch of CMC that did not evolve from the old ARPANET networks or the grassroots BBS culture, but from a surprisingly old and often-failed attempt to apply the broadcast paradigm to CMC, known as videotex. The idea is that people will pay, and even subject themselves to advertising, in exchange for information presented on a screen that the human viewer can browse by means of a telephone touchpad, keyboard, or other control device. The problem, as failed videotex experiments funded by governments Britain's Prestel and newspapers (Knight-Ridder's Viewtron) have demonstrated over and over, is that people aren't all that interested in information on screens, if that is all you have to sell—unless you also offer a way for people to interact with one another. Minitel, part of France Telecom's Teletel version of videotex, was so successful because of the chat services, the *messageries*, that were available along with the canned information.

Prodigy is modeled on the old consumers-as-commodity model that works for mass-market magazines. You use the services and contents of the magazine or television network (or online service) to draw a large population of users, who give you detailed information about their demographics, and then you sell access to those users to advertisers. You tailor the content of the magazine or television program or online service to attract large numbers of consumers with the best demographics, you spend money on polls and focus groups to certify the demographics of your consumers, and then advertising agencies buy access to the attention of those consumers you've "captured." This is the economic arm of the broadcast paradigm, extended to cyberspace. With a reported one million users, and both parent companies in trouble, it is not at all clear whether Prodigy will reach the critical mass of users to repay the investment, but this notion of online subscribers as commodities isn't likely to go away. It's based on one of the most successful money-making schemes in history, the advertising industry.

As a model of a future in which CMC services come to be dominated by a few very large private enterprises, Prodigy previews two key, chilling aspects of online societies that are far from the innocent dreams of the utopians. First there was a wave of paranoia among Prodigy subscribers, much discussed on the Net, regarding the way Prodigy's software works: to use the service, you grant Prodigy's central computers access to a part of your desktop computer (the infamous STAGE.DAT file that shows up on Prodigy users' computer disks) whenever you connect with the service via modem. The idea that Prodigy might be capable of reading private information off your personal computer from a distance, even though there was no proof that Prodigy was actually doing any such thing, stemmed from Prodigy's use of a technology that could, in principle, be used for such a purpose. The prospect of giving up parts of our privacy in exchange for access to information is the foundation of a school of political criticism of communications technologies that I'll come back to.

More chilling is the fact that all public postings on Prodigy are censored; there are actually banks of people sitting in front of monitors somewhere, reading postings from Prodigy subscribers, erasing the ones with offensive content. This measure dealt effectively with the outbreak of racist and anti-Semitic invective. It also dealt effectively with free and open public discussions among Prodigy subscribers of Prodigy's own policies. Prodigy's users sign a contract that gives Prodigy the right to edit all public messages before they are posted, and at the same time the contract absolves Prodigy of responsibility for the content of the messages that are posted by declaring them to be in the public domain. Then Prodigy subscribers used Prodigy's free e-mail feature to create mailing lists to get around Prodigy censorship. Private e-mail is protected by the Electronic Communications Privacy Act of 1986, which requires a court order for any third party to read a private message. So Prodigy management changed the pricing for e-mail, cutting off free messages after thirty per month, surcharging twenty-five cents for each additional message.

Prodigy as a private publisher claims First Amendment protection from government interference, so Prodigy users can't go to court to claim their rights to free speech without stepping on Prodigy's rights. Publishers in the United States have a right to publish what they want to publish; with the exception of libel, the courts have no business restraining editors from using their judgment. If you don't like Prodigy, you can go elsewhere—as long as there is an elsewhere. The presence of competition is the key. The Prodigy situation might be a preview of what could happen if a small number of large companies manages to dominate a global telecommunications industry that is now a competitive market of small and medium-size businesses that manage to survive and thrive along with the giants.

As long as BBSs remain legal and telephone carriers don't start charging by the amount of data users send and receive (instead of the amount of time they use the telephone connection), there will be a grassroots alternative to the giant services. But what if some big company comes along in the future and uses its deep pockets, economies of scale, and political power to squeeze out the WELLs and Big Sky Telegraphs and low-cost Internet access providers? Such tactics are not unknown in the history of the telecommunications industry. The telecommunications industry is a business, viewed primarily as an economic player. But telecommunications gives certain people access to means of influencing certain other people's thoughts and perceptions, and that access—who has it and who doesn't have it—is intimately connected with political power. The prospect of the technical capabilities of a near-ubiquitous high-band-width Net in the hands of a small number of commercial interests has dire political implications. Whoever gains the political edge on this technology will be able to use the technology to consolidate power.

There might be a fork in the road of technology-dependent civilization, somewhere in the mid- to late 1990s, forced by the technical capabilities of the Net. Two powerful and opposed images of the future characterize the way different observers foresee the future political effects of new communications technology. The utopian vision of the electronic agora, an "Athens without slaves" made possible by telecommunications and cheap computers and implemented through decentralized networks like Usenet and FidoNet, has been promoted by enthusiasts, including myself, over the past several years. I have been one of the cheerleaders for people like Dave Hughes and Mitch Kapor as they struggled to use CMC to give citizens some of the same media powers that the political big boys wield. And I admit that I still believe that this technology, if properly understood and defended by enough citizens, does have democratizing potential in the way that alphabets and printing presses had democratizing potential.

The critiques of the cheerleading for unproven technologies such as computer conferencing bear serious attention, and so do the warning signals from Prodigy, and the disturbing privacy issues that are raised by some of the same technologies that promise citizens so many benefits. What if these hopes for a quick technological fix of what is wrong with democracy constitute nothing more than another way to distract the attention of the suckers while the big boys divide up the power and the loot? Those who see electronic democracy advocates as naive or worse point to the way governments and private interests have used the alluring new media of past technological revolutions to turn democratic debate into talk shows and commercials. Why should this new medium be any less corruptible than previous media? Why should contemporary claims for CMC as a democratizing technology be taken any more seriously than the similar-sounding claims that were made for steam, electricity, and television?

Three different kinds of social criticisms of technology are relevant to claims of CMC as a means of enhancing democracy. One school of criticism emerges from the longer-term history of communications media, and focuses on the way electronic communications media already have preempted public discussions by turning more and more of the content of the media into advertisements for various commodities—a process these critics call commodification. Even the political process, according to this school of critics, has been turned into a commodity. The formal name for this criticism is "the commodification of the public sphere." The public sphere is what these social critics claim we used to have as citizens of a democracy, but have lost to the tide of commodization. The public sphere is also the focus of the hopes of online activists, who see CMC as a way of revitalizing the open and widespread discussions among citizens that feed the roots of democratic societies.

The second school of criticism focuses on the fact that high-bandwidth interactive networks could be used in conjunction with other technologies as a means of surveillance, control, and disinformation as well as a conduit for useful information. This direct assault on personal liberty is compounded by a more diffuse erosion of old social values due to the capabilities of new technologies; the most problematic example is the way traditional notions of privacy are challenged on several fronts by the ease of collecting and disseminating detailed information about individuals via cyberspace technologies. When people use the convenience of electronic communication or transaction, we leave invisible digital trails; now that technologies for tracking those trails are maturing, there is cause to worry. The spreading use of computer matching to piece together the digital trails we all leave in cyberspace is one indication of privacy problems to come.

Along with all the person-to-person communications exchanged on the world's telecommunications networks are vast flows of other kinds of personal information—credit information, transaction processing, health information. Most people take it for granted that no one can search through all the electronic transactions that move through the world's networks in order to pin down an individual for marketing—or political—motives. Remember the "knowbots" that would act as personal servants, swimming in the info-tides, fishing for information to suit your interests? What if people could turn loose knowbots to collect all the information digitally linked to *you*? What if the Net and cheap, powerful computers give that power not only to governments and large corporations but to everyone?

Every time we travel or shop or communicate, citizens of the credit-card society contribute to streams of information that travel between point of purchase, remote credit bureaus, municipal and federal information systems, crime information databases, central transaction databases. And all these other forms of cyberspace interaction take place via the same packet-switched, high-bandwidth network technology—those packets can contain transactions as well as video clips and text files. When these streams of information begin to connect together, the unscrupulous or would-be tyrants can use the Net to catch citizens in a more ominous kind of net.

The same channels of communication that enable citizens around the world to communicate with one another also allow government and private interests to gather information about them. This school of criticism is known as Panoptic in reference to the perfect prison proposed in the eighteenth century by Jeremy Bentham—a theoretical model that happens to fit the real capabilities of today's technologies.

Another category of critical claim deserves mention, despite the rather bizarre and incredible imagery used by its most well known spokesmen—the hyper-realist school. These critics believe that information technologies have already changed what used to pass for reality into a slicked-up electronic simulation. Twenty years before the United States elected a Hollywood actor as president, the first hyper-realists pointed out how politics had become a movie, a spectacle that raised the old Roman tactic of bread and circuses to the level of mass hypnotism. We live in a hyper-reality that was carefully constructed to mimic the real world and extract money from the pockets of consumers: the forests around the Matterhorn might be dying, but the Disneyland version continues to rake in the dollars. The television programs, movie stars, and theme parks work together to create global industry devoted to maintaining a web of illusion that grows more lifelike as more people buy into it and as technologies grow more powerful.

Many other social scientists have intellectual suspicions of the hyper-realist critiques, because so many are abstract and theoretical, based on little or no direct knowledge of technology itself. Nevertheless, this perspective does capture something about the way the effects of communications technologies have changed our modes of thought. One good reason for paying attention to the claims of the hyper-realists is that the society they predicted decades ago bears a disturbingly closer resemblance to real life than do the forecasts of the rosier-visioned technological utopians. While McLuhan's image of the global village has taken on a certain irony in light of what has happened since his predictions of the 1960s, "the society of the spectacle"—another prediction from the 1960s, based on the advent of electronic media—offered a far less rosy and, as events have proved, more realistic portrayal of the way information technologies have changed social customs.

The Selling of Democracy: Commodification and the Public Sphere

There is an intimate connection between informal conversations, the kind that take place in communities and virtual communities, in the coffee shops and computer conferences, and the ability of large social groups to govern themselves without monarchs or dictators. This social-political connection shares a metaphor with the idea of cyberspace, for it takes place in a kind of virtual space that has come to be known by specialists as the public sphere.

Here is what the preeminent contemporary writer about the public sphere, social critic and philosopher Jurgen Habermas, had to say about the meaning of this abstraction:

By "public sphere," we mean first of all a domain of our social life in which such a thing as public opinion can be formed. Access to the public sphere is open in principle to all citizens. A portion of the public sphere is constituted in every conversation in which private persons come together to form a public. They are then acting neither as business or professional people conducting their private affairs, nor as legal consociates subject to the legal regulations of a state bureaucracy and obligated to obedience. Citizens act as a public when they deal with matters of general interest without being subject to coercion; thus with the guarantee that they may assemble and unite freely, and express and publicize their opinions freely.

In this definition, Habermas formalized what people in free societies mean when we say "The public wouldn't stand for that" or "It depends on public opinion." And he drew attention to the intimate connection between this web of free, informal, personal communications and the foundations of democratic society. People can govern themselves only if they communicate widely, freely, and in groups—publicly. The First Amendment of the U.S. Constitution's Bill of Rights protects citizens from government interference in their communications—the rights of speech, press, and assembly are communication rights. Without those rights, there is no public sphere. Ask any citizen of Prague, Budapest, or Moscow.

Because the public sphere depends on free communication and discussion of ideas, as soon as your political entity grows larger than the number of citizens you can fit into a modest town hall, this vital marketplace for political ideas can be powerfully influenced by changes in communications technology. According to Habermas,

When the public is large, this kind of communication requires certain means of dissemination and influence; today, newspapers and periodicals, radio and television are the media of the public sphere.... The term "public opinion" refers to the functions of criticism and control or organized state authority that the public exercises informally, as well as formally during periodic elections. Regulations concerning the publicness (or publicity [Publizitat] in its original meaning) of state-related activities, as, for instance, the public accessibility required of legal proceedings, are also connected with this function of public opinion. To the public sphere as a sphere mediating between state and society, a sphere in which the public as the vehicle of publicness—the publicness that once had to win out against the secret politics of monarchs and that since then has permitted democratic control of state activity.

Ask anybody in China about the right to talk freely among friends and neighbors, to own a printing press, to call a meeting to protest government policy, or to run a BBS. But brute totalitarian seizure of communications technology is not the only way that political powers can neutralize the ability of citizens to talk freely. It is also possible to alter the nature of discourse by inventing a kind of paid fake discourse. If a few people have control of what goes into the daily reporting of the news, and those people are in the business of selling advertising, all kinds of things become possible for those who can afford to pay.

Habermas had this to say about the corrupting influence of ersatz public opinion:

Whereas at one time publicness was intended to subject persons or things to the public use of reason and to make political decisions subject to revision before the tribunal of public opinion, today it has often enough already been enlisted in the aid of the secret policies of interest groups; in the form of "publicity" it now acquires public prestige for persons or things and renders them capable of acclamation in a climate of nonpublic opinion. The term "public relations" itself indicates how a public sphere that formerly emerged from the structure of society must now be produced circumstantially on a case-by-case basis.

The idea that public opinion can be manufactured and the fact that electronic spectacles can capture the attention of a majority of the citizenry damaged the foundations of democracy. According to Habermas,

> It is no accident that these concepts of the public sphere and public opinion were not formed until the eighteenth century. They derive their specific meaning from a concrete historical situation. It was then that one learned to distinguish between opinion and public opinion.... Public opinion, in terms of its very idea, can be formed only if a public that engages in rational discussion exists. Public discussions that are institutionally protected and that take, with critical intent, the exercise of political authority as their theme have not existed since time immemorial.

The public sphere and democracy were born at the same time, from the same sources. Now that the public sphere, cut off from its roots, seems to be dying, democracy is in danger, too.

The concept of the public sphere as discussed by Habermas and others includes several requirements for authenticity that people who live in democratic societies would recognize: open access, voluntary participation, participation outside institutional roles, the generation of public opinion through assemblies of citizens who engage in rational argument, the freedom to express opinions, and the freedom to discuss matters of the state and criticize the way state power is organized. Acts of speech and publication that specifically discuss the state are perhaps the most important kind protected by the First Amendment to the U.S. Constitution and similar civil guarantees elsewhere in the world. Former Soviets and Eastern Europeans who regained it after decades of censorship offer testimony that the most important freedom of speech is the freedom to speak about freedoms.

In eighteenth-century America, the Committees of Correspondence were one of the most important loci of the public sphere in the years of revolution and constitution-building. If you look closely at the roots of the American Revolution, it becomes evident that a text-based, horseback-transported version of networking was an old American tradition. In their book *Networking*, Jessica Lipnack and Jeffrey Stamps describe these committees as

> a communications forum where homespun political and economic thinkers hammered out their ideological differences, sculpting the form of a separate and independent country in North America. Writing to one another and sharing letters with neighbors, this revolutionary generation nurtured its adolescent ideas

into a mature politics. Both men and women participated in the debate over independence from England and the desirable shape of the American future....

During the years in which the American Revolution was percolating, letters, news-sheets, and pamphlets carried from one village to another were the means by which ideas about democracy were refined. Eventually, the correspondents agreed that the next step in their idea exchange was to hold a face-to-face meeting. The ideas of independence and government had been debated, discussed, discarded, and reformulated literally hundreds of times by the time people in the revolutionary network met in Philadelphia.

Thus, a network of correspondence and printed broadsides led to the formation of an organization after the writers met in a series of conferences and worked out a statement of purpose—which they called a "Declaration of Independence." Little did our early networking grandparents realize that the result of their youthful idealism, less than two centuries later, would be a global superpower with an unparalleled ability to influence the survival of life on the planet.

As the United States grew and technology changed, the ways in which these public discussions of "matters of general interest," as Habermas called them—slavery and the rights of the states versus the power of the federal government were two such matters that loomed large—began to change as well. The text-based media that served as the channel for discourse gained more and more power to reshape the nature of that discourse. The communications media of the nineteenth century were the newspapers, the penny press, the first generation of what has come to be known as the mass media. At the same time, the birth of advertising and the beginnings of the public-relations industry began to undermine the public sphere by inventing a kind of buyable and sellable phony discourse that displaced the genuine kind.

The simulation (and therefore destruction) of authentic discourse, first in the United States, and then spreading to the rest of the world, is what Guy Debord would call the first quantum leap into the "society of the spectacle" and what Jean Baudrillard would recognize as a milestone in the world's slide into hyper-reality. Mass media's colonization of civil society turned into a quasi-political campaign promoting technology itself when the image-making technology of television came along. ("Progress is our most important product," said General Electric spokesman Ronald Reagan, in the early years of television.) And in the twentieth century, as the telephone, radio, and television became vehicles for public discourse, the nature of political discussion has mutated into something quite different from anything the framers of the Constitution could have foreseen.

A politician is now a commodity, citizens are consumers, and issues are decided via sound-bites and staged events. The television camera is the only spectator that counts at a political demonstration or convention. According to Habermas and others, the way the new media have been commoditized through this evolutionary process from hand-printed broadside to telegraph to penny press to mass media has led to the radical deterioration of the public sphere. The consumer society has become the accepted model both for individual behavior and political decision making. Discourse degenerated into publicity, and publicity used the increasing power of electronic media to alter perceptions and shape beliefs.

The consumer society, the most powerful vehicle for generating short-term wealth ever invented, ensures economic growth by first promoting the idea that the way to be is to buy. The engines of wealth depend on a fresh stream of tabloids sold at convenience markets and television programs to tell us what we have to buy next in order to justify our existence. What used to be a channel for authentic communication has become a channel for the updating of commercial desire.

Money plus politics plus network television equals an effective system. It works. When the same packaging skills that were honed on automobile tail fins and fast foods are applied to political ideas, the highest bidder can influence public policy to great effect. What dies in the process is the rational discourse at the base of civil society. That death manifests itself in longings that aren't fulfilled by the right kind of shoes in this month's color or the hot new prime-time candidate everybody is talking about. Some media scholars are claiming a direct causal connection between the success of commercial television and the loss of citizen interest in the political process.

Another media critic, Neal Postman, in his book *Amusing Ourselves to Death*, pointed out that Tom Paine's *Common Sense* sold three hundred thousand copies in five months in 1776. The most successful democratic revolution in history was made possible by a citizenry that read and debated widely among themselves. Postman pointed out that the mass media, and television in particular, had changed the mode of discourse itself, by substituting fast cuts, special effects, and sound-bites for reasoned discussion or even genuine argument.

The various hypotheses about commodification and mode of discourse focus on an area of apparent agreement among social observers who have a long history of heated disagreements.

When people who have become fascinated by BBSs or networks start spreading the idea that such networks are inherently democratic in some magical way, without specifying the hard work that must be done in real life to harvest the fruits of that democratizing power, they run the danger of becoming unwitting agents of commodification. First, it pays to understand how old the idea really is. Next, it is important to realize that the hopes of technophiles have often been used to sell technology for commercial gain. In this sense, CMC enthusiasts run the risk of becoming unpaid, unwitting advertisers for those who stand to gain financially from adoption of new technology.

The critics of the idea of electronic democracy have unearthed examples from a long tradition of utopian rhetoric that James Carey has called "the rhetoric of the 'technological sublime.'" He put it this way:

Despite the manifest failure of technology to resolve pressing social issues over the last century, contemporary intellectuals continue to see revolutionary potential in the latest technological gadgets that are pictured as a force outside history and politics.... In modern futurism, it is the machines that possess teleological insight. Despite the shortcomings of town meetings, newspaper, telegraph, wireless, and television to create the conditions of a new Athens, contemporary advocates of technological liberation regularly describe a new postmodern age of instantaneous daily plebiscitory democracy through a computerized system of electronic voting and opinion polling.

Carey was prophetic in at least one regard—he wrote this years before Ross Perot and William Clinton both started talking about their versions of electronic democracy during the 1992 U.S. presidential campaign. If the United States is on the road to a version of electronic democracy in which the president will have electronic town hall meetings, including instant voting-by-telephone to "go directly to the people" (and perhaps bypass Congress?) on key issues, it is important for American citizens to understand the potential pitfalls of decision making by plebiscite. Media-manipulated plebiscites as political tools go back to Joseph Goebbels, who used radio so effectively in the Third Reich. Previous experiments in instant home polling and voting had been carried out by Warners, with their Qube service, in the early 1980s. One critic, political scientist

Jean Betheke Elshtain, called the television-voting model an

interactive shell game [that] cons us into believing that we are participating when we are really simply performing as the responding "end" of a prefabricated system of external stimuli.... In a plebiscitary system, the views of the majority.... swamp minority or unpopular views. Plebiscitism is compatible with authoritarian politics carried out under the guise of, or with the connivance of, majority views. That opinion can be registered by easily manipulated, ritualistic plebiscites, so there is no need for debate on substantive questions.

What does it mean that the same hopes, described in the same words, for a decentralization of power, a deeper and more widespread citizen involvement in matters of state, a great equalizer for ordinary citizens to counter the forces of central control, have been voiced in the popular press for two centuries in reference to steam, electricity, and television? We've had enough time to live with steam, electricity, and television to recognize that they did indeed change the world, and to recognize that the utopia of technological millenarians has not yet materialized.

An entire worldview and sales job are packed into the word *progress*, which links the notion of improvement with the notion of innovation, highlights the benefits of innovation while hiding the toxic side-effects of extractive and lucrative technologies, and then sells more of it to people via television as a cure for the stress of living in a technology-dominated world. The hope that the next technology will solve the problems created by the way the last technology was used is a kind of millennial, even messianic, hope, apparently ever-latent in the breasts of the citizenry. The myth of technological progress emerged out of the same Age of Reason that gave us the myth of representative democracy, a new organizing vision that still works pretty well, despite the decline in vigor of the old democratic institutions. It's hard to give up on one Enlightenment ideal while clinging to another.

I believe it is too early to judge which set of claims will prove to be accurate. I also believe that those who would prefer the more democratic vision of the future have an opportunity to influence the outcome, which is precisely why online activists should delve into the criticisms that have been leveled against them. If electronic democracy advocates can address these critiques successfully, their claims might have a chance. If they cannot, perhaps it would be better not to raise people's hopes. Those who are not aware of the history of dead ends are doomed to replay them, hopes high, again and again.

The idea that putting powerful computers in the hands of citizens will shield the citizenry against totalitarian authorities echoes similar, older beliefs about citizen-empowering technology. As Langdon Winner (an author every computer revolutionary ought to read) put it in his essay "Mythinformation,"

Of all the computer enthusiasts' political ideas, there is none more poignant than the faith that the computer is destined to become a potent equalizer in modern society.... Presumably, ordinary citizens equipped with microcomputers will be able to counter the influence of large, computer-based organizations.

Notions of this kind echo beliefs of eighteenth-century revolutionaries that placing fire arms in the hands of the people was crucial to overthrowing entrenched authority. In the American Revolution, French Revolution, Paris Commune, and Russian Revolution the role of "the people armed" was central to the revolutionary program. As the military defeat of the Paris Commune made clear, however, the fact that the popular forces have guns may not be decisive. In a contest of force against force, the larger, more sophisticated, more ruthless, better equipped competitor often has the upper hand. Hence, the availability of low-cost computing power may move the baseline that defines electronic dimensions of social influence, but it does not necessarily alter the balance of power. Using a personal computer makes one no more powerful vis-à-vis, say, the National Security Agency than flying a hang glider establishes a person as a match for the U.S. Air Force.

The great power of the idea of electronic democracy is that technical trends in communications technologies can help citizens break the monopoly on their attention that has been enjoyed by the powers behind the broadcast paradigm—the owners of television networks, newspaper syndicates, and publishing conglomerates. The great weakness of the idea of electronic democracy is that it can be more easily commodified than explained. The commercialization and commoditization of public discourse is only one of the grave problems posed by the increasing sophistication of communications media. The Net that is a marvelous lateral network can also be used as a kind of invisible yet inescapable cage. The idea of malevolent political leaders with their hands on the controls of a Net raises fear of a more direct assault on liberties.

Caught in the Net: CMC and the Ultimate Prison

In 1791, Jeremy Bentham proposed, in *Panopticon; or, the Inspection House*, that it was possible to build a mechanism for enforcing a system of social control into the physical structure of a building, which he called the Panopticon. His design for this building was intended to be very general, an architectural algorithm that could be used in prisons, schools, and factories. Individual cells are built into the circumference of a circular building, around a central well. An inspection tower atop the well, in conjunction with a method for lighting the cells and leaving the inspection tower dark, made it possible for one person to monitor the activity of many people, each of whom would know he or she was under surveillance, none of whom would know exactly when. And the inspectors are similarly watched by other unseen inspectors. It was precisely this mental state of being seen without being able to see the watcher that Bentham meant to induce. When you can induce that state of mind in a population, you don't need whips and chains to restrain them from rebelling.

Historian and political philosopher Michel Foucault, in *Discipline and Punish*, examined the social institutions by which powerful people control the potentially rebellious masses. Foucault felt that the Panopticon as an idea as well as a specific architectural design was an important one, for it was a literal blueprint for the way future tyrants could use surveillance technologies to wield power. Just as the ability to read and write and freely communicate gives power to citizens that protects them from the powers of the state, the ability to surveil, to invade the citizens' privacy, gives the state the power to confuse, coerce, and control citizens. Uneducated populations cannot rule themselves, but tyrannies can control even educated populations, given sophisticated means of surveillance.

When you think of privacy, you probably think of your right to be undisturbed and possibly unembarrassed by intrusions into your personal affairs. It does not seem, on the surface, to be a politically significant phenomenon. Kevin Robins and Frank Webster, in their article "Cybernetic Capitalism: Information, Technology, Everyday Life," made the connection between Bentham, Foucault, and the evolution of the telecommunications network:

We believe that Foucault is right in seeing Bentham's Panopticon as a significant event in the history of the human mind. We want to suggest that the new communication and information technologies—particularly in the form of an integrated electronic grid—permit a massive extension and transformation of that same (relative, technological) mobilization to which Bentham's Panoptic principle aspired. What these technologies support, in fact, is the same dissemination of power and control, but freed from the architectural constraints of Bentham's stone and brick prototype. On the basis of the "information revolution," not just the prison or factory, but the social totality, comes to function as the hierarchical and disciplinary Panoptic machine.

The Panopticon, Foucault warned, comes in many guises. It is not a value-neutral technology. It is a technology that allows a small number of people to control a large number of others. J. Edgar Hoover used it. So did Mao tse-Tung. You don't need fiber optics to institute a surveillance state—but it sure makes surveillance easier when you invite the surveillance device into your home.

Critics of those who pin their hopes for social change on computer technology also point out that information and communications technologies have always been dominated by the military, and will continue to be dominated by the military, police, and intelligence agencies for the foreseeable future. A computer is, was, and will be a weapon. The tool can be used for other purposes, but to be promoted as an instrument of liberation, CMC technology should be seen within the contexts of its origins , and in full cognizance of the possibly horrific future applications by totalitarians who get their hands on it.

The first electronic digital computer was created by the U.S. Army to calculate ballistics equations for artillery. The military and intelligence communities, particularly in the United States, have always benefited from a ten- to twenty-year technological lead on civilian applications of the computer technology. The U.S. National Security Agency, the ultra-secret technosnoop headquarters that applies computers to signals intelligence and codebreaking, and the U.S. National Laboratories at Livermore and Los Alamos, where thermonuclear weapons and antimissile defenses are designed, have long been the owners of the most powerful collections of computing power in the world.

Computer and communications technologies outside the military sphere are applied with great effectiveness by public and private police agencies. One example that I saw with my own eyes is suggestive of the range of goodies available to police forces: at a laboratory outside Tokyo, I saw a video camera on a freeway zero in on the license plate of a speeder, use shape-recognition software to decode the license number, and transmit it to police computers, where a warrant search could be conducted. No human in the loop—the camera and computer determine that a crime has been committed and instantly identify the suspect. Just as grassroots citizens' networks have been interconnecting into a planetary Net, police information networks have been evolving as well. The problem there is that law enforcement officers have the authority to shoot you dead; if they shoot you on the basis of misinformation propagated on a Net (and it is far easier to broadcast bad information than to recall it), the Net helped kill you. Jacques Vallee, in the very beginning of his prophetic 1982 book *The Network Revolution*, told the true cautionary tale of the innocent Frenchmen who died under police gunfire as the result of a glitch in a poorly designed police computer network.

The more spectacularly overt images of a Panoptic society—the midnight knock on the door, the hidden microphones of the secret police— are genuine possibilities worth careful consideration. Now it isn't necessary to plant microphones when a remote and inaudible command can turn any telephone—while it is on the hook—into a microphone. The old scenarios aren't the only ones, now. Privacy has already been penetrated in more subtle, complex ways. This assault on privacy, invisible to most, takes place in the broad daylight of everyday life. The weapons are cash registers and credit cards. When Big Brother arrives, don't be surprised if he looks like a grocery clerk, because privacy has been turning into a commodity, courtesy of better and better information networks, for years.

Yesterday, you might have gone to the supermarket and watched someone total up the bill with a bar code reader. Perhaps you paid with an ATM card or credit card or used one as identification for a check. Last night, maybe the data describing what you bought and who you are were telecommunicated from the supermarket to a central collection point. This morning, detailed information about your buying habits could have been culled from one database and sold to a third party who could compile it tomorrow into another electronic dossier somewhere, one that knows what you buy and where you live and how much money you owe. Next week, a fourth party might purchase that dossier, combine it with a few tens of millions of others on an optical disk, and offer to sell the collection of information as a marketing tool.

All of the information on the hypothetical mass-dossier disk is available from public sources; it is in their compilation, the way that information is sorted into files linked to real citizens, that intrusion is accomplished. On each CD-ROM disk will be a file that knows a lot about your tastes, your brand preferences, your marital status, even your political opinions. If you contributed to a freewheeling Usenet newsgroup, all the better, for your political views, sexual preferences, even the way you think, can now be compiled and compared with the other information in your dossier.

The capabilities of information-gathering and sorting technologies that can harvest and sift mind-numbing quantities of individual trivial but collectively revealing pieces of information are formidable today. This Panoptic machinery shares some of the same communications infrastructure that enables one-room schoolhouses in Montana to communicate with MIT professors, and enables overseas Chinese dissidents to disseminate news and organize resistance. The power to compile highly specific dossiers on millions of people will become even more formidable over the next several years as the cost of computing power drops and the network of electronic transactions becomes more richly interconnected. The commodization of privacy is piggybacking on the same combination of computers and communications that has given birth to virtual communities. The power to snoop has become democratized.

When our individual information terminals become as powerful as supercomputers, and every home is capable of sending and receiving huge amounts of information, you won't need a dictatorship from above to spy on your neighbors and have them spy on you. Instead, you'll sell pieces of each other's individuality to one another. Entrepreneurs are already nibbling around the edges of the informational body politic, biting off small chunks of privacy and marketing it. Information about you and me is valuable to certain people, whether or not we actively choose to disclose that information. We've watched our names migrate from magazine subscription lists to junk mail assaults, but we haven't seen the hardware and software that has evolved for gathering and exploiting private information for profit.

The most insidious attack on our rights to a reasonable degree of privacy might come not from a political dictatorship but from the marketplace. The term "Big Brother" brings to mind a scenario of a future dictatorship held together by constant electronic surveillance of the citizenry; but today's technologies allow for more subtlety than Orwell could have been foreseen. There are better ways to build Panopticons than the heavy-handed Orwellian model. If totalitarian manipulators of populations and technologies actually do achieve dominance in the future, I predict that it will begin not by secret police kicking in your doors but by allowing you to sell yourself to your television and letting your supermarket sell information about your transactions, while outlawing measures you could use to protect yourself. Instead of just telephone taps, the weapons will include computer programs that link bar codes, credit cards, social security numbers, and all the other electronic telltales we leave in our paths through the information society. And the most potent weapon will be the laws or absence of laws that enable improper uses of information technology to erode what is left of citizens rights to privacy.

"Marketplace," a CD-ROM that contained the collected available information about you, your family, and 120 million other people, was announced in 1991 by Lotus. After public criticism, Lotus decided not to market the product. Interactive television systems are being installed now, systems that allows customers to download videos and upload information about their tastes, preferences, and opinions. With high-speed digital communication capabilities of future fiber-optic networks, there will be even more ways to move information about you from your home to the databases of others, with and without your consent.

Informational dossiers about individuals are marketing gold mines for those who know how to make money by knowing which magazines you subscribe to, what kind of yogurt you eat, and which political organizations you support. Invisible information—your name, address, other demographic information—is already encoded in certain promotional coupons you get in the mail. Ultimately, advertisers will be able to use new technologies to customize the television advertising for each individual household. Advertising agencies, direct mail marketers, and political consultants already know what to do with your zip code, your social security number, and a few other data. These professional privacy brokers have begun to realize that a significant portion of the population would freely allow someone else to collect and use and even sell personal information, in return for payment or subsidies.

Here is one obvious answer to the inequity of access to Net resources and the gap between information-rich and information-poor. Some people would be able to afford to pay for "enhanced information services." Others would be able to use those services in exchange for a little information-monitoring. For answering a few questions and allowing certain of your transactions to be monitored, for example, you would be granted a certain number of hours of service, or even paid for the information and the right to use it. Why should anybody go to the trouble of seizing our rights of privacy when so many of us would be happy to sell them?

Selling your privacy is your right, and I'm not suggesting that anyone stop you. In fact, it might be a viable solution to the problems of equity of access. There is, in medicine, the notion of informed consent, however, which obligates your physician to explain to you the risks and potential side effects of recommended medical procedures. I'd like people to know what it is they are giving away in exchange for convenience, rebates, or online hours on the latest MUD. Do people have a right to privacy? Where does that right begin and end? Without adequate protections, the same information that can flow laterally, from citizen to citizen, can be used by powerful central authorities as well as by grassroots groups.

The most important kind of protection for citizens against technology-assisted invasion of privacy is a set of principles that can help preserve individual autonomy in the digital age. Laws, policies, and norms are the various ways in which such principles, once articulated and agreed on, are enforced in a democratic society. But high technology is often very good at rendering laws moot. Another kind of protection for citizens is the subject of current intense scrutiny by cyberspace civil libertarians, a technical fix known as citizen encryption. A combination of principles, laws, policies, and technologies, if intelligently designed and equitably implemented, offer one more hopeful scenario in which citizens can continue to make use of the advantages of the Net without falling victim to its Panoptic potential.

Gary Marx, a professor of sociology at MIT, is an expert on technology and privacy. Marx suggests that

an important example of the kind of principles needed is the Code of Fair Information developed in 1973 for the U.S. Department of Health, Education, and Welfare. The code involves five principles:

There must be no personal-data record keeping whose very existence is secret.

There must be a way for a person to find out what information about him is in a record and how it is being used.

There must be a way for a person to prevent information that was obtained for one purpose from being used or made available for other purposes without his consent.

There must be a way for a person to correct or amend a record of identifiable information about himself.

Any organization creating, maintaining, using, or disseminating records of identifiable personal data must assure the reliability of the data for their intended use and must take precautions to prevent misuses of the data.

The highly interconnected, relatively insecure networks, with their millions and billions of bits per second, are a tough environment to enforce rules based on these suggested principles. Many of the nuances of public conferencing or private e-mail or hybrid entities such as e-mail lists will require changes in these principles, but this list is a good way to focus societal debate about values, risks, and liberties. If the profit or power derived from Net-snooping proves to be significant, and the technicalities of the Net make it difficult to track perpetrators, however, no laws will ever adequately protect citizens. That's why a subculture of computer software pioneers known as cypherpunks have been working to make citizen encryption possible.

Encryption is the science of encoding and decoding messages. Computers and codebreaking go back a long way. Alan Turing, one of the intellectual fathers of the computer, worked during World War II on using computational strategies to break the codes created by Germany's Enigma machine. Today, the largest assemblage of computer power in the world is widely acknowledged to be the property of the U.S. National Security Agency, the top-secret contemporary high-tech codebreakers. Computers and mathematical theories are today's most important weapons in the war between codemakers and codebreakers. Like computers themselves, and CMC, the mathematical complexities of encryption have begun to diffuse from the specialists to the citizens.

A tool known as public-key encryption is causing quite a stir these days, not just because it enables citizens to encode messages that their recipients can read but are not readable by even the most computationally powerful codebreakers, but also because citizen encryption makes possible two extremely powerful antipanoptic weapons known as digital cash and digital signature. With digital cash, it is possible to build an electronic economy where the seller can verify that the buyer's credit is good, and transfer the correct amount of money, without the seller knowing who the buyer is. With digital signature, it is possible in the identity-fluid online world to establish certainty about the sender of a message. This has important implications for intellectual property and online publishing, as well as personal security.

Key is a cryptographers' term for the codebook that unlocks a particular code. Until recently, code keys, whether made of metal or mathematical algorithms, were top secret. If someone steals your key, your messages are compromised. Public-key encryption makes use of recent mathematical discoveries that enable a person to keep one key private and distribute to everyone and anyone a public key. If anyone wants to use that person's public key, only the owner of the private key can read the message; both public and private keys are necessary, and the private key cannot be discovered by mathematical operations on the public key. Because encryption is based on precise mathematical principles, it is possible to demonstrate that a particular encryption scheme is inherently strong enough to survive brute-force mathematical assault by powerful supercomputers.

Public-key encryption as it exists today is unbreakable by all but the most powerful computers, such as those owned by the National Security Agency. Policy debate and legal challenges have revolved around citizens' rights to use mathematically unbreakable encryption. The National Security Agency sees this as a security nightmare, when it can no longer do its job of picking strategic signals out of the ether and inspecting them for content that threatens the security of the United States. Certain discoveries in the mathematical foundations of cryptography are automatically classified as soon as a mathematician happens upon them. John Gilmore, one of the founders of the EFF, recently filed suit against the National Security Agency for its classification and suppression in the United States of fundamental cryptography texts that are undoubtedly known to America's enemies. A few days after Gilmore filed suit and informed the press, the agency astonished everybody by declassifying the documents.

Think of digital cash as a kind of credit card that allows you to spend whatever credit you legitimately have without leaving a personal identifier linked to the transaction. The same techniques could be used to render other aspects of personal information—medical and legal records—far less vulnerable to abuse. Different applications of encryption technology already are being considered as safeguards against different kinds of panoptic danger. But ubiquitous encryption poses important problems: will citizen encryption, by making it impossible for any individual or group to crack encrypted messages, give the upper hand to criminals and terrorists, or will it force law enforcement and intelligence agencies to shift resources away from signals intelligence (monitoring communications) and into other, possibly even more invasive surveillance techniques? The impact of citizen encryption, for good or ill, looms as one of those unexpected applications of higher mathematics—like nuclear fission—that has the potential to change everything. There's still time to talk about it.

The third school of criticism builds on the foundation of commodification of the public sphere but veers off into a somewhat surrealistic dimension. Highly abstruse works of contemporary philosophy, much of it originating in France, have been proposing certain ideas about the psychological and social effects of previous communications technologies that raise disturbing resonances with the nature of CMC technologies.

The Hyper-realists

Hyper-realists see the use of communications technologies as a route to the total replacement of the natural world and the social order with a technologically mediated hyper-reality, a "society of the spectacle" in which we are not even aware that we work all day to earn money to pay for entertainment media that tell us what to desire and which brand to consume and which politician to believe. We don't see our environment as an artificial construction that uses media to extract our money and power. We see it as "reality"—the way things are. To hyper-realists, CMC, like other communications technologies of the past, is doomed to become another powerful conduit for disinfotainment. While a few people will get better information via high-bandwidth supernetworks, the majority of the population, if history is any guide, are likely to become more precisely befuddled, more exactly manipulated. Hyper-reality is what you get when a Panopticon evolves to the point where it can convince everyone that it doesn't exist; people continue to believe they are free, although their power has disappeared.

Televisions, telephones, radios, and computer networks are potent political tools because their function is not to manufacture or transport physical goods but to influence human beliefs and perceptions. As electronic entertainment has become increasingly "realistic," it has been used as an increasingly powerful propaganda device. The most radical of the hyper-realist political critics charge that the wonders of communications technology skillfully camouflage the disappearance and subtle replacement of true democracy—and everything else that used to be authentic, from nature to human relationships—with a simulated, commercial version. The illusion of democracy offered by CMC utopians, according to these reality critiques, is just another distraction from the real power play behind the scenes of the new technologies—the replacement of democracy with a global mercantile state that exerts control through the media-assisted manipulation of desire rather than the more orthodox means of surveillance and control. Why torture people when you can get them to pay for access to electronic mind control?

During the events of May 1968, when students provoked a revolt in the streets of Paris against the Gaullist regime, a radical manifesto surfaced, written by Guy Debord. *The Society of the Spectacle* made a startling tangential leap from what McLuhan was saying at around the same time. Cinema, television, newspapers, Debord proclaimed, were all part of worldwide hegemony of power in which the rich and powerful had learned to rule with minimal force by turning everything into a media event. The staged conventions of the political parties to anoint politicians who had already been selected behind closed doors were a prominent example, but they were only part of a web of headlines, advertisements, and managed events.

The replacement of old neighborhoods with modern malls, and cafés with fast-food franchises, was part of this "society of the spectacle," precisely because they help destroy the "great good places" where the public sphere lives. More than twenty years later, Debord looked back and emphasized this aspect of his earlier forecasts:

For the agora, the general community, has gone, along with communities restricted to intermediary bodies or to independent institutions, to salons or cafés, or to workers in a single company. There is no place left where people can discuss the realities which concern them, because they can never lastingly free themselves from the crushing presence of media discourse and of the various forces organized to relay it.... What is false creates taste, and reinforces itself by knowingly eliminating any possible reference to the authentic. And what is genuine is reconstructed as quickly as possible, to resemble the false.

Another French social critic, Jean Baudrillard, has been writing since the 1960s about the increasingly synthetic nature of technological civilization and a culture that has been irrevocably tainted by the corruption of our symbolic systems. This analysis goes deeper than the effects of media on our minds; Baudrillard claims to track the degeneration of meaning itself. In Baudrillard's historical analysis, human civilization has changed itself in three major stages, marked by the changes in meaning we invest in our symbol systems. More specifically, Baudrillard focused on the changing relationship between *signs* (such as alphabetical characters, graphic images) and *that which they signify*. The word dog is a sign, and English-speakers recognize that it refers to, signifies, a living creature in the material world that barks and has fleas. According to Baudrillard, during the first step of civilization, when speech and then writing were created, signs were invented *to point to reality*. During the second step of civilization, which took place over the past century, advertising, propaganda, and commodification set in, and the sign begins to *hide reality*. The third step includes our step into the hyper-real, for now we are in an age when signs begin to *hide the absence of reality*. Signs now help us pretend that they mean something.

Technology and industry, in Baudrillard's view, succeeded over the past century in satisfying basic human needs, and thus the profit-making apparatus that controlled technology-driven industry needed to fulfill desires instead of needs. The new media of radio and television made it possible to keep the desire level of entire populations high enough to keep a consumer society going. The way this occurs has to do with sign systems such as tobacco commercials that link the brand name of a cigarette to a beautiful photograph of a sylvan scene. The brand name of a cigarette is woven into a fabric of manufactured signifiers that can be changed at any time. The realm of the hyper-real. Virtual communities will fit very neatly into this cosmology, if it turns out that they offer the semblance of community but lack some fundamental requirement for true community.

Baudrillard's vision reminded me of another dystopian prophecy from the beginning of the twentieth century, E. M. Forster's chilling tale "The Machine Stops." The story is about a future world of billions of people, each of whom lives in a comfortable multimedia chamber that delivers necessities automatically, dispenses of wastes, and links everyone in the world into marvelously stimulating web of conversations. The only problem is that people long ago forgot that they were living in a machine. The title of the story describes the dramatic event that gives the

plot momentum. Forster and Baudrillard took the shadow side of telecommunications and considered it in light of the human capacity for illusion.
They are both good cautionary mythmakers, marking the borders of the
pitfalls of global, high-bandwidth networks and multimedia virtual
communities.

Virtual communitarians, because of the nature of our medium, must
pay for our access to each other by forever questioning the reality of our
online culture. The land of the hyper-real begins when people forget that
a telephone only conveys the illusion of being within speaking distance
of another person and a computer conference only conveys the illusion
of a town hall meeting. It's when we forget about the illusion that the
trouble begins. When the technology itself grows powerful enough to
make the illusions increasingly realistic, as the Net promises to do within
the next ten to twenty years, the necessity for continuing to question
reality grows even more acute.

What should those of us who believe in the democratizing potential of
virtual communities do about the technological critics? I believe we
should invite them to the table and help them see the flaws in our dreams,
the bugs in our designs. I believe we should study what the historians and
social scientists have to say about the illusions and power shifts that
accompanied the diffusion of previous technologies. CMC and technology in general has real limits; it's best to continue to listen to those who
understand the limits, even as we continue to explore the technologies'
positive capabilities. Failing to fall under the spell of the "rhetoric of the
technological sublime," actively questioning and examining social assumptions about the effects of new technologies, reminding ourselves that
electronic communication has powerful illusory capabilities, are all good
steps to take to prevent disasters.

If electronic democracy is to succeed, however, in the face of all the
obstacles, activists must do more than avoid mistakes. Those who would
use computer networks as political tools must go forward and actively
apply their theories to more and different kinds of communities. If there
is a last good hope, a bulwark against the hyper-reality of Baudrillard or
Forster, it will come from a new way of looking at technology. Instead of
falling under the spell of a sales pitch, or rejecting new technologies as
instruments of illusion, we need to look closely at new technologies and
ask how they can help build stronger, more humane communities—and

ask how they might be obstacles to that goal. The late 1990s may eventually be seen in retrospect as a narrow window of historical opportunity, when people either acted or failed to act effectively to regain control over communications technologies. Armed with knowledge, guided by a clear, human-centered vision, governed by a commitment to civil discourse, we the citizens hold the key levers at a pivotal time. What happens next is largely up to us.

11

Rethinking Virtual Communities

The world shifted into Internet overdrive soon after the 1993 publication of *The Virtual Community*. In the 1980s, when I began writing about online society, the many-to-many capabilities of the Internet were known to a relatively small subculture of early adopters, technophiles, and researchers. A rich ecology of different affinity groups, including scientists, scholars, and (mostly) programmers, thrived in an online culture that almost else nobody knew about. The total online population numbered in the tens of thousands. Less than a decade later, the Internet has made it possible for hundreds of millions of people to transform civilization's most powerful institutions—commerce, politics, science, scholarship, entertainment, education, health care. Our world has changed profoundly and swiftly in large part because of the phenomenon this book described—the sudden emergence of the Internet as a new communication medium.

The publication of this new edition by The MIT Press affords me the rare opportunity to revisit my views on online social communication. The world has changed, virtual communities have changed, my opinions have changed, and I have changed. More than ever before, we need to ask the right questions today about what kind of people, what kind of societies might emerge from social cyberspaces tomorrow. I hope this additional chapter will help provoke those questions.

Social communication in cyberspace is but a part of the global constellation of changes enabled by the Internet, but it's a part where humans have a chance of influencing our destiny. Before we can take actions that influence our future in more positive directions, however, we need to know how to act, and understand why. I originally wrote this book to introduce social cyberspace to the world. Now I feel obliged to help people think about what we're going to do about it.

This addendum is partially autobiographical because I moved beyond the boundaries of participant-observation and took on the roles of hands-on instigator, advocate, spokesman, straw man, and media persona. *The Virtual Community* led me into face-to-face meetings with the members of virtual communities in Sydney and Stockholm, London and Kyoto, Helsinki and Amsterdam. Scholars around the world published detailed studies of why I was wrong. I welcome this opportunity to add something of what I've learned in recent years to what I wrote about virtual communities long ago.

The Well changed in the years after I wrote about it. A new owner provoked an abortive revolution and the creation of a virtual community owned by its users. The growth of the Well's population from hundreds to thousands, the effect of this book and a cover article in *Wired*, the Well's role in celebrity hacker Kevin Mitnick's bust—all these events changed our little one-horse virtual community into a notorious cybertropolis.

In 1994 I helped create *HotWired*, the first commercial webzine/community and flagship of the brand-new digital culture. I quit *HotWired* and created my own Internet startup, *Electric Minds*. I've created a dozen virtual communities for pleasure, profit, and civic duty since this book was first published.

Since the publication of the first edition of *The Virtual Community*, critics have publicly challenged the book's assumptions, positions, arguments, and proposals. When you are the first person to write about a subject, new works emerge that are based in part on challenging your own. That's how scholarship is supposed to work, although I didn't have any notion that what I was doing was supposed to resemble scholarship. I just knew that there was something very wrong about the public image of online social life that existed in 1992. I was witnessing heartbreak and love and life-death struggles online. My family and I experienced numerous occasions when people cooperated in the physical world to help one another. The common wisdom of that time, however, was that only socially crippled adolescents would use the Internet to communicate with other people. Perhaps I put a rosier tint on my portrait of online socializing in reaction to the stereotype. Perhaps prospects for life online were brighter then, seven years before the dotcom era. And perhaps I've grown more critical of ideas I once proposed, out of more prolonged exposure to their shortcomings.

In which ways was I right in 1993, and in which ways was I wrong? More important, what are the main questions raised by these critical challenges?

Is the use of the phrase *virtual community* a perversion of the notion of community? What do we mean by community, anyway? What should we know about the history of technological transformations of community? Is the virtualization of human relationships unhealthy? Are virtual communities simulacra for authentic community, in an age where everything is commodified? Is online social behavior addictive? Most important, are hopes for a revitalization of the democratic public sphere dangerously naive? Will Internet-based publishing and communicating decentralize the distribution of political power and influence, or will many-to-many media be dominated by a few?

In the remainder of this chapter I cover in more detail the material I have sketched thus far. Some of this large territory will have to be covered more quickly than it deserves, and entire continents of social cyberspace, from instant-message-land and the many realms of chat to avatar worlds and graphical MOOs, have been skipped entirely, simply because this is a long updated chapter, not an entire new book. I have expanded the original bibliography to serve as a guide to the extensive scientific literature that has emerged since the publication of the first edition of *The Virtual Community*. For those readers who are engaged in studying social cyberspaces, the references included here will lead you far beyond the scope of this book.

The WELL Grows Up

Ironically, the deaths of Tom Mandel and Kathleen Creighton, two outspoken WELLites who would contest my use of "community" to describe the WELL, precipitated communion rituals among people for whom online and offline communities had fused. "Something about this online thing is realer than we had bargained for" was the unspoken message in our eyes when we gathered to say goodbye.

The "Homesteading..." subtitle of the first edition is obsolete and anachronistic today. Tom Mandel's death in 1995, a decade after the founding of the WELL, marked the end of much of the pioneer culture I described in 1992–93. Like all social groups that persist over time, relationships among the original WELL members shifted, warped, and broke; at the same time, new members continued to enter the group. The founding myths and norms also shifted, warped, and sometimes disappeared in this process.

Tom Mandel was a controversial character on the WELL and in real life. He was brilliant, funny, charming, ruthless, inventive, playful, cruel. He harbored a scary temper and a warm, gentle smile. He and I became friends. We saw each other face to face only a few times a year, but it seemed like we lived together online. We were among the first dozen people you could count on to be logged into the WELL most of the day, every day.

When *New York Times* reporter Katie Hafner looked for a narrative line to try to describe a decade of the WELL for a *Wired* cover story, she focused on "the Mandel incident," a brilliantly orchestrated online/offline brouhaha that Tom instigated when his fiancée, another WELLite, broke off their engagement (Hafner, 1997). The online wreckage was spectacular. More remarkably, Tom made his way back into the community, and remained a central figure in the community's life until the end of his own.

Tom announced his doom with characteristic flamboyance, by starting a discussion topic in the WELL's busiest conference, its virtual town square. The title of the topic was "My Turn." In his first post, he announced that he had been diagnosed with lung cancer. For too few weeks and months after that, the rest of us shared with Tom the terrifying periods of waiting for the results of medical tests. And the test results grew worse and worse. The disease progressed quickly. Friendships were mended, including mine. Feuds were resolved. Some were not resolved. Tom and his fiancée married. Toward the end, a WELLite who was a nurse in real life attended his deathbed.

Tom made his last entries in his online death-diary from a laptop plugged into his bedside telephone until the pain and weakness made typing impossible. He died with Beethoven's "Ode to Joy" playing in his hospital room, and with hundreds of people around the world sitting in front of computer screens with tears in their eyes.

I was asked to speak for Tom at his funeral. It's hard to sympathize with the charge that all online relationships are unreal when you've stood in front of a person's friends and family at their funeral, as I've done twice for WELL deaths (the first was Blair's funeral, described earlier).

Tom's wasn't the first online deathwatch; his title for the discussion was an ironic reference to a prior online death. Another WELLite, in my opinion a sometimes verbally caustic woman, also announced her fatal diagnosis online. Unlike Tom, "KJ" didn't have an extensive support network in real life. A dozen or more of us who had never met her organized shifts to sit with her and read to her when her eyesight failed. Without the WELL, how much lonelier would KJ's final weeks have been?

One of the ironies of KJ's death was that one of the WELLites who got to know her online was Cliff Stoll, author of the best-selling book *The Cuckoo's Egg* (Stoll, 1989). KJ posted that she thought it was a good book, and wondered in her blunt fashion who really wrote it. Cliff replied with good humor that he actually wrote the book himself. Stoll cited that same online exchange in his next book, *Silicon Snake Oil*, in which he more or less dismissed virtual community as a cruelly deceptive imitation of real community (Stoll, 1996). KJ started dying after *Silicon Snake Oil* was on its way to press. And Cliff Stoll was one of the people who spent time with KJ at her deathbed.

Not long after Tom's death, Kathleen Creighton died suddenly. Known to WELLites by her username "Casey," Kathleen transcribed the original interviews I taped for this book, and never hesitated to give me the benefit of her own opinions, always more skeptical than my own, along with the transcript. She provoked me to prove or abandon my assumptions about the meaning of cyberlife.

Casey had some health problems, and she didn't live in a healthy apartment. A number of her friends raised some money, provided a truck and labor, and helped her find a place in the country and move there. She died a few months later. When she died, an interesting thing happened. Casey wasn't aggressively nasty, but she didn't brook foolishness, and she eloquently ridiculed highfalutin talk or naive grandiosity. She claimed that the "community talk" was crap, and that she didn't "have a strong need for affiliation." But she cheerfully sold WELL posters of her own design and manufacture in order to help pay for an operation.

The day the news of Casey's death was announced, people started testifying online. Dozens of people revealed that their first welcoming email came from Casey, and that she had provided free, unpublicized technical support as they learned their way around the WELL. At her funeral, her family was surprised to find Casey's family and face-to-face friends outnumbered by a factor of ten by all these people she had known "through the Internet."

And there was Gabe Catalfo. The night, eight years ago, when Phil Catalfo started a topic in the parenting conference about Gabe's leukemia, and the next morning, when an online support group materialized, was certainly a conversion experience for many of us. Over the years, Phil and others continued that conversation, as other newly diagnosed leukemia patients found the discussion. Gabe went into remission. But then he had a setback. And the setback got worse. Finally, he had a bone marrow transplant. When the disease recurred, it was clear that the next step was death.

Gabe became a luminous spiritual teacher. The theologian Matthew Fox, local and Tibetan Buddhist adepts, his family and friends, and the extended online community watched and listened as he accepted the role of teacher. It can't be described by me. Perhaps by Phil. Tens of thousands of dollars had been contributed to the Catalfo family fund, and three pews were filled by WELLites. The 600-seat church was filled to capacity. Back then, the idea of an online support group seemed both natural and completely novel. Now, it's become an entire emerging industry.

Although Gabe's story was the first such tragedy I had encountered, unfortunately, it was not unique. Although socializing in cyberspace is a shallow experience for many, others find there a place to share their most intimate feelings and seek support from invisible strangers. In 1994, a *New York Times* story by Jon Katz quoted this posting from a Compuserve online community (Katz, 1994):

My daughter (Jennifer) has cancer. As some of you know, she is 8. In all the world I never conceived of all the sorrow I would feel at learning this, all the horror at watching her suffer so stoically through test after test. There is not a lot of hope, just a lot of medicine. We are preparing ourselves for the worst, which her doctor has hinted is what we should expect. I've decided to journal you everyday, those of you who can bear to read it. Feel free to answer, to offer sympathy, encouragement or whatever else you're feeling. Please feel free to check me if I am too sorry for myself or for her.... I do not know how to tell her grandparents, or even our friends, for she is much loved, inside and out of the house. We can start here. She asked me this morning, "Dad, does it get better? It does, doesn't it?" My mouth moved up and down, but nothing came out of it. I could sure use some words.

Is Jennifer's father's experience, the support he asks for and receives, the lives forever changed by all who participated, somehow less authentic because human hearts connected through the use of words and Internets? Did it matter that many of the hearts touched by Gabe Catalfo never met him?

Yes, it is important to question whether human lives are growing more mechanical and component-like. It is *all*-important to question the mechanization of human behavior. It is quite another thing to assume that true human emotions can't be transmitted through media, or that they don't count as much as face to face emotion. For some who are rarely seen, a mediated life is a better life than the one they would have otherwise.

I remember a high school student who sent me email about a school project. I get email from students often, but this message was different. He was asking various people about ethical and moral decisions regarding technology. If we could detect spina bifida and cerebral palsy early in pregnancy, would it be permissible to abort these fetuses? I wrote him that I thought it was a complex issue and that frankly I wasn't sure I knew the best answer.

He wrote back later, saying he had received responses from people in 50 countries. He had patiently sent out email to hundreds of people. He disclosed to those of us who had responded that he had been born with spina bifida and cerebral palsy and was glad he was born. I emailed and asked if we could talk and he replied that wasn't practical, since his mother was about the only person who could understand his speech. So I called his mother, who moved us both to tears. She said that she had a wonderfully bright and funny and warm son for whom the entire world constituted an obstacle. His speech is unintelligible. He pecks out messages on an oversized keyboard with a stick. He has little social life outside the Internet, but has a wide circle of friends in the online chess world and elsewhere. For this young man, there is no other way than cyberspace to socialize.

This young man is an extreme case. And there are many other extreme cases. We usually aren't aware of people like this young man because they stay indoors. They are hidden from public awareness, but they exist.

They are disabled, disfigured, frail, frightened, or shy. Before social cyberspaces, they were alone. Now they are not.

I don't tell this story in order to characterize online socializing as a panacea. I tell it to caution those who judge the experience of others to be inauthentic because they communicate with keyboards and screens. Is it good for our society to encourage more and more of the population to communicate by way of computer screens? I am uncertain of the answer. As we shall see, elevators and rubber tires are as implicated as computer screens in the trend toward alienation and mechanization of human life. I am more certain about this: It is dangerous to mindlessly invalidate the experiences of a person for whom Internet communication is not a luxury but a lifeline.

The times we helped each other, reached through the screens to touch each others' lives, were the times when something deserving of the word "community" manifested among people who spent most of our time sending words to each other across wires. But the years proved that, like communities in the real world, the WELL culture harbored its shadow side.

All online interactions are influenced by the lack of corporeality. In some cases, this works to the benefit of the communication; in other instances, it damages the communication. The absence of our bodies and the conveyance of nuance that accompanies body language and tone of voice, coupled with the ease of access to the attention of many people, also makes social cyberspaces susceptible to certain human foibles. Energy creatures, for example.

The energy creature is an online stereotype of a certain kind of pathological behavior that often infects listservs, newsgroups, BBSs, chatrooms—an articulate person with time to spare, access to the Net, and a need for negative attention. One person with this particular need and talent can stir up the emotions of hundreds or thousands of other online participants. Every response, from friendly and cajoling to flaming, encourages the energy creature to continue. Energy creatures received their name from a *Star Trek* episode where an alien seemed to grow stronger as the crew of the Enterprise shot it with their energy-blasters. As long as there is one remaining person who doesn't know that yelling at the EC will just feed him or her energy, one person can steal the attention of thousands. As such, an EC is a property of a group. For any sufficiently large number of human beings, there exists a potential EC with the power to waste the attention of many people.

There is also the invisibility of positive attention. While people often jump to disagree, dispute, disparage, or mock something they dislike, people don't spend as much time telling each other online how much they appreciate one another's contributions. Online peanut galleries are incubators for kibitzing—online book discussions can include heated arguments among people who haven't read the book yet. Character assassins and passive aggressive organizers of other people's feuds, gossips and snitches, bullies, charlatans, con-artists all make their way online, along with the authentically goodwilled. In the years since I first wrote about the phenomenon, I've seen far more of the dark side than I had witnessed before I wrote *The Virtual Community*.

The WELL was younger in 1992, and so was I. Many things happened to change the phenomenon that took root in 1985 into something very different by 1995: abortive revolutions and splinter colonies, feuds that continue to this day, new subcommunities full of people who neither knew nor cared about what the first WELLites did in 1985, mass media attention, the Internet population explosion.

The WELL's charmed history of absentee owners documented in the first edition of this book came to an end shortly after it was published. In 1994, an entrepreneur by the name of Bruce Katz bought the WELL from its owner, the Point Foundation. At this point, I enter the story as a character. At that time, I was the editor of the unprofitable magazine *Whole Earth Review*, which was on the brink of going under entirely. We were in the middle of creating *The Millennium Whole Earth Catalog*, which we hoped would solve our financial problems. The magazine and catalog publications were both owned by Stewart Brand's Point Foundation.

I approved the sale as a desperation measure to save the paper publications, because Bruce Katz had good intentions and deep pockets, and because the Point Foundation didn't have the resources or intention of growing the WELL before it suffered the fate of the quarterly and catalog. One of the conditions of the sale was that I would sit on the board of the WELL, a privately owned corporation controlled by Bruce Katz. This gave Katz a grace period of good will with the WELL community.

But Katz lacks good listening skills and didn't seem to understand that he needed to communicate with the WELL community himself, in our medium, in a way that showed some basic understanding of our norms. The tempest that followed was all a matter of respect, as tempests in social cyberspaces often are.

Around a hundred volunteer hosts like myself and Tom Mandel had spent years of our lives adding value to the enterprise that Bruce had bought, and presumably meant to profit from. It is an unusual business where your customers also create the value you sell them. We would have been happy to continue doing it, because we were giving it away to each other, and had no problem if the people who owned the hardware and paid for the telecommunications costs of running the server and hired the staff made some profit. But we needed the new owner to pay his respects. He failed to master the online Aikido that could have made the thousands of WELLites contented volunteers, and when he fired the general manager, himself a longtime WELLite, cabals began to form. I had not been consulted about the firing, which made it unproductive to remain on a powerless Board of Directors, so I resigned.

Because the WELL's software made it possible for members to form their own private conferences in parallel with the public discussions open to all members, cabals began to brew. One cabal in particular enlisted the temporary cooperation of a large group of hosts and others, including many people who didn't normally get along. The private conference for the cabal was expanding quickly as the momentum of revolution began to become a force of its own. First, we were shocked out of our own naivete. The WELL was owned by someone. That was enough of a shock. That the owner didn't know how to communicate with us but wanted to grow it to rival AOL threw the old-timers into a panic. The WELL might sink. We needed a lifeboat.

But not everybody was included in the private conference, and that turned the revolution into an online equivalent of a left-wing firing squad (first, you all get in a circle). The private communications and the exclusion of some others created the conditions for the kinds of malicious behavior that can erupt in such circumstances—snitches, flamewars, blood feuds that taint certain cyberspaces for years (sometimes continuing from one virtual community to another).

The conspirators decided to name the lifeboat "The River." I served as one of the "Octopod," a group of eight chosen by online consensus to meet face to face as well as online and draw up a social contract for the debate and approval of the group. We pooled our funds and quickly discovered we had enough money to buy a computer and connect it to the Internet, and enough expertise to install and maintain conferencing software. The big question was how we would run the thing, and of course, who would run it. The shock of the sale of the WELL convinced us that it was time for virtual community owned and governed by its members. We set up a California Cooperative Corporation, a legal entity that enabled each member to own one nontransferable share and one vote in the election of the directors. The idea is elegant, and it works in practice. However, the River was the first time but not the last that I observed how computer-mediated communication can make democratic decision-making a more onerous process than it has to be.

Democratic decision-making means a great deal of talking and arguing, and town hall meetings in colonial New England probably were susceptible to the same things that plague online decision-making—the small number of cranks and obsessives who can squander the group's time and attention, the many different conversations needed for people of different interests to agree on a compromise, factionalism and interpersonal conflict entangled with policy issues. When you try to do that process online, the naturally abrasive discourse of the public sphere is complicated by the lack of nuance that increases the probability of misunderstanding online. The intense controversy surrounding the River's private planning conference, coupled with all these factors, turned the online constitutional convention and first political campaign into an unpleasant process, punctuated by ugly eruptions. Many people left the River early because they wanted to have good conversations about things, not conversations about how they were going to have conversations. The critics of the notion of virtual community are right to point out that this kind of community is extremely easy to leave.

But the ownership and governance model works, the River survives (http://www.river.org), and the founders are still happy to share their organizational documents with others who are looking for an online governance model. Legislative processes, even those that produce workable results, can be unpleasant to behold. In the case of the River, the new owner neither grew the WELL into a rival of AOL, nor was he responsible for sinking it. Indeed, he spent millions of dollars upgrading the equipment needed to serve a population pushing ten thousand at its peak. The River has managed to survive and turn into a friendly little place for a couple hundred people, but without the shipwreck, the lifeboat wasn't necessary. The WELL sailed on in its own directions.

In 1998, shortly before it went public, the online culture and politics zine Salon.com bought the WELL. Katz converted his investment into shares in a publicly traded Internet company, and the WELLites didn't object too harshly. The whole Katz brouhaha had proved the counter-productivity of barking too loudly at a well-meaning owner, even if he isn't adept at the native lingo. And, ironically, the Community Director for Salon.com in 1999 was Cliff Figallo, former General Manager of the WELL.

For me and for much of the rest of the industrialized world, the smaller events on the WELL were overshadowed by another Internet event—the advent of the Web. From the first time I saw images and links on a pre-Mosaic browser in 1993, I saw the Web as not just a many-to-many multimedia broadcasting medium, but as a social medium. By the time I followed that vision to its conclusion, I had started an Internet company to marry content and community, raised and spent $2 million to launch it, created a cultural success, and watched the entire enterprise fail during the short, strangely unique venture capital drought of early 1997.

In 1996, I needed to promote the strange new idea that people could use the web to communicate as well as surf (e-commerce wasn't even a cloud on the horizon). So I started calling it "the social web."

The Social Web

The first time I saw the Web, I wanted to create communities there. Although I seek to apply standards of objective truth-seeking to my investigations of online social phenomena, I have come to understand that much of my participation in this new medium has been driven by my own personal longings for that participation. Lusting after tools that don't quite exist yet but that are clearly possible has motivated much of the effort that created the Web as we know it today—long before dreams of IPOs made simple avarice the driving force for Internet innovation.

In 1993, before Mosaic made the World Wide Web visible to millions of people with shocking suddenness, a fellow named Dale Daugherty who worked for an outfit called Global Network Navigator (GNN) showed me how you could display words and images and links to other pages. He had a pre-Mosaic browser and intended to publish a kind of dynamic magazine online, a guide or portal to the rest of the Web. His employer published a hugely successful book in the first years of the Internet's emergence into the public eye, called *The Whole Internet User's Guide* (Krol, 1994). At that time, I was editor of *Whole Earth Review* and Daugherty thought an alliance might be possible. GNN could have beaten Yahoo to market by two years, except there were no venture capitalists willing to invest in Internet ventures in 1993. I wrote about GNN for an early edition of *Wired*—the era of the webzine had arrived! But GNN was acquired by AOL, the graveyard of more than one promising venture, and disappeared from view around the time the Netscape browser detonated the Web's explosive growth.

What if you could have many-to-many conversations, WELL-style, and also include photographs, illustrations, and links? I conceived a passion for a mode of communication that had become technically possible but didn't exist yet—a community of publishers, where the audience is the entertainment, and the flat world of ASCII text in social cyberspace blossoms into a world of color and movement and sound. A new medium was emerging, as different from everything that preceded it, and as portentous, as the emergence of television.

"Internet time"—the furious pace of change in digital culture—compresses the timelines of events. I first encountered the Web in the same year this book was first published. The idea that you could do a magazine on the Web was fringey, the notion that you might make money on it completely ridiculous. People didn't make money off the Internet, even with pictures and links. But if anyone could invent a way to make money on the Web, *Wired* magazine was a promising candidate. In 1993, *Wired* online presence consisted of a folder on AOL. A graduate student at Stanford, Jonathan Steuer, was hired as "Online Tsar," and convinced Wired Ventures that they needed their own Internet presence. In the spring of 1994, Steuer and I, along with Kevin Kelly, met with *Wired* publishers and agreed to launch a commercial webzine. I agreed to be the executive editor.

If *Wired* publisher Louis Rossetto had taken the time for a cup of coffee or a walk around the block with me, it would have been clear to both of us that we would never work together harmoniously. He looked at our new e-zine and saw it as an extension of *Wired* magazine's brand into cyberspace, which it certainly was, and an extension of *Wired* magazine's role as fashion arbiter of the emerging digital culture, which many of us thought to be the wrong role online among technical sophisticates. I looked at the same enterprise and saw a community of the best of the digital culture online, the best of whose worldwide multimedia jam sessions would be featured in the e-zine. But Rossetto didn't want to provide resources for the community role. It was an electronic extension of letters to the editor, from where he sat. "I don't want to be the bozofilter for the Net," he barked, when I talked about user-generated content.

HotWired, designed and launched by the crew that Rossetto, Steuer, and I organized in the summer of 1994, did include a web-based conferencing community called "Threads," and it did have life to it. But it needed at least one person devoted to managing it. Having invented the online banner ad, *HotWired* was making money by publishing editorial content pages with advertisements on them.

I resigned from *HotWired* shortly after it launched. Within a month, close to half of the original staff left. But I couldn't forget my hankering for a worldwide multimedia jam.

What I had in mind had elements of a magazine (editorial discrimination, creative design, regular, high-quality, "content"), but was much more like a community (many to many, unfiltered, audience-created content). I spent most of 1995 having great fun updating my web page every day. I did all the writing, editing, design, illustrations, html. I talked friends in America, Europe, and Japan into writing for free. In late 1995, I became infected with the notion that I should expand what I was having such fun doing. When I sat down to figure out how to pay my writers and editors, hire a "real" designer, license a webconferencing system, it looked like it would cost tens of thousands per month, and take us three or four months to launch.

Lesson number one was that everything in an Internet startup that depends on cutting-edge technology takes longer and costs more than originally estimated, even when you take lesson number one into account. It took us eight months to launch and cost $2 million.

Deciding to pay people reasonably well (but by no means extravagantly) for editorial content, art and design, technical services, sales and marketing, finance and management, led me to need more money than I had. That's when I made what I now clearly see to be my most fundamental error. I got caught up in the intoxication of venture-capital financing, which was entering a state of mania in late 1995 that has continued since then, unabated except for a brief period in early 1997 when nobody wanted to invest in the notion of "the social web." I connected with a business partner I didn't know, but who knew how to go about securing financing and putting together a company—my second fundamental error. I failed to listen to my own nagging doubts and made a bad choice in partners.

I take responsibility for making the decisions that led to the business failure of Electric Minds. I made many bad decisions, although not many more than average for startups. The decision to go for venture capital made all the other decisions moot. My new partner introduced me to a fellow from Softbank Ventures, an early investor in Yahoo! that was investing billions in Internet ventures. I told the guy from Softbank that if we could figure out how to combine community and publishing, then the other companies in the Softbank investment portfolio could leverage that knowledge profitably. Electric Minds was supposed to be an experiment.

At that point, any business plan for an Internet business was a conjecture, and thinking about how virtual communities could be part of a profitable business was in the realm of science-fiction. We agreed that the first step was to build an exemplary product. We agreed that it would take at least three years to become profitable.

We were funded in March 1996 and launched in November. In December, *Time* magazine named us one of the ten best web sites of 1996 (*Time*, December 23, 1996). By July 1997 we were out of business. VCs want a return of ten times their initial investment, and they would prefer to get their money in three to five years. When Softbank started weeding out the investments that were less likely to achieve a ten times return on investment, they withdrew their verbal promises of bridge financing for Electric Minds. They even told us to keep operating, and thus accumulating debt, while seeking investment. When they backed out of their investment, they also backed out of their verbal promise to cover our debts. This left us with more debts than assets, so we settled with our creditors and dissolved the business. Entrepreneurs: Get it in writing!

The worst part of it, I realized when it was over, was that I had turned something that was fun into something that wasn't fun. When I had the time to think about where I had gone wrong, it became clear to me that if I had simply added conferencing software and continued doing my amateur editing and design, then grew a virtual community on my own,

I could have built something less fancy but more sustainable in cultural if not in financial terms. Venture capital, I concluded, might be a good way to ramp up a Yahoo or create a market for a kind of technology product that never existed before. But perhaps it isn't a healthy way to grow a social enterprise. Certainly, there is room for virtual community as part of a business strategy. Just as certainly, virtual communities would be meaningless if the only ones available were commercial enterprises.

Ethical issues occurred to me when I entered the business of growing virtual communities. Is building a virtual community for parents, for example, using money provided by a company that sells diapers, a way of turning community into a commodity? Is this a bad thing? Is it really right to call a collection of web pages or smutty chatrooms a "community?" How much commercial ownership are the members of a virtual community willing to accept, in exchange for the technical and social resources necessary for maintaining the community? Is it possible to be in the business of building communities for profit and still write about them?

A provocative twist to the Electric Minds story is that the community that grew up there survived the dissolution of the company that had fostered it. We laid off most of the staff in April, vainly sought bridge financing in May, started shutting down operations and getting ready to clear out of our offices in June. At the last minute, a company called Durand Communications offered to buy the Electric Minds name and logo, editorial database, and the right to make an offer to the community. Most of the tens of thousands of original registrants left the community when the company stopped paying editorial contributors and community facilitators, but hundreds of active participants stayed. When I told them that Durand would keep the community software running on their computer, after we moved out of our old office and unplugged the server, the enthusiasm among the several hundred hardcore "eMinders" was high. Then came my second experience, reminding me of the great River thrash, in the difficulties of trying to create a democracy online.

"Democracy online" refers to something distinctly different from "the impact of online culture on democracy," a larger subject covered later in this chapter. Democracy online refers to the ideal of governing a virtual community through online debates and votes. To those who seek to do this, I recommend that you start by composing a simple social charter *before* you go online. You need to specify the qualifications for voting membership, the mechanisms for campaigning and voting, the structure and powers of a governing body, and mechanisms for recalling or impeaching that ruling body. People can modify the template, which is far less contentious than creating one from scratch. Agree upon the compact and hold an election. Then let your elected leadership use their judgment instead of putting every issue to the vote. If you prepare the template for the social contract in advance, and ask your new members to agree to this means of governance, you will find it much smoother than proposing to an existing virtual community that it decide online how to adopt such a governance structure.

Asynchronous online communication spaces like Usenet or the WELL are not effective media for conducting meetings that result in documents that a diverse population of people agrees to. Collaborative document creation is well supported by the many-to-many medium, but consensus decision-making is not: online conversations tend to diverge and branch and digress, rather than converge. A computer conference is better for letting all opinions be heard than in creating something everyone can go along with.

An online chat conducted by Robert's *Rules of Order* might be an effective supplement to asynchronous discussion. Democracy is a cantankerous process. Many voices need to be heard, and many issues threaten to flare into conflict long before they promise to converge on agreement. People who are online to communicate about science fiction books or children with learning disabilities often want to discuss the subject matter, not engage in lengthy meta-discussion about how to have discussions about the subject matter. While the process-junkies grind on about fine points of jurisprudence, the people whose affinity is in the subject matter leak away and find other places to participate online. Activist and online pioneer Jon Lebkowsky has written online about the reasons "online democracy" is difficult to achieve: <http://www.socio.demon.co.uk/magazine/5/5jon.html>.

Virtual communities often go for years without feeling the need to have any kind of governance. Issues of governance only emerge from conflict. Norms that ought to be rules only become matters of serious discussion when they are transgressed. There are now several case histories or at least descriptive documents about the experiences of different virtual communities with online governance in the face of transgression. Julian Dibbell's book, *My Tiny Life* (Dibbell, 1999) about a "virtual rape" at LambdaMOO, a famous online community, is also about how the citizens of a community decided online about governance, and matters of crime and punishment. Anna du Val Smith's *Problems of Conflict Management in Virtual Communities* (Smith, 1998) chronicles how online jurisprudence and governance grew from attempts to deal with transgression in another famous community: MicroMUSE.

Smith concluded that "cyber communities, like any social system, must include diversity and find some way to integrate it if they are to thrive. Because open cyber communities are likely to be extremely diverse, managing the resultant inevitable conflict is an especially important task." Managing online conflict could be the subject of a book in its own right.

The social web, a notion journalists and investors found radical and futuristic in 1996, has emerged from both the grassroots and the big players in today's highly commercialized web enterprises. America Online continues to use the word "community" to sell their service ("I think AOL is one big community" is the primetime soundbite of the moment), despite their notorious disrespect for the unpaid community leaders whose allegiance to their breast cancer support group or investment club is what really draws them to AOL. GeoCities, a multi–billion dollar enterprise now owned by Yahoo, offers free web site hosting to millions of their "homesteaders," along with primitive, unsupervised, low-quality message boards, and bills itself as a virtual community. Huge Web "portal" sites that harvest the attention of tens of millions of people each day offer free mailing lists, forums, and chatrooms to anyone willing to eyeball their banner advertisements.

You used to need both money and expertise to set up a webconference, chatroom, or listserv. Now online communication tools are public goods, offered as marketing sizzle by web businesses that want us to pay with the coin of our attention. Billions of instant messages, posts to mailing lists, quips in chatrooms are exchanged every day, and new kinds of communities emerge daily. My infant daughter, whose words of alarm at my corporeal behavior while logged on to the WELL open this book, is now a teenager who routinely talks on the telephone, exchanges instant messages with her friends, and monitors a chatroom (all while working on her homework, she claims, apparently truthfully). A huge social experiment is taking place, as people and enterprises take up these tools, are changed by them, and change the way others live, work, and play.

One major difference between what I know now and what I knew when I wrote the first edition of this book is that I've learned that virtual communities won't automatically emerge or grow in a healthy manner simply by adding a forum or chatroom to a web page. The forces that draw people and our attention away from anything as abstract as written discussions in cyberspace are strong, and action must be taken to glue people together. Skilled facilitation, well-thought-out social contracts, social mechanisms, and multimedia material for initiating newcomers in the use of the medium—the "social infrastructure" for success in virtual-community building—has become valuable, now that tools are free.

If people know how to use many-to-many communication, they can amplify their ability to think and communicate, and if the people who use these tools don't understand how to use them, they can create a mess. Indeed, a business niche has emerged for virtual community design, consulting, building, and facilitation services. I'm in that business myself part of the time, and so is Cliff Figallo, former general manager of the WELL. Later in this chapter, when I examine social critiques of virtual community and the notion of community as commodity, Marxian analysis turns out to be one of the useful lenses we can use to try to see where we are going. Being a capitalist, starting a corporation, growing a small business, were also useful lenses for me at the dawn of the age of the commercialized Internet. (Does anyone remember that in the early 1990s it wasn't legal to use the Internet for commercial enterprise?)

Fifteen years ago, the idea that Cliff or I would engage in professional virtual community consulting would have been the cause for argument about "selling out" the noncommercial purity of online discourse. By now, however, the difference between well-maintained virtual communities and hellish juvenile flame-zones is growing clear to millions of people. Knowing how to use the tools of computer-mediated communication is now a specialized skill that is valuable enough for people to pay for it. In the future, if the new media are to be more useful than destructive, this know-how must become a literacy. The skill cannot remain the exclusive property of an elite, but the process of distributing the skill is necessarily a question of education.

In 1997, just as Electric Minds was circling the drain, a book began making the rounds of venture capitalists and entrepreneurs. John Hagel III and Arthur G. Armstrong, who both worked for the worldwide business consultancy, McKinsey & Co., wrote a book whose title signaled the beginning of the virtual community industry: *Net Gain: Expanding Markets through Virtual Communities* (Hagel and Armstrong, 1997). They connected the emergent properties of online communities with the new economics of increasing gains and showed how online enterprises could reap financial rewards by aggregating people in virtual communities organized around specific interests: sports communities, medical communities, travel communities, pet communities. The notion of e-commerce was only beginning to emerge in 1997. Few people had heard of Amazon, and not every Internet IPO was an instant success. But Hagel and Armstrong saw the social nature of marketplaces and predicted that communities of consumers would be able to use the many-to-many powers of the Internet to organize and begin demanding price discounts from vendors. Indeed, such communities are beginning to emerge. Social communication would bring people back to commercial web sites again and again, thus increasing revenues for advertising, and that social communication could furnish the context for economic transactions.

I agree with Hagel and Armstrong's insight that communities of consumers will use the Internet to their advantage, and that e-commerce communities can be profitable ventures. Whether or not the large profits Hagel and Armstrong forecast for such enterprises will be enjoyed by more than a handful of large media companies is yet to be determined. There are other ways for online communities to create commercial value, in marketing, customer support, and R&D. I have little doubt that some kinds of virtual communities will replace or reshape some kinds of present business practices.

I was involved in one of the early demonstrations of how freewheeling virtual community can serve the purposes of a commercial enterprise. In the spring of 1997, IBM wanted to let the new generations of web geeks know that IBM was still an innovator, and not just a historical name from the days of mainframes. The were confident that their chess-playing computer, "Deep Blue II," would defeat world chess grandmaster Gary Kasparov. So they contracted Electric Minds to create a webconference to accompany the match—an online virtual community of interest to draw together the chess aficionados, artificial intelligence researchers, programmers, and Netheads. We used WELL Engaged web-conferencing software. I hired Cliff Figallo to manage the project.

Figallo trained an international group of chessmasters in the art of online facilitation, and they helped a core of experienced online facilitators learn about the nuances of chess. Fifty thousand people registered to read the conversations, hundreds of people from more than twenty countries posted thousands of comments in scores of discussion topics. There was very little flaming. The level of discourse was high. And IBM made the point it wanted to make to the audience they wanted to reach.

IBM took a leap of faith, because it is difficult and counterproductive to try to control what people say in the context of a public webconference. If things went bad with IBM's web site during the match, as had happened during the 1994 Olympics, the publicity could backfire, as Electric Minds had created a forum where people from all over the world could jeer. Kasparov lost and IBM won. People who were passionate about programming and people who were passionate about chess had intelligent conversations on the play by play. But it could have turned out differently. Companies that aren't willing to take that kind of risk are better advised to avoid the use of virtual communities for brand-building.

As Figallo wrote in *Hosting Web Communities* (Figallo, 1998) and Amy Jo Kim wrote in *Community Building on the Web* (Kim, 2000), there are plenty of legitimate reasons for different kinds of commercial enterprises to use virtual communities.

Figallo wrote about smaller informal affinity groups, nonprofit organizations, and businesses. In regard to businesses, he wrote, among other things:

For a business intending to serve the needs of its customers, the Web can replace expensive 800-number help lines and paper manuals with interactive services and easily updated online information. This is a practice being adopted by more businesses as they discover how large a percentage of their customers have access to the Web. The investment in hosting such support communities can save money and please customers at the same time. A corporate site doesn't have to be based around support; it can host community activities relevant to its products and services as a public relation gesture and still be able to justify the expense. (Figallo, 1998, p. 363)

He's right. Webconferences and instant messages can augment or even replace telephone support for products. I can see the social critics chewing on this example. Is one of the founders of the WELL, who lived for twelve years on a self-sustaining commune and built irrigation systems in the Mayan highlands, actually saying community is now a business tool, a kind of sociable helpdesk for businesses to help their customers understand evermore complicated products? One criticism of this approach to virtual community as business practice is that this activity turns community into a commodity. Isn't there another way of looking at it? By building webs of ongoing conversation online, customer support communities can make relations between businesses and customers more humane and sociable.

Linux, the "open source" operating system that is challenging Microsoft's dominant Windows, is a collaborative enterprise that wouldn't exist without virtual communities. The source code for this valuable software product is free, and anybody who can improve it is free to do so, and to contribute their improvements to the entire community. Listservs, IRC Channels, the notorious Linux geek webconferencing community Slashdot <http://www.slashdot.org> enable independent operators to share code. Instead of owning the product the way Microsoft owns Windows, individual entrepreneurs and billion-dollar companies like Red Hat and VA Linux make their money by supporting and building tools for a product that belongs to everyone. Is this capitalism as we've known it? People are giving away valuable intellectual property, and making money at it. As business transforms the nature of virtual communities, it's worth paying attention to the way virtual communities are changing business.

Commercial communities are still evolving. There are branding communities, like IBM's experiment. There are communities of interest like Women.com, PlanetRx, or Petopia that make their money on e-commerce. There are purely social communities like TalkCity chatrooms that make their money on advertising. My gut feeling is that only a few large enterprises will profit purely by providing social cyberspaces. Only a few daring large companies will risk their brand by building online communities. But other enterprises that don't exist yet will find virtual communities to be rich webs of value for their own employees, customers, suppliers, value-added resellers. Future definitions of competition, customer, product, and service might well warp because of new ways for people to communicate with each other. Future best-selling books might contain chips that connect readers into virtual communities of interest, for example. The most significant impacts of virtual community on commercial enterprises are bound to be internal. Enterprises that have been undergoing profound internal transformations via intranets over the past five years will find that over the next five years, internal online knowledge communities will amplify the power of their most important assets—the intellectual capital and goodwill of their employees.

In addition to Figallo's and Kim's books, Jenny Preece's book *Online Communities: Supporting Sociability and Designing Usability* lays down the foundation for the emerging field of virtual community design (Preece, 2000). Virtual communities are a business, and might grow into an industry, whether anyone likes that or not. Virtual communities might influence changes in traditional business processes and become an integral part of creating and selling goods and services. But it doesn't look likely that "commercialization" is going to make noncommercial online culture disappear. It seems clear already that virtual communities will continue to emerge in a variety of media for a range of reasons, whether or not commercial virtual communities grow into a viable industry.

The business impact of virtual community is important, but it's certainly not the only or most important way socializing in cyberspace is changing us as individuals, communities, and societies. We know now that telephones and televisions changed the way people think and live. How will aspects of online culture change the world?

Rethinking Virtual Community

After more than a decade of discussing and debating the social impact of virtual communities, I have come to believe that this discussion only makes sense in a larger context. Questions about the social impact of digital media must be part of a broader debate that encompasses many communication tools and more than the past five years of history. Communication technologies, from alphabets to Internets, have been changing the nature of communities for nearly ten thousand years, although we didn't know anything about the way communication tools influence minds and communities until recently. Now that the social impact of Internet communication is sinking in, a key question is how to use what we know—and learn what we need to know—in order to influence events in our favor.

Technology doesn't have to dictate the way our social relations change, but we can only influence change if we understand how people use technologies. Although moderns are so thoroughly indoctrinated in the belief in "progress"—that science and technology will always continue to make tomorrow different and better than today—we also have the warning of Faust that certain kinds of knowledge and power come with a price for what we hold to be most uniquely human.

Plato warned in the allegorical tale of Thoth in *Phaedrus* that recording knowledge in books would destroy the oral tradition of knowledge and pedagogy (*Phaedrus* 275 a–b, p. 184). People would lose the skill of remembering, Plato's spokesman stated, and education would cease to be a living dialogue, where students and teachers discuss and argue the meaning of knowledge, but would become a solitary and lifeless decoding of facts from mute objects. He was probably right. Human civilization undoubtedly lost something as well as gained something when alphabetic writing, books, and libraries supplanted bards and peripatetic scholarship. Walter Ong in *Orality and Literacy: The Technologizing of the Word* (Ong, 1982), Harold Innis in *The Bias of Communication* (Innis, 1951), and more recently and more popularly Marshall McLuhan in *Understanding Media* (McLuhan, 1964) have amplified Plato's theme that our ways of knowing the world change when our modes of transferring knowledge change.

Elizabeth L. Eisenstein, historian of the impact of the printing press, noted that "getting the news" was a community event in pre-Gutenberg Europe. People in towns and villages would gather to hear the latest news from travelers, then linger in the town square and discuss it as a group (Eisenstein, 1983). When printed broadsides became economical, people retreated to an inn or their home to do their reading. Thus, the beginnings of the mass medium now known as the newspaper actually helped drain people's attention away from a certain kind of local community. At the same time printing was dissolving certain close social ties, it made possible larger, weaker ties, based on ideas, rather than kin, clan, or tribe. Not long after, and in large part because of the recent invention of printing, people all over Europe began to identify with other people who were not geographically adjacent. Luther's ideas about reformation of the Church spread at unprecedented speed. (This is a good place to note that care must be taken to avoid technological determinism—the printing press didn't "cause" the Reformation, but it was certainly a central enabling force for the spread of Luther's words.)

At the same time, the new medium contributed to and detracted from community—the way people used print for news distanced them in one way from other people in traditional local communities, and at the same time enabled them to bridge a distance that had previously separated people. People were willing to suffer martyrdom or wage war in alliance with strangers who shared religious values, but didn't live in the same territory or even speak the same language. That separation from traditional form of community and the invention of a new, more abstract—I'm tempted to call it "virtual"—kind of relationships among people was made possible by the printing press.

Important critical questions have been asked about the idea of virtual community and the influence of virtual communications on human relationships. We must all address these questions if we aspire to steer the course of the technology rather than passively experiencing the changes the technology triggers. If there is something disturbing about finding community through a computer screen (and who can deny that the image of disembodied geeks who move only our fingers while staring at a tube is disturbing?), we should also consider whether it is disturbing for hundreds of millions of people to drive for hours every day in our single-passenger automobiles to cities of inhuman scale, where we spend our days in front of screens inside cubicles within skyscrapers full of people who don't know each other. Yes, we should focus on the pitfalls of spending our days in front of screens, but we should not lose sight of those cubicles, skyscrapers, cities, and automobiles when we seek the sources of our alienation.

The rubber tire and the elevator both played their part in the construction of a technology-centric community. And they are both second-generation fruits of industrialized capitalism. Virtual community sits atop a hierarchy of abstractions—language, technology, computing, networking, many-to-many discussion. Virtual community is also built upon a succession of technologies and ways of life we chose to use and live in and be shaped by, because they gave many people freedom and power. Now, the biggest challenge to our freedom is our need to know how to wield the powers of new communication media. New tools exist. Who will use them, and how will they use them? Those who already have power and wealth to defend also have the knowledge of how to use media to influence and persuade others.

Technologies and literacies that help individuals and groups to dictate the conditions under which other people live are profoundly political instruments, although this seems to go against the grain of the common wisdom. Certain tools themselves are political by their nature. In order to frame critiques of the notion of virtual community, it helps to examine the ways in which the rapidly evolving communication media constitute a political environment—and look especially closely at the ways we choose not to examine that environment.

Langdon Winner stated it this way:

A crucial turning point comes when one is able to acknowledge that modern technics, much more than politics as conventionally understood, now legislates the conditions of human existence. New technologies are institutionalized structures within an existing constitution that gives shape to a new polity, the technopolis in which we do increasingly live. For the most part, this constitution still evolves with little public scrutiny or debate. Shielded by the conviction that technology is neutral and tool-like, a whole new order is built—piecemeal, step by step, with the parts and pieces linked together in novel ways, without the slightest public awareness or opportunity to dispute the character of the changes underway. It is somnambulism (rather than determinism) that characterizes technological politics—on the left, right, and center equally. (Winner, 1977)

Winner claims that technology, and the way it shapes our lives, is not an autonomous force. Humans have the power to influence the direction technologies take. I agree with Winner that our primary problem now is that we don't perceive that power. In that regard, we are indeed sleepwalkers. What do we need to know?

The first step is to read the critics and look at where they are pointing. A complete literature review requires more space than this chapter affords. However, the following quick review of the strongest critiques reveals a broad spectrum of criticism, from a variety of disciplines, including political polemics, social psychology experiments, and sociological arguments.

To me, the most penetrating technology critic in the largest sense today is Langdon Winner. In another article (Winner, 1996), Winner questions the notion that virtual communities will create a culture of participatory democracy. He convinced me that the notion of authentic community and civic participation through online discussion is worth close and skeptical examination. However, I would disagree that such media can never play such a role, on the same grounds that Chou En Lai refused to analyze the impact of the French Revolution: "It's too early to tell."

Another critic, Steven Jones (1995) bases his arguments on Effrat's notions of (1) community as solidarity institutions; (2) community as primary interaction; and (3) community as institutionally distinct groups. Jones suggests that the third of these, community as institutionally distinct groups, makes the most sense in the context of CMC. Jones argues that there is a need to conceptualize community as a complex of social relationships, which has not been sufficiently explored. He also argues that CMC is socially produced space that decenters place, and thus challenges the traditional framework as community being based on proximate geographic space. Jones states that "communities formed by CMC have been called 'virtual communities' and defined as incontrovertibly social spaces in which people still meet face-to-face, but under new definitions of both 'meet' and 'face'" (Jones, 1995).

Jones discusses the social science literature related to pseudocommunity and the decentering of place. Jones uses James Beniger's definition of pseudocommunity, a "reversal of a centuries old trend from organic community based on personal relationships, to impersonal associations integrated by mass means" (Beniger, 1987).

Peter Ludlow (1996) examines the social change brought about by the introduction of computer technology. He states that "with that change has come a sense of alienation and loss of community. Increasingly, though, it becomes possible to recreate that lost community in cyberspace, by forming communities of interest that are not bound by the accidents of geography. Ludlow asks whether they are really communities and raises the issue of whether you can call someone a "neighbor" if you can't see her face or hear her voice. He questions whether we might be abandoning our geographic communities in a sort of "urban flight" if we give our allegiances to virtual communities and also asks to what extent should other communities, and the legal system itself, acknowledge and respect virtual communities.

Clifford Stoll (1995) asserts that claims about the Internet as a community are false and that the Internet can only provide the illusion of community. Stoll says: "Computer networks isolate us from one another, rather than bringing us together."

Parks and Floyd (1996) indicate that other analysts have also questioned claims about the Internet as a community and have similarly stated that "only the illusion of community can be created by Cyberspace."

Calhoun (1991) argues that the modern condition is one of "indirect social relationships" in which connectivity with others is more imagined, or parasocial, than "real." The media's ability to broaden the range of our experiences creates the illusion of greater contact or membership in large-scale social organizations. Rather than creating "communities," however, were are merely developing "categorical identities" or "imagined communities" that are nothing more than the "feeling" of belonging to some group. He argues that a true "community" requires direct relationships among its members:

I want to argue that there is a great deal of difference between social groups formed out of direct relationships among their members, although often sharing an imaginatively constructed cultural identity, and social categories defined by common cultural or other external attributes of their members and not necessarily linked by any dense, multiplex, or systematic web of interpersonal relationships. (p. 107)

McClellan (1994,) claims that the character of virtual communities can be as provincial as small-town communities. He notes that the WELL has been criticized as too "New Agey" and "little more than a middle-class residents association in cyberspace" (p. 10). McClellan criticizes cyberspace communities as pseudocommunities that have only the appearance of true social bonding. He states:

Rather than providing a replacement for the crumbling public realm, virtual communities are actually contributing to its decline. They're another thing keeping people indoors and off the streets. Just as TV produces couch potatoes, so on-line culture creates mouse potatoes, people who hide from real life and spend their whole life goofing off in cyberspace. (p. 10)

In *The Future Does Not Compute: Transcending the Machines in Our Midst* (Talbott, 1995), Steve Talbott asks serious questions about how the Internet is affecting our culture and if, in fact, we are surrendering ourselves to it and constructing mechanized communities within its web, instead of a more humane world.

Spears and Lea (1994) claim that the anonymity inherent in CMC can be as oppressive in the hands of the powerful as it is liberating in the hands of the shy and introverted. Underscoring the fact that, in many CMC environments, existing social hierarchies supersede the aspatial characteristics of CMC, Spears and Lea explain that CMC should not be viewed as an alternative reality where "the individual can escape from the strictures of ordinary identity and interaction" (p. 449). Instead, they argue that "identity and interaction in CMC will often be grounded in the realities of identities and relations beyond CMC, which pervade the rest of our social lives."

Kiesler et al. (1984) identify four features that distinguish CMC from conventional forms of communication: 1) an absence of regulating feedback, 2) incomplete or limited expressions of emotion, 3) a lack of social status cues, and 4) social anonymity. In a subsequent paper, Kiesler (1986) elaborates on the impact anonymity can have on communication:

When communication lacks dynamic personal information, people focus their attention on the message rather than on each other. Communicators feel a greater sense of anonymity and detect less individuality in others than they do talking on the phone or face-to-face. They feel less empathy, less guilt, less concern over how they compare with others, and are less influenced by norms. (p. 48)

A guiding premise of CMC research since its inception is that CMC lacks nonverbal communication cues leaving the medium a hostile environment for communicators. Kiesler, Zubrow, and Moses (1985) found users of computer-mediated communication to "flame" users and exhibit other nonsupportive behavior.

Critics of both the armchair and experimental varieties have attacked the very use of the term *virtual community*, and have argued that the term debases real community, that online relationships degrade geographic community, that people are less humane to each other in cyberspace, that online discussion disempowers citizens who would otherwise be engaged in authentic civic involvement.

I suggest that we would most productively approach these critiques by maintaining the goal of raising our level of awareness about three levels of social impact of new media. Virtual communities affect the *minds* of individuals, the *interpersonal relationships* between people, and the *social institutions* that emerge from human relationships:

• Critiques at the *individual* level question whether the cognitive and emotional changes afforded by online socializing are healthy.
• Critiques on the *interpersonal* level look at the nature of community, offline and online, and question whether the online variety affects the offline kind in a healthy way.

• Critiques on the *social* level examine whether the kind of society that is emerging from the digital zeitgeist is humane and sustainable and, most important, about whether online communication strengthens or weakens democracy and civil society.

Minds Online

What kind of person do I become when I spend hours a day communicating through the mediation of virtual communities? Despite the obvious importance of this question, relatively little social science research has been directed at the cognitive and emotional effects of online communication. Probably the longest-term observations have been those of MIT professor Sherry Turkle. Her book, *Life On The Screen: Identity in the Age of the Internet* (Turkle, 1995), based on two decades of participant-observation, remains the fundamental work in the field.

Turkle asserts that the personal computer itself is an "object-to-think-with" for understanding the changes computers are inducing in our minds. "We come to see ourselves differently as we catch sight of our images in the mirror of the machine," Turkle writes.

The development of windows for computer interfaces was a technical innovation motivated by the desire to get people working more efficiently by cycling through different applications. But in the daily practice of many computer users, windows have become a powerful metaphor for thinking about the self as a multiple distributed system."

As human beings become increasingly intertwined with the technology and with each other via the technology, old distinctions about what is specifically human and specifically technological become more complex. Are we living life on the screen or in the screen? Our new technologically enmeshed relationships oblige us to ask to what extent we ourselves have become cyborgs, transgressive mixtures of biology, technology, and code. The traditional distance between people and machines has become harder to maintain.... The computer is an evocative object that causes old boundaries to be renegotiated.

Exactly how, and on what terms, are we renegotiating the boundaries between our selves and our technologized environment? What kind of multiple distributed system do I become when I live part of the day as a teenage girl in a chatroom, part of the day as a serious professional in a webconference, part of the day slaying enemies as Zaxxon, the steel-eyed assassin of an online gaming tribe? Turkle doesn't pretend to map the territory—indeed, she was the first to begin insisting that a vast psychic territory exists in cyberspace, waiting to be explored systematically by more than a few pioneer researchers. Although the question might sound esoteric, the answers it might provoke are as important as our humanity itself. To the degree that virtual communities support ways for humans to become more comfortable thinking of ourselves as components of a machine, they contribute to a large-scale change in what we regard humans to be. Changing our definition of human is something we probably all agree should be done with a degree of caution or, at least, knowledge.

One social critic, William Irwin Thompson, in *The American Replacement of Nature: The Everyday Acts and Outrageous Evolution of Economic Life* (Thompson, 1992), accused me and *Whole Earth Catalog* and WELL creator Stewart Brand by name of being agents of an ancient Zoroastrian demon of mindless mechanism. I am convinced that I am not the agent of any kind of demon, but seeing the charge in print startled me into thinking about the shadow side of our empowering devices —and reminded me to examine my enthusiasms more closely.

Almost half a century ago, Lewis Mumford, in *The Myth of the Machine* (Mumford, 1966), proposed that the most powerful and dehumanizing invention was not a visible machine but a social machine in which humans are treated as components in a massive hierarchical system for building pyramids and skyscrapers, empires, and civilizations. Jacques Ellul went further, and claimed the extreme deterministic position in the philosophy of technology by asserting that humans no longer guide or even influence technology. Ellul's powerful and depressing book *The Technological Society* (Ellul, 1964) presents argument after argument to demonstrate that "la technique"—the mechanical and relentless evolution of ever-more efficient ways to harness energies and accomplish tasks—is beyond even enlightened human influence. When I read today's cybercritics, with their sometimes pointed but often shallow critiques of digital culture, I'm sorry Mumford and Ellul don't seem to be read any more.

Whether or not you agree with their conclusions, these two technology critics looked into the future at the very beginning of the computer and communications revolution and saw developments that were deeply rooted in millennia of human history. We are changing what it means to be human, we have been doing it for a long time, and we have recently invented ways to accelerate the whole process.

More recently, in *Escape Velocity: Cyberculture at the End of the Century* (Dery, 1996), Mark Dery has examined the ways in which our psyches and societies are preparing us for the transition to the posthuman or transhuman age. There are those, the "extropians" and "transhumanists" who actively seek to jack in to the Net through neural implants. These extreme technophiles ask why we should put up with the messiness, mortality, limitations in intelligence and physical power that accompany the human body as it evolved biologically. Isn't it foolish, they propose, to refuse to research technologies of immortality when eternal life might be within the grasp of modern science? And there are those like Dery and others who warn that transhumanism might be leading us away from humanity as we know it, and into something Ellul might have predicted—a world in which we become fine-tuned down to our DNA as components in ever-consuming, ever-expanding, capitalist machinery, dominated and directed by an elite.

I'd put myself into the "wait a minute—do we really know what we are getting into?" camp. I want to ask technophiles whether we have learned anything from the drama of nuclear physicists in the 1940s. Have we gained sufficient collective wisdom to create technologies of immense power before we understand their consequences? To the most radical technology critics (I reject the pejorative term Luddite), I suggest that if you want to purify humanity by removing all technosocial systems that reduce us to components in larger machines, we'll probably have to do away with much of civilization from organized agriculture onward.

Certainly, mindless acceptance of tools and toys that tune our lives and sensibilities more and more acutely to the needs of machinery is dangerous. But extracting the humane powers from the diabolical forces enabled by technology is not a simple task. It might not even be possible. I see no alternative but to make the effort to find out.

Two other critiques of the individual impact of cybersociety are worth mentioning. First, there is the question of whether people who spend time online are happier or more depressed than those who don't, and then there's the question of addiction—is there a danger of abuse of social cyberspaces? These two critiques are only beginning, and are not the only kinds of questions to be asked about the cognitive and emotional impact of socializing in cyberspace. But they are the most sensational claims, and are certainly serious, even if the early research has been inadequate and misinterpreted. In discussing the social science of the Internet, the issue of media hype or media scare is always important to address from the beginning

In 1999, a headline in the *New York Times* proclaimed "Internet, Sad, Lonely Place, Researchers Find" (Harmon, 1998). The report cited in the Times, published in the *American Psychologist*, was titled "Internet paradox: A social technology that reduces social involvement and psychological well-being?" (Kraut, Patterson, Lundmark, Kiesler, Mukophadhyay, and Scherlis, 1998).

The researchers found 169 people who did not use computers or the Internet (not exactly a random sample, since the sample excludes all the people who were motivated to get online—maybe it's depressing to go online if you didn't really want to), lent them computers, furnished an Internet connection, and tested them for social-psychological satisfaction at the beginning of the study, then once again, two years later.

Humans are complicated creatures, and testing people regarding their mood once every two years isn't exactly a fine level of analysis. Such data are the beginning of a process of search and research. They certainly should not be mistaken for the end of the inquiry.

In its discussion of the "social use of the Internet," the study lumped email, listservs, newsgroups, BBSs, MUDs, chat, and conferencing into one category. Ignoring the difference between a hot singles chatroom, a listserv for immunologists, a webring of college students, and a message board for Alzheimer's caregivers doesn't make for strong inferences about people's behavior online. But this question of differentiating useful from wasteful social cyberspaces raises an important point. If Internet neophytes don't know what they are doing and aren't lucky their first few times out, it's much easier to find social interaction that is inane, obscene, or irate than it is to find a caring group of people who establish strong ties through online interaction. There are stupid and ugly online interactions and informative and compassionate ones, and like much of contemporary life online or off, the quality of your experience is influenced by which kind you find.

People who communicate via computer networks definitely need to learn about the dangers of mistaking messages on computer screens for fully authentic human relationships. People who suffer from pathologies of cognition or mood indeed can use communication media in pathological ways. Children and others can be preyed upon. Understanding what online conversation is good for and what its limitations are, and knowing where and how to look for healthy online social groups, seems to be an obvious prerequisite to a rewarding experience with the medium. And those people whose use of the Internet is part of a pattern of obsessive behavior such as compulsive gambling or consumption of pornography need help breaking their pathological patterns. This raises another recent claim regarding harmful effects of online social communication—the matter of "Internet addiction."

Approximately 11 million people around the world are Internet addicts, according to a paper presented by Doctor David Greenfield at the 1999 meeting of the American Psychological Association and reported by the Associated Press. Greenfield also happens to run a clinic <http://www.virtual-addiction.com/> for treating "Internet addiction."

The survey Greenfield cites in support of his claims was conducted by publishing the questionnaire on the ABC News web site last year <http://abcnews.go.com/sections/tech/DailyNews/netaddiction990823. html>. The survey consists of ten questions, such as whether respondents had used the Internet to escape from their problems, tried unsuccessfully to cut back on Internet use, or found themselves preoccupied with the Internet when they were no longer at the computer. Of the 17,251 people who voluntarily responded to the survey, 990 answered "yes" to five or more questions. That's approximately 5.7%. With an estimated 200 million Internet users, this finding was extrapolated to give a figure of 11 and a half million possible Internet addicts.

Is it really possible that 11.4 million people use the Internet in ways that damage their lives? Bold claims require strong evidence. It doesn't take an expert in research methodology to doubt the validity of a "five 'yes' answers out of ten" technique, applied to a self-selected population, with no control group, and no attempt to get a sample that represents the Internet-using population. In fact, a little digging reveals that the "disorder" was first proposed as a parody of the trend toward treating compulsive behaviors as addictions.

"Internet Addiction Disorder" was first proposed as a spoof in March 1995. Although nobody disputes that some individuals spend too much time gambling, downloading pornography, or chatting with fourteen-year-old boys posing as eighteen-year-old girls, the notion of a widespread outbreak of a new mental disorder has been floated annually ever since then. The experts quoted by the media almost always want to add "Internet Addiction Disorder" to the Diagnostic and Statistical Manual of Mental Disorders (DSM), the authoritative text on what mental disorders are diagnosable (and the guide to which treatments qualify for insurance compensation).

The whole hoo-ha started when a psychiatrist, Ivan Goldberg, sent out a message in 1995 claiming to have established the existence of a new disorder that should be added to the DSM. Borrowing language used to describe compulsive gambling as an addiction, Dr. Goldberg listed a set of symptoms <http://web.urz.uniheidelberg.de/Netzdienste/anleitung/wwwtips/8/addict.html>. When he started receiving email from people who claimed to be suffering from the disorder, Goldberg started a tongue-in-cheek online support group for Internet addicts. Although he does believe that some yet-undiscovered percentage of the online population suffer from what he now calls "pathological Internet use disorder," Goldberg told a writer for the *New Yorker* in 1997 that "To medicalize every behavior by putting it into psychiatric nomenclature is ridiculous. If you expand the concept of addiction to include everything people can overdo, then you must talk about people being addicted to books, addicted to jogging, addicted to other people" <http://www.psycom.net/iasg.html>.

Although Goldberg's original article was a hoax, Dr. Kimberly Young, an assistant professor of psychology at the University of Pittsburgh at Bradford, announced the opening of her Center for On-Line Addiction <http://www.netaddiction.com>. In 1997, Dr. Young urged the American Psychiatric Association to give official recognition to the disorder. Dr. Young's paper, "Internet Addiction Disorder: The Emergence of a New Clinical Disorder" <http://www.pitt.edu/~ksy/apa.html>, was based on the responses to a seven-item questionnaire she sent to 496 people who responded to online and offline advertisements for "avid Internet users." She concluded that 396 of the respondents were "dependent Internet users."

The first questions to ask about any scientific experiment, especially those conducted on human subjects, and especially those that are presented to promote a certain policy, are methodological questions: Does the sample represent the population it is supposed to describe? How are the subjects selected? Are the questions tested and verified? Are there control subjects? Are any relationships specifically implied by the data necessarily causal relationships?

Doctor Joseph B. Walther, associate professor of communication and information technology at Rensselaer Polytechnic Institute <http://www.rpi.edu/~walthj/>, objected to the methodology of the Greenfield study: "The checklist in the reported research includes items that have been shown to correlate statistically with greater Internet usage (although one could indicate 'yes' to five items but not use the Net very much), but have not been shown to predict any kind of dysfunction."

Doctor Walther also objected to "the fallacy of using analogous diagnostic criteria as a substitute for etiological (causative) criteria. That is, as these researchers draw from substance addiction or gambling addiction, they are focusing on tangentially-related aspects of some syndromes that have *nothing* to do with communicating with people or gathering information. No theory or conceptual framework has emerged to explain or predict *what* about Internet use is addictive, or what the underlying addictive mechanism is. If the Internet was addictive, like drugs, everyone who used it a lot would be addicted."

Another psychologist who thinks about the psychology of cyberspace is John Suler, Ph.D., professor of psychology at Rider University, and author of the excellent online hypertext book *The Psychology of Cyberspace* <http://www1.rider.edu/~suler/psycyber/psycyber.html>. He has a section on Internet Addiction on his site, so I asked him what he thought of the APA presentations:

In my opinion, the largest group of addicts are ghosts. They exist only in the minds of our media that loves to hype and scandalize and of some naive mental health professionals who want to lay claim to a new pathology. Another group gets caught up in the excitement and novelty of the many fascinating opportunities the Internet offers. Maybe they go overboard—causing problems in their "real world" life—but it's a phase. They realize what they can and can't get out of cyberspace, and return to the real world a bit wiser. The last group are those unfortunate, already vulnerable people who succumb to one or more of the many seductions of the Internet. They're unable to help themselves. These are the people that expert professionals are trying to help.

Storm King, president of International Society for Mental Health Online <www. www.ismho.org>, a doctoral candidate at Pacific Graduate School of Psychology in Palo Alto, first published "Is the Internet Addictive, or Are Addicts Using the Internet?" in December 1996

<http://www.concentric.net/~astorm/iad.html>. In his paper, which takes seriously the consequences of Internet addiction, King did what so many of today's research clearly failed to do: He sets out the methodological problems that must be overcome (how do you get someone whose behavior truly is pathological to report about it?), and acknowledges the complexities of attempting to attribute specific causes to human behavioral disorders. King, in recent communication, argued that the Internet does enable people who have an impulse control disorder such as pathological gambling to have greatly enhanced access to their vice via the Internet <http://www.concentric.net/~astorm/gamaddabs.html>.

Although I dispute the numbers, I don't dispute that some people spend inordinate amounts of time in chatrooms, MUDs, and BBSs, to the detriment of their social life and state of mind. People whose Internet use has damaged their lives deserve to be helped. Because people can use an otherwise helpful tool to accomplish harmful ends, a need remains for carefully designed research into the dynamics of pathological Internet use.

Another important issue remains to be considered—the persistence of the tale of Internet addiction and the societal opportunity cost associated with not publishing more relevant stories. Too many people who call themselves journalists have concentrated on the scare stories about Internet addicts, the sensational tales of online porno, sweeping claims based on research that is less than superficial. So many other stories need to be told about who has gained and lost power because of the Internet, who is profiting and who is losing because of the Internet, who has access and who doesn't, what opportunities the Internet provides for education, medicine, and citizen participation in civic affairs, what impacts Internet use might have on our thoughts, feelings, and social relationships. Scientists and communicators have to do a far better job than we have done so far if we're to use and regulate the new communication medium reasonably and knowledgeably.

Social Networks and the Nature of Communities

If I had encountered sociologist Barry Wellman and learned about social network analysis when I first wrote about cyberspace cultures, I could have saved us all a decade of debate by calling them "online social networks" instead of "virtual communities."

Social networks predated the Internet, writing, and even speech. Indeed, humans are not the only creature that makes use of social networks. When I met Wellman, author of many social science journal articles about social networks, he had just written an insightful paper comparing social networks to virtual communities.

Think of the people you encounter regularly—every month, let's say. Your biological family, the people from your job you hang out with, your congregation, service organization, the people in your neighborhood who would loan or borrow things, the people you talk with regularly on the telephone in the course of your professional or social activities, the delivery people who show up every day at your business, the people you email regularly.

In a recent email communication, Wellman added: "Ever since the late 1960s, I have arguing that community does not equal neighborhood. That is, people usually obtain support, sociability, information and a sense of belonging from those who do not live within the same neighborhood. They have done this through phoning, writing, driving, railroading, transiting, and flying. LA is the classic example of this, but in fact, this has been the prevalent means of connectivity in the western world at least since the 1960s" (Wellman, 2000).

Social networks emerge when people interact with each other continually, and they have to be useful or they wouldn't exist. Your social network can find you a job or a husband, information you need, recommendations for restaurants and investments, babysitters and bargains, a new religion, emotional support. Before writing letters became commonplace, social networks were confined to those people who saw each other face to face. Writing, public postal systems, telegraph, telephone, and the Internet each brought new means of extending one's social network to include people who are not in the immediate geographical vicinity, who share an interest rather than a location.

It has been argued that these increasingly mediated relationships are, for the most part, increasingly superficial. As I look at the way more and more of our social communication is migrating to email and cell phone, instant message and online greeting card, I tend to agree. At the same time, it certainly is possible to maintain deep relationships through letters, telephone calls, or online chats. Like all technologies, communication tools come with a price: Alienation might be the cost of the power of abstraction. We might do better by ourselves by paying more attention to how we're using the powers of abstraction.

Social network analysis provides a useful framework for discussing the impact of online socializing. It counters the critique of virtual communities as alienating, dehumanizing substitutes for more direct, less mediated human contact. The notion of "strong ties and weak ties" is a useful part of that conceptual framework. The classic document explicating this idea is "The Strength of Weak Ties" (Granovetter, 1973). A weak tie is an alumnus of your alma mater, a stronger tie would be members of your college sorority or fraternity you actually lived with, an even stronger tie would be your roommate. A social network with a mixture of strong ties, familial ties, lifelong friend ties, marital ties, business partner ties, is important for people to obtain the fundamentals of identity, affection, emotional and material support. But without a network of more superficial relationships, life would be harder and less fun in many ways. Weaker ties multiply people's social capital, useful knowledge, ability to get things done.

When asking questions about the impact of any technology on community, I have learned to avoid romanticizing the notion of community, of assuming a state of pastoral existence that once existed in pretechnology small towns. There is an indisputable merit to living your life in the same place, loving or hating or putting up with the same people day after day, making decisions together with people you don't necessarily like, reducing the number of your social relationships and perhaps increasing their depth. But there is a cost to this long lost *Gemeinschaft* of the village, the hamlet, the small town, as well. If the shadows of urban and mediated experience are alienation and superficiality, the shadows of the traditional community are narrow-mindedness and bigotry.

In *All That Is Solid Melts into Air: The Experience of Modernity* (Berman, 1982), Marshall Berman claims that Goethe's Faust is a tale of the transition to modernity and includes lessons about how cruel those pastoral communities of premodern times could be. When Faust bespoils the reputation of the maiden Gretchen, her warm, small, unmediated community of strong-tie relationships persecutes her to the point of suicide. How many people flee the idylls of small towns because they look or think or act differently than the local norm? Just as virtual communities have attractive and unattractive aspects, so do other forms of community. As Berman wrote: "So long as we remember Gretchen's fate, we will be immune to nostalgic yearning for the worlds we have lost."

I must therefore reconsider and retract the words I originally published here in 1993. I owe it to my critics Fernback and Thompson for pointing out <http://www.Well.com/user/hlr/texts/VCcivil.html> that I clearly proclaimed a nostalgia for community lost when I wrote:

Virtual communities might be real communities, they might be pseudocommunities, or they might be something entirely new in the realm of social contracts, but I believe they are in part a response to the hunger for community that has followed the disintegration of traditional communities around the world.

The disintegration, I discovered, has been an ongoing process ever since the development of the alphabet. And human relationships are too complex to be judged as either "deep" or "shallow," with nothing in between. But I have come to see how the benefits of communication tools have always come with a less visible cost. There is no denying that good things can be lost or destroyed by harmful use of tools and social systems, or there would be more redwoods, rainforests, town squares, and convivial public transit systems and less pavement, fewer vehicles, and cleaner air and water. Before we charge off to preserve those good things new media might threaten, we need to understand and agree upon what those good things are, who they are good for, and why we agree they are good. Do we want cohesive societies...or democratic ones? Do we want warm communities or innovative ones? Where are the spectrums of alternatives between these extremes? What are the right questions to ask about the impact of virtual communities on geographic community—the questions whose answers might improve our lives or defend against disaster?

The best attempt by social scientists to address some social critiques of virtual community is, in my opinion, "Virtual Communities as Communities: Net Surfers Don't Ride Alone" (Wellman and Gulia, 1999). Wellman and Gulia point out the vast excluded middle between virtual community utopianism and the most emphatic critics of life online, and review the findings of social science research to address seven key questions regarding virtual community:

1. Are relationships on the Net narrow and specialized or are they broadly based? What kinds of support can one expect to find in virtual community?

2. How does the Net affect people's ability to sustain weaker, less intimate relationships and to develop new relationships? Why do Net participants help those they hardly know?

3. Is support given on the Net reciprocated? Do participants develop attachment to virtual communities so that commitment, solidarity, and norms of reciprocity develop?

4. To what extent are strong, intimate relationships possible on the Net?

5. What is high involvement in virtual community doing to other forms of "real-life" community involvement?

6. To what extent does participation on the Net increase the diversity of community ties? To what extent do such diverse ties help to integrate heterogeneous groups?

7. How does the architecture of the Net affect the nature of virtual community? To what extent are virtual communities solidarity groups (like traditional villages) or thinly connected Webs? Are virtual communities like "real-life" communities? To what extent are virtual communities entities in themselves or integrated into people's overall communities?

Although they don't intend to argue for definitive answers, Wellman and Gulia look at the literature of social science research, especially social network analysis, and propose ways in which the existing data can illuminate these questions.

In regard to the first question, Wellman and Giulia wrote:

The standard pastoralist ideal of in-person, village-like community has depicted each community member as providing a broad range of support to all others. In this ideal situation, all can count upon all to provide companionship, emotional aid, information, services (such as child care or health care), money, or goods (be it food for the starving or a drill for the renovating).

It is not clear if such a broadly supportive situation has ever actually been the case—it might well be pure nostalgia—but contemporary communities in the western world are quire different. Most community ties are specialized and do not form densely knit clusters of relationships. For example, our Toronto research has found that except for kin and small clusters of friends, most members of a person's community network do not really know each other. Even close relationships usually provide only a few kinds of social support. Those who provide emotional aid or small services are rarely the same ones who provide large services, companionship, or financial aid. People do get all kinds of support from community members but they have to turn to different ones for different kinds of help. This means that people must maintain differentiated portfolios of ties to obtain a wide variety of resources. In market terms, they must shop at specialized boutiques for needed resources instead of casually dropping in at the general store. (Wellman, 1992)

Wellman and Gulia suggest that the nature of the Internet serves to amplify this specialization and diversification of personal portfolios of social ties. They point out how virtual communities can organize, segment, and separate kinds of social ties, from those that furnish professional information to those that provide emotional support. They note that "Emotional support, companionship, information, making arrangements, providing a sense of belonging are all non-material social resources that are relatively easy to provide from the comfort of one's computer."

In regard to their second question, Wellman and Gulia observed that people often provide information, support or favors for people they have never met—strangers. The weak ties enabled by online relationships, while perhaps reducing the depth of relationships, can help increase the diversity of relationships—the number of different kinds of people in one's social network.

To the third question, they cite evidence that there is reciprocity online and attachment to virtual communities. Indeed, the idea that cyberspace is a place where sharing is encouraged is itself a norm that influences behavior: "Norms of generalized reciprocity and organizational citizenship are another reason for why people help others online." In most of the rest of the world of human activities, competition is the ruling norm. Building something collaboratively that creates a value for all who use it was one of the enduring values of the people who built the antecedents of today's Internet back in the 1970s and 1980s.

The ARPAnet and Internet cultures that preceded the Web by thirty years were built on norms of collaboration and cooperation. The Net was a place where informal gift economies enriched life and thought for everyone who participated. Minimal "netiquette" in social dealings, a willingness to share resources when others request them, a commitment to put value in as well as take it out of the Net are what made the Internet attractive to grow to its present status. But many question whether those norms have survived the waves of millions of newcomers and the abuse of the commons in the form of spam, chain email, viruses, and virus hoaxes. If, as Wellman and Gulia assert, social science data shows that norms of reciprocity and organizational attachment exist online, will they continue to do so? Or are they a resource that can only live in the early stages of a network economy?

The all-important and much-obviated question of whether high involvement in virtual communities removes people from involvement in their physical communities led Wellman and Gulia to several questions about the question itself. First, they questioned the certainty that "community" is a zero-sum game, that online involvement necessarily displaces offline communication.

Second, they point out that fears of virtual community in this vein indirectly "demonstrate the strength and importance of online ties, and not their weakness."

Third, they note that the question is based on a false comparison between virtual communities and unmediated, face-to-face communities. Do the critics mean communities where nobody ever uses a telephone? Citing Wellman's own research, the authors claim: "In fact, most contemporary communities in the developed world do not resemble rural or urban villages where all know all and have frequent face to face contact. Rather most kith and kin live further away than a walk (or short drive), so that telephone contact sustains ties as much as face-to-face get-togethers" (Wellman, Carrington, and Hall, 1988).

Fourth, they point out that most people don't divide their worlds into strictly segregated online and offline portions: Online discussions are one way that people make friends offline.

Fifth, the existence of webs of personal relationships via private email is not visible to most research, and "provides the basis for more multiplex relationships to develop...." In particular, they cite the "invisible colleges" of scholars who know each other well, meet once a year at most, but stay in touch online much more intensively via email, listservs, newsgroups, and web conferences.

Wellman and Gulia concluded about the relationship between online and offline community:

In sum, the Net supports a variety of community ties, including some that are quite close and intimate. But while there is legitimate concern about whether true intimacy is possible in relationships that operate only online, the Net promotes the functioning of intimate secondary relationships and weaker ties. Nor are such weaker ties insignificant. Not only do such ties sustain important, albeit more specialized, relationships, but the vast majority of informal interpersonal ties are weak ties, whether they operate online or face-to-face. Current research suggests that North Americans usually have more than 1,000 interpersonal relations, but that only a half-dozen of them are intimate and no more than 50 are significantly strong (Kochen, 1989; Wellman, 1992). Yet, in the aggregate, a person's other 950+ ties are important sources of information, support, companionship, and a sense of belonging.

Wellman and Gulia are less sanguine about the data regarding whether the Net increases community diversity. Noting that all people in contemporary communities belong to a number of different partial communities, which expose them to a diverse set of social worlds, the authors remind us that the diversity of the online social world depends, first of all, on who is online: "Possibilities for diverse communities depend also on the population of the Net having diverse social characteristics." I'll address the issue of the "digital divide" later in this chapter.

Are virtual communities "real?" Wellman and Gulia argue that "The limited evidence available suggests that the relationships people develop and maintain in cyberspace are much like most of the ones they develop in their real life communities: intermittent, specialized, and varying in strength." The net supports exchanges of information strongly, but does not hinder the exchange of communications of emotional support, as well. Specialized communities "foster multiple memberships in partial communities. At the same time, the ease of group response and forwarding can foster the folding-in of formerly separate Net participants into more all-encompassing communities."

In their conclusion, Wellman and Gulia did not try to claim that social cyberspace is good or evil or that we know anywhere near enough to judge: "It is time to replace anecdote with evidence. The subject is important: practically, scholarly, and politically. The answers have not yet been found. Indeed, the questions are just starting to be formulated."

Formulating the right questions about radically new phenomena sometimes requires thinking about old ideas in new ways. Are entirely new methodologies for social scientific inquiry required to deal with entirely new forms and media for human relationships? Wellman and Gulia point in that direction. Another social scientist makes the claim more explicitly. K. A. Cerulo, Ph.D., claims, in "Reframing Social Concepts for a Brave New (Virtual) World," (Cerulo, 1997), that "Recent developments have touched issues at the very heart of sociological discourse—the definition of interaction, the nature of social ties, and the scope of experience and reality. Indeed, the developing technologies are creating an expanded social environment that requires amendments and alterations to ways in which we conceptualize social processes" (p. 49).

Cerulo questions the fundamental assumption made by many critics, that face-to-face communication is necessarily primary, more authentically human, than mediated communication.

Cerulo proposes that social scientists and communication researchers look again, and with new eyes, at the definitions they base their assumptions and theories on—definitions of social interaction, social bonding, and empirical experience. Must all assumptions about social interaction be framed in terms of face-to-face communications? Do social bonds require geographic co-presence? And is it possible for ethnographers of cyberspace to do their work without becoming participant observers in virtual communities?

Challenging the assumption that physical co-presence is the benchmark for social interaction, Cerulo says: "'We speak of the closeness and trust born of such mediated connections using terms such as pseudo-gemeinschaft, virtual intimacy, or imagined community. Such designations reify the notion that interactions void of the face-to-face connection are somehow less than the real thing."

The question of how virtual and geographic communities relate to each other has not been confined to theorists. In the first edition of *The Virtual Community*, I noted the birth of the "Freenet" and "Community Networking" movements in the early 1990s. Hundreds of experiments were spawned. What happened?

In 1996, Douglas Schuler's book *New Community Networks: Wired for Change* provided both a manifesto and a handbook for community network building (Schuler, 1996). Although space here does not permit an adequate review of community networks over the past seven years, it's worth noting that a whole class of community networks foundered on a weak business model (those that supported themselves by being Internet service providers), that well-funded and carefully designed experiments (like Blacksburg Electronic Village and Toronto's Netville) have thrived, that hundreds of others (like the Appalachian Center for Economic Networks) have managed to survive economically and slowly build social networks that bring people face to face rather than separating them by screens. I can only mention a few examples of the hundreds of community network enterprises all around the world.

Blacksburg Electronic Village (BEV) is the one most journalists write about, because it had the most going for it early in the game. BEV <http://www.bev.net/> has succeeded because it grew out of a collaboration among knowledgeable community institutions that were willing to experiment, a local communications corporation, and a research university that was willing to contribute staff and resources to find out what would happen if you gave an entire community ready access to high-speed Internet connections and community services.

Virginia Tech, the Town of Blacksburg, and Bell Atlantic set out in 1991 to offer Internet access to every citizen in town. BEV launched in October 1993. By the summer of 1997, more than 60 percent of the town's 36,000 citizens regularly used the Internet, 70 percent of the local businesses (more than 250) advertised online. Blacksburg senior citizens meet via listserv <http://www.bev.net/community/seniors/>. Instead of watching local dollars flow through the Internet on their way out of town, hundreds of local merchants participate in main street e-commerce through an online mall <http://www.bev.net/mall/>. By late 1999, more than 87 percent of town residents were online and more than 400 area businesses were listed on the BEV Village Mall.

Another "wired neighborhood" in Toronto was the subject of research by sociologists Keith N. Hampton and Barry Wellman, who reported their results online ("Netville Online and Offline: Observing and Surveying a Wired Suburb" [Hampton and Wellman, 1999]). In their abstract, the authors state:

A connected society is more than a populace joined through wires and computers. It's a society whose people are connected to each other. For the past two years we have been looking for community online and offline, locally and globally, in the wired suburban neighborhood of "Netville." We want to find out how living in a residential community equipped with no cost, very high speed access to the Internet affects the kinds of interpersonal relations people have with coworkers, friends, relatives, and neighbors.

In their conclusion, they write:

Preliminary analysis suggests that the Internet supports a variety of social ties, strong and weak, instrumental, emotional, social and affiliative. Relationships are rarely maintained through computer-mediated communication alone, but are sustained through a combination of online and offline interactions. Despite the ability of the Internet to serve as a global communication technology, much online activity is between people who live (or work) near each other, often in Netville itself. In Netville, the local network brought neighbors together to socialize, helped them to arrange in-person get-togethers—both as couples and as larger groups (barbecues, etc.)—facilitated the provision of aid, and enabled the easy exchange of information about dealing with the developer. The high rate of online activity led to increased local awareness, high rates of in-person activity, and to rapid political mobilization at the end of the field trial.

Although many efforts in community networking failed because they lacked the funds and institutional resources available to BEV, many communities have succeeded in urban and rural middle class and lower-income communities. On January 8, 2000, the *Charlotte News and Observer* published a story entitled "A World Wide Web of cul-de-sacs" by staff writer Sarah Lindenfield <http://www.news-observer.com/daily/2000/01/08/tri00.html>:

John Wyman remembers the old days, before his neighborhood went online with a Web page. Every couple of weeks, he would pay $20 to make 170 copies of a community flier. Then he would drive up to each home to deliver them.

"Do you know what that does to your clutch, and do you know how long that takes?" Wyman asked. "With the Web site, I can go in there and, in 10 seconds, have it updated for everybody."

Today, Wyman is out of the printing business. Of the 170 homes in the Hardscrabble Plantation subdivision in northern Durham County, 155 have access to e-mail and the Web. Residents read neighborhood announcements and newsletters online, and they pass the information to the 15 neighbors who aren't connected.

Hardscrabble Plantation is among at least 65 Triangle neighborhood groups that have ventured out on the Internet. Planters Walk in Knightdale, Alyson Pond in Raleigh, Park Village in Cary and Walden Pond in Durham are also among those that write newsletters, name board members or simply list social activities on Web sites.

A small, but growing, group of for-profit and nonprofit firms are designing sites just for neighborhoods. And more of the 5,100-plus Triangle subdivisions are looking for new ways to connect.

***

Internet neighborliness isn't completely replacing knocking on doors with fresh-baked brownies, or strolling down the street and waving to people on front porches.

Instead, residents see the Web as another way to communicate within the community.

Consider ACEnet, the Appalachian Center for Economic Networking <http://www.seorf.ohiou.edu/~acenet/>, "a community-based economic development organization located in rural, southeastern Ohio. Our purpose is to work with others in the area to create a healthy regional economy with many successful businesses and good jobs. Our goal is for people with low incomes to move out of poverty permanently through employment or business ownership." As the name reveals, and as a closer inspection of their programs makes clear, ACEnet is an economic network. Relationships with banks, businesses, and educational organizations are the core of the project. It's not about technology, but technology helps it happen, and helps tie together the different parts of the community involved in the effort. In particular, ACEnet uses the Internet to link businesses with new markets and market resources such as trend information; with resources both near and far through their community network; with one another through an electronic mailing list; and to link their Appalachian community with similar communities across the country.

These examples are not offered as evidence that electronic utopia through many-to-many communications is around the corner, but as a small sample of the large number of active experiments that are still going on. Before theorists whose research is conducted primarily in libraries dismiss unequivocally the possibility that online communication can enhance rather than erode face-to-face communication in geographic communities, perhaps they should also pay attention to the results of these experiments.

One of the early enthusiastic backers of community networking, Mario Morino, now believes that community networks have failed, thus far, to live up to the promise we saw in them at the original Ties That Bind conference. Organized by Steve Cisler, a librarian at Apple Computer, this was the first annual face-to-face get-together of international networkers. The Morino Foundation was one of the sponsors of that first meeting, and of several efforts in the years since. Says Morino today:

Community networking has been a movement in search of a cause and this has been its curse. It appeared that community networking never clearly articulated its purpose and this ambiguity caused some to view it from a technical perspective, others to view it as the electronic town, while others saw it as a means of activism. Its real potential lay in bringing people together, to help people connect with one another, and more importantly, to help them toward an outcome. I wonder what would have happened had the talent and innovative minds that went into community networking focused on worker preparation programs. What would have happened if community networks had rallied around the challenge of eliminating illiteracy, eradicating lead poisoning for children, preparing our teachers to integrate technology into their curriculums and learning delivery, or delivering health information to our most impoverished neighborhoods?

Instead, I believe the self-imposed limitation on community networking was the lack of a real vision for how it could have helped society in a focused way. The concept still holds remarkable potential. The world still hasn't grasped the potential of the online learning community. (Morino, 2000)

The foundation of a modern technological society is a population of educated individuals—humans who have been trained how to think. When new phenomena (alphabets, Internets) enable people to change the way we think, we then change the way we relate to one another. When human relationships change, human institutions change. What effects do virtual community and many-to-many communication technologies have on that fragile and precious institution, democracy? Will our grandchildren be citizens of a human-guided social system or components in a social system that guides humans? The question that trumps all the other questions is whether life online will contribute to political liberty, or diminish it.

The Prospects for the Public Sphere

Will citizens use the Internet to influence the nations of the world to become more democratic? Or will our efforts be ineffectual or even work to amplify the power of state or corporate autocracies? All other social questions about the impact of life online are secondary to this one.

Is the virtual community simply a self-hypnotizing subset of the culture industry? Previously (chapter 10, "Disinformocracy"), I pointed to the more skeptical worldviews of Baudrillard and Debord (global media productions as "simulacra" and "the society of the spectacle," respectively). I didn't get into Adorno and Horkheimer of the "Frankfurt School" of political-cultural theory. It has been made clear to me more recently that no analysis of the virtual community's political significance should ignore these thinkers who deliberated about the political implications of mass entertainment in the decades preceding the emergence of computer technology.

In the first edition of *The Virtual Community*, I coined the neologism *disinfotainment* to describe that sphere in which special effects, television laugh tracks, manufactured "news" programming, and cross-media promotion of cultural products serve to distract and misinform a pacified population of unprotesting consumers, as well as to return profits to the owners of the cultural producers. I also dabbled in the work of Jürgen Habermas, because his notion of the "public sphere" intuitively seemed to me the best way to frame the political import of social cyberspace. If I can be allowed to temporarily jack up the theoretical infrastructure for a social theory of cyberspace I started building into the clear blue sky of 1993, I need to insert Adorno and Horkheimer's ideas.

Adorno and Horkheimer were concerned with the fusion between the culture industry and mindless entertainment. Amusement is specific to the twentieth century mass cultural industry and is simply another part of the cycle of routinization. Their attack on the culture industry, first published in 1944, claimed that mass art was based on "a medicinal bath" of amusement and laughter, rather than on transcendence or happiness (Adorno and Horkheimer, 1972). People were amused and liberated from the need to think and their laughter affirmed existing society.

Are virtual communities part of a last hold out from the commodification of media culture, a place of resistance and autonomy and self-empowerment? A place where we have a chance of seeing reality for what it is, so that we can refuse to accept the present and try to change the future. Or are they disinfotainment in the guise of antidisinfotainment? Is it another way to amuse ourselves to death? These are the key questions Adorno and Horkheimer would most likely raise about the new phenomena of social cyberspaces. (Adorno died in 1969, the year the ARPAnet was born.)

Adorno and Horkheimer saw the culture industry as one that no longer tolerated autonomous thought or deviation to any degree because of the economic necessity for rapid return of capital investment. More than that, mass culture does not question the society it exists in and, instead, continually "confirms the validity of the system"(Adorno and Horkheimer, 1972, p. 129). Adorno and Horkheimer saw how acceptance and reaction were permeating more and more spheres of life, and how the culture of mass society with its corporate rather than aesthetic ideology eroded cultural standards in order to quell any forms of expression that might contest the given order, producing less freedom, less individuality, and ultimately, less happiness.

Their primary concern was the transformation of society, for the continuance of civilized humanity. They saw democracy and freedom to choose as diverging paths, but they found that "freedom to choose an ideology proved only to be freedom to choose what is always the same" (Adorno and Horkheimer, 1972, p. 167). For them, autonomy allows a conception of a different world and communicates the possibility that reason can penetrate existing barriers, allowing some to take a stance against modern culture to give the world a new direction, with a hope for the liberation of the human spirit.

Their boldest claim was that culture had become a form of domination, that the culture industry operates to diffuse oppositional consciousness and individualism. For them, the industry was selling packages of ideas and beliefs. People no longer had to think for themselves, since "the product prescribes every reaction by signals" (Adorno and Horkheimer, 1972, p. 137). It is characterized by a pervasive manipulation of the consumer whose intellectual capacity is continually underestimated. There is a profusion of sameness and repetition by using sets of interchangeable details, sweeping away all particularity and flattening out anything distinct, changing the nature of society as well as the way we perceive reality. One of the conclusions of the Frankfurt School was that the consumer society encouraged social and political apathy, even before the television era. I offer this extended quote not as an endorsement of this rather determinist view, but because it's a sobering attack on the foundations of any utopian ideas about democratizing media, from the earliest days of mass media.

The sociological theory that the loss of the support of objectively established religion, the dissolution of the last remnants of precapitalism, together with technological and social differentiation or specialization, have led to cultural chaos is disproved every day; for culture now impresses the same stamp on everything. Films, radio and magazines make up a system which is uniform as a whole and in every part.

Even the aesthetic activities of political opposites are one in their enthusiastic obedience to the rhythm of the iron system. The decorative industrial management buildings and exhibition centers in authoritarian countries are much the same as anywhere else. The huge gleaming towers that shoot up everywhere are outward signs of the ingenious planning of international concerns, toward which the unleashed entrepreneurial system (whose monuments are a mass of gloomy houses and business premises in grimy, spiritless cities) was already hastening. Even now the older houses just outside the concrete city centers look like slums, and the new bungalows on the outskirts are at one with the flimsy structures of world fairs in their praise of technical progress and their built-in demand to be discarded after a short while like empty food cans. Yet the city housing projects designed to perpetuate the individual as a supposedly independent unit in a small hygienic dwelling make him all the more subservient to his adversary—the absolute power of capitalism.

Because the inhabitants, as producers and as consumers, are drawn into the center in search of work and pleasure, all the living units crystallize into well-organized complexes. The striking unity of microcosm and macrocosm presents men with a model of their culture: the false identity of the general and the particular. Under monopoly all mass culture is identical, and the lines of its artificial framework begin to show through. The people at the top are no longer so interested in concealing monopoly: as its violence becomes more open, so its power grows. Movies and radio need no longer pretend to be art. The truth that they are just business is made into an ideology in order to justify the rubbish they deliberately produce. They call themselves industries; and when their directors' incomes are published, any doubt about the social utility of the finished products is removed.

Interested parties explain the culture industry in technological terms. It is alleged that because millions participate in it, certain reproduction processes are necessary that inevitably require identical needs in innumerable places to be satisfied with identical goods. The technical contrast between the few production centers and the large number of widely dispersed consumption points is said to demand organization and planning by management. Furthermore, it is claimed that standards were based in the first place on consumers' needs, and for that reason were accepted with so little resistance. The result is the circle of manipulation and retroactive need in which the unity of the system grows ever stronger. No mention is made of the fact that the basis on which technology acquires power over society is the power of those whose economic hold over society is greatest.

A technological rationale is the rationale of domination itself. It is the coercive nature of society alienated from itself. Automobiles, bombs, and movies keep the whole thing together until their leveling element shows its strength in the very wrong which it furthered. It has made the technology of the culture industry no more than the achievement of standardization and mass production, sacrificing whatever involved a distinction between the logic of the work and that of the social system. This is the result not of a law of movement in technology as such but of its function in today's economy. The need which might resist central control has already been suppressed by the control of the individual consciousness. The step from the telephone to the radio has clearly distinguished the roles. The former still allowed the subscriber to play the role of subject, and was liberal. The latter is democratic: it turns all participants into listeners and authoritatively subjects them to broadcast programs which are all exactly the same.

No machinery of rejoinder has been devised, and private broadcasters are denied any freedom. They are confined to the apocryphal field of the "amateur," and also have to accept organization from above. But any trace of spontaneity from the public in official broadcasting is controlled and absorbed by talent scouts, studio competitions and official programs of every kind selected by professionals. Talented performers belong to the industry long before it displays them; otherwise they would not be so eager to fit in. The attitude of the public, which ostensibly and actually favors the system of the culture industry, is a part of the system and not an excuse for it.

Assuming that the prospect for individual liberty is as bleak as the neo-Marxist Frankfurt School portrayed it, has the technical power of the Net changed the culture machine portrayed by Adorno and Horkheimer? Is there is a loophole in their critique that many-to-many communication might exploit? The broadcast technologies the Frankfurt School wrote about in 1944 centralized the power to produce and distribute cultural material, and continued to grow and consolidate as cultural products grew digital in the 1990s. The owners of the culture industry did not create the Internet, however. The Internet descended from the atomic bomb, not the silver screen. Does many-to-many turn the tables on culture monopoly, or will it be absorbed? While Sony is not the same as your desktop video on the Web, the monopolies and near-monopolies that used to control the culture industry through the high cost of culture-producing technology now are no longer alone in the mediasphere.

The Internet didn't matter to the powers that be when I first wrote about virtual communities. When I interviewed executives at American, Japanese, and French telecommunications companies in 1992, they were unanimous in their claim that their more serious enterprises regarded the Internet as a toy. A VP from Cap Cities, the company that owned the ABC network, told me at a lunch in 1992 that communicating via the Internet was a temporary fad, like CB radio in the 1980s. The Netscape-Yahoo-AOL-Microsoft Internet industry changed all that. When AOL bought Time-Warner in 2000, a milestone was established. At this point, Adorno and Horkheimer would remind us that when there is money to be made, when economic aspects of media culture become entrenched, then more controls will be instituted because there is more at stake.

"No machinery of rejoinder has been devised, and private broadcasters are denied any freedom." Is many-to-many a machinery of rejoinder that empowers media freedom for many who have been denied such power, as the printing press was? The difference, I am convinced, lies not in the nature of the technology, but in the way it is used. Manipulation, deception, and marketing are not the only imaginable uses for new media. What happens when millions of people begin to create their own cultures and communicate with each other, even giving them away to each other?

The most serious critique of this book and the most serious concern about the social impact of the Internet is the challenge to my claim that many-to-many discussions could contribute to the health of democracy by making possible better communications among citizens. It seems that a great deal of the critique, although not all, is directed at one specific paragraph. I wrote this in 1993:

We temporarily have access to a tool that could bring conviviality and understanding into our lives and might help revitalize the public sphere. The same tool, improperly controlled and wielded, could become an instrument of tyranny. The vision of a citizen-designed, citizen-controlled worldwide communications network is a version of technological utopianism that could be called the vision of "the electronic agora." In the original democracy, Athens, the agora was the marketplace, and more—it was where citizens met to talk, gossip, argue, size each other up, find the weak spots in political ideas by debating about them. But another kind of vision could apply to the use of the Net in the wrong ways, a shadow vision of a less utopian kind of place—the Panopticon.

Two of the criticisms directed at this paragraph have caused me to reconsider my original statement. The phrase "tool that could bring" has an implication of technological determinism that I simply let slip through because I wasn't paying sufficient attention. Now, I pay more attention when discussing the way people, tools, and institutions affect each other. It's not healthy to assume we don't have a choice. Tools aren't always neutral. But neither do they determine our destinies, immune to human efforts. The rest of the book isn't overly deterministic, but that paragraph is probably cited and challenged by dozens of scholarly essays over the years for reasons I have humbly come to understand.

Another flaw in my original draft is that I failed to make it clear that I was identifying, not advocating, the utopian version of an "electronic agora." I also should have mentioned that the affluent zeitgeist of Athenian democracy rested on the backs of slaves. As David Silver, one of the most thoughtful critical commentators, told me: "I'd make it clear in your new edition: neither Athens nor America nor cyberspace is a utopia."

I agree, now that critics have helped educate me. I would argue that we can still learn something from both experiments about the social nature of democracy, and about the influence of public communications on political action.

Some critics have claimed that by concentrating on the Panoptic aspects of possible Internet futures as the only dystopian alternatives, I neglected to say anything about the influence of global capitalism. In fact, the Panoptic aspects of the Web today have less to do with the government spying on your every move, but with invisible and commonplace events that take place with the click of a mouse—information snooped out about your habits by web sites that install information on your hard disk and read information previously stored on your computer. Capitalist competition, not totalitarian surveillance, has forced the rapid evolution of technologies that help vendors to zero in on precisely the products they need to bring to your attention.

These critics have their own evidence. It can't be denied that over the past five years the Internet has been a powerful an instrument of globalization and the centralization of great wealth in organizations like Sprint, MCI-Worldcom, Microsoft, Newscorp, AOL-Turner-Time-Warner. It is not outlandishly imaginative to think that a future Microsoft-AOL-Time-Warner-Sprint-MCI-Disney-Sony might merge into being. What kind of choice of access to the Web or variety of opinion or many-to-many broadcast capabilities will citizens have then? More important, will it put us back in the broadcast age, where a small number of people controlled the power to inform, influence, and persuade? What happens when the decentralized network infrastructure and freewheeling network economy collides with the continuing growth of mammoth, global, communication empires? We'll know soon. The experiment is just beginning, but well underway.

Which citizens are going along for the ride as broadband and wireless networks enmesh every part of the human environment? Who will benefit from the replacement of physical goods by knowledge products? Who will fail to benefit?

In recent years, strong evidence has emerged of a "digital divide" between poor and middle-class households, white and nonwhite households, in regard to ownership of personal computers and access to the Internet. As long as that divide continues to grow even while usage of new media grows explosively, no discussion of technology-assisted democracy can begin without mentioning the key question of who can afford to take advantage of new media.

One thing all of the people online have in common today is that we have access to a computer and an Internet account. There are 200 million Internet users in a global population of 6 billion. According to a 1999 report from the U.S. National Telecommunications and Information Administration, forty percent of American families have computers, but only eight percent of households earning less than $10,000 a year have PCs, and just three percent of that group have access to the Internet. The disparity between the highest and lowest income levels increased between 1997 and 1998. Urban households with incomes above $75,000 are more than 20 times more likely than low income rural households to have home Internet access.

On February 2, 2000, President Clinton toured a Washington, D.C., school with AOL CEO Steve Case and proposed spending more than $2 billion in tax breaks over 10 years as incentive for large-scale donations of computer gear and community technology centers. The idea of community technology centers where people can come to learn how to use Internet technology in their lives was a direct appropriation of an activist effort that has struggled on a shoestring for years, "CTCnet" <http://www2.ctcnet.org/ctcweb.asp>. Clinton also called for $150 million in federal funds to train teachers and $100 million for low-income urban and rural communities.

A group of Silicon Valley executives have initiated an organization called "ClickStart," a nonprofit devoted to connecting low-income people to the Internet, ideally with the help of government subsidies. For a copayment from the citizen of $5 per month, each participant in the proposed program would receive a $10 monthly voucher to buy hardware and Internet access from those vendors who make their products and services available at low rates to the program. The program resembles in some ways the Rural Electrification Administration, a federal program initiated in 1935 to bring electrical power and telephone service to rural regions.

The millions of lower-income citizens who might go online as the result of ClickStart's efforts will also increase tomorrow's market for high-tech product and services. From the point of view of the socially conscious Silicon Valley libertarian, this is a simple answer to social inequality that's also good business. They might be right. It's hard to imagine a future for public-private partnerships if there isn't something to gain for the private part of the enterprise.

Henry Ford paid his workers well enough, and made his Model T automobiles inexpensively enough that his employees could afford to buy them. In February 2000, perhaps taking a leaf from the founder, the Ford Motor Company announced that it would make a personal computer, color printer, and Internet access available to each of its 350,000 employees for $5/month (http://dailynews.yahoo.com/h/ap/20000203/ tc/ford_computers_2.html).

Nobody will know for years to come whether or not these programs or other government or nonprofit attempts to address the problem of the digital divide will actually be implemented, or whether they will succeed. The question remains: Will the advantages of online community be limited to those who can afford it at market rates? Is this a fundamental social inequality that must be addressed on all levels of community, society, and nation-state? Or is the idea of a "digital divide" simply a marketing device for describing fundamental economic disparity in terms of consumption of technology products? If our concern as a society is for the welfare of our poorest citizens, perhaps food and shelter should have higher priority on taxpayer money. Or perhaps the inherent wealth captured by Moore's Law and knowledge communities can create a rising economic tide that will lift all boats, as Silicon Valley libertarians claim.

This book was not intended to be a critique of global capitalism or the problems the culture industry poses for democracy, but the power and gravitational pull of corporate power and opinion-shaping cannot be ignored in any speculation about the future of media. The matter of the public sphere is a most serious one. Without liberty, all the other questions are irrelevant.

In an age in which most of the journalism seen by most of the world is produced by a subsidiary of one of a few multinational entertainment companies, the question of what will remain truly "public" about communications is central today. It might not make sense tomorrow. If a theme park is all you know, you aren't going to be asking where all the real parks are. In America, the idea of "public property" has grown increasingly unfashionable in the physical world of freeways, malls, and skyscrapers. Is there still space in cyberspace for public property, public discourse, public opinion that emerges from informed deliberation among citizens?

Which brings us to the most serious challenge to the original draft of this book, that virtual communities might be bogus substitutes for true civic engagement or outright directly harmful to the public sphere. In 1995, two scholars, Jan Fernback and Brad Thompson, presented a talk, "Computer-Mediated Communication and the American Collectivity," at the annual convention of the American Communication Association. With the permission of the authors, I've hosted it on my web site since then <http://www.Well.com/user/hlr/texts/VCcivil.html>.

How certain can I be, sitting at my desk, tapping on my keyboard, about the reality and limits of the Net's political effectiveness? Would I bet my liberty on the democratizing potential of the Net? I'll have to say that the answer has to be "no." But that doesn't mean that I am convinced that we should do nothing about the way Internet media are used. To agree in theory that an action can have no consequences is to create a self-fulfilling prophecy. Therefore, I frame their critique by stating my belief that until it is proved impossible, it is important for citizens to attempt to influence the public sphere by their use of many-to-many media.

Fernback and Thompson present several arguments, but to me, the most serious paragraphs are these:

For the reasons stated in the preceding section, the likely result of the development of virtual communities through CMC will be that a hegemonic culture will maintain its dominance. Certainly, it cannot be assumed that the current political and technical elites would willingly cede their position of dominance or knowingly sow the seeds of their own destruction.

Indeed, it seems most likely that the virtual public sphere brought about by CMC will serve a cathartic role, allowing the public to feel involved rather than to advance actual participation. Communities seem more likely to be formed or reinforced when action is needed, as when a country goes to war, rather than through discourse alone. Citizenship via cyberspace has not proven to be the panacea for the problems of democratic representation within American society; although communities of interest have been formed and strengthened (as noted previously) and have demonstrated a sense of solidarity, they have nevertheless contributed to the fragmented cultural and political landscape of the United States that is replete with identity politics and the unfulfilled promise of a renewed vita activa.

This research poses a larger question that has been addressed by other scholars (see Elshtain, 1995 and Lasch, 1995) which emphasizes the connection between the condition of fragmentation that exists within the American collectivity and democracy in theoretical terms. CMC does not, at this point, hold the promise of enhancing democracy because it promotes communities of interest that are just as narrowly defined as current public factions defined by identity (whether it be racial, sexual, or religious). Public discourse ends when identities become the last, unyielding basis for argumentation that strives ideally to achieve consensus based on a common good.

If nothing else, the expressions of hope and desire for new modes of communication such as CMC speak volumes about the failures of present and past technologies to help create a just and equitable society. Perhaps these failures should prompt us to re-examine why we continue to place so much hope in technology after so many disappointments. Ultimately, we believe, the hope placed in CMC is misplaced because change will occur not by altering the technology but by reforming the political and social environment from which that technology flows.

Finally, we suggest that the term virtual community is more indicative of an assemblage of people being "virtually" a community than being a real community in the nostalgic sense that advocates of CMC would seem to be endorsing. Our comments should not be construed as protests against the corruption of a term; we recognize that community has a dynamic meaning. Our concern is that the public is more likely to forget what it means to form a true community. If, on the other hand, virtual communities can lead to action, that may be the basis for the formation of real and lasting communities of interest. But until then, any change in the communications structure, such as the widespread use of CMC, is likely to be unsettling. Therefore, we must agree with Cooley, who wrote in 1909:

> [A] rapid improvement in the means of communication, as we see in our own time, supplies the basis for a larger and freer society, and yet it may, by disordering settled relations, and by fixing attention too much upon mechanical phases of progress, bring in conditions of confusion and injustice that are the opposite of free. (Cooley, 1909, p. 55)

Have we fixed "attention too much upon mechanical phases of progress?" Are we facing "conditions of confusion and injustice" at the same time that so many people are prospering and learning in the Net-enabled environment? The questions are sobering, but are the questions alone sufficient to prevent us from investigating further the potential of many-to-many media? So many experiments are springing up on the Internet to bridge the digital divide, to make tools available to citizens, teach media literacy. I would not stop watching these experiments to see if they work simply because good critics raise good questions about the democratizing potential of CMC. No theory can be any good if its effect is to prevent people from trying to improve their institutions. Are the critics themselves taking a deterministic stance that the hegemonic culture will maintain its dominance?

Perhaps the most useful point Fernback and Thompson raise is: "Ultimately, we believe, the hope placed in CMC is misplaced because change will occur not by altering the technology but by reforming the political and social environment from which that technology flows." If any population is to succeed in this alteration, are we to do it without tools? And assuming the success of such a reformation of the political and social environment, aren't we still faced with the challenge of learning how to use technology? Or are we to abandon the factories and office buildings and return to hunting and gathering? I agree, and must emphasize, that hopes placed in CMC or any technology are false hopes. Hopes must be placed in humans. I believe that knowing how to use tools is part of any successful human enterprise.

Fernback and Thompson's serious challenges must also be weighed in the light of reports such as Christopher Mele, who documents the story of how a group of low-income residents of public housing, all African-American women, used online communications to transform and empower the residents association in a two-year battle with the housing authority: "Once wired, it is difficult to predict the effects of online communication for collective action conducted by disempowered groups. For the women activists at Jervay, their connection to the Internet peeled away some of the historic and systematic layers that blanketed access to essential information. Whether it translates to long-term success is perhaps less important than the positive effect upon the activist role of the women themselves" (Mele, 1999).

The power to publish and communicate has no magical ability to make democracy happen. Only people can do that. No tool can make democracy happen without the actions of millions of people—but those millions of people won't succeed without the right tools. Most of what needs to be done has to be done face to face, person to person—civic engagement means dealing with your neighbors in the world where your body lives. But an important part of the work to be done will be mediated by new communication technologies. We need to relearn and continue to teach the communication skills necessary for maintaining healthy democracies.

Information sources and communication media that were until recently the province of the wealthy and powerful are used daily by millions. Discourse among informed citizens can be improved, revived, restored to some degree of influence—but only if a sufficient number of people learn how to use communication tools properly, and apply them to real-world political problem-solving. Surely, this opportunity is worthy of serious consideration. Surely, we owe it to ourselves to make an effort to discover whether the charges of Fernback and Thompson and other critics are true in practice as well as theory.

The global corporations that have consolidated control of distribution of news and entertainment will continue to command attention, reap profits, and exert influence. But they are no longer the only game in town. If there is one question that lies at the foundation of the uncertainty about the Internet's future it is whether the technical democratization of publishing will prove to be a credible challenge to existing publishing interests.

I believe the publicness of democracy has been eroded, for the reasons Neil Postman cited in *Amusing Ourselves to Death* (Postman, 1985): The immense power of television as a broadcaster of emotion-laden images, combined with the ownership of more and more news media by fewer and fewer global entertainment conglomerates, has reduced much public discourse, including discussions of vital issues, to soundbites and barrages of images.

In theory and a few practical examples, centralized opinion-shaping mechanisms are challenged by the decentralization afforded by many-to-many media. But that is far from saying that the future will be less manipulated and more freely chosen by informed citizens. Much remains to be done for that rosy scenario to become a reality.

Theories and opinions about the Internet are plentiful. A good question to ask is how many real online tools exist for citizens to use today? Are there examples of successful experiments in online civic involvement that ought to be widely replicated? As a definition of " civic involvement," I suggest the one offered in Robert Wuthnow's *Loose Connections: Joining Together in America's Fragmented Communities*: "Broadly conceived, civic involvement consists in participation in social activities that either mediate between citizens and government or provide ways for citizens to pursue common objectives with or without the help of government."

The public sphere is where Kim Alexander operates when her organization, the California Voter's Foundation <http://www.calvoter.org /aboutcvf.html>, uses email to organize a campaign to require political candidates to put their financial disclosures on the Internet. Civic involvement is what Paul Resnick and his students are trying to foster when they go door to door in their neighborhoods in Ann Arbor, Michigan, creating web pages and email lists intended to help people who live on the same block get to know one another <http://www.whothat.org>. The public sphere is what Steven Clift and colleagues at the Minnesota E-Democracy project <http://www.e-democracy.org> seek to extend when they bring candidates for state office online to publish position statements and field questions from citizens. A little investigation reveals that dozens, probably hundreds, of profit-making and nonprofit enterprises are experimenting with different tools for civic involvement. Among the most notable are:

• CapAdvantage <http://www.capitoladvantage.com/> for communication with officials, and other citizens. Their page, titled "Tools for Online Grassroots Advocacy and Mobilization," offers a comprehensive guide to Congressional publications, directories to identify state and national congressional representatives. spot news and issues tracking.

• E-The People <http://www.ethepeople.com/> for petitions. "Welcome to America's Interactive Town Hall: Where Active Citizens Connect with Their Government and Each Other"

If your car is swallowed up by a pothole the size of Poughkeepsie, E-The People can help you find the person you need to tell about it. Simply come to our site, click on "roads and transportation," type in your address and we'll forward your note to the right officials in your city. And if your public works commissioner doesn't have Internet access, we'll convert your concern to a fax! Are you an organizer? With E-The People, you can start a petition about the same pothole and contact 10 neighbors to sign it—all on one site.

• Freedom Forum <http://www.freedomforum.org/> is a good example of vibrant discussion of political issues via message boards, along with Internet radio and news on rights. "The Freedom Forum is a nonpartisan, international foundation dedicated to free press, free speech and free spirit for all people."

• Civic Practices Network <http://www.cpn.org/> describes itself thus: "Born of the movement for a "new citizenship" and "civic revitalization," CPN is a collaborative and nonpartisan project dedicated to bringing practical tools for public problem solving into community and institutional settings across America."

• The title of the Freespeech.org page <http://www.freespeech.org/>. is "Free Speech Internet Television."

• VolunteerMatch <http://www.volunteermatch.org) matches volunteers with opportunities, enables nonprofit organizations and potential volunteers to get together. Since 1987, CompuMentor (http://www.compumentor.org/> has provided volunteer-based technology assistance to nonprofits.

• National Strategy for Nonprofit Technology <http://www.nten.org/nsnt.htm> is "a leadership network of nonprofit staff members, funders, and technology assistance providers working together to analyze the technology needs of the nonprofit sector, and to develop a blueprint for how it can use technology more effectively and creatively."

• Guidestar <http://www.guidestar.org> is a clearinghouse for financial information: "Find information on the activities and finances of more than 650,000 nonprofit organizations, the latest news on philanthropy, and resources for donors and nonprofits."

• While many big organizations are incorporating donation activities into their web sites, smaller sites are going with a donation service like i-charity <http://www.i-charity.net/>: "Free Internet fundraising service and online donations portal."

• Cause-related marketing type services like GreaterGood <http://www. greatergood.com/> provide online consumers the ability to send a portion of product purchase prices to designated organizations: "Shop where it matters."

• VoxCap <http://www.voxcap.com> aggregates tools and resources for online civic engagement as well as for "building a community of engaged citizens, where social capital can be accumulated and brought to bear," according to Jeff Fisher, VoxCap's Director of Community Development.

• Two enterprising political satirists quit their jobs in the winter of 2000 and hit the road in a van, following the early stages of the presidential campaign from the road, updating their web site daily from their own zany and well-informed angle. The site <http://www.y2kwhistlestop .com/> is well designed and informative as well as funny. Perhaps political journalism might follow their lead and loosen up.

• The Association for Community Networking <http://www.bcn.boulder.co.us/afcn/> is a community of interest and support for the hundreds of people working to use Internet communications to improve social capital in face to face communities.

• The Living Constitution Society <http://www.wethepeople.org> is dedicated to creating a continuous flow of interrelationship between government, industry, academia, citizens, and nonprofit organizations.

If the public sphere is where people act as citizens by discussing the issues that concern them, and civil society is the general name for the associations that citizens organize for social, charitable, and political purposes, the name for the common wealth that they gain from acting cooperatively, in concert, rather than competitively as individuals seeking to maximize individual gain, is "social capital."

Civic Practices Network defines social capital this way (http://www. cpn.org/sections/tools/models/social_capital.html):

Social capital refers to those stocks of social trust, norms and networks that people can draw upon to solve common problems. Networks of civic engagement, such as neighborhood associations, sports clubs, and cooperatives, are an essential form of social capital, and the denser these networks, the more likely that members of a community will cooperate for mutual benefit. This is so, even in the face of persistent problems of collective action (tragedy of the commons, prisoner's dilemma, etc.), because networks of civic engagement:

• foster sturdy norms of generalized reciprocity by creating expectations that favors given now will be returned later;

• facilitate coordination and communication, and thus create channels through which information about the trustworthiness of other individuals and groups can flow, and be tested and verified;

• embody past success at collaboration, which can serve as a cultural template for future collaboration on other kinds of problems;

• increase the potential risks to those who act opportunistically that they will not share in the benefits of current and future transactions.

Social capital is productive, since two farmers exchanging tools can get more work done with less physical capital; rotating credit associations can generate pools of financial capital for increased entrepreneurial activity; and job searches can be more efficient if information is embedded in social networks. Social capital also tends to cumulate when it is used, and be depleted when not, thus creating the possibility of both virtuous and vicious cycles that manifest themselves in highly civic and uncivic communities.

The question of how to measure social capital is central to understanding the health of the public sphere. Indeed, as I will show later, there are those who question the idea that the social should be considered to be a form of capital. In an influential article, "Bowling Alone: America's Declining Social Capital" (*Journal of Democracy* 6:1, January 1995, 65–78), Robert Putnam documented a broad decline in civic engagement and social participation in the United States over the past 35 years. Citizens vote less, go to church less, discuss government with their neighbors less, are members of fewer voluntary organizations, have fewer dinner parties, and generally get together less for civic and social purposes. Putnam argues that this social disengagement is having major consequences for the social fabric and for individual lives. At the societal level, social disengagement is associated with more corrupt, less efficient government and more crime. When citizens are involved in civic life, their schools run better, their politicians are more responsive, and their streets are safer. At the individual level, social disengagement is associated with poor quality of life and diminished physical and psychological health. When people have more social contact, they are happier and healthier, physically and mentally

Putnam concluded his article prescriptively:

In the established democracies, ironically, growing numbers of citizens are questioning the effectiveness of their public institutions at the very moment when liberal democracy has swept the battlefield, both ideologically and geopolitically. In America, at least, there is reason to suspect that this democratic disarray may be linked to a broad and continuing erosion of civic engagement that began a quarter-century ago. High on our scholarly agenda should be the question of whether a comparable erosion of social capital may be under way in other advanced democracies, perhaps in different institutional and behavioral guises. High on America's agenda should be the question of how to reverse these adverse trends in social connectedness, thus restoring civic engagement and civic trust.

The questions raised Putnam's articles are about as serious as questions get: Is the social "glue" that holds together democratic societies going to dissolve as we retreat from civic participation into more private pursuits? If, as Putnam proposed in a follow-up article, "The Strange Disappearance of Civic America," (PS, American Political Science Association, winter 1996), the diffusion of television through the population over the past forty years was strongly correlated with the disintegration of civic participation during that time, it is indeed important to ask now which way the Internet might push us in the future—toward or away from authentic community and deep personal ties. Or are we using the wrong assumptions and terminology when addressing the way civic practices are changing, the way Wellman and Cerulo believe we are misframing social science research in cyberspace?

Another contemporary student of community, also a Harvard professor, Robert Wuthnow, recently wrote a book, *Loose Connections: Joining Together in America's Fragmented Communities* (Cambridge: Harvard University Press, 1998), that addresses the way social affiliations seem to be changing. These paragraphs describing the book <http://hupress.harvard.edu/Fall98/catalog/loose_connect.html> summarize Wuthnow's thesis, offering an alternative to Putnam's view of the changes that seem to be taking place:

It has become common to lament Americans' tendency to pursue individual interests apart from any institutional association. But to those who charge that Americans are at home watching television rather than getting involved in their communities, Robert Wuthnow answers that while certain kinds of civic engagement may be declining, innovative new forms are taking their place.

Acknowledging that there has been a significant change in group affiliations—away from traditional civic organizations—Wuthnow shows that there has been a corresponding movement toward affiliations that respond to individual needs and collective concerns. Many Americans are finding new and original ways to help one another through short-term task-oriented networks. Some are combining occupational skills with community interests in nonprofit and voluntary associations. Others use communication technologies, such as the World Wide Web, to connect with like-minded people in distant locations. And people are joining less formal associations, such as support groups and lobbying efforts, within their home communities.

People are still connected, but because of the realities of daily life, they form "loose connections." These more fluid groups are better suited to dealing with today's needs than the fraternal orders and ladies' auxiliaries of the past. Wuthnow looks at the challenges that must be faced if these innovative forms of civic involvement are to flourish, and calls for resources to be made available to strengthen the more constructive and civic dimensions of these organizations.

Defining, measuring, valuing, growing, and preserving "social capital" is hotly disputed territory. A group from the University of Victoria, British Columbia, maintains a literature review online: "Space Between the Market and the State: A Social Capital Literature Review and Conceptual Framework" at <http://web.uvic.ca/cpss/npsri/lit_rev.html.> The World Bank has a social capital web site at <http://www.worldbank.org/poverty/scapital/index.htm>. The British Columbia group defines social capital as: "the intangible social features of community life—such as trust and co-operation between individuals and within groups, actions and behaviour expected from community members, networks of interaction between community members, and actions taken by community members for reasons other than financial motives or legal obligations—that can potentially contribute to the wellbeing of that community."

In a recent online exchange, Christopher London pointed out that this economic definition of one of the most uniquely human traits, the ability to cooperate, presupposes a certain economic worldview, free-market capitalism:

Marx argued that in capitalist social relations it is possible for social life to be reduced to the mere exchange of tokens of exchange value and for the relationship between the things that people produce and the people themselves to get reversed. Rather than products existing to serve human needs, humans exist to serve products, that is, to make products come to life so that they may circulate freely in a market. Built into this monetary and exchange system is the subordination of masses of people, and their figurative and often literal degradation, so that the product of their labor may be profitably circulated by others. For capital to exist entails a host of social (institutional and cultural) arrangements to make this circulation of "surplus value" continue and for it to be characterized by continuous growth. This is a massive simplification, but I think it applies to the issue of social capital because in treating social relations as "stocks" that can be "accumulated," the relations themselves are treated as mere means to an end: that of (physical or financial) capital accumulation. Though the social capital people claim to be putting social relations at the center of economic relations (and so supposedly illustrate that economic relations are social through and through), they don't do that at all. Rather, they reduce social relations to just another factor in an economic calculation. It's culturally premised on the idea that people come to their social relations only by thinking in terms of "what can I get out of this" and not in terms of "what do these people mean to me and me to them." (London, 2000)

The phrase "commodification of community" has been used by some social critics of virtual community. London pointed me to this passage from Marx's *Capital* in which Marx introduces (in colorful language) the notion that capitalism can turn human relations into commodities:

A commodity appears, at first sight, a very trivial thing, and easily understood. Its analysis shows that it is, in reality, a very queer thing, abounding in metaphysical subtleties and theological niceties. So far as it is a value in use, there is nothing mysterious about it, whether we consider it from the point of view that by its properties it is capable of satisfying human wants, or from the point that those properties are the product of human labour. It is as clear as noon-day, that man, by his industry, changes the forms of the materials furnished by Nature, in such a way as to make them useful to him. The form of wood, for instance, is altered, by making a table out of it. Yet, for all that, the table continues to be that common, every-day thing, wood. But, so soon as it steps forth as a commodity, it is changed into something transcendent. It not only stands with its feet on the ground, but, in relation to all other commodities, it stands on its head, and evolves out of its wooden brain grotesque ideas, far more wonderful than "table-turning" ever was.

* * *

A commodity is therefore a mysterious thing, simply because in it the social character of men's labour appears to them as an objective character stamped upon the product of that labour; because the relation of the producers to the sum total of their own labour is presented to them as a social relation, existing not between themselves, but between the products of their labour. This is the reason why the products of labour become commodities, social things whose qualities are at the same time perceptible and imperceptible by the senses. In the same way the light from an object is perceived by us not as the subjective excitation of our optic nerve, but as the objective form of something outside the eye itself. But, in the act of seeing, there is at all events, an actual passage of light from one thing to another, from the external object to the eye. There is a physical relation between physical things. But it is different with commodities. There, the existence of the things qua commodities, and the value-relation between the products of labour which stamps them as commodities, have absolutely no connexion with their physical properties and with the material relations arising therefrom. There it is a definite social relation between men, that assumes, in their eyes, the fantastic form of a relation between things. In order, therefore, to find an analogy, we must have recourse to the mist-enveloped regions of the religious world. In that world the productions of the human brain appear as independent beings endowed with life, and entering into relation both with one another and the human race. So it is in the world of commodities with the products of men's hands. This I call the Fetishism which attaches itself to the products of labour, so soon as they are produced as commodities, and which is therefore inseparable from the production of commodities. This Fetishism of commodities has its origin, as the foregoing analysis has already shown, in the peculiar social character of the labour that produces them. (Marx, 1987, 76–77)

Outlining a program for measuring the health of civil society and defining social capital in a way that doesn't transform human relationships into commodities is beyond the scope of this book. However, it is at the very heart of the kinds of discussions that must take place on a broad basis, online and offline, among millions of people. It is in the service of this broad, citizen-driven, democratic discourse that online tools for publishing and communicating hold out a hope. If online community is NOT a commodity, it is only because people work to make it so. The hope I hold out for myself and suggest to others is that people will accomplish a task using a tool. Hope should not be vested in the tool itself. One important way of using tools wisely is informed government regulation. A tax break for corporations that donate to the public sphere, for example, might do more good than all the rhetoric and all the books decrying the deterioration of civic engagement. Consider the following scenario, not as a recipe for utopia, but a thought-experiment.

A tiny proportion of the gargantuan profits reaped by telecommunications service providers could be contributed to a well-managed fund (with its own budget and expenditures open for public inspection) that insures that every citizen has access to publicly available terminals, a free email account, and free access to introductory classes on citizen use of the Net. In a world where everyone has affordable access and citizens become actively engaged in informing themselves and communicating with one another, will it be possible to make government more responsive to citizen needs—and perhaps more responsible to the public trust? All proceedings and filings at the city, state, and national level could be made available to all citizens in dynamically updated databases, with easy-to-use web interfaces. GIS systems could enable citizens to visualize the impacts of proposed development on regional cultural and ecosystems. We could know when our legislators trade stock in companies their legislation affects.

The scenario offered in the previous paragraph is offered as an example of what I believe we should work to build, not as an unattainably ideal society expected to emerge magically from technology. There is no guarantee that the potential power of many-to-many communications will make a difference in political battles about the shape of our future. Indeed, the odds are against a media-literate population seizing the opportunities the Internet offers. But I believe the opportunity for leverage is there, waiting to be seized, ignored, or mishandled. The hegemony of culture, power, and capital that critics from Marx to Fernback and Thompson describe is a potent force to be reckoned with. But if we don't try to make a difference in the way tools are used and people are treated, we definitely *won't* make a difference.

The first step in acting effectively is to know what you are acting on. Collectively, we know only a small amount about human behavior in social cyberspaces. We need to know a lot more. I hope that this chapter, and the updated bibliography, helps inspire and orient those who pursue that knowledge, debate its meaning, and put it into action in meaningful ways.

Afterword (1994)

When *The Virtual Community* went to press in the summer of 1993, the subtitle reflected the zeitgeist of that moment—"homesteading on the electronic frontier." By the time the book arrived in bookstores in November 1993, the media were buzzing about something called "the information superhighway." By the beginning of 1994, the information superhighway metaphor had saturated mass-culture.

The heretofore underground online subculture was reported, hyped, spoofed, incisively analyzed, and grossly misinterpreted by the networks and national news magazines, intellectual and technical publications, *Doonesbury* gags and cartoons in the *New Yorker*, jokes on sit-coms—the modern American media food-chain. In a few months, the public image of cyberspace changed from homesteaders on the frontier to highway developers. (By mid-1994, Net cognoscenti were calling it "the infobahn.")

The public is waking up. So are the biggest players in the telecommunications industry. Something has happened recently in the minds of the people who control the largest communications and entertainment corporations in the world, something significant enough to shape the market strategies of NTT and Time-Warner, Microsoft and Sprint, Viacom and Disney, Apple and IBM.

The grassroots movements described in *The Virtual Community* are beginning to intersect with movements that originated in board rooms and government offices. The big players in business and government are newer at CMC than the Internet pioneers and BBSers, but they bring a lot more weight to bear on the market and on political regimes when they devote their resources to it.

When a representative of a regional Bell operating company called me in the summer of 1992 to find out whether his CEO ought to pay attention to (then Senator) Albert Gore's National Education and Research Network legislation, I was astonished to realize that the highest levels of American telecommunications industries had not awakened to the revolution that was overtaking them, an impression that grew stronger as I talked with managers in other telecommunications companies. Then it all changed rapidly.

By the summer of 1993, telephone companies were merging and flirting with cable companies, software companies were entering joint ventures with entertainment companies, newspapers were establishing media laboratories.

Events related to the emergence of a new global communications infrastructure have been moving rapidly in Japan, as well as in the US—in fact, events have been moving rapidly in Japan *because* events have been moving rapidly in the US. Computer networks and virtual communities were futuristic fantasies when I talked about them with NTT researchers two years ago. Researchers were eager to speculate, but many-to-many communications technology wasn't part of their companies' business strategy.

Japan's largest players seem to have restructured their entire global telecommunications strategy in response to America's information superhighway initiative. NTT researchers told me in 1994 that their company was refocusing its energies on Internet-like interactive services to individuals, rather than just the few-to-many applications for high-bandwidth networks they had been developing previously.

The battle over whether Japan joins the Net in a big way—which was still unpredictably far in the future when Izumi Aizu, Joichi Ito, and I discussed it two years ago—broke out in earnest in late 1993, when TWICS drew the ire of a government ministry by offering full worldwide Internet access to all subscribers. Their access was suddenly cut off, and restored after unexpected publicity. A power struggle between the old guard, with its bureaucratic networks in Tokyo ministries, and the grassroots Internet activists in the Universities and virtual communities elsewhere in Japan, was joined. In the case of TWICS, the old guard didn't listen, and when the young generation of activists tried to end-run them, the old boys got angry.

When I attended my third Hypernetwork Conference in Oita, in 1994, COARA had become an Internet site, Governor Hiramatsu talked of adding "Broadband ISDN" services (billions of bits per second) to Oita Prefecture's free network, and the research managers from techno-Japan, Inc., who had in years past listened to me futurize about citizen-to-citizen, many-to-many networks at previous conferences, were joined by their bosses, who were talking openly about finding their companies' places in the emerging "global information superhighway."

Two powerful forces drove the rapid emergence of the superhighway notion in 1994. First, the proposed mergers of multi-billion dollar companies, and sometimes their decisions not to merge, as happened to Bell Atlantic and TCI, are always news. Tens of billions of dollars start to add up to real money, not just in the minds of the public who read about it in the newspaper, but in the minds of the people who control companies. It doesn't matter that most people in the world had never heard of networked desktop communications before last year; everybody in the world understands what tens of billions of dollars means.

The second driving force behind the superhighway idea continued to be Vice-President Gore. In late 1993, the Clinton-Gore administration began to present their vision, to be backed up by legislative and regulatory actions, of a "National Information Infrastructure"—known inside the beltway as "the NII." But the US government's entry into the discussion was punctuated by continuing front-page news from the business world.

The Bell-Atlantic/TCI proposed merger galvanized public attention for months. In early 1994, in the wake of an FCC-imposed cut in cable rates, the merging parties called off the deal. Barely had the news stories about the failure of the merger begun to fade when in March, 1994, the dark prince of cyberspace, Bill Gates, the young Microsoft software magnate, announced he was teaming up with another very rich young boy-wizard of the info-industry, Craig McCaw. McCaw had just sold his cellular communications company, and Gates was positioning Microsoft for the new era.

The Gates-McCaw company, Teledesic, was set up to bypass the cables and fiber optics the other companies were fighting over. Gates and McCaw proposed making voice communications and enhanced data services available worldwide (especially in formerly hard-to-reach areas) through a network of 840 low-orbit satellites that would transfer information to and from the earth-bound portion of the Net via ultra-high radio frequencies.

One week after the Gates-McCaw announcement, NTT (Nippon Telephone and Telegraph) announced a partnership with Gates to develop services "to allow users to access multimedia information on a communications network in Japan," according to a March 24 Reuters announcement. By the end of 1994, Gates has emerged as the man to watch. The reason Gates is feared by those who favor wide-open competition and fear monopoly-like control of the new media is that all the other players, with their billions of dollars and global technical infrastructures, don't understand and appreciate the way Bill Gates does the unique characteristics of the new medium emerging from the convergence of computing and communications.

Gates has the understanding, the platform, the money, the power, and the will to go for a dominant position in the emerging industry, the way he achieved a dominant position in the personal computer software industry. Whether or not he manages to make himself the John D. Rockefeller of cyberspace, Bill Gates rang the bell that woke up the big money. It looks like he plans to keep ringing it.

Vice President Gore seemed to have listened to both the big money and the grassroots activists, judging from the proposals Gore outlined in a speech to the National Press Club in December, 1993. He talked about a National Information Infrastructure that would be a platform for economic growth and competition, but would also serve the public good. Gore pledged the Clinton-Gore administration to five "guiding principles."

The administration, Gore proclaimed, would act through legislative and regulatory initiatives to encourage private investment, provide and protect competition, provide open access to the network, avoid creating information "haves and have-nots," and encourage flexible and responsive government action.

The first principle represented a major policy shift. As an advocate of NREN in the Senate, Gore had spoken forcefully for a strong government role in building and regulating the new technology. In the early days of the Clinton-Gore administration, Gore clashed with industry figures over the role of the government in the emerging media. Gore was signalling a policy shift when he emphasized in his Press Club speech that private industry was going to build the new infrastructure. When Gore promised to remove some of the regulations that restrained cable and telephone companies from certain kinds of services, he was offering to deregulate something that had remained tightly controlled even during the deregulatory heyday of Reagan and Bush.

If the first principle could have been dictated by TCI's Tom Malone or Microsoft's Bill Gates, the second principle, a commitment to "protect competition," could have been written by Mitch Kapor. In fact, Gore acknowledged Kapor, the Electronic Frontier Foundation, and the EFF's "Open Platform" proposal in his declaration of principles. The vice-president agreed with the industrialists that they should be cut loose to compete and build something far too big for the government to build or administer. But immediately after that, with his second guiding principle, Gore agreed with the Open Platform activists that the huge players in the telecommunications marketplace should be prevented from controlling the content of the communications they carry, and should be restrained from using their wealth to squeeze out competition from entrepreneurs and other smaller businesses.

By combining the offer to deregulate companies that were hungry to invest big money in the new media with a commitment on the part of the Administration to protect competition, Gore proposed a compromise that was strongly influenced by the political realities of 1994. From the Administration side, Gore knew that if they did not make the NII happen before the next election, the telecommunications industry's biggest players would be tempted to wait for the possibility of a Republican administration in 1997 that presumably would deregulate without restraining the biggest players.

From the industry side of the same problem, the technology and the industry were moving too quickly for major players to hesitate for long. The outcome of the next presidential election is always far from clear when there are still 2 years until the next election. And a lot can happen in a volatile global industry. Especially now that the Japanese are starting to wise up.

Gore stressed, in his third guiding principle, the need to design an information infrastructure that would not further exacerbate the split between the information-and-education haves and have-nots. He called upon the private sector to take the initiative in helping pay for extending the information highway into every school, library, and hospital in America. Those who have hopes of using CMC technology as a tool for restoring community and conviviality applauded this point.

Evidence of great economic disparities and hardships by the less well-educated is not disputed. Everybody knows that a two-tiered society is in trouble and headed for bigger trouble. It is more cost-effective to educate people than to incarcerate them later. But nobody wants to pay for it. Perhaps Gore will succeed in luring the private sector into putting up a few billion to extend their infrastructure to a few repositories of public interest. It seems certain that taxpayers aren't going to pay for it, even though an equal-access superhighway might sound like a good idea in theory.

The "flexible and responsive government action" mentioned by Gore was the vaguest of the principles, but it was an acknowledgement that a major overhaul of communications policy is underway at the same time that the technological basis for the regulated industries is itself changing: cable television companies turn out to be high-bandwidth communication carriers that want to add voice and data communications to their entertainment fare, and telephone companies want to provide interactive multimedia point-click-and buy- services.

To complicate the picture, an "interactive television" vision of the new media emerged in 1994 as a Hollywood-Madison Avenue-Silicon Valley hybrid that might be a huge ball of hype or the beginning of yet another epic wealth-gathering scheme: imagine stopping the action in a sit-com or movie-of-the-week, zooming in on an actor's sweater, clicking on it to get more information, and clicking on it again to buy it and arrange shipping. The final digital commodification of entertainment will open vast new horizons to the consumer society via the same technologies that online activists can use for political work and educators employ to link remote classrooms and online libraries. Everything is happening at once. A good time to be flexible.

Although Gore acknowledged the EFF Open Platform vision in regard to the importance of competitiveness in the telecommunications market, he and the administration very quickly clashed about the matter of allowing citizens to have access to strong encryption. The "Clipper Chip" proposal that Clinton inherited from a multi-year National Security Agency effort, began to sound more sinister as more was disclosed about it. The

Clipper Chip is an encryption technology built into a microchip that can be manufactured in telephones and other communication devices. People who use Clipper-equipped devices can engage in secure communications.

The fly in the ointment is that the Federal Government holds the keys to a backdoor to everybody's Clipper Chip, which it can use to decode private conversations whenever it needs to defend national security. Remember J. Edgar Hoover? Wouldn't he have enjoyed that. Back to the FBI in a moment—they are indeed in the game.

The most ominous thing about the Clipper proposal, to many, is the fact that the government doesn't have to get the key to your private communications to learn a lot about you; Clipper devices emit identification signals that allow government traffic analysts to track where and when the devices were used. Clipper defenders pointed out that the government wasn't restraining people from using stronger forms of encryption, but citizen-encryption advocates, like gun-owners, feel like they are on a slippery slope. By creating a de facto standard through the purchasing power of the Federal Government, the administration can make Clipper an accepted part of the landscape before most people understand what it is.

Civil libertarians point out that it is incumbent upon the government to make a case for taking any right that belongs to citizens, not upon the citizens to make a case for restraining the government. The fact that encryption involves esoteric mathematics doesn't help the issue. It will take time, at best, to explain the implications of these technical issues to the citizens whose liberties will be affected.

Along with the Clipper proposal put forward by the Clinton-Gore administration in 1993 and pushed in 1994 despite wide opposition from cryptography experts, civil libertarians, and mainstream business-people, was the revival of the "Digital Telephony" Bill. The FBI was at it again, trying to force the telephone companies to install FBI-operable central snooping power in the new digital communications networks. Remember the Panopticon? Keep in mind that less than 1000 legal wire-taps are granted every year for investigation of serious crimes, out of the millions of crimes and billions of conversations. Instead of obtaining a court order and going to the telephone company to install a tap, the FBI would like the telephone company to, in effect, give them the power to tap any conversation they deem necessary. Everything is happening at once. The Net is liberating; the Net is a trap.

John Perry Barlow "shmoozed" his way onto Air Force Two after Gore made a much-publicised follow-up to his Press Club speech at an "Information Superhighway Summit" in early 1994. Gore evaded his questions about the civil liberty implications of Clipper and Digital Telephony. And White House staffers who had been friendlier about other NII issues, began to use the "if you knew what we know" justification for sticking with a policy that could put a national digital surveillance state into place. It wasn't the Clinton administration that Barlow, the Wyoming libertarian, feared—it was putting certain kinds of power in the hands of any government.

Barlow responded with a hot rant, which proliferated through the Net for weeks before it appeared in print in *Wired* magazine: "... we could shortly find ourselves under a government that would have the automated ability to log the time, origin, and recipient of every call we made, could track our physical whereabouts continuously, could keep better account of our financial transactions than we do, and all without a court-ordered warrant. Talk about crime prevention!"

"Worse, under some vaguely defined and surely mutable "legal authority," they also would be able to listen to our calls and read our e-mail without having to do any backyard rewiring. They wouldn't need any permission at all to monitor overseas calls."

"If there's going to be a fight, I'd rather it be with this government than the one we'd likely face on that hard day."

"Hey, I've never been a paranoid before. It has always seemed to me that most governments are too incompetent to keep a good plot strung together all the way to quitting time. But I am now very nervous about the government of the United States of America."

"Because Bill 'n' Al, whatever their other new-paradigm virtues, have allowed the old-paradigm trogs of the Guardian Class to define as their highest duty the defense of America against an enemy that exists primarily in the imagination—and is therefore capable of anything."

"To assure absolute safety against such an enemy, there is no limit to the liberties we will eventually be asked to sacrifice. And, with a Clipper Chip in every phone, there will certainly be no technical limit on their ability to enforce those sacrifices."

"In his Los Angeles speech, Gore called the development of the NII "a revolution." And it is a revolutionary war we are engaged in here.

Clipper is a last ditch attempt by the United States, the last great power from the old Industrial Era, to establish imperial control over cyberspace. If they win, the most liberating development in the history of humankind could become, instead, the surveillance system that will monitor our grandchildren's morality. We can be better ancestors than that."

Just as CMC decentralizes control of communication and publication, it decentralizes surveillance, as well. Before we argue about the best way to build utopia, it might be time for citizens to unite against the encroachments of tyranny in the guise of technology. Tell-tale chips are embedded in our purchases, bar-codes track our smallest transaction, electronic telltales in our credit-cards and telephones broadcast our location and activities, and powerful, high bandwidth information superhighways carry information into—and out of—our homes. If there is a chance to stop the installation of a Panoptic super-surveillance state, that time is before it is installed. If Barlow is to be believed, that time is now.

Along with the economic and political infrastructures and the enabling technologies, the human interface to the Net is changing rapidly. It took Joi Ito, on my last trip to Tokyo, to show me the visible window into the Net. What had previously been a silent alphanumeric abstraction for years popped into full sensory reality for me.

Joichi Ito's family stone might record the names of 27 generations, but Joi is a distinctly 21st century lad. After a late dinner in Roppongi, on a rare snowy night in Tokyo in early 1994, we went to his apartment to kill some time on the Net before the Tokyo rave scene woke up. A Mosaic page painted itself on his PowerBook screen. Along the left side were postage-stamp pictures of galaxies and pop groups. Next to the pix were headlines and subheads. Even before he issued a command, I knew I was looking at a new world. I literally jumped, the first time Joi pointed at the picture of a pop group and music came out of his computer's speaker.

"I've been teaching myself hypertext markup language," he remarked. Joi is always teaching himself something I've never heard about before. This language is a code that gives him the power to broadcast video, graphics, and text stored on his computer to tens of millions of Internet nodes.

I remember my first sight of a Macintosh in 1984. I remember the first time I logged onto the WELL in 1985. I remember the vertigo of reading through the names of 3000 newsgroups. I've learned to recognize those moments when a technological breakthrough sucks us all into a new dimension. Mosaic in Joi's hands had that instantly-recognizable look of the future to it. Mosaic might be the "killer app"—the unexpected application of a technology that drives the technology to become a mass-medium, like spreadsheets were for personal computers. It definitely has a beat you can dance to.

Outside Joi Ito's apartment, in the streets of Harajuku, Tokyo teenagers were cycling through a well-designed media loop: Fashion designers and retailers decide what trend to sell next month, their new look is trans-mitted at precisely-timed intervals to the appropriate tribes via popular magazines and ""idol" singers. Joi Ito, however, rolls his own media.

A Mosaic home page looks like the table of contents from a full-color, slick-paper magazine. There are menus directing you to some of Joi's personal information—multimedia self-portraits. There's a video of Joi jumping out of an airplane. But Joi wanted to soar higher.

"First, let's see space," he said, and Joi clicked on the menu item for "Hubble Pictures." It took a minute to suck down the image from its home on a computer 15 time zones away. Then a detailed color image of a distant galaxy, beamed to Earth from the Hubble Space Telescope that morning, popped up on his screen.

"How about the weather?" I pick one of the little pictures of parts of planet Earth—the North Pacific, because that's where we were at that moment. In a few seconds, I was watching a weather movie on the screen, beamed down from a satellite an hour ago.

MTV.COM's server was cool. This was a digital outpost that MTV had set up on the Internet. Clicking on an icon on Joi's screen connected his computer in Tokyo to MTV's Internet site in the U.S. I browsed album covers, tried a few samples of the songs on the albums. There's a short video of a VJ (I guess he's now an "EJ") blasting off in a rocket ship, to the accompaniment of Elton John's "Rocketman."

Joi Ito's Tomogaya is a Net-zine, an online, multimedia version of an only slightly older cultural phenomenon that bubbles up from popula-tions that have access to communications technology. Zines came from a generation who don't care about the mass-media. Zinesters want to get together with a few friends, jam with xerox machines and computer paint programs, print it out at night on the boss's laser printer, and put it out there for a select cult audience.

Joi and his nethead friends have their own ideas of where techno-culture is headed. They want to play the Net like their parents wanted to play electric guitar. I watch where they're pointing because they might know something about where we're going.

The battle for the shape of the Net is joined. Part of the battle is a battle of dollars and power, but the great lever is still *understanding*—if enough people can understand what is happening, I still believe that we can have an influence. Whether we live in a Panoptic or Democratic Net ten years from now depends, in no small measure, on what you and I know and do now. The outcome remains uncertain. What the Net will become is still, in large part, up to us.

Bibliography

Adorno, T. W., and M. Horkheimer. *The Culture Industry: Enlightenment as Mass Deception. In The Dialectic of Enlightenment*, trans. John Cumming. New York: Herder and Herder, 1972.

Agre, P. E., and D. Schuler, eds. *Reinventing Technology, Rediscovering Community: Critical Studies in Computing as a Social Practice*. Stamford, Conn.: Ablex Publishing Corporation, 1997.

Agres, C., D. Edberg, and M. Igbaria. "Transformation to Virtual Societies: Forces and Issues." *The Information Society* 14, no. 2 (1998): 71–82.

Allison, Jay. "Vigil." *Whole Earth Review* 75 (Summer 1992): 4.

Amara, Roy, John Smith, Murray Turoff, and Jacques Vallee. "Computerized Conferencing, a New Medium." *Mosaic* (National Science Foundation) (January–February 1976).

Anderson, Benedict. *Imagined Communities: Reflections on the Origin and Spread of Nationalism*. London: Verso, 1983.

Anderson, T., and H. Kanuka. "On-Line Forums: New Platforms for Professional Development and Group Collaboration." *Journal of Computer-Mediated Communication* 3, no. 3 (1997).

Arrow, Holly, et al. "Time, Technology and Groups: An Integration." *Computer Supported Cooperative Work* 4, no. 2/3 (1995–1996): 253–261.

Aycock, Alan. "Technologies of the Self: Foucault and Internet Discourse." *Journal of Computer-Mediated Communication* 1, no. 2 (1995).

Bagdikian, Ben. "The Lords of the Global Village." *Nation* (12 June 1989): 805.

Bagdikian, Ben. *The Media Monopoly*. Boston: Beacon Press, 1983.

Bajan, P. "New Communities, New Social Norms?" *Studia Psychologica* 40, no. 4 (1998): 361–366.

Baker, Andrea. "Two by Two in Cyberspace: Getting Together and Connecting Online," *Cyberpsychology and Behavior* 3, no. 2 (2000) 237–242.

Barak, A. "Psychological Applications on the Internet: A Discipline on the Threshold of a New Millennium." *Applied and Preventive Psychology* 8, no. 4 (1999): 231–245.

Baran, Paul. "On Distributed Communications Networks." *IEEE Transactions on Communications Systems* CS–12 (1964): 1–9.

Baran, Paul. "On Distributed Communications." In *Rand Memoranda*, vols. 1–11. Santa Monica, Calif.: Rand Corporation, August 1964.

Barbatsis, G., and K. Hansen. "The Performance of Cyberspace: An Exploration into Computer-Mediated Reality." *Journal of Computer-Mediated Communication 5*, no. 1 (1999).

Barlow, John Perry. "Crime and Puzzlement." *Whole Earth Review* 68 (Fall 1990): 44.

Barnes, S., and L. M. Greller. "Computer-Mediated Communication in the Organization." *Communication Education* 43, no. 2 (1994): 129–142.

Barrett, Neil. *The State of Cybernation: Cultural, Political and Economic Implications of the Internet*. London: Kogan Page Publishers, 1997.

Bartle, Richard. "Interactive Multi-User Computer Games." Internal study for British Telecom, Colchester, England, 1990.

Baudrillard, Jean. *Selected Writings*. Edited by Mark Poster. Stanford, Calif.: Stanford University Press, 1988.

Baym, N. "Agreements and Disagreements in a Computer-Mediated Discussion." *Research on Language and Social Interaction* 29, no. 4 (1996): 315–345.

Baym, N. "From Practice to Culture on Usenet." *Sociological Review Monograph* (1995): 29–52.

Baym, N. "The Performance of Humor in Computer-Mediated Communication." *Journal of Computer-Mediated Communication* 1, no. 2 (1995).

Behar, Joseph E., ed. *Mapping Cyberspace: Social Research on the Electronic Frontier*. New York: Dowling College Press, 1997.

Bellah, Robert N., R. Madsen, W. Sullivan, A. Swindler, and S. Tipton. *Habits of the Heart: Individualism and Commitment in American Life*. Berkeley, Calif.: University of California Press, 1985.

Bellah. *The Good Society*. New York: Knopf, 1991.

Beniger, James. "The Personalization of Mass Media and the Growth of Pseudo-Community." *Communication Research* 14, no. 3 (1987): 369.

Bentham, Jeremy. *Works*, vol. 4. Edited by J. Bowring. Edinburgh: William Tait, 1843.

Berdahl, J. L., and K. M. Craig. "Equality of Participation and Influence in Groups: The Effects of Communication Medium and Sex Composition." *Computer Supported Cooperative Work* 4, no. 2/3 (1995–1996): 179–201.

Berleur, J., and D. Whitehouse, eds. *Ethical Global Information Society: Culture and Democracy Revisited*. Norwell, Mass.: Kluwer Academic Publishers, 1999.

Berman, Marshall. *All That Is Solid Melts into Air: The Experience of Modernity*. New York: Simon & Schuster, 1982.

Berthold, Michael, et al. "Clustering on the Nets: Applying an Autoassociative Neural Network to Computer-Mediated Discussions." *Journal of Computer-Mediated Communication* 2, no. 4 (1997).

Blanchard, A., and T. Horan. "Virtual Communities and Social Capital." *Social Science Computer Review* 16, no. 3 (1998): 293–307.

Bollier, D., and C. M. Firestone. *The Future of Community and Personal Identity in the Coming Electronic Culture.* Washington, D.C.: Aspen Institute Publications Office, 1996.

Bordia, P. "Face-to-face Versus Computer-Mediated Communication: A Synthesis of the Experimental Literature." *The Journal of Business Communication* 34, no. 1 (1997): 99–120.

Bordia, P., N. DiFonzo, and A. Chang. "Rumor as Group Problem Solving: Development Patterns in Informal Computer-mediated Groups." *Small Group Research* 30, no. 1 (1999): 8–28.

Borsook, Paulina. *Cyberselfish: How the Digital Elite Is Undermining Our Society, Culture and Values.* Des Plaines, Ill.: Bantam Books, 1999.

Boyer, M. Christine. *CyberCities: Visual Perception in the Age of Electronic Communication.* New York: Princeton Architectural Press, 1996.

Brand, Stewart. *II Cybernetic Frontiers.* New York: Random House, 1974.

Brand, Stewart. *The Media Lab: Inventing the Future at MIT.* New York: Penguin, 1987.

Breen, Marcus. "Information Does Not Equal Knowledge: Theorizing the Political Economy of Virtuality." *Journal of Computer-Mediated Communication* 3, no. 3 (1997).

Brignall, Wells. "The Internet as a Tool for a Community: Virtual Citizens and the New Technocracy." *Society for the Study of Social Problems* (1999).

Brook, J., and I.A. Boal, eds. *Resisting the Virtual Life: the Culture and Politics of Information.* San Francisco: City Lights, 1995.

Bruckman, Amy, and Mitchel Resnick. "Virtual Professional Community: Results from the MediaMOO Project." Paper submitted to the Third International Conference on Cyberspace. Austin, Texas, March 1993.

Bruckman, Amy. "Finding One's Own Space in Cyberspace." *Technology Review* 99, no. 1 (1996): 48–54.

Bruckman, Amy. "Identity Workshops: Emergent Social and Psychological Phenomena in Text-Based Virtual Reality." Master's thesis, MIT Media Laboratory, 1992.

Bruhat, Thierry. "Messageries Electroniques: Grétel à Strasbourg et Télétel a Vélizy." In *Télématique: Promenades ans les Usages.* Edited by Marie Marchand and Clair Ancelin. Paris: La Documentation Francaise, 1984.

Calhoun, C. *Indirect Relationships and Imagined Communities: Large-Scale Social Integration and the Transformation of Everyday Life.* Pp. 95–120 in *Social Theory for a Changing Society,* edited by Pierre Bourdieu and James S. Colemen. Boulder, Colo.: Westview Press, 1991.

Calhoun, Craig. "Community Without Propinquity Revisited: Communications Technology and the Transformation of the Urban Public Sphere." *Sociological Inquiry* 68, no. 3 (1998): 373–397.

Capussotti, Enrica. "Italian Cyberpunk: A Networked Community." *Quaderni di Sociologia* 41, no. 13 (1997): 59–77.

Carey, James. "The Mythos of the Electronic Revolution." In *Communication as Culture: Essays on Media and Society*. Winchester, Mass.: Unwin Hyman, 1989.

Carpignano, Paolo, Robin Anderson, Stanley Aronowitz, and William Difazio. "Chatter in the Age of Electronic Reproduction: Talk Television and the Public Mind." *Social Text* 25, no. 6 (1990).

Cerulo, Karen A. "Reframing Social Concepts for a Brave New (Virtual) World." *Sociological Inquiry* 67, no. 1 (1997): 48–58.

Cherny, L. *Conversation and Community: Discourse in a Social MUD*. Cambridge: Cambridge University Press, 1999.

Cherny, L., and E.R. Weise, eds. *Wired Women: Gender and New Realities in Cyberspace*. Seattle, Wash.: Seal Press, 1996.

Christensen, Ward, and Randy Seuss. "Hobbyist Computerized Bulletin Boards." *Byte* (November 1978): 150.

Christensen, Ward. "History: Me, Micros, Randy, Xmodem, CBBS." Posting on Chinet conferencing system, 18 March 1989.

Clapp, T. J. Burnside. "Weekend-Only World." Fesarius Publications, 1987.

Coate, John. "Innkeeping in Cyberspace." Paper read at the Directions in Advanced Computing Conference. Berkeley, Calif., 1991.

Cohill, A. M., and A. L. Kavanaugh, eds. *Community Networks: Lessons from Blacksburg, Virginia*. Norwood, Mass.: Artech House, 1997.

Coleman, L.H., C.E. Paternite, and R.C. Sherman. "A Reexamination of Deindividuation in Synchronous Computer-Mediated Communication." *Computers in Human Behavior* 15, no. 1 (1999): 51–65.

Congress of the United States, Office of Technology Assessment. *Critical Connections: Communication for the Future*. Washington, D.C.: United States Government Printing Office, 1990.

Cooley, C. H. *The Extension of Primary Ideals*. In *Social Organization*. New York: Charles Scribner's Sons, 1909.

Coyne, Richard. *Technoromanticism: Digital Narrative, Holism, and the Romance of the Real*. Cambridge, Mass.: MIT Press, 1999.

Cubitt, Sean. *Digital Aesthetics*. Thousand Oaks, Calif.: Sage Publications, 1998.

Curtis, Pavel, and David A. Nichols. *MUDs Grow Up: Social Virtual Reality in the Real World*. Palo Alto, Calif.: Xerox PARC, 1993.

Curtis, Pavel. Panel on MUDs at the Directions in Advanced Computing Conference. Berkeley, Calif., 1991.

Cutler, R. H. "Distributed Presence and Community in Cyberspace." *Interpersonal Computing and Technology* 3, no. 2 (1995).

D'Ambra, J., R.E. Rice, and M. O'Connor. "Computer-Mediated Communication and Media Preference: An Investigation of the Dimensionality of Perceived

Task Equivocality and Media Richness." *Behaviour and Information Technology* 17, no. 3 (1998): 164–174.

Davis, B. H., and J. P. Brewer. *Electronic Discourse: Linguistic Individuals in Virtual Space.* New York: State University of New York Press, 1997.

Debord, Guy. *Comments on the Society of the Spectacle.* London: Verso, 1992.

Denning, P. J., and R. M. Metcalfe. *Beyond Calculation: The Next Fifty Years of Computing.* Germany: Springer Verlag, 1998.

Dennis, A. R., S. T. Kinney, and Y. T. Hung. "Gender Differences in the Effects of Media Richness." *Small Group Research* 30, no. 4 (1999): 405–437.

Dery, Mark. *Escape Velocity: Cyberculture at the End of the Century.* New York: Grove Press, 1996.

DeSanctis, G., and P. Monge. "Communication Processes for Virtual Organizations." *Journal of Computer-Mediated Communication* 3, no. 4 (1998).

Dibbell, Julian. *My Tiny Life.* New York: Henry Holt, 1999.

Doheny-Farina, Stephen. *The Wired Neighborhood.* New Haven, Conn.: Yale Uni-versity Press, 1998.

Donath, J., K. Karahalios, and F. Viégas. "Visualizing Conversation." *Journal of Computer-Mediated Communication* 4, no. 4 (1999).

Douglas, M., and G. Pallotti. "The Home as a Virtual Community." *Rassegna Italiana di Sociologia* 36, no. 2 (1995): 229–250.

Druckrey, T., and A. R. Stone, eds. *Electronic Culture: Technology and Visual Representation.* New York: Aperture Publishing, 1997.

Du Pont, Pete. "Yesterday, Today and Tomorrow: How the Internet Will Revolutionize Public Policy." *Vital Speeches of the Day* 65, no. 15 (1999): 477–479.

Dyson, Esther, et al. "Cyberspace and the American Dream: A Magna Carta for the Knowledge Age." *Information Society* 12, no. 3 (1996): 295–308.

Dyson, Esther. *Release 2.0: A Design for Living in the Digital Age.* New York: Broadway Books, 1997.

Ebo, B. L. *Cyberghetto or Cybertopia: Race, Class, and Gender on the Internet.* Westport, Conn.: Praeger Publishers, 1998.

Eisenstein, E.L. *The Printing Revolution in Early Modern Europe.* Cambridge: Cambridge University Press, 1983.

Ellul, Jacques. *The Technological Society.* New York: Knopf Publishing, 1964.

Elshtain, Jean Betheke. "Interactive TV—Democracy and the QUBE Tube." *The Nation* (7–14 August 1982): 108.

Endo, Kaoru. "Projection into Virtuality: Modernity and Virtual Communities." *Japanese Sociological Review* 48, no. 4 (1998): 50–64.

Engelbart, Douglas C. "A Conceptual Framework for the Augmentation of Man's Intellect." In *Vistas in Information Handling,* vol. 1. Edited by Paul William Howerton and David C. Weeks. Washington, D.C.: Spartan Books, 1963, pp. 1–29.

Engelbart, Douglas C. "Intellectual Implications of Multi-Access Computing." Proceedings of the Interdisciplinary Conference on Multi-Access Computer Networks, April 1970.

Engelbart, Douglas C. "NLS Teleconferencing Features: The Journal and Shared-Screen Telephoning." *IEEE Digest of Papers* (CompCon) (Fall 1975): 175–76.

Escobar, Arturo, et al. "Welcome to Cyberia: Notes on the Anthropology of Cyberculture." *Current Anthropology* 35, no. 3 (1994): 211–223.

Escobar, Arturo. "Anthropology and the Future: New Technologies and the Reinvention of Culture." *Futures* 27, no. 4 (1995): 409–421.

Ess, Charles, ed. *Philosophical Perspectives on Computer-Mediated Communication.* New York: State University of New York Press, 1996.

Evenson, Laura. "Future TV Will Shop for You and Talk for You." *The San Francisco Chronicle*, 8 June 1993.

Featherstone, M., and R. Burrows, eds. (1996). *Cyberspace, Cyberbodies, Cyberpunk: Cultures of Technological Embodiment.* London: Sage Publications, 1996.

Feenberg, Andrew. "From Information to Communication: The French Experience with Videotext." In *The Social Contexts of Computer-Mediated Communication.* Edited by Marin Lea. Englewood Cliffs, N.J.: Simon & Schuster/Harvester-Wheatsheaf, 1992.

Fernback, J., and B. Thompson. "Computer-Mediated Communication and the American Collectivity: The Dimensions of Community Within Cyberspace." *International Communication Association* (1995).

Ferris, Sharmila Pixy. "Women On-Line: Cultural and Relational Aspects of Women's Communication in On-Line Discussion Groups." *Interpersonal Computing and Technology* 4, no. 3/4 (1996): 29–40.

Figallo, Cliff. *Hosting Web Communities: Building Relationships, Increasing Customer Loyalty, and Maintaining a Competitive Edge.* Somerset, N.J.: John Wiley & Sons, 1998.

Fischer, C. S. "Technology and Community: Historical Complexities." *Sociological Inquiry* 67, no. 1 (1997): 113–18.

Forster, E. M. "The Machine Stops." *In The Eternal Moment and Other Stories.* New York: Harcourt Brace Jovanovich, 1929.

Foucault, Michel. *Discipline and Punish: The Birth of the Prison.* Translated from the French by Alan Sheridan. New York: Pantheon, 1977.

Fuller, R. "Human-Computer-Human Interaction: How Computers Affect Interpersonal Communication." *The Electronic Journal on Virtual Culture* 2, no. 2 (1994).

Furger, Roberta. *Does Jane Compute? Preserving Our Daughters' Place in the Cyber Revolution.* New York: Warner Books, 1998.

Gackenbach, Jayne, ed. *Psychology and the Internet: Intrapersonal, Interpersonal, and Transpersonal Implications.* San Diego: Academic Press, 1998.

Galegher J., L. Sproull, and S. Kiesler. "Legitimacy, Authority, and Community in Electronic Support Groups." *Written Communication* 15, no. 4 (1998): 493–530.

Garcia, A.C., and J. B. Jacobs. "The Eyes of the Beholder: Understanding the Turn-taking System in Quasi-Synchronous Computer-Mediated Communication." *Research on Language and Social Interaction* 32, no. 4 (1999): 337–367.

Garton, L., C. Haythornthwaite, and B. Wellman. "Studying Online Social Networks." *Journal of Computer-Mediated Communication* 3, no. 1 (1997).

Geertz, Clifford. *The Interpretation of Cultures: Selected Essays.* New York: Basic Books, 1973, p. 44.

Gergen, Kenneth J. *The Saturated Self: Dilemmas of Identity in Contemporary Life.* New York: Basic Books, 1991.

Gibson, William. *Neuromancer.* New York: Ace, 1984.

Goffman, Erving. *The Presentation of Self in Every Day Life.* Garden City, N.Y.: Doubleday, 1959.

Graetz, K.A., et al. "Information Sharing Face-to-face Teleconferencing, and Electronic Chat Groups." *Small Group Research* 29, no. 6 (1998): 714–743.

Granito, A. J., L. Groarke, and J. Kohls. "Open Peer Commentaries on Virtuality, Conversation, and Morality." *Technology Studies* 3, no. 2 (1996): 215–226.

Granovetter, Mark. "The Strength of Weak Ties." *American Journal of Sociology* 78 (1973): 1360–1380.

Gregson, K. "Conversation and Community or Sequential Monologues: An Analysis of Politically Oriented Newsgroups." *Proceedings of the ASIS Annual Meeting* 35 (1998): 531–541.

Griffith, T.L., and G.B. Northcraft. "Distinguishing Between the Forest and the Trees: Media, Features, and Methodology in Electronic Communication Research." *Organization Science* 5, no. 2 (1994): 272–285.

Grodin, D., and T.R. Lindlof, eds. *Constructing the Self in a Mediated World: Inquiries in Social Construction.* Thousand Oaks, Calif.: Sage Publications, 1996.

Grossman, L.K. *The Electronic Republic: Reshaping Democracy in the Information Age.* New York: Penguin, 1996.

Gruber, S. "Communication Gone Wired: Working Toward a Practiced Cyberfeminism." *Information Society* 15, no. 3 (1999): 199–208.

Habermas, Jürgen. Extensive discussion of the public sphere was published in *Strukturwandel der Öffentlichkeit* (Neuwied, 1962). A discussion of this book, translated into English, appeared in *New German Critique* no. 3 (Fall 1974): 45–55.

Habermas, Jürgen. *The Theory of Communicative Action.* Vol. 1, *Reason and the Rationalization of Society.* Translated by Thomas McCarthy. Boston: Beacon Press, 1984.

Hacker, K. L., and M. A. Todino. "Virtual Democracy at the Clinton White House: An Experiment in Electronic Democratisation." *Javnost /The Public* 3, no. 1 (1996): 71–86.

Hafner, Katie. "The Epic Saga of The Well: The World's Most Influential Online Community (and it's not AOL)." *Wired* 5.05 (1997): 100–144.

Hagel, John, III, and Arthur G. Armstrong. *Net Gain: Expanding Markets through Virtual Communities*. Boston: Harvard Business School Press, 1997.

Hampton, K. N., and B. Wellman. "Netville Online and Offline: Observing and Surveying a Wired Suburb." *American Behavioral Scientist* 43, no. 3 (1999): 475–492.

Haraway, Donna J. *Modest-Witness, Second-Millennium: Femaleman Meets Oncomouse: Feminism and Technoscience*. New York: Routledge, 1996.

Harcourt, Wendy, ed. *Women Internet: Creating New Cultures in Cyberspace*. New York: Zed Books, 1999.

Harmon, Amy. "Researchers Find Sad, Lonely World in Cyberspace." *New York Times*, August 30, 1998.

Hart, Jeffrey, R. Reed, and F. Bar. "The Building of the Internet: Implications for the Future of Broadband Networks." *Telecommunications Policy* (November 1992): 666–89.

Hauben, Michael. "The Social Forces Behind the Development of Usenet News." Unpublished paper, Columbia University, 1992.

Hauben, R., and M. Hauben. *Netizens: On the History and Impact of Usenet and the Internet*. Los Alamitos, Calif.: IEEE Computer Society, 1997.

Hayles, Katherine. *How We Became Posthuman: Virtual Bodies in Cybernetics, Literature, and Informatics*. Chicago: University of Chicago Press, 1999.

Haythornthwaite, C. "Work, Friendship, and Media Use for Information Exchange in a Networked Organization." *Journal of the American Society for Information Science* 49, no. 12 (1998): 1101–1114.

Haythornthwaite, C., B. Wellman, and M. Mantei. "Work Relationships and Media Use: A Social Network Analysis." *Group Decision and Negotiations* 4, no. 3 (1995): 193–211.

Hearst, M. A., and J. Grudin. "The Changing Relationship Between Information Technology and Society: Has the Ice Man Arrived? Tact on the Internet." *IEEE Intelligent Systems and their Applications* 14, no. 1 (1999): 8–15.

Herring, Susan. "Interactional Coherence in CMC." *Journal of Computer-Mediated Communication* 4, no. 4 (1999).

Herring, Susan. "Linguistic and Critical Analysis of Computer-Mediated Communication: Some Ethical and Scholarly Considerations." *Information Society* 12, no. 2 (1996): 153–168.

Herring, Susan. "The Rhetorical Dynamics of Gender Harassment Online." *Information Society* 15, no. 3 (1999): 151–168.

Hill, K. A., and J. E. Hughes. "Computer-Mediated Political Communication: The USENET and Political Communities." *Political Communication* 14, no. 1 (1997): 3–27.

Hill, K.A., and J.E. Hughes. *Cyberpolitics: Citizen Activism in the Age of the Internet (People, Passions, and Power).* Lanham, Md.: Rowman & Littlefield, 1998.

Hiltz, S. R., and B. Wellman. "Asynchronous Learning Networks as a Virtual Classroom." *Communications of the ACM* 40, no. 9 (1997): 44–49.

Hiltz, S.R., and M. Turoff. *The Network Nation: Human Communication Via Computer,* revised edition. Cambridge, Mass.: MIT Press, 1993.

Hiltz, Starr Roxanne, and Murray Turoff. *The Network Nation: Human Communication via Computer.* Reading, Mass.: Addison-Wesley, 1978, p. 102.

Hinds, P., and S. Kiesler. "Communication Across Boundaries: Work, Structure, and Use of Communication Technologies in a Large Organization." *Organization Science* 6, no. 4 (1995): 373–393.

Hiramatsu, Morihiko. "Towards a More Autonomous Region through Informatization and Revitalization." Speech given at the Apple Hakone Multimedia and Arts Festival, Hakone, Japan, 1 August 1992.

Holeton, Richard. *Composing Cyberspace: Identity, Community, and Knowledge in the Electronic Age.* Columbus, Ohio: McGraw-Hill College Division, 1997.

Holmes, David, ed. *Virtual Politics: Identity and Community in Cyberspace.* London: Sage, 1998.

Horn, Stacy. *Cyberville: Clicks, Culture, and the Creation of an Online Town.* New York: Warner Books, 1998.

Howard, Tharon W. *A Rhetoric of Electronic Communities.* Stamford, Conn.: Ablex Publishing Corporation, 1997.

Innis, Harold. *The Bias of Communication.* Toronto: University of Toronto Press, 1951.

Ito, M. "Theory, Method, and Design in Anthropologies of the Internet." *Social Science Computer Review* 14, no. 1 (1996): 24–26.

Jacobson, David. "Contexts and Cues in Cyberspace: The Pragmatics of Naming in Text-Based Virtual Realities." *Journal of Anthropological Research* 52, no. 4 (1996): 461–479.

Jacobson, David. "Impression Formation in Cyberspace: Online Expectations and Offline Experiences in Text-based Virtual Communities." *Journal of Computer-Mediated Communication* 5, no. 1 (1999).

Jenkins, Henry. *Textual Poachers: Television Fans and Participatory Culture.* New York and London: Routledge, 1992.

Johnson, Dan. "Do-it-Yourself Governance?" *The Futurist* 33, no. 5 (1999): 12.

Johnson, Steven. *Interface Culture: How New Technology Transforms the Way We Create and Communicate.* San Francisco: Harper, 1997.

Jones, Quentin. "Virtual-Communities, Virtual Settlements and Cyber-Archaeology: A Theoretical Outline." *Journal of Computer-Mediated Communication* 3, no. 3 (1997).

Jones, Steve. "Using the News: An Examination of the Value and Use of News Sources in CMC." *Journal of Computer-Mediated Communication* 2, no. 4 (1997).

Jones, Steven G., ed. *Cybersociety 2.0: Revisiting Computer-Mediated Communication and Community (New Media Cultures, V. 2).* New York: Sage, 1998.

Jones, Steven G., ed. *Cybersociety: Computer-Mediated Communication and Community.* Thousand Oaks, Calif.: Sage Publications, 1995.

Jones, Steven G., ed. *Virtual Culture: Identity and Communication in Cybersociety.* London: Sage, 1997.

Jordan, T., and P. Taylor. "A Sociology of Hackers." *Sociological Review* 46, No. 4 (1998): 757–780.

Jordan, Tim. *Cyberpower: The Culture and Politics of Cyberspace and the Internet.* London: Routledge, 1999.

Kahai, S., and R.B. Cooper. "The Effect of Computer-Mediated Communication on Agreement and Acceptance." *Journal of Management Information Systems* 16, no. 1 (1999): 165–188.

Kahin, B., and J. Keller, eds. *Public Access to the Internet.* Cambridge, Mass.: MIT Press, 1995.

Katz, Jon. "The Tales They Tell in Cyberspace Are a Whole Other Story." *New York Times*, January 23, 1994, pp. A1, A30.

Kayany, Joseph M. "Contexts of Uninhibited Online Behavior: Flaming in Social Newsgroups on Usenet." *Journal of the American Society for Information Science* 49, no. 12 (1998): 1135–1141.

Kiesler, S., D. Zubrow, and A. Moses. "Affect in Computer-mediated Communication: An Experiment in Synchronous Terminal-to-terminal Discussion." *Human-Computer Interaction* 1 (1985): 77–104.

Kiesler, S., ed. *Culture of the Internet.* London: Lawrence Erlbaum Associates, 1997.

Kiesler, S., J. Siegel, and T. W. McGuire. "Social Psychological Aspects of Computer-mediated Communication." *American Psychologist* 39, no 10 (1984): 1123–1134.

Kiesler, Sara. "The Hidden Messages in Computer Networks." *Harvard Business Review* (January–February 1986).

Kim, Amy Jo. *Community Building on the Web.* Berkeley, Calif.: Peachpit Press, 1999.

King, Storm A. "Commentary on Responses to the Proposed Guidelines." *Information Society* 12, no. 2 (1996): 199–201.

King, Storm A. "Researching Internet Communities: Proposed Ethical Guidelines for the Reporting of Results." *Information Society* 12, no. 2 (1996): 119–127.

Kling, Rob, ed. *Computerization and Controversy: Value Conflicts and Social Choices*, 2nd ed. San Diego, Calif.: Academic Press, 1996.

Kling, Rob. "Synergies and Competition Between Life in Cyberspace and Face-to-Face Communities." *Social Science Computer* Review 14, no. 1 (1996): 50–54.

Kochen, Manfred, ed. *The Small World*. Norwood, N.J.: Ablex, 1989.

Kollock, Peter. "The Economies of Online Cooperation: Gifts and Public Goods in Cyberspace," 1999 [cited February 14, 2000]. Available at <http://www.research.microsoft.com/vwg/papers/KollockEconomies.htm>.

Komito, Lee. "The Net as a Foraging Society: Flexible Communities." *Information Society* 14, no. 2 (1998): 97–106.

Kraut Robert, et al. "Internet Paradox: A Social Technology that Reduces Social Involvement and Psychological Well-Being?" *American Psychologist* 53, no. 9 (1998): 1017–1031.

Kraut, Robert, et al. "Social Impact of the Internet: What Does it Mean?" *Association for Computing Machinery* 41, no. 12 (1998): 21–22.

Krol, Ed. *The Whole Internet User's Guide & Catalog*. Sebastopol, Calif.: O'Reilly & Assoc., 1992.

Kumon, Shumpei, and Izumi Aizu. "Co-emulation: The Case for a Global Hypernetwork Society." In *Global Networks: Computers and International Communication*. Edited by Linda Harasim. Cambridge, Mass.: MIT Press, 1993.

Kumon, Shumpei. "Japan as a Network Society." In *The Political Economy of Japan*. Vol. 3, *The Social and Cultural Dynamics*. Edited by Shumpei Kumon and Henry Rosovsky. Stanford, Calif.: Stanford University Press, 1992, pp. 109–41.

LaQuey, Tracy. *The Internet Companion: A Beginner's Guide to Global Networking*. Reading, Mass.: Addison-Wesley, 1992.

Laurel, Brenda. *Computers as Theater*. Menlo Park, Calif.: Addison-Wesley, 1991.

Leer, Anne C., ed. *Masters of the Wired World: Cyberspace Speaks Out*. London: Financial Times Pitman Publishing, 1999.

Leeson, L. H., ed. *Clicking In: Hot Links to a Digital Culture*. Seattle, Wash.: Bay Press, 1996.

Lemke, Dwight K. "Cyberia." *Journal of Management Inquiry* 7, no. 3 (1998): 270–272.

Lemke, J. "Cultural Dynamics and Virtual Culture." *The Electronic Journal on Virtual Culture* 2, no. 1 (1994).

LeValley, Janet. "Doing It in Cyberspace: Cultural Sensitivity in Applied Anthropology." *Anthropology of Consciousness* 8, no. 4 (1997): 113–132.

Levy, Pierre. *Collective Intelligence: Mankind's Emerging World in Cyberspace*. New York: Plenum Press, 1997.

Licklider, J. C. R. "Man-Computer Symbiosis." *IRE Transactions on Human Factors in Electronics* HFE–1 (March 1960): 4–11.

Licklider, J. C. R., Robert Taylor, and E. Herbert. "The Computer as a Communication Device." *International Science and Technology* (April 1968).

Lievrouw, Leah A. "Our Own Devices: Heterotopic Communication, Discourse and Culture in the Information Society." *Information Society* 14, no. 2 (1997).

Lindlof, T.R., and M.J. Shatzer. "Media Ethnography in Virtual Space: Strategies, Limits, and Possibilities." *Journal of Broadcasting and Electronic Media* 42, no. 2 (1998): 170–189.

Lipnack, Jessica, and Jeffrey Stamps. *Networking: The First Report and Directory.* Garden City, N.Y.: Doubleday, 1982.

Liu, Geoffrey Z. "Virtual Community Presence in Internet Relay Chatting." *Journal of Computer-Mediated Communication* 5, no. 1 (1999).

Loader, B., and B. N. Hague, eds. *Digital Democracy: Discourse and Decision Making in the Information Age.* London: Routledge, 1999.

Locke, John L. *The De-Voicing of Society: Why We Don't Talk to Each Other Anymore.* New York: Simon & Schuster, 1998.

London, Christopher. Email communication with author, February 7, 2000.

Ludlow, Peter, ed. *High Noon on the Electronic Frontier: Conceptual Issues in Cyberspace.* Cambridge, Mass.: MIT Press, 1996.

Luke, T. *Community and Ecology.* Pp. 207–221 in *Changing Community: The Graywolf Annual Ten,* edited by S. Walker. St. Paul, Minn.: Graywolf Press, 1993.

Luke, Timothy. "The Politics of Digital Inequality: Access, Capability and Distribution in Cyberspace." *New Political Science* 41–42 (1997): 121–144.

Lunenfeld, Peter, ed. *The Digital Dialectic: New Essays on New Media.* Cambridge, Mass.: MIT Press, 1999.

Maltz, Tamir. "Customary Law and Power in Internet Communities." *Journal of Computer-Mediated Communication* 2, no. 1 (1996).

Mannecke, B. E., and J. S. Valacich. "Information is What You Make of It: The Influence of Group History and Computer Support on Information Sharing, Decision Quality, and Member Perceptions." *Journal of Management Information Systems* 15, no. 2 (1997): 173–197.

Mantovani, G. "Is Computer-Mediated Communication Intrinsically Apt to Enhance Democracy in Organizations?" *Human Relations* 47, no. 1 (1994): 45–62.

Mantovani, G. "Social Context in HCI: A New Framework for Mental Models, Cooperation, and Communication." *Cognitive Science* 20, no. 2 (1996): 237–269.

Mantovani, G., and G. Riva. "Real Presence: How Different Ontologies Generate Different Criteria for Presence, Telepresence, and Virtual Presence." *Presence-Teleoperators and Virtual Environments* 8, no. 5 (1999): 540–550.

Marchand, Marie. *A French Success Story: The Minitel Saga.* Translated by Mark Murphy. Paris: Larousse, 1988.

Markoff, John. "Microsoft and Two Cable Giants Close to an Alliance." *The New York Times* (13 June 1993).

Markoff, John. "U.S. Said to Play Favorites in Promoting Nationwide Computer Network." *The New York Times* (18 December 1991).

Marx, Gary T. "Privacy and Technology." *The World and I* (September 1990).

Marx, Karl. *Capital: A Critique of Political Economy*, Vol. 1, edited by Frederick Engels. New York: International Publishers, 1987.

McChesney, R. W. "The Internet and U.S. Communication Policy-making in Historical and Critical Perspective." *Journal of Communication* 46 (1996): 98–124.

McClellan, J. "Netsurfers." *The Observer*, February 13, 1994.

McKenna, K. Y., and J. A. Bargh. "Coming Out in the Age of the Internet: Identity Demarginalization Through Virtual Group Participation." *Journal of Personality and Social Psychology* 75, no. 3 (1998): 681–694.

McLuhan, Marshall. *Understanding Media: The Extensions of Man*. New York: McGraw-Hill, 1964.

Mehta, M. D., and E. Darier. "Virtual Control and Discipline on the Internet: Electronic Governmentality in the New Wired World." *Information Society* 14, no. 2 (1997).

Mele, Christopher. *Cyberspace and Disadvantaged Communities: The Internet as a Tool for Collective Action*. In *Communities in Cyberspace*, edited by Marc A. Smith and Peter Kollock. London: Routledge, 1998.

Meyrowitz, J. *No Sense of Place: The Impact of Electronic Media on Social Behavior*. New York: Oxford University Press, 1985.

Miller, Steven E. *Civilizing Cyberspace*. New York: ACM Press, 1996.

Morino, Mario. Email communication with author, February 4, 2000.

Morningstar, Chip, and F. Randall Farmer. "The Lessons of Lucasfilm's Habitat." In *Cyberspace: First Steps*. Edited by Michael Benedikt. Cambridge, Mass.: MIT Press, 1991.

Mumford, Lewis. *The Myth of the Machine*. New York: Harcourt, Brace, & World, 1966.

Myers, Daniel J. "Communication Technology and Social Movements: Contributions of Computer Networks to Activism." *Social Science Computer Review* 12, no. 2 (1994): 250–260.

Nardi, B. A., and V. L. O'Day. *Information Ecologies: Using Technology with Heart*. Cambridge, Mass.: MIT Press, 1999.

Negroponte, Nicholas. *Being Digital*. New York: Alfred A. Knopf, 1995.

Nora, Simon, and Alain Minc. *L'informatisation de la société*. Paris: Editions du Seuil, 1978.

Notess, Greg R. "Communications and Community on Web sites." *Online* 23, no. 4 (1999): 65–68.

Odasz, Frank. "Big Sky Telegraph." *Whole Earth Review* 71 (Summer 1991): 32.

Odzer, Cleo. *Virtual Spaces: Sex and the Cyber Citizen*. New York: Berkley Books, 1997.

Okleshen, C., and S. Grossbart. "Usenet Groups, Virtual Community and Consumer Behaviors." *Advances in Consumer Research* 25 (1998): 276–282.

Olaniran, Bolanle A. "Group Performance in Computer-Mediated and Face-to-Face Communication Media." *Management Communication Quarterly* 7, no. 3 (1994): 256–281.

Oldenburg, Ray. *The Great Good Place: Caf,s, Coffee Shops, Community Centers, Beauty Parlors, General Stores, Bars, Hangouts, and How They Get You through the Day*. New York: Paragon House, 1991.

Oldenburg, Ray. *The Great Good Place: Cafes, Coffee Shops, Bookstores, Bars, Hair Salons, and Other Hangouts at the Heart of the Community*, 3rd ed. New York: Marlowe & Company, 1999.

Olson, Mancur. *The Logic of Collective Action*. Cambridge, Mass.: Harvard University Press, 1965.

Ong, Walter. *Orality and Literacy: The Technologizing of the Word*. New York: Routledge, 1982.

Ono, R., and K. Aoki. "Convergence and New Regulatory Frameworks: A Comparative Study of Regulatory Approaches to Internet Telephony." *Telecommunications Policy* 22, no. 10 (1998): 817–838.

Paccagnella, Luciano. "A Cyberspace Sociology: A Case Study of a Cyberpunk Electronic Conference." *Quaderni di Sociologia* 41, no. 13 (1997): 33–57.

Paccagnella, Luciano. "Getting the Seats of Your Pants Dirty: Strategies for Ethnographic Research on Virtual Communities." *Journal of Computer-Mediated Communication* 3, no. 1 (1997).

Paccagnella, Luciano. "How to Regulate the Use of Electronically Registered Messages in Research on Computer-Assisted Communication?" *Quaderni di Sociologia* 41, no. 15 (1997): 159–163.

Paccagnella, Luciano. "Language, Network Centrality, and Response to Crisis in On-line Life: A Case Study in the Italian Cyberpunk Computer Conference." *Information Society* 14, no. 2 (1997).

Paolillo, John. "The Virtual Speech Community: Social Network and Language Variation on IRC." *Journal of Computer-Mediated Communication* 4, no. 4 (1999).

Parks, M. R., and K. Floyd. "Making Friends in Cyberspace." *Journal of Communication* 46, no. 1 (1996): 80–97.

Parks, M.R., and L.D. Roberts. "Making MOOsic: The Development of Personal Relationships Online and a Comparison to their Offline Counterparts." *Journal of Social and Personal Relationships* 15, no. 4 (1998): 517–537.

Peck, M. Scott. *The Different Drum: Community-Making and Peace*. New York: Touchstone, 1987.

Pfaffenberger, Bryan. "If I Want It, It's OK: Usenet and the (Outer) Limits of Free Speech." *Information Society* 12, no. 4 (1996): 365–386.

Phillips, David J. "Defending the Boundaries: Identifying and Countering Threats in a Usenet Newsgroup." *Information Society* 12, no. 1 (1996): 39–62.

Plant, Sadie. *Zeros and Ones: Digital Women and the New Technoculture.* Doubleday Books, 1997.

Plato. "Phaedrus." In *The Dialogues of Plato*, trans. B. Jowett. Oxford: Clarendon Press, 1953.

Porter, David, ed. *Internet Culture.* New York: Routledge, 1997.

Postman, Neal. *Amusing Ourselves to Death: Public Discourse in the Age of Show Business.* New York: Viking Penguin, 1985.

Postman, Neil. *Amusing Ourselves to Death: Public Discourse in the Age of Show Business.* New York: Viking Press, 1985.

Postmes, T., R. Spears, and M. Lea. "Breaching or Building Social Boundaries: Side-effects of Computer-Mediated Communication." *Communication Research* 25, no. 6 (1998): 689–715.

Preece, J. Online *Communities: Supporting Sociability, Designing Usability.* Chichester, England: John Wiley & Sons, 2000.

Putnam, Robert. "Bowling Alone: America's Declining Social Capital." *Journal of Democracy* 6, no 1 (1995): 65–78.

Quarterman, John. "How Big Is the Matrix?" *Matrix News* 2, no. 2. Matrix Information and Directory Services, Austin, Texas, 1992.

Quarterman, John. "The Global Matrix of Minds." In *Global Networks: Computers and International Communication.* Edited by Linda Harasim. Cambridge, Mass.: MIT Press, 1993.

Quarterman, John. *The Matrix: Computer Networks and Conferencing Systems Worldwide.* Bedford, Mass.: Digital Press, 1990.

Quittner, Joshua. "Internet Faces Gridlock." *Newsday* (1 November 1992).

Rafaeli, S., and F. Sudweeks. "Networked Interactivity." *Journal of Computer-Mediated Communication* 2, no. 4 (1997).

Rapaport, Mathew J. *Computer-Mediated Communications.* New York: Wiley, 1991.

Rash, Wayne Jr. *Politics on the Nets: Wiring the Political Process.* New York: W. H. Freeman & Co, 1997.

Reich, Robert. *The Work of Nations: Preparing Ourselves for 21st-Century Capitalism.* New York: Random House, 1991.

Reid, Elisabeth. "Electropolis: Communications and Community on Internet Relay Chat." Electronically distributed version of honors thesis for the Department of History, University of Melbourne, 1991.

Reid, Elizabeth. "Informed Consent in the Study of On-Line Communities: A Reflection on the Effects of Computer-Mediated Social Research." *Information Society* 12, no. 2 (1996): 169–174.

Rheingold, Howard, ed. *The Millennium Whole Earth Catalog.* San Francisco: Harper, 1994.

Rheingold, Howard. "Electronic Democracy." *Whole Earth Review* 71 (Summer 1991): 4.

Rheingold, Howard. *Tools for Thought.* New York: Simon & Schuster, 1985.

Rheingold, Howard. *Virtual Reality.* New York: Summit, 1991.

Rhodes, Sarah N. *The Role of the National Science Foundation in the Development of the Electronic Journal.* Washington, D.C.: National Science Foundation, Division of Information Science and Technology, 1976.

Ribeiro, Gustavo L. "Transnational Virtual Community? Exploring Implications for Culture, Power and Language." *Organization Science* 4, no. 4 (1997): 496–505.

Riedel, E., et al. "Electronic Communities: Assessing Equality of Access in a Rural Minnesota Community." *Social Science Computer Review* 16, no. 4 (1998): 370–390.

Rintel, E. S., and J. Pittam. "Strangers in a Strange Land: Interaction Management on Internet Relay Chat." *Human Communication Research* 23, no. 4 (1997): 507–534.

Riva, G., and C. Galimberti. "Computer-Mediated Communication: Identity and Social Interaction in an Electronic Environment." *Genetic, Social, and General Psychology Monographs* 124, no. 4 (1998): 434–464.

Robertson, Douglas S. *The New Renaissance: Computers and the Next Level of Civilization.* Oxford: Oxford University Press, 1998.

Robins, Kevin, and Frank Webster. "Athens without Slaves . . . or Slaves without Athens? The Neurosis of Technology." *In Science as Culture*, vol. 1. London: Free Association Books, 1987.

Robins, Kevin, and Frank Webster. "Cybernetic Capitalism: Information, Technology, Everyday Life." In T*he Political Economy of Information.* Edited by V. Mosco and J. Wasko. Madison: The University of Wisconsin Press, 1988.

Rodino, Michelle. "Breaking Out of Binaries: Reconceptualizing Gender and its Relationship to Language in Computer-Mediated Communication." *Journal of Computer-Mediated Communication* 3, no. 3 (1997).

Rothkopf, David. "Cyberpolitik: The Changing Nature of Power in the Information Age." *Journal of International Affairs* 51, no. 2 (1998): 325–359.

Rothman, David H. *Networld! What People Are Really Doing on the Internet, and What It Means to You.* Roseville, Calif.: Prima Publishing, 1995.

Rowe, John Carlos. "Cybercowboys on the New Frontier: Freedom, Nationalism, and Imperialism in the Postmodern Era." *Information Society* 12, no. 3 (1996): 309–314.

Ryan, Alan. "Exaggerated Hopes and Baseless Fears." *Social Research* 64, no. 3 (1997): 1167–1190.

Sardar, Z., and J. R. Ravetz, eds. *Cyberfutures: Culture and Politics on the Information Superhighway.* New York: New York University Press, 1996.

Savicki, V., D. Lingenfelter, and M. Kelley. "Gender, Language, Style, and Group Composition in Internet Discussion Groups." *Journal of Computer-Mediated Communication* 2, no. 3 (1996).

Savicki, V., M. Kelley, and D. Lingenfelter. "Gender, Group Composition, and Task Type in Small Task Groups Using Computer-mediated Communication." *Computers in Human Behavior* 12, no. 4 (1996): 549–565.

Savicki, V., M. Kelley, and E. Oesterreich. "Judgments of Gender in Computer-Mediated Communication." *Computers in Human Behavior* 15, no. 2 (1999): 185–194.

Schiano, D. J. "Convergent Methodologies in Cyber-Psychology: A Case Study." *Behavior Research Methods, Instruments, and Computers* 29, no. 2 (1997): 270–273.

Schiano, D. J. "Lessons from LambdaMOO: A Social, Text-based Virtual Environment." *Presence-Teleoperators and Virtual Environments* 8, no. 2 (1999): 127–139.

Schuler, Douglas. *New Community Networks: Wired for Change*. New York: ACM Press, 1996.

Sculley, John, with John A. Byrne. *Odyssey: Pepsi to Apple—A Journey of Adventure, Ideas, and the Future*. New York: Harper & Row, 1987.

Seabrook, John. *Deeper: A Two-Year Odyssey in Cyberspace*. New York: Simon & Schuster Books, 1998.

Sexton, Richard, ed. *Parallel Utopias: The Quest for Community*. San Francisco, Calif.: Chronicle Books, 1995.

Shapiro, Andrew L. "Street Corners in Cyberspace." *The Nation* (July 3, 1995): 10–14.

Shapiro, Andrew L. "The Net That Binds: Using Cyberspace to Create Real Communities." *The Nation* (June 21, 1999).

Shields, Rob, ed. *Cultures of Internet: Virtual Spaces, Real Histories, Living Bodies*. London: Sage Publications, 1996.

Silver, David. *Communication, Community, Consumption: An Ethnographic Exploration of an Online City*. In *Virtual Publics: Policy and Community in an Electronic Age*, edited by Beth E. Kolko. New York: Columbia University Press, forthcoming 2000.

Silver, David. *Localizing the Global Village: Lessons from the Blacksburg Electronic Village*. Pp. 79–92 in *The Global Village: Dead or Alive?*, edited by Ray B. Browne and Marshall W. Fishwick. Bowling Green, Ohio: Popular Press, 1999.

Silver, David. *Margins in the Wires: Looking for Race, Gender, and Sexuality in the Blacksburg Electronic Village*. In *Race in Cyberspace*, edited by Beth E. Kolko, Lisa Nakamura, and Gilbert B. Rodman. New York: Routledge, forthcoming 2000.

Smith, Anna Du Val. *Problems of Conflict Management in Virtual Communities*. In *Communities in Cyberspace*, edited by Marc A. Smith and Peter Kollock. London: Routledge, 1998.

Smith, C. B., M.L. McLaughlin, and K.K. Osborne. "Conduct Control on Usenet." *Journal of Computer-Mediated Communication* 2, no. 4 (1997).

Smith, M. A., and P. Kollock. "Managing the Virtual Commons: Cooperation and Conflict in Computer Communities." *American Sociological Association* (1994).

Smith, Marc A., and Peter Kollock, eds. *Communities in Cyberspace.* London: Routledge, 1998.

Smith, Marc. "Voices from the WELL: The Logic of the Virtual Commons." Master's thesis, Department of Sociology, UCLA, 1992.

Soukup, Charles. "The Gendered Interactional Patterns of Computer-Mediated Chatrooms: A Critical Ethnographic Study." *Information Society* 15, no. 3 (1999): 169–176.

Spears, R., and M. Lea. "Panacea or Panopticon? The Hidden Power in Computer-Mediated Communication." *Communication Research* 21, no. 4 (1994): 427–459.

Spender, Dale. *Nattering on the Net: Women, Power, and Cyberspace.* Melbourne: Spinifex Press, 1996.

Springer, Claudia. *Electronic Eros: Bodies and Desire in the Postindustrial Age.* Austin: University of Texas Press, 1996.

Sproull, Lee, and Sara Kiesler. *Connections: New Ways of Working in the Networked World.* Cambridge, Mass.: MIT Press, 1991.

Stefik, Mark. *Internet Dreams: Archetypes, Myths, and Metaphors.* Cambridge, Mass.: MIT Press, 1996.

Sterling, Bruce. *Hacker Crackdown.* New York: Bantam, 1992.

Stoll, Clifford. *Silicon Snake Oil: Second Thoughts on the Information Highway.* New York: Anchor Books, 1996.

Stoll, Clifford. *The Cuckoo's Egg: Tracking a Spy Through the Maze of Computer Espionage.* New York: Doubleday, 1989.

Stone, Allucquère Rosanne. *The War of Desire and Technology at the Close of the Mechanical Age.* Cambridge, Mass.: MIT Press, 1996.

Stone, Allucquere Roseanne. "Will the Real Body Please Stand Up? Boundary Stories about Virtual Cultures." In *Cyberspace: First Steps.* Edited by Michael Benedikt. Cambridge, Mass.: MIT Press, 1991.

Strate, L., R. Jacobson, and S. B. Gibson, eds. *Communication and Cyberspace: Social Interaction in an Electronic Environment.* Cameron Park, Calif.: Hampton Press, 1996.

Streck, John M. "Pulling the Plug on Electronic Town Meetings: Participatory Democracy and the Reality of the Usenet." *New Political Science* 41–42 (1997): 17–46.

Stuhlmacher, A. F., and A. E. Walters. "Gender Differences in Negotiation Outcome: A Meta-Analysis." *Personnel Psychology* 52, no. 3 (1999): 653–677.

Sudweeks, F., M.L. McLaughlin, and S. Rafaeli. *Network and Netplay: Virtual Groups on the Internet.* Cambridge, Mass.: MIT Press, 1998.

Suler, J. R. "Psychotherapy in Cyberspace: A Five Dimension Model of Online and Computer-mediated Psychotherapy." *CyberPsychology and Behavior* (forthcoming in 2000).

Suler, J. R., and W. Phillips. "The Bad Boys of Cyberspace: Deviant Behavior in Multimedia Chat Communities." *CyberPsychology and Behavior* 1 (1998): 275–294.

Suler, J. R. "To Get What You Need: Healthy and Pathological Internet Use." *CyberPsychology and Behavior* 2 (1999): 385–394.

Talbott, Steve. *The Future Does Not Compute: Transcending the Machines in Our Midst*. Sebastopol, Calif.: O'Reilly & Associates, 1995.

Tan, Bernard C. Y., et al. "Reducing Status Effects with Computer-Mediated Communication: Evidence from Two Distinct National Cultures." *Journal of Management Information Systems* 15, no. 1 (1998): 119–141.

Tan, Bernard C. Y., et al. "Computer-mediated Communication and Majority Influence: Assessing the Impact in an Individualistic and a Collectivistic Culture." *Management Science* 44, no. 9 (1998): 1263–1278.

Terry, J., and M. Calvert. *Processed Lives: Gender and Technology in Everyday Life*. London: Routledge, 1997.

Thompson, William I. *The American Replacement of Nature: The Everyday Acts and Outrageous Evolution of Economic Life*. New York: Doubleday, 1992.

Tonnies, Ferdinand. *Community and Society/Gemeinschaft Und Gesellschaft*, trans. C. P. Loomis. New Brunswick, N.J.: Transaction, 1988. (Original work published in 1887.)

Tribe, Laurence H. "The Constitution in Cyberspace." *The Humanist* (September–October 1991.)

Tsagarousianou, R., D. Tambini, and C. Bryan, eds. *Cyberdemocracy: Technology, Cities and Civic Networks*. London: Routledge, 1998.

Turkle, Sherry. "Multiple Subjectivity and Virtual Community at the End of the Freudian Century." *Sociological Inquiry* 67, no. 1 (1997): 72–84.

Turkle, Sherry. "Virtuality and its Discontents: Searching for Community in Cyberspace." *The American Prospect* 24 (1996): 50–57.

Turkle, Sherry. *Life on the Screen: Identity in the Age of the Internet*. New York: Simon & Schuster, 1995.

Turkle, Sherry. *The Second Self: Computers and the Human Spirit*. New York: Simon & Schuster, 1984.

Turoff, M., and S. R. Hiltz. "Superconnectivity. Association for Computing Machinery." *Communications of the ACM* 41, no. 7 (1998): 116.

Turoff, Murray, and Starr Roxanne Hiltz. "Meeting through Your Computer." *IEEE Spectrum* (May 1977): 58–64.

Uncapher, Willard. "Rural Grassroots Telecommunication: Big Sky Telegraph and Its Community." Master's thesis, Annenberg School for Communication, University of Pennsylvania, 1991.

Uncapher, Willard. "Trouble in Cyberspace." *The Humanist* (September–October 1991).

Valacich, J. S., A. R. Dennis, and T. Connolly. "Idea Generation in Computer-Based Groups: A New Ending to an Old Story." *Organizational Behavior and Human Decision Processes* 57, no. 3 (1994): 448–467.

Vallee, Jacques. *The Network Revolution: Confessions of a Computer Scientist.* Berkeley, Calif.: And/Or Press, 1982.

Van Gelder, Lindsy. "The Strange Case of the Electronic Lover." Reprinted in *Computerization and Controversy.* Edited by Charles Dunlop and Robert Kling. San Diego, Calif.: Academic Press, 1991.

Van Vliet, W., and J. Burgers. *Communities in Transition: From the Industrial to the Postindustrial Era.* In *Neighborhood and Community Environments*, edited by I. Altman, and A. Wandersman. New York: Plenum Press, 1987.

Varley, Pamela. "What's Really Happening in Santa Monica." *Technology Review* (November/December 1991).

Virnoche, M. E., and G. T. Marx. "Only Connect: E. M. Forster in an Age of Electronic Communication: Computer-Mediated Association and Community Networks." *Sociological Inquiry* 67, no. 1 (1997): 85–100.

Wachte, R. M. "The Effect of Gender and Communication Mode on Conflict Resolution." *Computers in Human Behaviour* 15, no. 6 (1999): 763–782.

Wallace, Patricia M. *The Psychology of the Internet.* Cambridge: Cambridge University Press, 1999.

Walsh, J. P., and T. Bayma. "Computer Networks and Scientific Work." *Social Studies of Science* 26, no. 3 (1996): 661–703.

Walther, Joseph B. "Anticipated Ongoing Interaction Versus Channel Effects on Relational Communication in Computer-mediated Interaction." *Human Communication Research* 20, no. 4 (1994): 473–501.

Walther, Joseph B. "Computer-Mediated Communication: Impersonal, Interpersonal, and Hyperpersonal Interaction." *Human Communication Research* 23, no. 1 (1996): 3–43.

Walther, Joseph B. "Group and Interpersonal Effects in International Computer-Mediated Collaboration." *Human Communication Research* 23, no. 3 (1997): 342–369.

Walther, Joseph B. "Interpersonal Effects in Computer-Mediated Interaction: A Meta-Analysis of Social and Antisocial Communication." *Human Communication Research* 21, no. 4 (1994): 460–487.

Walther, Joseph B. "Relational Aspects of Computer-Mediated Communication: Experimental Observations Over Time." *Organization Science* 6, no. 2 (1995): 186–203.

Walther, Joseph B., et al. "Interpersonal Deception: Effects of Suspicion on Perceived Communication and Nonverbal Behavior Dynamics." *Human Communication Research* 22, no. 2 (1995): 163–196.

Ward, K. J. "Cyber-Ethnography and the Emergence of the Virtually New Community." *Journal of Information Technology* 14, no. 1 (1999): 95–105.

Waskul, D., and M. Douglass. "Cyberself: The Emergence of Self in Online Chat." *Information Society* 13, no. 4 (1997): 375–398.

Weinberg, Nancy. "Compassion by Computer: Contrasting the Supportiveness of Computer-Mediated and Face-to-Face Interactions." *Computers in Human Services* 13, no. 2 (1997): 51–63.

Weisband, S. P., S. K. Schneider, and T. Connolly. "Computer-Mediated Communication and Social Information: Status Salience and Status Differences." *Academy of Management Journal* 38, no. 4 (1995): 1124–1151.

Wellman, B. "The Road to Utopia and Dystopia on the Information Highway" *Contemporary Sociology* 26, no. 4 (1997): 445–449.

Wellman, B. "Which Types of Ties and Networks Give What Kinds of Social Support?" *Advances in Group Processes* 9 (1992): 207–235.

Wellman, B., and M. Gulia. *Net Surfers Don't Ride Alone: Virtual Community as Community*. Pp 331–67 in *Networks in the Global Village*, edited by B. Wellman. Boulder, Colo.: Westview Press, 1999.

Wellman, B., and S. Wortley. "Different Strokes from Different Folks: Community Ties and Social Support." *American Journal of Sociology* 96 (1990): 558–588.

Wellman, B., et al. "Computer Networks as Social Networks: Collaborative Work, Telework, and Virtual Community." *Annual Review of Sociology* 22 (1996): 213–238.

Wellman, B., P. Carrington, and A. Hall. *Networks as Personal Communities. In Social Structures: A Network Approach*, edited by B. Wellman and S.D. Berkowitz. Cambridge: Cambridge University Press, 1988.

Wellman, Barry, ed. *Networks in the Global Village: Life in Contemporary Communities*. Boulder, Colo.: Westview Press, 1999.

Wellman, Barry. Email communication with author, January 11, 2000.

Whittle, David B. *Cyberspace: The Human Dimension*. New York: W. H. Freeman and Co, 1997.

Wiesenfeld, B., S. Raghuram, and R. Garud. "Communication Patterns as Determinants of Organizational Identification in a Virtual Organization." *Journal of Computer-Mediated Communication* 3, no. 4 (1998).

Winner, Langdon. "Who Will We Be in Cyberspace?" *Information Society* 12, no. 1 (1996): 63–72.

Winner, Langdon. *Autonomous Technology: Technics-out-of-Control as a Theme in Political Thought*. Cambridge, Mass.: MIT Press, 1977.

Winner, Langdon. *The Whale and the Reactor*. Chicago: University of Chicago Press, 1986, p. 112.

Wise, John M. Exploring *Technology and Social Space* (New Media Cultures). Thousand Oaks, Calif.: Sage Publications, 1997.

Witmer, D. F., and S. L. Katzman. "On-Line Smiles: Does Gender Make a Difference in the Use of Graphic Accents?" *Journal of Computer-Mediated Communication* 2, no. 4 (1997).

Wittig, Michelle. "Electronic City Hall." *Whole Earth Review* 71 (Summer 1991): 24.

Wolfe, Tom. *The Electric Kool-Aid Acid Test*. New York: Farrar, Straus and Giroux, 1968.

Woolley, Benjamin. *Virtual Worlds: A Journey in Hype and Hyperreality*. New York: Penguin, 1994.

Wuthnow, Robert. *Loose Connections: Joining Together in America's Fragmented Communities*. Cambridge, Mass.: Harvard University Press, 1998.

Xiaoming, H., K. Zhang, and H. Yu. "The Internet and Information Control: The Case of China." *Javnost /The Public* 3, no. 1 (1996): 117–130.

Yates, Simeon J. "Gender, Identity and CMC." *Journal of Computer Assisted Learning* 13, no. 4 (1997): 281–290.

Yoshida, Atsuya, and Jun Kakuta. "People Who Live in an On-Line Virtual World." Department of Information Technology, Kyoto Institute of Technology, Matsugasaki, Sakyoku, Kyoto 606, Japan, 1993.

Zdenek, S. "Rising Up From the MUD: Inscribing Gender in Software Design." *Discourse and Society* 10, no. 3 (1999): 379–409.

Index

Acceptable use, 77, 80, 169
ACEnet, 369–370
Acid Phreak (hacker), 267–270,
  272–273
Activism, 397. *See also* Politics
  Apple Computer and, 282
  Barlow and, 267–271
  BBSs and, 257–258
  big business and, 290–292
  Hughes and, 255–267
  Kapor and, 267, 271–272
  online, 255–293
ADAnet, 146–147
Addiction, 18–19, 156–158, 169, 237
  Greenfield on, 356
  Internet Addiction Disorder and,
    356–357
  IRC and, 188, 191
  medical views on, 356–359
  Minitel and, 240–241
  MUDs and, 150
Adorno, T. W., 371–375
Advertising, 295–296, 299
Agent Baxter, 269–271
Agora, 50, 376
Aizu, Izumi, 205–206, 232–233, 394
  background of, 207–208
  CMC and, 211
  COARA and, 212–215
  emulation and, 220
  Kumon and, 218–219
  Oita conference and, 211–212
  Tomino and, 209–210

Alexander, Kim, 383
Allison, Jay, 3–4
*All That Is Solid Melts into Air:
  The Experience of Modernity*
  (Berman), 361
Alternate identities
  Cyberion City and, 160–167
  deception and, 169–172
  depersonalization and, 151–152
  Habitat and, 194–203
  IRC and, 181–203
  mimesis theory and, 159–160
  Minitel and, 242
  powers and, 153, 159
  self identity and, 352–359
  sex chat and, 242–246
  social problems and, 174–175
  text and, 158–159
Alto (computer), 71
American Information Exchange
  (Amix), 199
America On-Line, 200, 333, 335, 340
  future and, 375, 377–378
American Psychiatric Association,
  357
American Psychological Association,
  356
American Psychologist, 355
*American Replacement of Nature:
  The Everyday Acts and Outrageous
  Evolution of Economic Life, The*
  (Thompson), 353
Amherst University, 169

Amnesty International, 280
Amusing Ourselves to Death
  (Postman), xxix, 305, 383
Anarchy, 119, 139
Anderson, Benedict, 54
Animateurs, 235, 242
Anonymity, 38
ANS corporation, 80–81
AOL, 200, 333, 335, 340
  future and, 375, 377–378
Apple Computers, 60, 113, 208, 260
  activism and, 282
  France and, 234
  future and, 393
  hackers and, 269, 272
  Japan and, 222
  multimedia and, 200
  personal communicators and,
    283–284
  text search and, 102–103
ARC, 64, 113
Archie (software), 47, 102
Armstrong, Arthur G., 342
ARPA (Advanced Research Projects
  Agency), xxvi
  bootstrapped research and, 65–66
  hackers and, 36
  interactive computing and, 59
  PC revolution and, 71
ARPANET, xxi–xxiii, 64
  beginning of, 9
  e-mail and, 69
  FidoNet and, 141
  groupminds and, 111
  growth of, 73
  MILNET and, 76
  networking and, 78
  transfer rates and, 72
  Unix and, 77
  Usenet and, 121–122
Artificial Intelligence Laboratory, 64,
  166
Asahi Shimbun (magazine), 205
Aspnes, James, 167–168
Association for Community
  Networking, The, 385

Association for Progressive
  Communications (APC), 253, 282
AT&T, 61, 77, 82
Atsuya, Yoshida, 194, 202
"Augmentation of Human Intellect,
  The" (Engelbart), 63
Augmentation Research Center
  (ARC), 64, 113
Autodesk, 270–271
Avatars, 196–199
Awaken community, 115

Baba, Masaharu, 214
Bagdikian, Ben, xxix
Bandy, 20–22
Baran, Paul, 67
Barlow, John Perry, 24, 68, 400
  hackers and, 267–271
  Japan 212
  Kapor and, 272
  video and, 177
Bartle, Richard, 198
  MUDs and, 149, 155, 159–160,
    168–169
Baudrillard, Jean, 304, 318–319
Bay Area Skeptic, 146
BBSs (Bulletin Board Systems),
  xxii–xxiii, 225
  birth of, 59–60
  Brand and, 25
  CalvaCom and, 234
  counterculture of, 133–148
  electronic democracy and, 295
  extent of, xxiv
  grassroot projects and, 110
  Internet and, xxiv
  political activism and, 257–258
  power of, 133
  religion and, 146
Bell Atlantic, 395
Bell Labs, 121
Ben-Horin, Dan, 277
Bentham, Jeremy, xxx, 300, 308–310
Berkeley, 76, 169
Berlin airlift, 110–111
Berman, Marshall, 361–362

Bible, 146
BIG BOARD, 148
Big Brother, 312
Big business, 393
  activism and, 290–292
  ClickStart and, 378
  commodification and, 299, 301–308
  hackers and, 269, 271
  influence and, 382–383
  mergers and, 377, 394–396
  networking and, 79–84
  politics and, 395–398
  private information and, 313
  public sphere and, 371–375
  telecommunications service and, 297
Big Sky Telegraph (BST), 258,
  260–264
Bill Graham Presents, 27
Bill of Rights, 276
BITNET, 77, 279–280, 283
Bitzer, Don, 111
Biwa-Net, xxvi
Blacksburg Electronic Village (BEV),
  367–369
Blair Newman Memorial Newuser
  Report, 42
Blink connection, 147
Boardwatch, 134
Body Dharma, 146
Bolt, Beranek, and Newman (BBN),
  63, 66, 166
  packet switching and, 67–68
Bootstrapped research, 65–66
Bots, 47, 103–104, 182, 299
"Bowling Alone: America's Declining
  Social Capital" (Putnam), 386
Bozo filter, 119
Brand, Stewart, 9, 25–26
  anonymity and, 38
  Brilliant and, 27–28
  Farm alumni and, 29
  hackers and, 267, 272
  PC revolution and, 36
  Thompson's accusation and, 353
  WBSI and, 27
  WELL birth and, 26–30

Breakfast in bed for 400,000, 28
Brilliant, Larry, 27–28
Britain, 237, 247–253
Brown, Deborah, 189–190
Bruckman, Amy, 150, 155, 185, 188
  ideals and, 168
  "Identity Workshops" and,
    156–157, 173, 178
  Jenkins and, 174
  MediaMOO and, 157, 178–180
Builders, 167
Bulletin-board systems. *See* BBSs
Burns, Frank, 209, 286
Bush, George, 80
Business Week, 37
Byte, 37, 135

Cabals, 332
Calhoun, Craig, 350
California Cooperative Corporation,
  333
California Rural Legal Assistance,
  278
California Voter's Foundation, 383
CalvaCom, xvii, 231–233
  Lumbroso and, 234–237
Calvados, 233–235
Campus Wide Information System,
  104
Canal Plus, 236
CapAdvantage, 384
Cap Cities, 375
Captain Crunch (John Draper), 270
Carey, James, 306
Carlson, Lisa, 207, 209, 286
Carnegie-Mellon University, 167–168
Case, Steve, 378
Casey (Kathleen Creighton), 13, 17,
  327–328
Catalfo, Gabe, 328
Catalfo, Phil, 4–8, 328
Catholic Information Network (CIN),
  146
Caucus, 228, 286
CBBS, 135–136, 138
Censorship, 296–297

Center for On-Line Addiction, 357
Cerf, Vinton, 103
Cerulo, K. A., 366–367
Channels, 182, 186. See also IRC
Chanops, 186–187, 190
Chariot, 259
Chat, 60, 99. See also Internet Relay
    Chat; WELL
  France and, 231–253
  Japan and, 205–229
  messageries and, 232, 240–246, 296
  Minitel and, 231
  MUDs and, 149–180
Children, 356
Chinet, 136
Christensen, Ward, 134–136
CIA, 85
Cisler, Steve, 103, 370
Citizen encryption, 314–315
City Council Telecommunications
    Policy Advisory Committee, 257
Civic Practices Network, 384–386
Civil liberty, 266–273
CIX, xvii, 247–253
C language, 36
ClickStart, 378
Clift, Steven, 383
Clinton administration, xxvi, 378,
    395–396
  Clipper Chip and, 399
  electronic democracy and, 306
  national information and, 207
Clipper Chip, 399–401
Club Caribe, 200
CMC (Computer-Mediated
    Communications), xix–xxi
  BBSs and, xxii–xxiv
  birth of, 58
  Brand and, 25
  Britain and, 247–253
  circle of friends and, 11
  Clipper Chip and, 399–401
  commodification and, 301–308
  community and, xxviii
  cooperation and, 109
  countercultures and, 27–28. See also
    Countercultures

dangers of, 352–359
diffusion of, 75
EIES and, 111, 113–116
electronic democracy and, 295–321
escapism and, xxvi
France and, 231–253
future of, 69
globalism and, 276–284
groupminds and, 109–118
growth of, 401–403
human interaction and, 8
impact on business, 52–53
intellectual property and, 99–100
interactive computing and, 59
interfaces and, 38
IRC and, 181–203
Japan and, 205–229
MUDs and, 149–180
municipal systems and, xxv–xxvi
political activism and, xxix,
    255–293
potential influence of, xxxi–xxxii
privacy and, 296–300
private sector and, 78–79
progress of, 106–107
public sphere and, 371–391
software and, 46–47
transfer rates and, 72
ultimate prison and, 308–317
Utopia and, 115–116
COARA, xxvi, 211–218, 221–222,
    224
Coate, John "Tex", 28–29, 41
Co-Evolution Quarterly, 26–27
Collective goods, xxviii
Colleges, 60–61
Colorado, 255–258
COMBAT ARMS, 142–145
Commercial interests. See Big
    business
Commodification, 299, 317, 372
  public sphere and, 301–308
  social capital and, 386–391
Commodore 64, 196, 200, 260
Common room, 177–178
Common Sense (Paine), xxix, 255,
    305

Communication. *See also* CMC
  Avatars and, 196–199
  Baran scheme and, 67
  BBSs and, 133–148
  big business and, 79–84
  commodification and, 301–308
  dangers of, 352–359
  France and, 231–253
  future of, 69
  groupminds and, 109–118
  IRC and, 181–203
  Japan and, 205–229
  MUDs and, 149–180
  Net information and, 84–102
  packet-switching and, 66–68
  PARC and, 70–71
  privacy and, 299–300
  social impact of, 345–352
  Unix and, 76
  video linking and, 176–178
CommuniTree, 136–139
Community, xxviii, 9, 178. *See also*
  Virtual communities
  standards and, 132
  technology centers and, 378
Community Building on the Web
  (Kim), 343
Compconf Psychserv, 18
CompuMentor, 253, 277–278
CompuServe, 117, 170, 183
"Computer as a Communication
  Device, The" (Herbert, Licklider,
  and Taylor), 69
Computer-based Education Research
  Laboratory (CERL), 111
Computer Bulletin Board System
  (CBBS), 135–136, 138. *See also*
  BBSs
Computer conferencing, xxi–xxii
  BBSs and, 133–148
  birth of, 64
  Brilliant and, 28
  circle of friends and, 11
  Deadheads and, 30
  EIES and, 111, 113–115
  electronic democracy and, 298
  Experts on the Well and, 50–52

Fidonet and, 138–148
  future of, 69
  groupminds and, 109–118
  history and, 29
  military and, 111–112
  modern state of, 340–341
  municipal, 209–210
  NETI and, 28
  PC revolution and, 36
  SRI International and, 40
  Threads and, 336
  True Confessions and, 30
  TWICS and, xvii, 31, 207, 215, 394
  Japan and, 224–227
  Usenet and, 118–133
  WELL's list of, 32–35
"Computer-Mediated Communication
  and the American Collectivity"
  (Fernback and Thompson), 379
Computer-mediated communications.
  See CMC
Computer Press Association, 208
Computer Professionals for Social
  Responsibility, 275
Computers
  birth of Internet and, 58–59
  early history of, 58
  emulation and, 220
  Engelbart and, 57–58
  enlarged use of, 60
  extent of, 377–378
  graphics and, 63–65, 71
  multiple-access and, 66
  PCs and, 36, 58, 60, 71, 133–148
  rural education and, 259–266
  supercomputers, 77–78
  symbols and, 57
  as weapons, 310
Computers, Freedom, and Privacy,
  274, 276
Computers As Theater (Laurel), 159
Computer-supported cooperative play,
  194–203
Computer-supported cooperative
  work (CSCW), 194
ConflictNet, 280, 282
Connect Ed, 266

Connections: New Ways of Working in the Networked World (Sproull and Kiesler), 47
Cook, Gordon, 82
Cooperation, 109
Corporation for National Research Initiatives, 103
Corporations. *See* Big business
Countercultures, 53. *See also* Virtual communities
  alternate identities and, 149–180
  Awaken, 115
  BBSs and, 133–148
  colleges and, 60–61
  CommuniTree and, 136–138
  computer revolution and, 59–60
  Deadheads, 37
  Habitat and, 194–203
  Hog Farm and, 27–28
  IRC and, 181–203, 205
  media and, 393
  Merry Pranksters and, 27
  newsgroups and, 122–123
  PC revolution and, 36
  SF-LOVERS, 70
  tiprudder analogy and, 26–27
  WELL birth and, 26–30
  Whole Earth and, 25–26
Creighton, Kathleen, 288, 325, 327–328
"Crime and Puzzlement" (Barlow), 267
CSNET, 77
CTNet, 378
Cuckoo's Egg, The (Stoll), 267, 327
Culture
  public sphere and, 301–308, 333
  prospects for, 371–391
Curtis, Pavel, 149, 156, 171–172, 175
Cyberion City (MUD), 160–167
"Cybernetic Capitalism: Information, Technology, Everyday Life" (Robins and Webster), 309
Cyberspace, xxxi
  alternate identities and, 149–180
  big business and, 82–84

  Britain and, 247–253
  cities in, 284–293
  Clipper Chip and, 399–401
  commodification and, 301–308
  cost and, 25
  counterculture of, 25–55
  deceit and, 12
  democracy and, 295–321
  Fidonet and, 138–148
  France and, 231–253
  gift economics and, 45–55
  groupminds and, 109–118
  growth of, 401–403
  Habitat and, 194–203
  hackers and, 266–269
  history of, 57–62
  hosting and, 26
  hyper-realism and, 317–321
  information in, 84–102
  IRC and, 181–203
  Japan and, 205–229
  minds online and, 352–359
  PC revolution and, 36, 58, 60, 71
  physical attributes and, 11
  political activism and, 255–293
  privacy and, 296–300
  public sphere prospects and, 371–391
  self identity and, 352–359
  social contracts and, 45–55
  society and, 53–54, 334–345
  toolbuilders' quest and, 62–84

Dante, 100
DARPA, 77, 80
Daugherty, Dale, 334–335
Deadheads, 30, 37, 39, 173
Debord, Guy, 304, 318
DEC (Digital Equipment Corporation), 61, 63
  Unix and, 77
  Usenet and, 121
Deceit, 12, 331, 375
  commodification and, 299, 301–308
  gender-switching, 169–172, 189
  hyper-realism and, 300
  IRC and, 181

Deep Blue II, 342–343
Delphi method, 112
de Maublanc, Henri, 241–242
Democracy, xxx, 376, 403. *See also*
  Electronic democracy
  erosion of, 383
  Frankfurt School and, 371–375
  online, 338–340
de Moor, Aldo, 279
Denis, 242, 244–245
Department of Commerce, 80
Department of Defense, 63, 70
Dernieres Nouvelles d'Alsace (news-
  paper), 239
Dery, Mark, 354
DFS Action, 278
d'Estaing, Valery Giscard, 238
Determinism, 346, 376
Deutsch, Peter, 102
DGT, 237–238, 241, 245
Dhawk (David Hawkins), 38
Dibbell, Julian, 340
Digital cash, 315–317
Digital convergence, 68
Digital divide, 377–379
Digital signature, 315
Digital Telephony Bill, 399–400
Digital trails, 299–300
Direction Generale des Telecommuni-
  cations (DGT), 237–238, 241, 245
Dirigiste (cultural regulation), 237,
  246
Discipline and Punish (Foucault),
  xxx, 309
Discourse, 305–306
Disinformocracy, 295–296, 371, 383.
  See also Democracy
  commercial interests and, 297–298
  commodification and, 299–308
  hyper-realism and, 320–321
Disney, 300, 393
Divina Commedia (Dante), 100
DNA, 354
Dourish, Paul, 176–177
Dow Jones, 102–103
Draper, John, 270–271
Drucker, Peter, xxvii, 40

Drugs, 101
Duke University, 61, 117
Durand Communications, 338
Durkheim, Emile, 54

EARN (European Academic Research
  Network), 280
Earth Trust, 278
Echomail, 141
*Ecolinking: Everyone's Guide to
  Online Environmental Organiza-
  tion*, 279
Econet, 253, 280, 282
Educational theory, 166–167
EFF. *See* Electronic Frontier
  Foundation
EIES (Electronic Information
  Exchange System), 111, 113–116,
  207
Eisenhart, Mary, 39
Eisenstein, Elizabeth L., 346
Electric Kool-Aid Acid Test (Wolfe),
  27
Electric Minds, 324, 336–338,
  342–343
Electronic Communications Privacy
  Act, 275, 297
Electronic democracy, 295–296,
  383
  commercial interests and, 297–298
  commodification and, 299–308
  hyper-realism and, 320–321
Electronic Frontier Foundation (EFF),
  81, 220
  birth of, 266–276
  encryption and, 316
  Gore and, 397–398
Electronic mail. *See* E-mail
Electronic Networking Association,
  225
"Electropolis: Communication and
  Community on Internet Relay
  Chat" (Reid), 186
Ellis, James, 118
Ellul, Jacques, 353
Elly (Elly van der Pas), 13–17
Elshtain, Jean Betheke, 307

E-mail, xxii, 29, 42, 95, 205
  ARPANET and, 69, 185
  birth of, 60–61, 183
  FidoNet and, 141
  first lists of, 70
  future of, 69
  Gulf War and, 283
  hackers and, 266
  House of Representatives and,
    88–90
  IRC and, 184
  MUDs and, 152
  personal communicators and, 284
  political campaigns and, 383
  privacy and, 297
  Usenet and, 118–133
  White House and, 86–87
Emergency Management Information
  System and Reference Index
  (EMISARI), 112–113
Emergent behaviors, 72–73
E-Minders, 338
Emoting, 152–153, 182
Emulation, 220
Enabling technology, 60
Encryption, 314–316
Energy creature, 330
Engelbart, Douglas, 40, 112
  ARC and, 113
  bootstrapped research and, 65–
    66
  crusade of, 57–58
  hypertext and, 96
  PARC and, 71
  SRI and, 62–63, 65–66
Enhanced information services,
  313–314
Environmentalists, 278–280
*Escape Velocity: Cyberculture at the
  End of the Century* (Dery), 354
Escapism. *See* Fantasy
E-The People, 384
Ethics, 98, 338
  intellectual property and, 99–101
EuroPARC, 176
Experts on the WELL, 50–53

E-zines, 335–336

Falk, Bennet, 39
Fantasy, xxvi, 53. *See also* MUDs;
  Sex
  Habitat and, 194–203
  IRC and, 188–189
Fanzines, 134
FAQs, 128–130
Farallones Institute, 282
Farber, David, 81
Farmer, Randy, 195–201
FBI, 270–271, 276
  Clipper Chip and, 399
  hacking and, 266–273
FCC, 134, 395
FDA, 101
Federal Preparedness Agency, 112
Feenberg, Andrew, 246
FEMA, 147
Fernback, Jan, 379–382, 391
FidoNet, xxiv
  beginnings of, 138–139
  cost of, 139–140
  Internet and, 141–142
  various BBSs of, 143–148
Figallo, Clifford, 12–13, 31, 341
  Deep Blue II and, 343
  EFF and, 274
  Salon.com and, 334
  WELL and, 28–29
Finkel, Bruria, 285
First Amendment, 301–303
First Conference on Cyberspace, 137,
  195
Flaming, 332, 343, 351
  big business and, 82–84
  Fido and, 139
  WELL and, 41–42
Flash Gordon, 17, 40
Floyd, K., 350
FM-Towns, 201
Foley, Timothy, 275
Ford Motor Company, 378–379
Forster, E. M., 319–320
FORTRAN, 62

Foucault, Michel, xxx, 309–310
France, 248–253
  CalvaCom and, 231–237
  DGT and, 237–238, 241, 245
  Minitel surprises and, 237–247
  sex chat and, 242–246
  Telematique and, 238–239
  videotext and, 237–239
Frankfurt School, 371–375
Frederick, Howard, 280–281
Freedom
  Clipper Chip and, 399–401
  Frankfurt School and, 371–375
  of speech, 301–304, 312, 384
Freedom Forum, 384
Free-Net, 289
Free software, 99–100
Freespeech.org, 384
Friends, 11–12
  Blair and, 18–24
  Elly and, 13–17
  social contracts and, 45–55
Frivolity, 123
FTP (file transfer protocol), 95, 98,
  105
Fujino, Yukitsugu, 214–215
Fujitsu, 183–184, 207
  play and, 194–203
Fuller, Buckminster, 26–27, 259
Future Does Not Compute:
  Transcending the Machines in Our
  Midst, The (Talbott), 350

Gans, David, 39–40
Gates, Bill, 99, 395–397
Gates, Rick, 92
Gateway computers, xxiv
Geertz, Clifford, 187
Gemeinschaft, 54
Gender-switching, 169–172, 189
General Atomics, 82
General Electric, 304
General Instrument, 292
General Magic, 283–284
GeoCities, 340
Geonet, 253

Gergen, Kenneth J., 174
Gesellschaft, 54
Gibson, William, xx, 139
Gift economics, 45–55
Gilder, George, xxvii
Gilmore, John, xxii, 272, 316
GlasNet, 281–282
Globalization, 301, 377
Global Network Navigator (GNN),
  334–335
GLOCOM, 220
Goebbels, Joseph, 306
Goffman, Erving, 245
Goldberg, Ivan, 357
Good Society, The, xxviii
Gopher (software), 47, 104–105
Gordon, Flash, 17, 40
Gore, Al, xxvi, 73, 79
  big business and, 395–398
  Clipper Chip and, 399
  deregulation and, 397
Government, 62. *See also* Politics
  big business and, 395–398
  computer conferencing and,
    109–112
  grassroot projects and, 110
  networking and, 116
  privacy and, 299–300
Graphics, 63–65, 71, 200
Grassroot projects, 393
  activism and, 255–293
  BBSs and, 133–148
  globalism and, 276–284
  groupminds and, 109–118
  Japan and, 205–229
  Usenet and, 118–133
Grateful Dead conference, 37
Grateful Med, 147
GreaterGood, 385
Great Good Place, The (Oldenburg), 9
Greenfield, David, 356
GreenNet, 253, 280, 282
Gretel project, 239
Groupminds
  BBSs and, 133–148
  Berlin airlift and, 110–111

Groupminds (*cont.*)
 computer conferencing and,
  109–118
 Usenet and, 118–133
Grundner, Tom, 289
Guidestar, 385
Gulf War, 191–193, 282–283
Gulia, M., 362–366

Habermas, Jurgen, 301–305, 372
Habitat, 184
 play and, 194–203
 religion and, 199
Habits of the Heart, xxviii
Hackers, 36–37, 64, 271
 EFF and, 272–273
 ethics and, 99
 fear of, 266
 original meaning of, 270
 WELL conference and, 267–269
Hacker's Conference, 30, 36,
  270–271
*Hackers: Heroes of the Computer
  Revolution* (Levy), 64, 270
Hafner, Katie, 326
Hagel III, John, 342
Haight-Ashbury, 26
Hall, Kevin, 252
Hampton, Keith N., 368–369
Hardware, 66
Harper's, 37, 266–268
Harrington, Ken, 141
Hart, Michael, 101
Harvard, 68
Harvard Business Review, 11, 52
Hattori, Katsura, 205–232–233
Hawkins, David, 38
Herbert, E., 69
Herestoby, 248, 252
Hierarchy, 123–124
High-bandwidth, 299
High Performance Computing Act,
 xxvi, 79–80
High Technology Communications,
 208
Hiltz, Starr Roxanne, 116, 207

Hiramatsu, 216–218, 221–222, 395
"Hobbyist Computerized Bulletin
 Boards" (Christensen and Suess),
 136
Hog Farm, 27–29
Home interactive information services
 industry, xxvii
Hoover, J. Edgar, 310
Hori-gotatsu (warming pit), 208
Horkheimer, M., 371–375
Horton, Mark, 121
Hosting, 26, 30
Hosting Web Communities (Figallo),
 343
HotWired (webzine), 324
House of Representatives, 88–90
"How Big Is the Matrix?"
 (Quarterman), 73
Hughes, Dave, 298
 activism and, 255–258
 BBS of, 133
 EIES and, 207
 hackers and, 267
 Odasz and, 259–266
HUMAN-NETS, 70, 121
Hypernetwork conference, 212–213,
 395
Hypernetwork Society, 205, 221
Hyper-realism, 300
 commodification and, 301–304
 disinformocracy and, 317–321
Hypertext, 64, 96, 96–98, 100

IBM, 78, 295, 393
 BITNET and, 77
 Deep Blue II and, 342–343
 Net management and, 80–81
I-charity, 385
Identity Workshops. See MUDs
"Identity Workshops" (Bruckman),
 173, 178
Illinois Benedictine College, 101
Imagined Communities (Anderson),
 54
Income levels, 377–378
Industry. *See* Big business

Information. *See also* Knowledge
  commodification and, 301–308
  digital trails and, 299–300
  Fidonet and, 138–148
  home interactive, xxvii
  intellectual property and, 99–101
  Internet and, 84–102
  knowbot agents and, 103–104
  marketing and, 313–314
  minds online and, 352–359
  pornography and, 99
  privacy and, 311–312
  Prodigy and, 295–296
  search tools for, 103–107
  superhighway of, 393, 395
  technology and, 72
  WAIS and, 102–103
Information Processing Techniques
  Office, 64
Information Superhighway Summit,
  400
Institute for Defense Analysis, 111
Institute for Global Communications
  (IGC), 281–282
Institute for Networking Design, 211
Institute for the Future, The (IFTF),
  116
Intel Corporations, 292
Intellectual property, 99–101, 315,
  344
Interaction, 8, 59, 398
Interfaces, 38
Internet
  alternate identities and, 149–180
  BBSs and, xxiv
  big business and, 79–84
  birth of, 58–59
  Britain and, 247–253
  Clipper Chip and, 399–401
  commodification and, 301–308
  complexity of, 102–103
  cyberspace cities and, 284–293
  dangers of, 356
  democracy and, 295–321
  Engelbart and, 57–58
  Fidonet and, 138–148

France and, 231–253
  future of, xxi, 393–403
  GNN and, 334–335
  government access and, 86–92
  groupminds and, 109–118
  growth of, 73, 401–403
  hackers and, 266–269
  Hunt and, 92–95
  information on, 84–102
  IRC and, 181–203
  Japan and, 205–229
  management of, 79–80
  minds online and, 352–359
  network protocol and, 122
  political activism and, 255–293
  privacy and, 296–300
  private sector and, 78–79
  public access to, 377–378
  public sphere prospects and,
    371–391
  science and, 75
  search tools for, 103–107
  self-governance and, 54–55
  self identity and, 352–359
Internet Addiction Disorder,
  356–357
Internet Relay Chat (IRC), xxvi,
  xxxii, 61, 106, 205
  actions and, 182
  addiction and, 188, 191
  antisocial behavior and, 191
  beginning of, 184
  communication and, 181–183
  Gulf War and, 191–193
  Internet and, 183–184
  nicknames and, 181
  romance and, 189–190
  taboos and, 186–187
IRL (in real life), xvi
IRS, 112
Islandia (TinyMUD), 169
Ito, Joichi, 394, 401–403
  grassroots projects and, 207–209
  kansei and, 203
  TWICS and, 224–225, 227–229

Jackson, Steve, 269, 272, 274–275
Jaffe, Louis, 260
Janet and John books, 250
Japan, 205, 219–220, 394–395
  COARA and, 211–218, 221–222, 224
  infrastructure of, 207
  Ito and, 227–229
  JUNET and, 202
  karaoke and, 212–213
  municipal computer conferencing and, 209–210
  Net policies of, 222–223
  Oita conference and, 211–217, 221–222, 395
  similarities and, 206–207
  technology and, 207–209
  TWICS and, 224–227
Jenkins, Henry, 173–174
Jennings, Tom, 138–141
Jobs, Steve, 36
Johansen, Robert, 212
Johnson-Lenz, Trudy, 114–115, 207, 212
Johnson-Lenz, Peter, 114–115, 207, 212
Jones, Steven, 349
Journalists, 30, 37
JUNET (Japanese University NETwork), 202

Kahle, Brewster, 102
Kahn, Robert, 67–68, 80
Kakuta, Jun, 194, 202
Kaleida labs, 291–292
Kansei (rightness), 203, 206
Kapor, Mitchell D., 36, 81
  hackers and, 267, 271–272
  Japan and, 220
  politics and, 298
  principles and, 397
Karaoke, 212–213
KarlsGirl (Deborah Brown), 189–190
Kasparov, Gary, 342–343
Katz, Bruce, 331–334
Katz, Jon, 328–329
Kay, Alan, 65, 70–71

Kelly, Kevin, 30, 267, 335
Kesey, Ken, 27
Keshernet, 146
Kiesler, Sara, 11, 47, 52–53, 190, 351
Kill file, 119
Kim, Amy Jo, 343
King, Storm, 358–359
Kiosque system, 242
KJ, 327
Kleinpaste, Karl, 189–190
Knowbots, 47, 103–104, 182, 299
Knowledge. See also Information
  Amix and, 199
  computers and, 57
  as currency, 48
  Experts on the WELL and, 50–51
  Fidonet and, 138–148
  groupminds and, 118–148
  minds online and, 352–359
  Net information and, 84–102
  products of, 377
  virtual communities and, 48
  worker, 40
KPMC, 102
Kubaki, Masato, 215
Kumon, Shumpei, 218–220
Kyoto Institute of Technology, 194, 202

Lai, Chou En, 349
LambdaMOO, 175, 340
Landaret, Michel, 239–240
LANs, 71
Lanzmann, Chine, 236–237
Laurel, Brenda, 159
LDSnet, 146
Lea, M., 350–351
Le Monde (newspaper), 238
"Lessons of Lucasfilm's Habitat, The" (Morningstar and Randall), 195
Levenson, Paul, 266
Levy, Steven, 64, 270
Library of Congress, 72–73, 80, 85, 100
Licklider, J. C., 9, 66
  ARPA and, 63
  on future communication, 69

Life On The Screen: Identity in the Age of the Internet (Turkle), 352
Lim, Stan, 166–167
Lincoln Laboratory, 63–65, 67
Linux, 344
Lipnack, Jessica, 210, 303–304
Living Constitution Society, The, 385
London, Christopher, 388–389
Loney, Tina, 38–39
Loose Connections: Joining Together in America's Fragmented Communities (Wuthnow), 383, 387
Lotus Development Corporation, 81, 271, 313
Love, 42
Lucasfilm Games, 195–196, 200
Ludlow, Peter, 349
Lumbroso, Lionel, 231–232
  CalvaCom and, 234–237
  description of, 233

McCaw, Craig, 395–396
McClellan, J., 350
McClure, Matthew, 26, 28–31
McCullough, Peter, 70
"Machine Stops, The" (Forster), 319–320
McKinsey & Co., 342
McLuhan, Marshall, 151, 346
Maddog (David Gans), 39–40
Malone, Tom, 397
"Man-Computer Symbiosis" (Licklider), 63
Mandel, Tom, 38, 40, 325–327
Mao tse-Tung, 310
Marketing, 313, 342. *See also* Big business
Frankfurt School and, 371–375
Markoff, John, 81, 292
Marwick, Peat, 102
Marx, Gary, 314–315
Mass-scribbling, 20–22
Mathematics, 315–316
Matrix, The (Quarterman), xxiii, 225
Matters of general interest, 304
MCI Communications, 78, 80–81, 377

Media, xxix–xxx, 304–305. *See also* Communication; CMC
  commodification and, 301–308
  Frankfurt School and, 371–375
  influence of, 345–352, 371–391
Media Lab, The (Brand), 9
Media Monopoly, The, xxix
MediaMOO, 157, 178–180, 193
Medicinal bath, 372
Mele, Christopher, 382
Mendel, Gregor, 75
Merit Network, Inc., 78
Merry Pranksters, 27
Messageries, 240–241, 296
  pink, 242–246
  rose, 232
Messages, 112–113
  BBSs and, 133–148
  Usenet and, 118–133
Metadescription, 182
Metanetwork, 209–210
Metasystems Design Group (MDG), 286
Metaview, 18, 22
MicroMUSE, xvii, 160–167, 340
Microsoft, 99
  market strategies of, 393, 395, 397
  mergers and, 292, 377, 395
  open source and, 344
Millennium Whole Earth Catalog, The, 331
MILNET, 76–77
Mimesis, 159
Minc, Alain, 237–238
Minitel, xviii, xxvi, 183, 296
  Paris chat scene and, 231–232, 234
  sex chat and, 242–246
  surprises of, 237–247
Minnesota E-Democracy project, 383
MIT, 63
  Artificial Intelligence Lab, 64, 166
  Lincoln Laboratory, 67
  Media Lab, 9, 150, 178–180
  packet-switching and, 67–68
  time-sharing and, 64–65
Mitchell, Albert, 5

MITI (Ministry of International Trade and Industry), 217
Mitnick, Kevin, 324
MITRE, 166
MODEM program, 134–135
Modems, 135–136, 208, 223, 296
Montana, 259, 265–266
  Big Sky Telegraph (BST) and, 258, 260–264
Moore, James F., 292
Morel, Annick, 231–233
Morino Foundation, 370–371
Mormons, 146
Morningstar, Chip, 195–201
Morris Worm, 81
Mosaic, 334
Moses, A., 351
Motorola, 291
Moulton (Barry Kort), 161–167
Mouse device, 64
Mr. T., 202
MTV, xxvii, 402
MUDs (Multi-User Dungeons), xviii, xxvi, 53, 61, 227–228
  addiction and, 156–158, 169
  antisocial behavior and, 167
  artificial worlds of, 154–157
  colleges and, 155
  communication boundaries and, 150–151
  computer memory and, 169
  Cyberion City and, 160–167
  deception and, 169–172
  educational theory and, 166–167
  emoting and, 152–153
  "get a life" and, 150, 172–175
  growth of, 149–150
  ideals and, 167–168
  identity problems and, 174–175
  IRC and, 182–183, 188
  MediaMOO and, 178–180
  mimesis theory and, 159–160
  multimedia, 178
  narrative and, 160
  Project Jupiter and, 175, 178
  romance and, 172
  virtual building and, 175

  Xerox PARC and, 175–178
MUFON, 148
Mumford, Lewis, 353
MUSE (Multi-User Simulation Environment), 160–167
"Mythinformation" (Winner), 308
Myth of the Machine, The (Mumford), 353
My Tiny Life (Dibbell), 340

Nagano, Mieko, 216
Naisbitt, John, xxvii
NASA, 97–98
National Fido Hour, 140–141
National Information Infrastructure (NII), 395, 397
National Institute of Standards and Technology, 80
National Library of Medicine, 103
National Physical Laboratory, 67
National Public Telecomputing Network, 289–290
National Research and Education Network, xviii, xxvi, 265
National Research and Education Network (NREN), 62, 72
  activism and, 265, 396
  legislation and, 79–82
National Science Foundation (NSF), 60, 77, 82
  EIES and, 114
  private sector and, 80
  NSFNET and, 72, 78, 80–81
National Security Agency, 315–316, 398
National Strategy for Nonprofit Technology, 384
Native Americans, 264, 279
Neidorf, Craig, 269, 272
Nelson, Ted, 96, 100
Net. *See* Internet
Net Gain: Expanding Markets through Virtual Communities (Hagel and Armstrong), 342
NETI, 28
Netiquette, 54, 98–99, 364
Net.sleazing, 154

Networking
  BBSs and, 133–148
  big business and, 79–84
  commodification and, 301–308
  Congress and, 77–78, 80
  EIES and, 111–116
  encryption and, 314–315
  Fidonet and, 138–148
  groupminds and, 109–118
  Japan and, 205–229
  minds online and, 352–359
  nature of communities and, 359–371
  political activism and, 255–293
  privacy and, 296–300
  protocol of, 122
  self identity and, 352–359
  Source and, 117
  supercomputers and, 78
  transfer rates and, 72
  Unix and, 76–77
  Usenet and, 118–133
*Networking, People Connecting with
  People, Linking Ideas and
  Resources* (Lipnack and Stamps),
  210, 303–304
Network Nation (Hitz and Turoff),
  116
Network Revolution, The (Vallee),
  110, 311
Net-zines, 402
Neuromancer (Gibson), xx, 139
*New Community Networks: Wired
  for Change* (Schuler), 367
NewLife Christian Network, 146
Newman, Blair, 18–24, 272
New Media Committee, 228
Newsgroups
  Usenet and, 118–133
  WELL and, 125, 127
New Yorker, 357
New York Times, 37, 81, 326,
  328–329, 355
Nicknames, 12, 181
NIFTY-serve, 201, 203
Nixon, Richard, 112
NLS (oNLineSystem), 112–114,
  116

Non-governmental organizations
  (NGOs), 276, 280–281
Nora, Simon, 237–238
Nora-Minc report, 238, 245
NordNet, 282
North American Defense Command,
  63
NREN, 62, 72
  activism and, 265, 396
  legislation and, 79–82
NSF, 60, 77, 82
  EIES and, 114
  private sector and, 80
  NSFNET and, 72, 78, 80–81
NTT(Nippon Telephone and Tele-
  graph), 207, 229
  high-speed communication and, 200,
  223
  marketing strategies and, 393–394,
  396
Nuclear attack, 66–67
NuPrometheus League, 269–270, 272

Octopod, 332
Odasz, Frank, 258–265
Odasz, Reggie, 258–262
Office of Science and Technology, 79
Office of Technology Assessment
  (OTA), 48
Oikarinen, Jarkko, 184
Oita, Japan, 211–213, 395
  COARA and, 214–218, 221–222
Oldenburg, Ray, 9–10, 177
Onezie (Tina Loney), 38–39
Ong, Walter, 346
*Online Communities: Supporting
  Sociability and Designing Usability*
  (Preece), 345
Online service. *See* Cyberspace
Online Tsar, 335
Ono, Toru, 213–214
Open Platform, 397–398
Operating systems, 76
Operation Sun Devil, 269, 271–274
*Orality and Literacy: The
  Technologizing of the Word* (Ong),
  346

Order of the Holy Walnut, 199
ORIGINS, 137
Orwellian model, 312–313

Packet-switching, 66–68, 76–77, 111
Paine, Thomas, xxix, 255, 305
Panopticon, xxx, 376, 403
  criticism and, 300
  networking and, 309–310
  privacy and, 311–312
Panopticon; or, the Inspection House
  (Bentham), 308–309
PARC (Palo Alto Research Center),
  70–71
  MUDs and, 175–178
Parenting conference, 1–3, 53. *See
  also* WELL
  leukemia discussion and, 5–8
Parks, M. R., 350
Participate, 117
Paschal, Don, 287
PC (personal computer)
  BBSs and, 133–148
  revolution, 36, 58, 60, 71
PDP–1, 63, 66, 121
Peace, 115–116
Peacenet, 253, 280, 282
Peeking, 176
"People Who Live in an On-line
  Virtual World" (Atsuya and Jun),
  195
Performance Systems International, 81
Perot, Ross, 306
Peter+Trudy (Johnson-Lenz),
  114–115, 208, 212
Peterson, Keith, 135
Phaedrus (Plato), 346
Phiber Optik (hacker), 267–269, 272
Phillips, Ken, 287–288
Phrack (e-newsletter), 269
Piaget, Jean, 166, 194
Pickle Family Circus, 5
Picospan, 28, 38
Pink messages, 242–246. *See also* Sex
Place, 9–10, 37
PLANET (PLAnning NETwork), 116
Plato, 346

PLATO system, 111,
*Plato: The Emergence of Online
  Community* (Woolley), 111
Playgrounds, 184–186
  mediated, 194–203
Plenty, 29
Plummer, Steve, 233–234
Point and click, 65, 114
Point Foundation, 331
Politics, xxix, 27, 36
  big business and, 82–84, 290–292,
    395–398
  Clipper Chip and, 399
  computer conferencing and,
    209–210
  electronic democracy and, 295–321
  electronic pioneering and, 255–293
  globalism and, 276–284
  hacking and, 266–273
  Hughes and, 255–258
  hyper-realism and, 300
  mass entertainment and, 371
  NGOs and, 276, 280–281
  public sphere and, 371–391
  technology and, 116
Pollenator (Howard Rheingold), 151,
  158, 164–165
Popravka, Nina, 235–236
Poptart (Karl Kleinpaste), 189–190
Populopolis, 201–202
Pornography, 99, See also Sex
Posing, 152–153, 182
Postman, Neal, xxix, 305–306, 383
Pozar, Tim, 138, 141
Preece, Jenny, 345
Presentation of Self in Every Day Life
  (Goffman), 245
Prestel, 250–251, 295
Prestige Game, 219
Privacy, 296–298, 309, 377
  Clipper Chip and, 399–401
  digital trails and, 299–300
  encryption, 314–316
  high bandwidth and, 299
  Orwellian model of, 312–313
  Panopticon and, 311
  technology and, 311–312

Privacy Protection Act, 275
Private sector, 79–81
Problems of Conflict Management in Virtual Communities (Smith), 340
Prodigy, 295–298
Programmers, 46
Progress, 109, 307, 381
Project Gutenberg, 101
Project Jupiter, 175, 178, 193
Pseudonyms, 38
Psychology, 54, 150, 356, 358
Psychology of Cyberspace, The (Suler), 358
Public domain, 135–136, 379
Public Electronic Network (PEN), 253, 284–288
Public-key encryption, 315–316
Public sphere, 333
  commodification and, 301–308
  prospects for, 371–391
Publishers Weekly, 27
Publishing, 297
Putnam, Robert, 386–387

QuantumLink Communications, 195–196, 200
Quarterman, John, xxiii, 73, 225

Rain Forest Network Bulletin, 279
RAND Corporation, xxi–xxii, 66, 111
Randall, F., 195
Readers Digest, 117
Reagan, Ronald, 304
Reality, 300, 366, 379–380. *See also* Hyper-realism
Reciprocity, 49–50
Red Hat, 344
Reformation, 347
Reich, Robert, 46
Reid, Elizabeth M., 185–187, 191, 226
Religion, 137, 145–146, 199
Rensselaer Polytechnic Institute, 358
Request for proposals (RFP), 67
Resnick, Mitchel, 179
Resnick, Paul, 38

Resource Interruption Monitoring Systems (RIMS), 112
RFC (Request for Comment), 73–74
Rheingold, Howard, 323–324
  democracy online and, 338–340
  Electric Minds and, 336–338, 342–343
  HotWired and, 335–336
  parenting conference and, 1–7
  resigns from WELL, 332
  retraction of, 362
  social web and, 334–345
  Thompson's accusation and, 353
  on webconferencing, 340–345
Rheingold, Judy, 1
Rider University, 358
Rising Storm BBS, 147
River project, 332–333, 338
Roberts, Lawrence, 67
Robins, Kevin, 309
Rolling Stone, 37
Romance, 189–190
Rosebud (software), 47, 103
Rossetto, Louis, 335–336
Royalties, 100–101
Rules of Order (Robert), 339
Rural Grassroots Telecommunications, 261

St. Anthony's Dining room, 278
SALEMDUG, 147
Salons, 29–30, 334
San Francisco Chronicle, 37
Saturated Self: Dilemmas of Identitity in Contemporary Life, The (Gergen), 174
Schrader, William L., 81
Schuler, Douglas, 367
Science, 75–77, 110. *See also* Technology
Scientific American, 73
Scientific Atlanta, 291–292
Scorpion (hacker), 272
Scribbling, 20–22
Sculley, John, 36, 222
Secret Service, 275–276
  hacking and, 266–273

Self-governance, 54–55
Sequent, 13
Seva Foundation, 28
Sex, 99, 147–148
  IRC and, 189
  messageries rose and, 232
  Minitel and, 242–246
  Tinysex, 154
SF-LOVERS, 70, 121, 185
Shapard, Jeffrey, 207, 224–227
Shatner, William, 172
SHWASHLOCK, 284–287
Silicon Snake Oil (Stoll), 327
Silicon Valley, 378, 398
Silver, David, 376
Slashdot, 344
Smith, Anna du Val, 340
Smith, Marc, xxviii, 54, 185
Social capital, 386–391
Society. *See also* Communication;
  Virtual communities
  contracts and, 45–55
  Frankfurt School and, 371–375
  of the spectacle, 304, 318, 371
  Wellman on, 359–366
Society of the Spectacle, The
  (Debord), 318
Sociology, 54–55
Softbank, 337
Software, 46–47
Sony, 375
Source, 25, 115, 117, 207–208
Soviet Union, 58, 64, 133
Spacewar, 185
Spears, R., 350–351
Sprint, 377, 393
Sproull, Lee, 47
Sputnik, 58, 64
STAGE.DAT, 296
Stamps, Jeffrey, 210, 303–304
Stanford Research Institute, 40, 64,
  71, 96, 116, 141
Star Trek, 172, 173
Steele, Shari, 274–275
Steuer, Jonathan, 335
Stevens, Harry, 114–115
Stoll, Clifford, 267, 327, 349

Stone, Allucquere Rosanne, 137
"Strange Case of the Electronic Lover,
  The" (Van Gelder), 170
"Strange Disappearance of Civic
  America, The" (Putnam), 387
Suess, Randy, 134–136
Suicide, 20–23
Suler, John, 358
Sun Microsystems, 77, 272
Supercomputers, 77–78
Superficiality, 360–362
Survnet, 147
Sutherland, Ivan, 63–66
Symbols, 46, 57
Sysops, 134, 139, 141
System cracking. *See* Hackers

Talbott, Steve, 350
Talk program, 184
Taxpayers, 184
Taylor, Robert, 9, 64, 66
  on future communication, 69
  packet-switching and, 67–68
  PARC and, 70
TCI, 395, 397
TCP/ICP protocol suite, 76
Technological Society, The (Ellul),
  353
Technology
  Britain and, 247–253
  commercial interests and, 297–298
  digital trails and, 299–300
  France and, 231–247
  groupminds and, 109–118
  growth of, 401–403
  hyper-realism and, 317–321
  information and, 72
  Japan and, 205–229
  privacy and, 311–312
  private sector and, 78–79
  reality and, 300
  social impact of, 109, 345–352,
    359–371
  transfer and, 78
Technology Review (MIT Press), 287
Telecom, 228
TeleCommunications Inc., 292

Telecomputing Corporation of
   America, 117
Teledesic, 395–396
Telematique, 250
Teleports, 256
Teletel, 232, 238–239, 241
Television, xxxi, 68, 300, 305, 398
Telnet, 95, 105
Tennessee colony, 29
Tex (John Coate), 28–29, 41
*Textual Poachers, Television Fans and
   Participatory Culture* (Jenkins), 173
Thinking Machines, 102–103
Third places, 10
Thompson, Brad, 379–382, 391
Thompson, William Irwin, 353
Thornley, Frank, 251
Thornley, Sylvia, 251
Threads, 336
Tiananmen Square, 132
Time, 37, 337
Time-sharing, 64–66, 71, 99
Time-Warner, 291–292, 375, 377,
   393
Tinysex, 154
Tiprudder analogy, 26–27
Toby, 249, 252
Toffler, Alvin, xxvii
Tokens, 199
Tomino, Kichiro, 133, 209–210
Trek-MUSE, 155
Trips Festival, 27
Trubshaw, Roy, 155
Truscott, Tom, 118, 120–121
Truth 'N Fun productions, 39
Turf (private region), 197
Turing, Alan, 315
Turkle, Sherry, 157, 188, 352
Turoff, Murray, 111–114, 116, 207
TWICS, xvii, 207, 215, 394
 Japan visit and, 224–227
 people's importance and, 31

UCLA, 68
Uncapher, Willard, 259, 261–262
Understanding Media (McLuhan),
   346

United States, xxi–xxii, 220–221, 228
 Clinton administration, xxvi, 378,
   395–396
 Clipper Chip and, 399
 Congress, 48, 77–78
 electronic democracy and, 306
 freedom of speech and, 301–304
 national information and, 207
 White House, 86–87
University of California, 76, 169
University of Essex, 61, 227
University of Illinois, 111
University of Minnesota, 105
University of North Carolina, 61, 117
University of Oulu, 184
University of Pennsylvania, 81
University of Pittsburgh, 357
University of Utah, 65
University of Victoria, 388
Unix, 36
 groupminds and, 116–117
 hackers and, 272
 TCP/ICP and, 76–77
 Usenet and, 121
 User's conference, 118
 UUCP and, 76, 116–121
U.S. Department of Defense. *See*
   ARPA
Usenet, xvii–xxxii
 anarchy and, 119
 birth of, 59–62
 description of, 118–120
 grassroot projects and, 110
 growth of, 120–133
 hierarchy and, 123–124
 newsgroups and, 118, 125
 posting examples of, 126–131
 science and, 75
U.S. Office of Emergency
   Preparedness, 112
Utopia, 115–116
UUCP (Unix to Unix Copy Program),
   76, 116–117
 Usenet and, 118–121

Vallee, Jacques, 40, 110, 116, 311
van der Pas, Elly, 13–17

Van Gelder, Lindsy, 170–171
Varley, Pamela, 287–288
Velizy experiment, 239
Viacom, 393
Video
  games, 185
  linking, 176–178
  on demand, 291
  text, 237–239, 295
Vietnam War, 70
Viewtron, 295
Virtual communities, xii–xiii
  BBS and, 133–148
  Britain and, 247–253
  CIX and, 247–253
  CMC technology and, xix–xx. *See also* CMC
  COARA and, 211–218, 221–222, 224
  cyberspace cities and, 284–293
  democracy and, 295–321, 338–340
  ethics and, 338
  fear of, 8
  future of, xxi
  France and, 231–253
  GeoCities, 340
  globalism and, 276–284
  groupminds and, 109–118
  growth of, xvi, 323–325
  hyper-realism and, 317–321
  invasion of, xv
  Japan and, 205–229
  Library of Congress and, 72–73
  marketing and, 342
  minds online and, 352–359
  modern state of, 340–341, 344–345, 367–370
  MUDs and, 149–180
  nature of, 359–371
  people of, 45–46
  public sphere and, 371–391
  reality and, 366
  rethinking, 345–352
  social capital and, 386–391
  social impact of, 54–55, 334–359
  Threads and, 336
  Usenet and, 118–133

WELL and, 25–55, 325–334. *See also* WELL
Virtual reality, 195
Viruses, 104
Volunteermatch, 384
VoxCap, 385

WAIS (Wide Area Information Servers), 47, 102–103
Walker, John, 271
Wall Street Journal, 37
Walther, Joseph B., 358
Wavy Davey (Dave Winder), 248
WBSI, 27–28
Wealth Game, 219
Webster, Frank, 309
Webster, Jody, 262
Webzines, 335–336
Weird Conference, 20
WELL (Whole Earth 'Lectronic Link), xv, xvii, xxxi–xxxii
  accomplishment and, 12–13
  addiction and, 18–19
  Aizu and, 209
  birth of, 26–30
  Brand and, 25
  cabals of, 332
  Catalfo death and, 328–329
  COARA and, 215
  collective goods and, xxviii
  CompuMentor and, 277–278
  conference structure of, 31–35
  Creighton death and, 325, 327–328
  cruelty and, 20–21
  Deadheads and, 37
  design goals of, 30–31
  EFF and, 274
  Elly and, 13–17
  Experts and, 50–52
  growth of, xvi, 29, 324
  hackers and, 36–37, 266–269, 271–272
  hosting and, 26
  human interaction and, 8
  hypertext and, 96–98
  integration of, xxiv–xxv
  Katz and, 331–332

leukemia discussion and, 5–8
Mandel's death and, 325–327
Newman and, 18–24
newsgroups and, 122, 125
parenting conferences and, 1–4
PC revolution and, 36
people of, 4–5, 38–45
place and, 9–10
science and, 75
scribbling and, 20–22
security and, 1
socializing and, 4–5, 38–55,
  329–330
success of, 27
troubles of, 331–334
Usenet and, 62, 120–121
Wellman, Barry, 359–363
 on community, 365–366
 on Net relationships, 363–364
 on reciprocity, 364
 on wired neighborhood, 368–369
Western Behavioral Sciences Institute
  (WBSI), 27–28
Whisper, 15
White, Don, 278
White House, 86–87
Whole Earth
 as a counterculture, 25–26
 WELL birth and, 36
Whole Earth Catalog, 25, 27
 Thompson's accusation and, 353
Whole Earth Review, 4, 138, 331,
  335
 computer conferencing and, 28
 Kelly and, 30
 survival of, 26–27
Whole Earth Software Review, The,
  27
Whole Internet User's Guide, The,
  335
Winder, Dave, 247–252
Winner, Langdon, 168, 308, 348
Wired, 326, 335, 400
Wisdom Game, 219
Wit, 181, 188
Wittig, Michele, 285
Wolfe, Tom, 27

Women's refuge, 278
Women's Resource Center, 262–263
Woodstock, 28
Woolley, David, 111
Word processors, 64
Work of Nations, The (Reich), 46
World Bank, 388
World Factbook, 85
World Health Organization, 28
Worms, 104
Wozniak, Steve, 272
Written words, 181–182, 186, 205
Wuthnow, Robert, 383, 387–388

Xanadu, 100–101
Xerox, 70–71,
  MUDs and, 175–178
XMODEM, 135–136

Yahoo, 335, 340
Young, Kimberly, 357

Zubrow, D., 351
Zushi, Japan, 209–210